OTHER A TO Z GUIDES FROM THE SCARECROW PRESS, INC.

55. *The A to Z of the War of 1812* by Robert Malcomson, 2009.
56. *The A to Z of Feminist Philosophy* by Catherine Villanueva Gardner, 2009.
57. *The A to Z of the Early American Republic* by Richard Buel Jr., 2009.
58. *The A to Z of the Russo–Japanese War* by Rotem Kowner, 2009.
59. *The A to Z of Anglicanism* by Colin Buchanan, 2009.
60. *The A to Z of Scandinavian Literature and Theater* by Jan Sjåvik, 2009.
61. *The A to Z of the Peoples of the Southeast Asian Massif* by Jean Michaud, 2009.
62. *The A to Z of Judaism* by Norman Solomon, 2009.
63. *The A to Z of the Berbers (Imazighen)* by Hsain Ilahiane, 2009.
64. *The A to Z of British Radio* by Seán Street, 2009.
65. *The A to Z of The Salvation Army* by Major John G. Merritt, 2009.
66. *The A to Z of the Arab–Israeli Conflict* by P R Kumaraswamy, 2009.
67. *The A to Z of the Jacksonian Era and Manifest Destiny* by Terry Corps, 2009.
68. *The A to Z of Socialism* by Peter Lamb and James C. Docherty, 2009.
69. *The A to Z of Marxism* by David Walker and Daniel Gray, 2009.
70. *The A to Z of the Bahá'í Faith* by Hugh C. Adamson, 2009.
71. *The A to Z of Postmodernist Literature and Theater* by Fran Mason, 2009.
72. *The A to Z of Australian Radio and Television* by Albert Moran and Chris Keating, 2009.
73. *The A to Z of the Lesbian Liberation Movement: Still the Rage* by JoAnne Myers, 2009.
74. *The A to Z of the United States–Mexican War* by Edward H. Moseley and Paul C. Clark Jr., 2009.
75. *The A to Z of World War I* by Ian V. Hogg, 2009.
76. *The A to Z of World War II: The War Against Japan* by Anne Sharp Wells, 2009.
77. *The A to Z of Witchcraft* by Michael D. Bailey, 2009.
78. *The A to Z of British Intelligence* by Nigel West, 2009.
79. *The A to Z of United States Intelligence* by Michael A. Turner, 2009.

The A to Z of Journalism

Ross Eaman

The A to Z Guide Series, No. 117

The Scarecrow Press, Inc.
Lanham • Toronto • Plymouth, UK
2009

Published by Scarecrow Press, Inc.
A wholly owned subsidiary of
The Rowman & Littlefield Publishing Group, Inc.
4501 Forbes Boulevard, Suite 200, Lanham, Maryland 20706
http://www.scarecrowpress.com

Estover Road, Plymouth PL6 7PY, United Kingdom

British Library Cataloguing in Publication Information Available

Library of Congress Cataloging-in-Publication Data

The hardback version of this book was cataloged by the Library of Congress as
follows:

Eaman, Ross Allan, 1945–
   Historical dictionary of journalism / Ross Eaman.
     p. cm. — (Historical dictionaries of professions and industries)
   Includes bibliographical references.
   1. Journalism—History—Dictionaries. I. Title.
   PN4728.E37 2009
   070.9—dc22   2008037829

ISBN 978-0-8108-7154-0 (pbk. : alk. paper)
ISBN 978-0-8108-7067-3 (ebook)

Printed in the United States of America

Contents

Editor's Foreword

Journalism, more than most other professions, is often seen as a higher calling, since journalists are expected to dig up the facts, assemble them logically, and then present them cogently in order to provide the knowledge so other people can make good choices in their lives. There are lazy and incompetent journalists—and editors—and others who just want to promote their own views; but on the whole, journalists have been crucial over the past several centuries and will probably remain so well into the future, even if their work assumes new forms. Journalism is also an industry, since it costs money to produce newspapers, newsletters, and even blogs, so financial concerns enter the picture and muddy the waters. While there have been some very enlightened, progressive, and even fearlessly crusading newspapers, there have also been many of lesser value, more interested in just providing entertainment or turning a profit.

The A to Z of Journalism shows both sides of the picture. The dictionary presents entries on some of the finest newspapers as well as those of lesser repute, many exceptional journalists as well as others the profession would rather forget, major advances such as investigative reporting and more questionable practices such as yellow journalism, and important topics like censorship and the continuing struggle for freedom of the press. It covers a long period of time, from the very first practitioners whose news was often sung to the most recent whose news appears in a computerized format. Last but not least, it traces the history of journalism in a large number of countries in a lengthy chronology and then an introduction, which analyzes individual developments thematically, showing how the discursive practices of journalism have evolved within a larger political, economic, and cultural context. Despite the breadth of coverage, the field of journalism history is so large that any work of this kind can constitute only a starting point for further research and study, so the substantial bibliography organizes recent literature in the field to facilitate this task.

This new addition to the Historical Dictionaries of Professions and Industries series was written by Ross Eaman, who has been a full-time member of faculty in the School of Journalism and Communication at Carleton University in Canada since 1980. His earlier publications include *The Media Society: Basic Issues and Controversies* (1987) and *Channels of Influence: CBC Audience Research and the Canadian Public* (1994). This volume builds on his interest in communication and democracy and the role of public broadcasting, but it reaches further, covering the lengthy history of journalism within a global context. It also provides the wide variety of topics, issues, and considerations related to understanding journalism as an industry and profession.

Jon Woronoff
Series Editor

Preface

The story of journalism is first and most visibly a tale of changing media, from ballads and chronicles to newsletters and newsbooks, newspapers and magazines, and eventually newscasts and websites. But this story begins to come alive only when the focus shifts to the texts conveyed through those media and the way these have evolved as a form of discourse over the past five centuries. Most of the components of this discourse--the news report, the editorial, the column, the *feuilleton*, the interview, the photograph, the inverted pyramid, the news lead, the by-line—are familiar enough to us. But when, how, and why these components first emerged as a product of culture is more complex than we might imagine. In most cases, their genesis is tied to a cast of characters who generally nurtured and shaped rather than "invented" them. Some of these figures are well known: Daniel Defoe, Joseph Addison, Benjamin Franklin, James Gordon Bennett, Joseph Pulitzer, William T. Stead, Walter Lippmann, Henry Luce, and Edward R. Murrow. But many others are largely unknown: from Pietro Aretino, John Wolfe, Ben Jonson, and John Crouch in the 16th and 17th centuries to William "Memory" Woodfall, Francis Jeffrey, Faddej Bulgarin, Liang Qichao, Walter Williams, and Lillian Ross in the 18th, 19th, and 20th centuries. In several cases, these pioneers were the owners or producers of a journalistic enterprise or product. But their number also includes practicing journalists, social critics of journalism, and journalism educators. Each of these groups has had an important impact on journalism as it exists today and will continue to influence its nature in accordance with its own goals and ideals.

Acronyms and Abbreviations

ABC	American Broadcasting Company
AEJMC	Association for Education in Journalism and Mass Communication (U.S.)
AFP	Agence France-presse
AIM	Accuracy in Media (U.S.)
ANG	American Newspaper Guild
ANPA	American Newspaper Publishers Association
AP	Associated Press (U.S.)
ASJMC	Association of Schools of Journalism and Mass Communication (U.S.)
ASNE	American Society of Newspaper Editors
BBC	British Broadcasting Corporation
CBC	Canadian Broadcasting Corporation
CBS	Columbia Broadcasting System (U.S.)
CJR	Columbia Journalism Review (U.S.)
CPI	Committee on Public Information (U.S.)
CPJ	Committee to Protect Journalists (New York)
C-SPAN	Cable Satellite Public Affairs Network (U.S.)
EJC	European Journalism Centre (The Netherlands)
ENPA	European Newspaper Publishers Association (Belgium)
FCC	Federal Communications Commission (U.S.)
FRC	Federal Radio Commission (U.S.)
GIZh	State Institute of Journalism (Soviet Union)
Glavlit	Main Administration for Literary and Publishing Affairs (Soviet Union)
IAPA	Inter-American Press Association (Latin America)
IFJ	International Federation of Journalists (Belgium)
IJ	Institute of Journalists (Great Britain)
INA	Irish News Agency

INS	International News Service
IRE	Investigative Reporters and Editors (U.S.)
NAA	Newspaper Association of America
NAB	National Association of Broadcasters (U.S.)
NABJ	National Association of Black Journalists (U.S.)
NBC	National Broadcasting Company (U.S.)
NG	Newspaper Guild (U.S.)
NSK	Japanese Newspaper Publishers & Editors Association
NSNC	National Society of Newspaper Columnists (U.S.)
NUJ	National Union of Journalists (Great Britain)
OC	Office of Censorship (U.S.)
PBS	Public Broadcast System (U.S.)
RSF	Reporters sans frontières
SNJ	Syndicat national des journalistes (France)
SPJ	Society of Professional Journalists (U.S.)
TASS	Telegraph Agency of the Soviet Union
UP	United Press (U.S.)
UPA	United Press Associations (U.S.)
UPI	United Press International (U.S.)
WAN	World Association of Newspapers (Paris)

Chronology

59 B.C.E. Julius Caesar ordered publication of the *acta diurna*.

c. 1350 Spanish chroniclers began recording events of interest to the *Generalitat*, or Catalan Legislative Assembly.

1476 William Caxton established the first printing press in England.

1493 Pedro Martir de Angleria from Italy gathered news about the Spanish Conquest from returning captains and sent it to European courts in his *decadas*, or newsletter.

1513 Richard Faques's pamphlet *Trewe Encounter* told of the Battle of Flodden Field.

1530 The first licensing system in England was established.

1535 The *poligraphi* used pamphlets to satirize Renaissance humanism.

1536 The Spanish bishop Juan de Zumárraga brought the first printing press to the Americas (Mexico City).

1566 The first printed newssheet, the *Gazzetta de la novità*, appeared in Venice.

1583 Printer Antonio Ricardo began operating the second press in the Americas (Lima).

1589 John Wolfe and other London printers began publishing regular news quartos about the fate of English soldiers fighting for Henry of Navarre.

1605 Abraham Verhoeven began publishing *Nieuwe Tidinghe* in Antwerp on a weekly and later thrice-weekly basis.

1609 Regularly published newssheets appeared in Strassbourg and Wolfenbüttel.

1615 Newssheets known as *kawaraban* (tile engraving) made their appearance in Japan.

1620 The English poet and playwright Ben Jonson satirized news publications in his masque *Newes from the New World Discover'd in the Moone.*

1621 The London printer Nicholas Bourne began to adapt Dutch corantos for English readers.

1620s Printing speed was increased from 15 to 150 impressions per hour through the use of a counterweight.

1627 The English newssheet *A Iournall* reported on the Duke of Buckingham's expedition against the French. The Greek Patriarch Cyril Lucaris founded the first Greek printing press in Constantinople with the protection of the English ambassador, though the Turks destroyed it a year later.

1631 The first French newspaper, Théophraste Renaudot's *Gazette de France*, was given a monopoly over political news by Cardinal Richelieu.

1637 The Spanish friar Tomas Pinpin, the "Prince of Filipino Printers," began *Sucesos Felices*, the first Philippine newsletter.

1638 The first printing press in the American colonies was established under the supervision of Harvard College.

1639 The first newspaper in Italy was established in Genoa.

1641 Nicholas Bourne and Nathaniel Butter began the first regularly published newsbook in London. The first newspaper in Spain, the *Gaceta semanal de Barcelona*, began publication on a weekly basis.

1642 Samuel Pecke, one of the foremost English journalists of his day, began the weekly newsbook *A Perfect Diurnall*.

1644 John Milton created a powerful set of arguments against prepublication censorship in *Areopagitica*.

1647 Marchamont Nedham switched from writing *Mercurius Britannicus* on behalf of Parliament to producing *Mercurius Pragmaticus* for the royalists.

1650 Nedham became editor of the official English newsbook, *Mercurius Politicus*, under the general supervision of Milton. The first daily newspaper, the *Einkommende Zeitung*, was established in Leipzig by the book merchant and printer Tomotheus Ritzsch.

1652 The first coffeehouses opened in London.

1653 Henry Muddiman's *Kingdom's Intelligencer* was given a monopoly over news in England.

1660 The English Parliament issued an injunction against printing any of its votes or proceedings. The first Scottish newspaper, *Mercurius Caledonius*, began publication in Edinburgh.

1661 The first vernacular newspaper in Eastern Europe, the *Merkuriusz Poliski Ordynaryjny*, was founded in Krakow. The *Gaceta de Madrid* (or *Gazzetta nueva*) began publication on an annual basis.

1662 Under a new Licensing Act, Roger L'Estrange became Surveyor of the Press in England.

1664 The *Journal des sçavans* under Denis de Sallo was awarded a *privilège* for scientific information.

1665 Muddiman's *Oxford Gazette* (later the *London Gazette*) provided news for the monarchy and Parliament during their relocation because of the plague.

1666 The Danish poet Anders Bording began a versified monthly newspaper called *Den Danske Mercurius* to pay homage to the new monarchy in Denmark.

1667 The *Gaceta de Madrid* began weekly publication.

1672 The *Mercure galante* was founded in France.

1674 The British East India Company set up a printing press in Bombay.

1680 The *Edinburgh Gazette* began publication.

1681   John Houghton, the "father of English advertising," began *A Collection of Letters for the Improvement of Husbandry and Trade*, a profitable monthly serial.

1690   Tobias Peucer submitted "De Relationibus Novellis," the first doctoral thesis on journalism, to the University of Leipzig. **25 September:** Benjamin Harris published the first and only issue of *Publick Occurrences, Both Foreign and Domestick.*

1692   Mail service was authorized between the American colonies.

1694   The *Mercure galante* became the *Mercure de France.*

1695   Failure to renew the Regulation of Printing Act marked the end of pre-publication controls over the press in England.

1700   Postmaster John Campbell began the *Boston News-Letter* as a handwritten publication.

1702   The *Daily Courant*, the first daily newspaper in England, was founded.

1704   **February:** Daniel Defoe began the *Review*. **April:** Campbell began printing the *Boston News-Letter*.

1709   **April:** Richard Steele began the *Tatler.*

1711   **January:** Edinburgh law student Robert Hepburn produced some 40 numbers of *The Tatler, by Donald MacStiff of the North*, an imitation of Steele's publication. **March:** Steele and Joseph Addison began the *Spectator*.

1715   The official *Gaceta de Lima* began publication in the viceroyalty of Peru.

1719   Postmasters William Brooker and Andrew Bradford founded the *Boston Gazette* and the *Philadelphia American Weekly Mercury* respectively.

1720   John Trenchard and Thomas Gordon began writing "Cato's Letters" in *The London Journal.*

1721   **August:** James Franklin established the *New-England Courant* in Boston.

1722   After Franklin was jailed for criticizing the local authorities during a controversy over inoculation, the *Courant* was issued by his younger half-brother Benjamin.

1725   The first newspaper in colonial New York, the *New-York Gazette*, was founded by William Bradford. Nathaniel Ames began compiling his best-selling *Astronomical Diary and Almanack*, a model for Benjamin Franklin's *Poor Richard's Almanack*.

1727   The first newspaper in Maryland, the *Maryland Gazette*, was founded by printer William Parks in Annapolis.

1728   **December:** Samuel Keimer, an eccentric religious enthusiast, established *The Universal Instructor in all Arts and Sciences: and Pennsylvania Gazette* in Philadelphia.

1729   **October:** Benjamin Franklin purchased Keimer's publication and shortened its title to *Pennsylvania Gazette*.

1731   The first periodical to describe itself as a magazine, *The Gentleman's Magazine*, was founded by Edward Cave in Britain. The first newspaper in the Caribbean, the *Barbados Gazette*, was founded by Samuel Keimer.

1732   The first newspaper in South Carolina, the *South Carolina Gazette*, was founded by Thomas Whitmarsh in Charleston with the financial help of Benjamin Franklin.

1733   **November:** John Peter Zenger founded the *New-York Weekly Journal*.

1734   **November:** Zenger was jailed on a charge of seditious libel, but later found not guilty.

1737   The *Belfast Newsletter*, one of the oldest newspapers in the world, began publication. The Spanish literary newspaper, *El Diario de los literatos*, was founded.

1741   The first newspaper merger in America occurred when the *Boston Gazette* joined with the *New-England Weekly Journal*. **January:** Andrew Bradford began the short-lived *American Magazine*, three days before Benjamin Franklin's *General Magazine*, making it the first magazine in the American colonies.

1752 The first newspaper in Canada, the *Halifax Gazette*, was founded by John Bushell. Printer James Parker apologized to a grand jury for printing a "Speech of an Indian" in his New York *Gazette,* or *Weekly Post-Boy.*

1754 **May:** The first newspaper cartoon in the American colonies, featuring a snake divided into eight sections with each identified as a colony and captioned "Join, or Die," was designed by Benjamin Franklin for his *Pennsylvania Gazette.*

1758 The first daily newspaper in Spain, the *Diario noticiosa, curiosa, edudito, comercial y politico* (later the *Diario de Madrid*), was founded by Francisco Mariano Nipho with a special privilege from King Fernando VI.

1759 The first women's magazine, the *Journal des dames*, began publication in France.

1760 The annual circulation of London newspapers reached almost 10 million copies.

1763 **April:** The British House of Commons declared no. 45 of John Wilkes's *The North Briton* a seditious libel. The liberal *Public Register or Freeman's Journal* began publication in Ireland.

1764 William Brown and Thomas Gilmore established the *Québec Gazette*. The monthly newspaper *La Gazeta* began publication in Argentina.

1765 **March:** The Stamp Act taxed the American colonies directly for the first time.

1766 **March:** The Stamp Act was repealed following a newspaper campaign against "taxation without representation."

1767 The first daily newspaper in Sweden, the *Dagligt Allehandra*, was founded. **November:** The *Pennsylvania Chronicle* began publishing "Letters from a Farmer in Pennsylvania to the Inhabitants of the British Colonies" by John Dickinson.

1769 In Britain, Henry Sampson Woodfall published the writings of "Junius," a political essayist of unknown identity, in his *Public Advertiser.*

1770 New England printer James Parker was arrested for printing an article by a "Son of Liberty," but died before trial. Isaiah Thomas and Zechariah Fowle founded the *Massachusetts Spy.*

1771 In Britain, the House of Commons ended its ban on parliamentary reporting.

1774 In Britain, the House of Lords allowed reporters to cover its proceedings. Isaiah Thomas founded the *Royal American Magazine* in Boston.

1775 In France, a network of journals began engaging in "Frondeur journalism."

1777 The first daily newspaper in France, the *Journal de Paris*, was founded.

1779 The first Sunday newspaper, the *British Gazette and Sunday Monitor*, began publication, ignoring the sabbatarian prohibition.

1780 The first newspaper on the Indian subcontinent, the *Bengal Gazette* or *Calcutta General Advertiser*, was founded by J. A. Hicky.

1781 Gottlob Benedikt von Schirach founded the commercially successful *Politische Journal.*

1783 **May:** The *Pennsylvania Evening Post*, founded by Benjamin Towne in 1775, became the first daily newspaper in America, but folded less than a year later.

1784 The first of a series of repressive Press Acts was instituted in Ireland. The first successful daily newspaper in the United States, the *Pennsylvania Packet and Daily Advertiser*, was established. The official *Gazeta de México* was established.

1788 **1 January:** In Britain, *The Daily Universal Register* was renamed *The Times* by John Walter.

1789 **April:** Reporters were allowed access to the U.S. House of Representatives. Thomas Lloyd began publishing the *Congressional Register.* John Fenno founded the *Gazette of the United States* as a Federalist newspaper.

1790   Benjamin Franklin Bache founded the Philadelphia *Aurora*, the first anti-Federalist newspaper. **31 December:** The first Greek newspaper, *Ephemerís*, began publishing in Vienna until the office in which it was printed was shut down for issuing a revolutionary proclamation by the poet and patriot Rhégas of Velestino.

1791   Philip Freneau established the anti-Federalist Philadelphia *National Gazette*. *El Mercurio Peruano* began publication in Lima. The first newspaper in present-day Columbia (at the time, New Granada), the *Papel Periódico de la Ciudad de Santafé de Bogatá*, was founded.

1792   The First Amendment to the U.S. Constitution, guaranteeing freedom of the press, was passed. A new U.S. Postal Act continued to allow publishers to exchange newspapers without charge. The New England journalist Robert Bailey Thomas began the long-running *Farmer's Almanac*.

1793   Louis Roy, the King's Printer in present-day Ontario, began publishing the *Upper Canada Gazette,* or *American Oracle.* New York City's first daily newspaper, the Federalist *American Minerva*, was founded by Noah Webster.

1794   The French Revolutionary journalist Camille Desmoulins was executed after calling for moderation against the Girondins in his journal *Le Vieux cordelier.* Journalist Jacques Hébert was guillotined after challenging Robespierre's authority in his newspaper *Le Père Duchesne.* Benjamin Franklin's best-selling *Autobiograhy* was published posthumously.

1796   **September:** President George Washington summoned the publisher of *Claypoole's American Daily Advertiser* to announce he was leaving public office.

1797   In Britain, George Canning began publication of the *The Anti-Jacobin* to attack those who sympathized with the French Revolution. Federalist supporters wrecked the office of the *Aurora* in Philadelphia.

1798   Johann Cotta began the *Allgemeine Zeitung* in Germany. The Alien and Sedition Acts were passed by the U.S. Congress in an attempt to control the anti-Federalist press.

1800 Samuel Harrison Smith founded *National Intelligencer* to cover the proceedings of the U.S. Congress.

1801 Alexander Hamilton helped to found the Federalist *New York Evening Post*. The newspaper *Telégrafo mercantil, rural, político-económico e historiográfo del Río de la Plata* was founded in Buenos Aires by Francisco A. Cabello. The official *Sierra Leone Gazette*, probably the first newspaper in sub-Saharan black Africa, began publication.

1802 William Cobbett founded the *Political Register*, one of the leading reform journals of the era.

1803 The first weekly newspaper in Mexico, *El Noticioso*, began publication in Mexico City. The first newspaper in Australia, the *Sydney Gazette*, was founded.

1805 The first daily newspaper in Mexico, the *Diario de México*, began publication in Mexico City. New York enacted a new libel law based on Alexander Hamilton's defense of Harry Croswell against a charge of libelling President Thomas Jefferson; other states later followed suit.

1808 The first periodical in Brazil, the *Gazeta de Rio Janeiro*, began publication.

1810 Isaiah Thomas published *The History of Printing in America*. The *Correo de Comercio* and the *Gaceta de Buenos Aires* were established to promote Argentine independence from Britain.

1811 Hezekiah Niles began publishing the influential political news magazine *Niles' Weekly Register* in Baltimore.

1812 The Cortes de Cádiz abolished political censorship of books and newspapers throughout Spain and its empire. A new law in Sweden gave the king the power to suppress any newspaper "imperilling the public safety." The *New England Journal of Medicine and Surgery* (eventually the *New England Journal of Medicine*) was founded in Boston.

1813 The first daily newspaper in Greek began publication in Vienna. The English poet, critic, and journalist Leigh Hunt and his brother John were jailed for derogatory remarks about the prince regent in their journal the *Examiner*, which they continued to edit from prison. Nathan Hale founded the *Boston Daily Advertiser*, the first successful daily newspaper in New England and one of the first American papers to feature editorials.

1814   Historian Joseph von Görres began to develop a more political approach to newspaper journalism in Germany as editor of the *Rheinische Merkur*.

1815   The annual circulation of London newspapers exceeded 25 million copies. The Cadiz periodical *La Abeja Espanola* was placed on the Index of Prohibited Books for satirizing the Spanish Inquisition. Robert Morrison and William Milne created the first missionary periodical in China, the *Chashisu Meiyue Tongji*.

1817   The Gagging Acts were passed in Britain to suppress radicalism. The *Scotsman* and the *Dundee Courier* began publication in Scotland. James Harper and his brother John founded the Harper publishing house in New York. The Argentine soldier, journalist, and future statesman Manuel Dorrego was banished from Buenos Aires after attacking the government in print.

1819   The French government instituted a system of "caution" or guarantee money to check the growth of the press. The Karlsbad Decrees forbade publication of anything "inimical to the maintenance of peace and quiet in Germany."

1821   The first newspaper actually published in Greece, the *Salpìnx Helleniké*, appeared in Kalamata during the War of Independence. In Mount Pleasant, Ohio, Quaker Benjamin Lundy founded the *Genius of Universal Emancipation*, one of the first abolitionist newspapers. Charles Alexander and Samuel Coate Atkinson founded the *Saturday Evening Post* in Philadelphia. The Spanish founded the newspaper *Ramillete Patriotico* in the Philippines. Alexander Boswell, the son of Samuel Johnson's biographer James Boswell, was mortally wounded in a duel to which he was challenged by Whig politician James Stuart after Boswell's slanderous attack upon him in the *Glasgow Sentinal*.

1823   Peter Force established the daily *National Journal* in Washington, D.C., to support John Quincy Adams for the presidency. Journalist and poet José María Heredia was permanently exiled from Cuba as a revolutionary.

1825 The *Journal of the Philadelphia College of Pharmacy*, later the *American Journal of Pharmacy*, began pharmaceutical journalism in the United States. The Russian journalist and novelist F. V. Bulgarin founded the daily newspaper *Northern Bee* with Nicholas Grech.

1826 The conservative French newspaper *Le Figaro* was founded in Paris.

1827 Arthur and Lewis Tappan founded the *New York Journal of Commerce*. Samuel E. Cornish and John B. Russwurm founded *Freedom's Journal*, the first abolitionist newspaper published by African Americans. Reporters began covering Congress on a continuous basis.

1828 The weekly *Mechanics' Free Press*, the first successful labor paper, was founded in Philadelphia. The first Native American newspaper, the *Cherokee Phoenix*, began publication. Bermuda's only daily newspaper, the *Royal Gazette*, was established.

1829 In New York City, George Henry Adams founded the *Working Man's Advocate* and Frances Wright founded the *Free Enquirer* to promote the cause of labor. Ion Heliade Raduescu founded *Curierul Romanesc*, the first newspaper in Romanian.

1830 The *Penny Magazine* went on sale in Britain. The French historian and future statesman Adolphe Thiers helped to found the journal *National*, which contributed to the July Revolution. Francis P. Blair began the *Washington Globe* as the official organ of the Jackson administration. Thurlow Weed founded the *Albany Evening Journal*, which became a leading Whig organ.

1831 William Lloyd Garrison began his campaign against American slavery in *The Liberator*. William Trotter Porter founded the *Spirit of the Times*, an American sports magazine. Anne Royall, arguably the first professional woman journalist in the United States, began producing the small muckraking newspaper *Paul Pry*. The first newspaper in Turkish was established.

1833 Benjamin Day founded the *New York Sun*, the first penny paper. The *Pfennig Magazin* (Penny Magazine) began publication in Germany.

1834 George Wisner began his "Police Office" column for the *New York Sun.*

1835 The French news agency, Agence Havas, was established. James Gordon Bennett Sr. established the *New York Herald* as a penny paper. The *New York Sun* perpetrated the moon hoax. Regulation XI formally eliminated the licensing system in India.

1836 The Helen Jewett murder trial generated a moral panic in the New York press.

1837 American novelist James Fenimore Cooper filed the first of 16 libel suits against newspapers and their "atmosphere of falsehoods."

1838 Orestes Brownson founded the *Boston Quarterly Review*, later *Brownson's Quarterly Review*, to spread his religious and political views. *The Times of India* was founded as an English-language weekly.

1839 Louis Daguerre presented the first practical method of photography to the French Academy of Sciences. The future Canadian statesman Sir Francis Hincks promoted responsible government as editor of the Toronto *Examiner*.

1840 In Britain, George Graham merged the *Casket* and *Gentlemen's* magazines into *Graham's* and began the practice of paying writers a sliding fee based on talent. New Zealand's first newspaper, the *New Zealand Gazette*, was founded by Samuel Revens.

1842 Herbert Ingram founded the *Illustrated London News*. Charles Dickens criticized corrupt journalists in *American Notes for General Circulation*, which described his tour of the United States.

1843 Lord Campbell's Libel Act reformed the law of libel in Britain. *The Economist* was founded in London by James Wilson. Walt Whitman became editor of the *Brooklyn Eagle*, an influential liberal newspaper.

1844 James Gordon Bennett Sr. began printing a daily column of news in the *New York Herald* entitled "By Magnetic Telegraph." The *New York Sun* published the balloon hoax of Edgar Allan Poe.

1846 The American penny press used the Pony Express and telegraphy to cover the war with Mexico. Margaret Fuller reported from Europe for Horace Greeley's *New York Tribune*, becoming the first woman foreign correspondent.

1848 Karl Marx established the *Neue Rheinische Zeitung*. The first American news agency, the Harbor News Association, began operations in New York City. A *New York Herald* reporter was jailed briefly for refusing to tell a U.S. senate committee how he obtained a copy of a treaty under its consideration. The American emancipationist Amelia Jenks Bloomer began promoting her revolutionary ideas about dress in her periodical *The Lily*.

1849 In Italy, Thomas Reggio, rector of a seminary in Chiavari and future archbishop of Genoa, founded *The Catholic Standard*, the first Catholic newspaper. The German news agency Wolff was founded. The *Deaf Mute*, the first of the "little papers," was established at the North Carolina Institute for the Deaf and Blind to provide training in printing and journalism.

1850 Britain was connected by cable with France. The London *Morning Chronicle* published a series of articles on prison reform by Henry Mayhew. *Harper's Monthly Magazine* began publication. *The Times of India* became a daily.

1851 In London, Baron Paul Julius Von Reuter, a German-born British journalist, founded Reuter's, one of the first international news agencies. The Qing court in China dismissed Zhang Fu's proposal to replace the traditional *Dibao* or *Jingbao* with a modern official newspaper.

1853 The British government began eliminating the so-called "taxes on knowledge." Frank Queen founded the *New York Clipper*, a leading sports journal.

1856 James P. Casey, publisher of the San Francisco *Sunday Times*, shot and killed James King, editor of the San Francisco *Bulletin*, after being attacked by King in one of his columns; vigilantes lynched Casey on the day of King's funeral.

1857 The *Atlantic Monthly*, devoted to literature, art, and politics, was founded in Boston by a number of leading New England literary figures, including Oliver Wendell Holmes, who gave it its name. Hinrich Johannes Rink introduced printing to Greenland.

1858 **17 August:** President James Buchanan and Queen Victoria exchanged the first message over the Atlantic cable.

1859 The Concordia Press Club, a professional organization of reporters, editors, and publishers, was founded in Vienna. Journalist Lambert A. Wilmer published *Our Press Gang*, the first book devoted entirely to press criticism. The *New York World* was founded.

1860 The establishment of the U.S. Government Printing Office ended the system of awarding government printing contracts to Washington newspapers such as the *National Intelligencer*.

1861 Englishman Albert William Hansard began the *Nagasaki Shipping List and Advertiser*, the first foreign newspaper in Japan. In Greenland, Hinrich Rink founded the magazine *Atuagagdliutit* and hired Lars Moller as printer and later editor.

1863 Polydore Milhaud founded the *Petit journal*, the first mass circulation daily in France. Union patriots destroyed the press of the *Columbus* (Ohio) *Crisis*, edited by Samuel Medary, a Democrat who opposed President Abraham Lincoln's policies. A. A. Kraevsky founded *Golos*, the first independent, privately owned daily newspaper in Russia.

1864 The Newspaper Press Fund was established for impoverished journalists in Britain. Joseph Heco (Hamada Hikozo), a Japanese sailor who had received an American education after being shipwrecked near the United States, founded the *Kaigai Shimbun* (Overseas News), the first Japanese-language newspaper.

1865 E. L. Godkin founded *The Nation*.

1866 The transatlantic cable was completed.

1867 In London, George W. Smalley organized the first American foreign newspaper bureau for Horace Greeley's *Tribune*. The Missouri Press Association was established. Henry Watterson, the leading Southern journalist in the post-Civil War period, became editor of the *Louisville Daily Journal*. Ali Suavi founded the political newspaper *Muhbir* in Turkey.

1868 Charles A. Dana became editor of the *New York Sun*. The American reformer Elizabeth Cady Stanton began to edit the militant feminist magazine *Revolution*, published by fellow women's suffrage leader Susan B. Anthony. The Press Association was created in New Zealand.

1869 January: E. L. Godkin's essay "Interviewing" was published in *The Nation*. Norman J. Colman proposed the creation of a school of journalism at the University of Missouri.

1870 Britain, France, and Germany designated zones of exclusive reporting for their respective news agencies.

1871 The first daily newspaper in Japan, the *Yokohama Mainichi Shimbun*, began publication. A direct cable link was established between Britain and Australia.

1872 Thomas Nast's cartoons in *Harper's Weekly* helped to overthrow the Tweed Ring in New York City. The first daily newspaper in Tokyo, the *Tokyo Nichi-ninchi Shimbun*, began publication. The British merchant Ernest Major founded the commercial newspaper *Shenbao* in the treaty port of Shanghai.

1873 Frederic Hudson published *Journalism in the United States*. The first newspaper owned and operated by the Chinese, the *Zhaowen Xinbao*, was established in Hankou under the protection of foreign jurisdiction.

1874 Joseph Medill, part owner of the *Chicago Tribune* since 1855, acquired a controlling interest and as editor began to turn it into one of the most powerful newspapers in the United States. Charles Nordhoff, a leading political commentator of his day, began a 15-year stint as Washington correspondent for the *New York Herald*. The *Xun Huan Ribao*, the second Chinese-owned and operated treaty port newspaper, was established in Hong Kong.

1875 Cornell University established the first degree in journalism. Ansell Kellogg introduced the use of pre-etched printing plates, or boiler-plating, which enabled local newspaper editors to graft news, features, and columns prepared by distant reporters and editors into their own papers. The Japanese government made it an offense for foreign residents to publish newspapers in Japanese. The English-language newspaper *The Statesman* was founded in India.

1876   Melville E. Stone founded the *Daily News*, the first penny paper in Chicago. The trans-Tasman submarine cable was completed, linking New Zealand to Australia at La Perouse near Sydney.

1878   Godwin Parke, former editor of the Fourierist magazine *Harbinger*, became editor of the *New York Evening Post*, succeeding William Cullen Bryant.

1879   A new U.S. Postal Act gave the press second-class mailing privileges. *Novoe vremia* installed the first rotary press in Russia.

1881   An act was passed in France allowing greater freedom of the press. *La Vanguardia*, a conservative newspaper, began publication in Barcelona. William O'Brien, author of the famous "No Rent Manifesto" during the Irish land war, became editor of the nationalist newspaper *United Ireland*. The United Press began operations in the United States. The first Chinese daily, *Lat Pau*, was founded by Ewe Lay in Singapore to protect the Chinese way of life.

1882   The Women's National Press Association was created in Washington.

1883   Joseph Pulitzer took over and began reviving the *New York World*. The U.S. magazine *Ladies' Home Journal* began publication. The Washington Press Club was created as a male social institution. Edwin Samuel Gaillard established the *American Medical Weekly*.

1884   *The Journalist*, a weekly magazine, began publication in the United States. The Japanese stenographer Wakabayashi Kanzō began using a new method of shorthand (*sokki*) developed by Takusari Koki to transcribe oral tales for the publisher Tōkyō Haishu Shuppansha, a practice which soon spread to newspapers and magazines.

1885   The Associated Press adopted typewriters. The New England Woman's Press Association was established.

1886   **July 3:** The *New York Tribune* typeset the first stories using Ottmar Mergenthaler's invention of the Linotype, which Thomas Edison called the eighth wonder of the world.

1887   The American Newspaper Publishers Association (ANPA), later the Newspaper Association of America (NAA), was founded as a trade association to help daily newspapers obtain national advertising and deal with problems such as mail rates, newsprint supply, new technologies, and labor relations.

1888 Britain's first mass readership daily newspaper, the evening *Star*, was created in London.

1889 The Institute of Journalists was created in Britain. Journalists in Chicago organized the short-lived Whitechapel Club. The *Wall Street Journal* began publication.

1890 *De Telegraaf*, the leading daily newspaper in the Netherlands, was founded.

1891 Frank A. Munsey founded *Munsey's Magazine*, one of the first mass market magazines.

1892 The newspaper industry trade journal *Newspaperdom* was established. A mob destroyed the offices of the *Memphis Free Speech* in retaliation for articles by Ida B. Wells attacking the practice of lynching.

1893 Peter Finley Dunne introduced readers of the Chicago *Sunday Post* to "Mr. Dooley," a saloonkeeper who philosophized in a humorous, practical vein about human affairs in an Irish dialect. Joseph French Johnson, former financial editor of the *Chicago Tribune*, organized the first college-based training in journalism at the University of Pennsylvania. In a speech to the Portland Press Club, Alice G. Friedlander called for equal rights for women in journalism and other careers.

1894 The International Congress of the Press was created to discuss issues such as copyright protection for news. Jane Cunningham Croly created the first women's pages for the *New York Daily World*. Józef Piłsudski began the underground journal *Robotnik* to promote Polish independence.

1895 William Randolph Hearst purchased the *New York Journal* and began a circulation war with Joseph Pulitzer's *New York World*. William W. Price became the first White House correspondent. William Allen White purchased the *Emporia Gazette* in Kansas.

1896 Lord Northcliffe founded the *Daily Mail* in London, Britain's first tabloid. Richard Felton Outcault began drawing the popular comic

"The Yellow Kid" in the *New York World*. The Qing court in China decided to issue modern official newspapers to help control public opinion.

1897   Li Boyuan began publication of *Youxi bao*, the first "small paper" in late Qing China. The Anglican Church's Missionary Society began the first periodical publication in the British colony of Uganda. Hearst began a campaign in the *New York Journal* to free Evangelina Cisneros, a beautiful young Cuban woman charged with conspiracy to assassinate a government official during the Spanish–American War. Francis Pharharcellus Church wrote the editorial "Is there a Santa Claus?" in the *New York Sun*. The epithet "yellow journalism" began to gain currency. In New York City, Abraham Cahan helped to found both the Social Democratic Party and the influential *Jewish Daily Forward*. A breakthrough occurred in the application of halftone technology in daily newspapers.

1898   Englishman Thomas Gowan founded the *Manila Times*, the first English-language daily in the Philippines.

1900   The American sociologist Josiah Flynt published "True Stories of the Underworld," a predecessor of muckraking journalism. Walter Hines Page, former editor of *Forum* and the *Atlantic Monthly*, founded and edited *World's Work*. Arthur Pearson founded the London *Daily Express*.

1901   The weekly trade magazine *Editor & Publisher* was founded in New York City. William T. Stead was nominated for a Nobel Peace Prize. V. I. Lenin described the role of journalism for revolution in *What Is to Be Done?* Following the shooting and death of President William McKinley at the Pan-American Exposition in Buffalo by Leon Czolgosz, many newspapers blamed "yellow journalism" for contributing to the assassination. **January 1:** Wearing formal evening attire, Alfred Harmsworth and the staff of Pulitzer's *New York World* produced the first tabloid as a one-time publicity stunt featuring "All the News in Sixty Seconds." **25 September:** The *New York Times* published its Jubilee Issue, including a 40-page supplement on its history.

1902   Joseph Pulitzer offered Columbia University $2 million to establish a school of journalism. *McClure's* magazine began publishing the muckraking journalism of Ida Tarbell, Lincoln Steffens, and Ray

Stannard Baker. The German inventor Arthur Korn transmitted photographs using a forerunner of the fax machine. The African Political Organization founded the bilingual newspaper *APO* to promote the equality of South Africans of mixed race.

1903 The transpacific cable was completed. Lord Northcliffe founded the London *Daily Mirror*. Julian Ralph's *The Making of a Journalist* was published. The editors of *Suabao* were prosecuted under the Chinese law against *Writing Books or Speaking About Sorcery*. John L. Dube and Nganzana Luthuli cofounded the *Hanga Lase Natal*, the first Zulu-language newspaper.

1904 Frank W. Scott set up the first full program in journalism at the University of Illinois.

1905 Robert S. Abbott founded the *Chicago Defender* to fight for racial equality. Ogden Mills Reid succeeded his father, Whitelaw Reid, as editor of the *New York Tribune*.

1907 The United Press news agency and the National Union of Journalists were founded in the United States. Frank E. Gannett began the process of building a newspaper empire by merging his newly acquired *Elmira* (New York) *Gazette* with the *Elmira Star* to establish the *Star-Gazette*. *Editor & Publisher* absorbed *The Journalist*. The Empire Press Union was founded in Britain. In Vienna, the exiled Russian revolutionary Leon Trotsky began writing polemical political articles for the press in order to support himself.

1908 Mary Baker Eddy founded the *Christian Science Monitor* in Boston as a counterweight to journalistic sensationalism. Walter Williams established a school of journalism at the University of Missouri. The National Press Club was created for male reporters in Washington. The Nobel Peace Prize was awarded jointly to Fredrik Bajer and Swedish journalist and peace advocate Klas Pontus Arnoldson. Hani Motoko founded *Fujin no tomo*, Japan's first women's magazine.

1909 The Society of Professional Journalists was founded to defend the First Amendment rights of American journalists.

1910 The first newsreels were shown in England and France. President Theodore Roosevelt unsuccessfully prosecuted Joseph Pulitzer for libel for publishing false stories about the construction of the Panama

Canal based on information gathered from a group of blackmailers posing as journalists, the so-called "blue pencil gang." The Kansas Editorial Association adopted one of the first codes of ethics for journalists. Two laborers were convicted of dynamiting the newspaper plant of the *Los Angeles Times* under the anti-union management of Harrison Gray Otis. The Korean newspaper *Mael Sinbo* was founded one day after the Japanese annexation.

1911 The French company Pathé Frères introduced the newsreel *Pathés Weekly* to the United States. Will Irwin's series on "The American Newspaper" was published by *Collier's Magazine. The Practice of Journalism* by Walter Williams and Frank L. Martin was published. E. W. Scripps began publishing the *Chicago Day Book* without ads, but the paper failed to reach its circulation target and later folded.

1912 The *Herald* was founded in London as a socialist newspaper. The U.S. Newspaper Publicity Act required disclosure of ownership, identification of advertisements, and truthful circulation statements. Frank E. Gannett began building the largest newspaper chain in the United States with the purchase of the *Ithaca Journal*. The American sociologist and reformer Paul Kellogg began editing *The Survey*, a magazine devoted to social issues.

1913 Lord Beaverbrook acquired control of the *Daily Express*.

1914 The price of *The Times* of London was reduced to 1d. Willard Straight founded *The New Republic* with Herbert Croly as editor. H. L. Mencken and George Nathan began co-editing *Smart Set*.

1916 With the aid of a line from the New York *American*, wireless pioneer Lee De Forest broadcast the presidential election returns, erroneously reporting that Charles Evans Hughes had defeated Woodrow Wilson.

1917 Floyd Gibbons filed a 4,000-word story on the sinking of the *Laconia* on which he had been sailing to France as a correspondent for the *Chicago Tribune*.

1918 Herbert Bayard Swope won a Pulitzer Prize for his reports on Germany in the *New York World*. Newspaper publisher E. W. Scripps made a personal appeal to President Woodrow Wilson to grant amnesty to war protestors jailed under the Military Service Act. **7 November:** Americans began celebrating the end of World War I prematurely when the United Press announced the signing of an armistice based on a cable from UP in France; a few hours later, the Associated Press and the U.S. secretary of state denied the story.

1919   Joseph M. Patterson founded the *New York Daily News*, the first American tabloid. The Women's National Press Association Club was organized in Washington, D.C. Upholding wartime restrictions on freedom of speech and the press, Supreme Court Justice Oliver Wendell Holmes Jr. declared in *Schenck v. United States* that "no citizen has the right to cry 'fire' falsely in a crowded theater."

1920   The *New Republic* published "A Test for the News," a study of news bias by Walter Lippmann and Charles Merz. The English journalist Philip Gibbs was knighted for his service as a front-line correspondent for the *London Daily Chronicle* during World War I. Sefanio Sentongo and Daudi Bassude founded *Sekanyoyla*, the first East African newspaper owned and edited by Africans. **2 November:** The Westinghouse radio station KDKA began operations by broadcasting presidential election bulletins provided by the Pittsburgh *Post*.

1921   The family of Joseph Medill endowed the Medill School of Journalism at Northwestern University. Clarence Walker Barron began the weekly American magazine *Barron's* for investors. Elmer Davis, an editorial writer for the *Times*, published a *History of the New York Times*. The State Institute of Journalism was established in Moscow. The Bolsheviks created *Krest'ianskaia gazeta*, a tabloid published weekly in Moscow.

1922   The Northcliffe estate sold *The Times* to John Jacob Astor. Five midwestern editors founded the American Society of Newspaper Editors (ASNE). The Women's National Press Association was replaced by the Women's National Press Club. Glavlit, the official organ for censorship and the protection of "state secrets," was organized in the Soviet Union. The Bataka founded *Munyonyozi* in Kampala, Uganda, with Daudi Bassude as editor, to pursue land redistribution.

1923   The opening of Congress was broadcast for the first time. Henry R. Luce and Briton Hadden began *Time Magazine*. The American Society of Newspaper Editors (ASNE) developed its Canons of Journalism, the first national code of ethics for the press. W. M. Kiplinger began the *Kiplinger Newsletter*, a weekly Washington publication for businessmen.

1924 The first European school of journalism, the ecole supérieure de journalisme, was founded in association with the Catholic University of Lille. H. L. Mencken and George Nathan cofounded (and jointly edited) the *American Mercury*. *The Ethics of Journalism* by Nelson A. Crawford was published. Benito Mussolini founded the Fascist newspaper *Il Tevere*.

1925 Mussolini founded the Istituto Nazionale L'Unione Cinematographica Educative (LUCE Institute) to coordinate the distribution of newsreels to an international network of cinemas.

1926 The International Federation of Journalists was established. The Inter-American Press Association was created to promote freedom of the press and journalism in Latin America. The *Dagong bao* was founded by Wu Dingchang and edited by Zhang Jiluan in China. Pietro Nenni, editor of the Italian Socialist party's newspaper *Avanti*, was forced by the Fascists to emigrate to France.

1927 *Editor & Publisher* merged with *The Fourth Estate*. Silas Bent criticized newspaper chains and sensationalistic tabloids in *Ballyhoo: The Voice of the Press*. Willard Bleyer's *Main Currents in the History of American Journalism* was published.

1928 The *Scotsman* became the first newspaper to transmit pictures from Europe by telegraph. Columnist Heywood Broun shifted "It Seems to Me" to the *New York Telegram*.

1929 Julias Elias, later Lord Southwood, took over the *Daily Herald* and launched a series of sales gimmicks to expand circulation. The *Athens Times* began publication using a press provided by Colonel Leicester Stanhope over a century earlier. **August:** In a radio address on the state of American journalism, novelist Sherwood Anderson lamented the dullness and standardization of the press.

1930 Two news reporters accompanied the U.S. delegation to the naval conference in London. American Anna Louise Strong founded the English-language *Moscow News* as a pro-Soviet journal.

1931 *Keesing's Contemporary Archives*, a weekly documentation of world events, began publication in London. Cheng Shewo established one of China's first independent journalism schools.

1932 The *Palestine Post*, later the *Jerusalem Post*, was founded to improve relations between the Jews and their British occupiers. **4 December:** *Walter Winchell's Journal* began on NBC's Blue Network.

1933 Austrian novelist and journalist Joseph Roth moved to Paris, where he continued his outspoken criticism of Adolf Hitler and German militarism. The American Newspaper Guild was founded to represent editorial workers. Journalist Dorothy Day founded the *Catholic Worker*, a radical monthly publication. **March 12:** The Nazis established the Reichministerium für Volksaufklärung und Propaganda by presidential decree.

1934 Louisiana governor Huey "Kingfish" Long tried to curb opposition newspapers through a 2 percent tax (later declared unconstitutional) on gross advertising receipts.

1935 Norway's journalist Carl von Ossietzky won the Nobel Peace Prize for his role in German-Norwegian relations. The *March of Time* made its debut in American and foreign movie theaters. Arthur Krock won the first of two Pulitzer prizes (the second was in 1938) as Washington correspondent for the *New York Times*. Cheng Shewo founded the *Libao*, a popular news tabloid in Shanghai. **20 October:** Journalism teacher George Gallup launched "America Speaks," a syndicated public opinion poll, in some 30 American newspapers. **December:** After exposing connections between the criminal underworld and Minnesota officials, Walter Liggett, publisher of the *Midwest American*, was gunned down in front of his wife and young daughter.

1936 Publication of *First Principles of Typography* by Stanley Morrison, who designed the new typeface Times Roman in his capacity as typographical advisor to *The Times*. Ishbel Ross's *Ladies of the Press*, the first book-length history of American women journalists, was published. **February:** The British-owned *Japan Chronicle* was raided by Japanese army officers during the White Rainbow (or *Osaka Asahi*) incident.

1937 Alice Mae Lee Jemison began campaigning for native American causes in her Washington, D.C. newsletter, *The First American*. Journalist

Karl Radek was among the high-profile communists who confessed to treason during the (show) Trial of the Seventeen in the Soviet Union. **November:** Nnamdi Azikiwe founded the *West African Pilot* in Nigeria.

1938 Most of Austria's dailies were forced to close following the Nazi takeover. CBS's Edward R. Murrow led the coverage of the Munich Crisis by radio reporters. Gilbert Seldes's *Lords of the Press* was published.

1939 Albert Camus began to work as a journalist in Paris, where he joined the resistance and edited the underground paper *Combat*.

1940 Veteran newsman George Seldes began publication of *In Fact*, a critical review of the press distributed with the help of the Congress of Industrial Organizations (CIO). *P.M.*, a liberal tabloid without advertising, was established by Ralph Ingersoll in New York City. Efforts by the National Union of Journalists in Portugal to establish a journalism education program were scuttled by the Salazar government. **6 February:** John H. Sengstacke, editor of the *Chicago Defender*, founded the National Negro Publishers Association.

1941 Frank Luther Mott's *American Journalism: A History* was published. The first American TV station went on the air. **January:** *Time* editor Henry Luce wrote an editorial announcing the "American Century."

1942 Former *Times'* editor and CBS commentator Elmer Davis was appointed chief of the U.S. Office of War Information. French historian Marc Bloch, cofounder of the *Annales d'histoire, économique et sociale*, helped to publish the Resistance newspaper *Franc-Tireur*.

1944 The Vichy government's press agency Agence Havas was renamed Agence France-presse (AFP). *Le Monde*, France's newspaper of record, was founded in Paris by Hubert Beuve-Méry as replacement for the discredited *Le Temps*. The novelist and political thinker Ignazio Silone returned from exile in Switzerland to edit the newspaper *Avanti* in Italy. The Commission on Freedom of the Press (Hutchins Commission) was created by Henry Luce. American Lawrence Dennis, publisher of the fascist *Weekly Foreign Letter* and later *Appeal to Reason*, was tried for sedition, but the charges were dismissed after a mistrial. *Many a Watchful Night*, a collection of journalist John Mason Brown's broadcasts to the American fleet during the invasion of Normandy, was published.

1945 Stanley Morrison, who later wrote a multi-volume history of *The Times*, became editor of *The Times Literary Supplement*. The Italian journalist and novelist Giovanni Guareschi helped to found the popular weekly *Candido*. Kyodo News was established as a nonprofit cooperative news agency in Tokyo. Martha Rountree and Lawrence E. Spivak created the radio interview program *Meet the Press*. AP correspondent Joe Morton died at the Mauthausen concentration camp, the only known journalist to have been executed by the Nazis. The American journalist Robert Henry Best was convicted of treason in the United States for broadcasting Nazi propaganda from Vienna during the war. James "Scotty" Reston of the *New York Times* won the first of two Pulitzer prizes (the other was in 1957) for his reporting. A. J. Liebling began "The Wayward Press" department for *The New Yorker*. The first school of journalism in Canada was founded at Carleton University in Ottawa.

1946 The Japanese Newspaper Publishers and Editors Association (NSK) was established to promote ethical standards in reporting. **August 31:** *The New Yorker* devoted its entire issue to "Hiroshima" by John Hersey.

1947 American editors formed the National Conference of Editorial Writers to help preserve their role. Newsmen with fellowships at Harvard University began *Nieman Reports*, a critical review published five times a year. Helen Rogers Reid succeeded her husband, Ogden Mills Reid, as editor of the *New York Tribune*. **6 November:** *Meet the Press* began on NBC television.

1948 Network TV news began in the United States with CBS's *Douglas Edwards and the News* and NBC's *The Camel News Caravan*. **October 4:** The popular comic strip *Pogo*, a satirical commentary on current political events by Walt Kelly, made its first appearance in the *New York Star*.

1949 The Pacifica Foundation, a small network of noncommercial FM stations, was organized by Lewis Hill in Los Angeles to provide hard news and in-depth commentary along with various forms of alternative programming.

1950   Radio Free Europe was established by the United States to broadcast news to countries behind the "Iron Curtain." The *Sangbad*, one of Bangladesh's leading national dailies, was founded. *Journalism Quarterly* published David Manning White's "The 'Gate Keeper': A Case Study in Selection of News" on how an editor at a small midwestern newspaper decided which wire service stories to run.

1951   **18 November:** *See It Now* began on CBS television.

1952   Fred L. Packer won a Pulitzer Prize for his cartoon lampooning Harry S. Truman after the president had attacked newspapers for printing information about American military installations contained in government press releases; the cartoon was captioned "Your Editors Ought to Have More Sense Than to Print What I Say!"

1953   The U.S. television program *Person to Person* went on the air. *One*, the first widely circulated gay and lesbian publication, was founded in Los Angeles.

1954   **19 November:** CBS-TV began *Face the Nation*, a Sunday afternoon interview program featuring public figures.

1955   William F. Buckley Jr. founded the *National Review* as a conservative journal of opinion. Edwin Fancher, Daniel Wolf, and Norman Mailer founded the *Village Voice* as an underground weekly tabloid in New York's Greenwich Village.

1956   Abigail Van Buren began her "Dear Abby" advice column for the lovelorn in the *San Francisco Chronicle*.

1957   AFP began to acquire a measure of independence. Glavlit hid knowledge of a major catastrophe in the South Urals from the Soviet people.

1959   "The Safe Car You Can't Buy" by Ralph Nader appeared in the *Nation*. Ralph Emerson McGill, editor of the Atlanta *Constitution,* was awarded a Pulitzer Prize for editorials condemning anti-civil rights violence. Journalism education began in South Africa at the Afrikaans-language Potchefstroom University.

1960   The U.S. Congress temporarily suspended the requirement that broadcasters offer political candidates "equal time" in order to allow four prime time debates between presidential candidates John F. Kennedy and Richard M. Nixon. Former journalist Carl E. Lindstrom published *The Fading American Newspaper.*

1961 The European Newspaper Publishers Association (ENPA), a nonprofit organization based in Brussels, was founded to promote freedom of the press and protect intellectual property rights. The *Columbia Journalism Review* was founded under the auspices of Columbia University's School of Journalism.

1962 *Der Spiegel* was accused of treason and temporarily shut down after publishing an article critical of German military preparedness. Some 387 news documentaries flooded American prime time television. Walter Cronkite succeeded Douglas Edwards as the evening newscaster for CBS-TV.

1964 NBC News broadcast Robert F. Rogers's hour-long documentary *Vietnam: It's a Mad War.* The "May Craig Amendment," which Maine political columnist May Craig succeeded in making part of the federal Civil Rights Act, prohibited employment discrimination on the basis of sex. William Gieber challenged White's 1950 gatekeeping study by showing how bureaucratic routines affect the choices of wire editors.

1965 A professional training center for journalists was established at the University of Madagascar.

1966 A new press law in Spain allowed for the expansion of news through self-censorship. The U.S. federal government enacted the Freedom of Information Act (FOIA).

1967 Universal News, the last of the major U.S. newsreel companies, ceased operations. The Astor family sold *The Times* to Canadian Roy Thomson. Robert Maynard became the *Washington Post*'s first African American national correspondent.

1968 **September:** *60 Minutes* began on CBS television. Following police violence against the press during the Democratic Convention in Chicago, a number of journalists began the *Chicago Journalism Review.*

1969 **13 November:** In a televised speech to a Republican party conference in Des Moines, the American vice president Spiro T. Agnew began a series of attacks on the credibility and integrity of network news.

1970 The Women's National Press Club changed its name to the Washington Press Club. A department of journalism was created at Rhodes University in South Africa.

1971 CBS president Frank Stanton successfully countered government efforts to interfere with editorial freedom in connection with the documentary "The Selling of the Pentagon." The National Press Club opened its membership to women under pressure from President Lyndon Johnson.

1972 The first edition of Gloria Steinem's feminist magazine *Ms.* appeared as an insert in *New York* magazine.

1973 Following a study commissioned by the Twentieth Century Fund, the National News Council was established in New York City to provide the public with a way to complain about press performance without having to engage in lawsuits, but later dissolved because of lack of media support.

1974 The periodical *Journalism History* began publication.

1975 The National Association of Black Journalists (NABJ) and Investigative Reporters and Editors (IRE) were founded in the United States.

1976 *La Republica* began publication in Italy as an independent newspaper, but was later purchased by the Mondadori publishing house. The government of Angola nationalized the press, radio, and television.

1977 Larry Maddry, a columnist at Norfolk Virginian-Pilot, organized the National Society of Newspaper Columnists (NSNC). American publishers, editors, and advertisers began a Newspaper Research Project to look for ways of creating a better product. CBS began *Lou Grant*, a popular weekly one-hour TV drama dealing with newspaper journalism.

1978 **June:** ABC began broadcasting *20/20*. A new constitution in Spain declared full freedom of expression.

1979 Brian Lamb formed the U.S. cable network C-SPAN (Cable Satellite Public Affairs Network) to provide 24-hour coverage of national events such as political conventions and debates in Congress.

Robert Maynard became the first African American editor of a major daily newspaper in the United States, the Gannett company's *Oakland Tribune*.

1981 The American Newspaper Guild became the Newspaper Guild. The *Washington Post* returned a Pulitzer Prize awarded to one of its reporters who had fabricated a story about an eight-year-old heroin addict. Australian media baron Rupert Murdoch purchased *The Times*. The Canadian Royal Commission on Newspapers issued its report. The Asian American Journalists Association was founded.

1982 *USA Today* was established as a national newspaper. The *Wall Street Journal* was embroiled in scandal after one of its columnists sold information to a stockbroker. An internal investigation of the CBS-TV documentary "The Uncounted Enemy: A Vietnam Deception" found that the documentary had violated network standards. PBS refused to broadcast the final episode of Peter Davis's documentary "Middletown," which showed high school students using drugs and swearing.

1983 The periodical *American Journalism* began publication.

1984 The American Association of Schools and Departments of Journalism (AASDJ) merged with the American Society of Journalism School Administrators (ASJSA) to become the Association of Schools of Journalism and Mass Communication (ASJMC). Also in the United States, the National Association of Hispanic Journalists and Native American Journalists Association were organized, while the National News Council ceased operations.

1985 Robert Ménard and Jean-Claude Guillebard founded Reporters sans frontières in Montpelier, an international organization to promote alternative journalism and later freedom of the press. The Washington Press Club merged with the National Press Club to become the National Press Club in Washington, D.C.

1986 The Chernobyl nuclear disaster forced Soviet authorities to modify their longstanding practice of secrecy about natural and industrial catastrophes.

1987 *Ms.* magazine was closed, but revived four years later. The first news agency in Sierra Leone (SLENA) began operations.

1989 Warner Communications merged with Time, Inc. to form Time Warner, one of the world's largest media companies.

1990 The Society of Environmental Journalists was founded in the United States to improve environmental reporting.

1991 The creation of the independent Republic of Armenia was accompanied by privatization of the newspaper industry.

1992 The European Journalism Centre (EJC), a nonprofit organization based in the Netherlands, was founded to provide training support for journalists and journalism educators. RSF organized the inaugural International Day of Freedom of the Press. The American Newspaper Publishers Association (ANPA) merged with the Newspaper Advertising Bureau and six other related associations to form the Newspaper Association of America (NAA). NBC was forced to apologize for a *Dateline* story on unsafe gas tanks that used incendiary devices to ensure an explosion.

1993 The Syndicate of Journalists in Portugal adopted a Deontological Code setting forth 10 duties for journalists. The University of Sierra Leone created the country's first academic program to train journalists.

1996 Time Warner purchased Turner Broadcasting System, becoming the world's largest media conglomerate.

1997 The 35,000-member Newspaper Guild joined the 600,000-member Communication Workers of America. Photojournalist José Luis Cabezas was murdered in Argentina.

1998 The first blog was created where readers could add comments to other writers' entries.

1999 Associated Press reporter Myles Tierney was killed in Freetown, Sierra Leone, by Revolutionary United Front rebels.

2000 Journalists at *La Presencia* in La Paz, Bolivia, received death threats and a bomb scare while investigating a drug trafficking story.

2001 Following the attacks of 9/11 in New York and Washington, U.S. network evening news coverage of foreign policy and global conflict increased substantially.

2002 Mohammed al Mukhtar, editor of the daily *Al-Madina* in Saudi Arabia, was dismissed by the government after publishing a cartoon criticizing the judicial system.

2003 Private Jessica Lynch, whose alleged capture by Iraqi soldiers and subsequent rescue by U.S. special operations forces became a major news story, later accused the government of fabricating the story as part of its propaganda efforts.

2004 *Le Figaro*, the flagship of the French publishing group Socpresse, was purchased by the giant armaments maker Groupe Industriel Marcel Dassault, raising concerns about its future independence.

2005 News agencies like Reuters and the Associated Press began competing with newspapers by providing some of their content through websites and mobile phone feeds.

2006 A photographer working for Reuters was found to have digitally altered pictures of the Israel-Lebanon conflict. **30 September:** The Danish newspaper Jyllands-Posten published 12 cartoons depicting the prophet Muhammad, setting off an escalating chain of Muslim protests that ended with the death of over 300 people.

2007 Freedom House found a decline in freedom of the press in both democratic and non-democratic regimes.

2008 A survey by the World Association of Newspapers reported that Japan led the world in daily newspaper sales per thousand (627), followed by Norway (580), Finland (503), and Sweden and Singapore (449), while readers spent the most time with newspapers in Turkey (74 minutes a day), Belgium (54 minutes), and Finland and China (48 minutes). **August:** An estimated 21,600 accredited journalists covered the Beijing Olympic Games amidst outside protests against the continuing incarceration of journalists in China.

Introduction

Journalist. 1. A person who earns a living by writing for or editing a newspaper or periodical. Also, a reporter for radio or television.

— *Shorter Oxford English Dictionary*, 5th ed. (2002), p. 1464

Journalist. n (1693). 1a: a person engaged in journalism; esp: a writer or editor for a news medium. 1b: writer who aims at a mass audience.

— *Merriam-Webster's Collegiate Dictionary*, 11th ed. (2003), p. 676

Journalism. [Early 19c: from French *journalisme* . . .]. The enterprise of producing newspapers and magazines (including reporting, writing, editing, photographing, and managing) as well as the styles of writing used in such publications.

— *Oxford Companion to the English Language* (1992), p. 554

The word *journalist* started to become common in the early 18th century to designate a new kind of writer, about a century before *journalism* made its appearance to describe what those writers produced. Despite its **etymology**, however, journalism originated as a form of discourse long before it became a stable and readily identifiable means of gainful employment. From the outset, this discourse was closely related to, but also transcended, the writing of news. Though varying in form from one age and society to another, it gradually distinguished itself from ballads, chronicles, history, and the novel through its focus on the unfolding present, its eyewitness perspective on current events, and its reliance on everyday language, among other characteristics. These discursive features later influenced the working arrangements and internal hierarchies governing journalism as an institutionalized occupation.

They contributed, for example, to the general openness of journalism to new practitioners, sometimes regardless of formal training, which has limited the degree to which journalism is considered to be a profession. At the same time, however, the evolution of production practices has also affected the nature of journalistic discourse. This reverse pressure has led to periodic crises among those who regard journalism as essential for civil society and a healthy **public sphere**. For much of its history, therefore, journalism has been subject to an inner tension between its discursive ideals and its occupational realities.

As both a form of discourse and an occupation, journalism has been shaped by three main forces or factors. The first of these factors is what might be called the resources principle, according to which those individuals, groups, or institutions with the greatest resources in society will normally be in the best position to use or control communication, including journalism, to enhance their own power. This principle does not assume that wealthy individuals, well-resourced groups, or even the state will necessarily invest resources in this manner or do so effectively; it merely assumes that all communication and its control requires an expenditure of resources such that, all other things being equal, the possession of greater resources naturally entails better means and opportunities for using or controlling communication.

In contrast to the resources principle, which has operated throughout the history of journalism, the market principle is essentially the application of the capitalist law of supply and demand to media content. It assumes that in a reasonably free market, the greater willingness of audiences to pay for one kind of material or set of ideas rather than another exerts a substantial influence over the production of media messages. From its initial introduction in the West in the late medieval period, this principle has struggled to extricate itself from the resources principle, which has compromised and manipulated it at every turn. In some parts of the world, it has successfully established itself, in conjunction with advertising, as a countervailing factor in the development of journalistic content; in others, it has remained largely ineffectual. Its operation was first recognized by late 19th-century English writers such as G. H. Lewes and Anthony Trollope, who challenged the prevailing idea of journalism as a kind of literary schoolroom in which journalists have a substantial degree of autonomy. Anticipating modern academic critiques of the mass media, they argued that the newspaper is part of the marketplace and is thus governed by relationships between buyers and sellers. For Trollope, the journalist is less a philanthropic mentor than a self-interested writer who must keep a close eye on what readers are willing to pay for.[1]

Trollope's recognition of the market principle as a factor in shaping journalism was shared by the American philosopher George Herbert Mead in "The Nature of Aesthetic Experience" (1926). At the same time, however, Mead suggested that there is a third principle, which also governs journalism to some extent. Like Trollope, Mead emphasized how audiences determine what is news through their purchasing choices. Calling news a commodity in an "acquisitive society," he argued that the "value" of most news varies not only "with its truth" but also in accordance with its "enjoyability." For that reason, "the reporter is generally sent out to get a story, not the facts," and must produce the kinds of "reverie" desired by "certain fairly defined groups." Whether this amusement constitutes an "aesthetic experience" depends, in Mead's view, on whether it also "serves to interpret to the reader his experience as the shared experience of the community of which he feels himself to be a part." However, despite stressing that a newspaper could "never get far away from the form of the news which their reveries demand," Mead still allowed that it might try to "lead its readers" to a larger sense of community.[2] It could, in other words, try to promote what had come to be known as the "public interest."

Like the market principle, the public interest principle is historically contingent and vulnerable to manipulation by the resources principle. Its operation is perhaps most clearly visible in the creation of public broadcasting institutions and their news and public affairs programming in the 1930s and 1940s. It is not limited, however, to public service broadcasters or to broadcasting generally; it first emerged in print journalism in the 18th century in conjunction with the development of a sphere of public information, discussion, and debate about matters of general social concern. Although this public sphere was influenced by both the resources and market principles, its shift from coffeehouses and salons to newspapers was dependent on journalists with a sense of purpose that transcended party interests and profits. Stimulated by related ideas about public opinion, popular sovereignty, democracy, and nationalism, the ideal of serving what was initially referred to as the common or general interest was further developed in the context of the

penny press, the so-called New Journalism, **muckraking**, and **investigative journalism**. While not immune to resources or market considerations, these new forms of journalism sought to promote the general welfare of society as their practitioners understood it. Of the three main principles shaping journalistic practice, to be sure, the public interest has generally been the weakest. However, the rise of journalism **education and training**, **codes of ethics**, and **professional organizations** have contributed to its survival as a force in modern journalism. "What distinguishes journalism from other media activities," writes Lynette Sheridan Burns, "is the notion of *service to the public interest*."[3]

EARLY JOURNALISM AND THE RESOURCES PRINCIPLE

Wealth or resources have long been used to stimulate, produce, manipulate, or suppress journalism on behalf of certain vested interests. States, churches, classes, businesses, unions, and various social groups and powerful individuals have all invested resources in an effort to create or control journalism on behalf of their own particular ends. According to Sian Lewis, the democratic city-states of ancient Greece opposed the creation of a system for gathering and exchanging news for fear that centralized control over information might deprive them of their independence.[4] But the use of resources to control and manage news for political purposes soon became common. In ancient Rome, Julius Caesar inaugurated the *acta diurna* so as to "strip the aristocratic senate of some of its mystique and hence authority."[5] In Han China, the *dibao* was used to provide official reports and interpretations of events; it also served as a means of communication among the political elite. A similar publication known as the *Chobo* ("court gazette") was begun by royal officials in Korea in 1392; it continued on an irregular basis until 1895.[6] In **India**, the Mughal Emperor Akbar (1556–1605) had clerks or *akhbār nawīs* ("newswriters") prepare a somewhat more restricted form of court diary.

Despite their underlying political purpose, there was some recognition in these early news vehicles of the need to maintain their audience's interest. The anonymous compilers of the *acta diurna* provided an element of entertainment by including stories about things like "a dog's exceptional loyalty, or the exhibition of the bird Phoenix on the forum."[7]

The *dibao* also understood the value of popular news items. Even the *akhbār nawīs*, who had to adhere to a strict formula and use deferential Persian language, tried to enliven their reports with advice or predictions.[8] However, the primary objective of these enterprises was political propaganda or, in the case of the Mughal court diary, political surveillance. No thought was given to recouping the resources invested in these instruments through sales or any other system of remuneration.

In medieval and early modern Europe, royal proclamations were used to control the dissemination of news. In addition to requiring the performance or cessation of certain actions, proclamations informed the public about matters of governance. In England, royal messengers delivered them to the Crown's chief officers in the counties, who then used paid criers and other means to ensure that they were heard. "Whatever its deficiencies," writes James A. Doig, ". . . few people in the kingdom would not have attended, or heard of, a royal proclamation at a town cross or standard or some other designated public place, whether to hear orders or decrees which directly affected them, or to learn of news at Westminster or across the Channel."[9] In addition to severe penalties, proclamations and other official news notices were used in part to counter rumormongers, for as C. A. J. Armstrong has noted, governments had "no doubt that in a society relying on oral information, whispering could be a dangerous weapon in the hands of subversive elements."[10]

The Crown was not alone in investing some of its resources on the dissemination of news. Though reaching smaller audiences, minstrels and balladeers also expended time and energy purveying non-official news in the streets of Europe. The *joculatores* (Latin) and *jongleurs* (French) were usually the servants of barons and ecclesiastics, but occasionally men of knightly rank or clerical training.[11] They generally provided less in the way of local news and innuendo than balladeers, who initially circulated their rhymes on manuscript broadsheets and played a significant role well into the 16th century. With the spread of printing, the "black-letter" ballad (so named because of the typeface used until about 1700) came into its own. Printed on coarse paper, filled with typographical errors, and utilizing primitive woodcuts, the broadside ballad was so popular by the mid-16th century that steps were taken to restrain its circulation. An early study found a number of points of comparison with journalism. The Renaissance balladist, wrote Hyder

Rollins, "fully understood the value . . . of dispensing news while it was news," suffered from "the interviewing mania," and was not averse to drawing moral lessons. Balladeers "were not trying to write poetry, or even ballads," he concluded somewhat anachronistically; "they were writing news-stories and editorials."[12]

Ballads were also made up by ordinary men and women with the intention of defaming someone's character, written down or printed by literate members of their circle, and then sung, recited, or otherwise made public among their neighbors.[13] In the case of the professional versifier whose ballads dealt with news, however, a patron or independent wealth of some kind was usually necessary to sustain his activity. This requirement was even more applicable to the medieval and early modern chronicler. The roots of journalism in the chronicle are suggested, as D. R. Woolf has pointed out, by "the number of newspapers which today call themselves chronicles."[14] Like the balladeer, the chronicler was limited to what he either saw himself as an "eyewitness" or was "reported to him."[15] Similarly, he did not consider what he recorded as constituting a continuum of action. As one medievalist has explained, "every new page of the clerical chronicle was potentially, at least, a new beginning; interest, not relevance, was the criterion determining selection."[16] Unlike the historian, the chronicler did not try to integrate the information he received into a single, uniform narrative, a characteristic which also generally distinguishes journalism from history.

By the 16th century, the most important news medium for literate members of European society was the printed pamphlet, or small book of news of about 20 pages. In England, where their publication was largely unregulated until the 1580s, news **pamphlets** grew steadily in number and sought to capture the immediacy of events. As John Timpane has noted, their authors engaged in "linear composition at great speed, often without looking back. The resulting energetic prose [was] often very close to speech, complete with syntax switched in midsentence, tedious subjects thrown out in midparagraph, and many inconsistencies, all carried on with a vivid awareness of the reader."[17] Even so, their publication remained irregular; they waited upon events and thus had an indeterminate, but generally quite expansive, concept of present time.

In **France**, the unofficial news pamphlets known as *canards* often made use of the term *veritable* in their titles "to reassure their readers that the report being retailed was just unembellished fact."[18] But for most pamphleteers, the primary purpose of relating news was to comment upon it. As M. A. Shaaber's pioneering work put it, 16th-century news was "almost invariably partial, without scruple or apology. Commentary never lagged far behind it." News pamphlets were used not only by governments and their sympathizers, both openly and surreptitiously, but to an even greater extent by "various parties, sects, groups, and organizations" so as to "benefit their cause and put in print their own versions and interpretations of passing events."[19] Indeed, a recent study of early modern Italian news publications has suggested that they were so slanted by political ideology as to imperil effective government and contribute to an age of skepticism generally.[20]

Among the more accomplished of Italian pamphleteers was the versatile satirical writer Pietro Aretino (1492–1556), whom Jacob Burckhardt described as the father of modern journalism, though more in disgust than admiration. In crafting a popular persona as an indignant moral critic, Aretino anticipated the modern columnist through his emphasis on his own personality, his presumption that all forms of human activity were grist for his mill, and his rejection of the artifice and pedantry of the humanists in favor of plain language. It has been suggested that the spontaneity of his writings was "an act of sprezzatura, the artful concealment of art. In fact, Aretino seems to have studied carefully and assimilated thoughtfully the literary targets that he pretends to disdain."[21] Aretino served as a model for a group of "low-born adventurers of the pen" known as the *poligraphi* who, according to Paul Grendler, were "the nearest thing to journalists or columnists that the sixteenth century possessed."[22]

In addition to satire, 16th-century pamphlets made increasing use of what looks to modern eyes like sensationalism.[23] In 1567, for example, a French *canard* reported the presence of a dragon over Paris, while a pamphlet printed in London in 1624 provided a graphic illustration of "the cruell and most horrible Butche of Mr. Trat, Curate of olde Cleatte; who was first murthe[red] as he trauailed upon the high way, then was brought home . . . and there was quartered and imboweld: his quarters and bowels being, afterwards perboyld and salted up, in a most strange and fearfull manner."[24] However, a recent study by Joy Wiltenburg argues that in the case of crime reporting, which is thought to have originated in 16th-century **Germany**, sensationalism served various political, religious, and social agendas, such as governmental authority and the patriarchal family. It was initially designed to influence respectable upper and middle-class members of society more than the lower orders.[25]

Regardless of motivation, news pamphlets did not provide any real continuity in their coverage of events. For more regular intelligence, therefore, government officials, prominent individuals, bankers, and wealthier merchants sometimes arranged for handwritten **newsletters** to be prepared on their behalf. In late 15th-century Italy, for example, Giovanni Sabadino degli Arienti of Bologna prepared a regular newsletter for Ercole d'Este, Duke of Ferrara.[26] During the 16th century, the Fuggers commissioned newsletters as a means of keeping informed about political and economic events. In the 1590s, private newsletter writers in England like John Chamberlain and Rowland Whyte came to be known as intelligencers. By then, however, a new force was beginning to shape the production of news. Instead of being entirely dependent on the investment of governmental, organizational, or personal resources, news and journalism began to come under the influence of capitalism.

JOURNALISM AND THE EMERGENCE
OF A LIMITED MARKET PRINCIPLE

For most of the Middle Ages in Europe, "publishing," in the sense of producing multiple copies of a text, was governed by the resources principle. In some cases, authors copied their own writing in order to circulate it among friends, present it to a patron, or simply make use of it themselves. In other cases, institutions such as monasteries had their own scriptoria to supply their internal needs for texts. Even individuals might have a copying facility; in the mid-14th century, Richard de Bury, an English bishop, had his own staff of copyists. In a few cases, authors and consumers jointly commissioned one or more copyists on an ad hoc basis.

During the 12th century, the rise of universities and the growth of literacy created more demand for books than could be met by the monastic scriptoria. In response, lay stationers (*stationarii*) in Paris, Bologna, Oxford, and elsewhere developed a *pecia* or putting-out system to serve the needs of teachers and students. Authorized exemplars of manuscripts were borrowed from the universities and then farmed out piecemeal in quires (*pecia*) to professional scriveners, usually women and students, who would copy them for a fixed fee. By the mid-15th century, there were apparently more than 10,000 copyists in the vicinity of Paris alone.[27] The early lay stationers were closely controlled by the universities and guilds. But in the late medieval period, some of them broke free from their control in response to growing demand for printed materials among the bourgeoisie. They began to engage in a degree of what Derek Pearsall calls "speculative, entrepreneur-initiated production, as distinct from commissioned or bespoke production."[28] In so doing, they introduced a limited market principle into the world of publishing; namely, the power of buyers to stimulate the production and influence the content of texts through their purchasing habits. An element of capitalism, or production for profit, was thus present in publishing *before* the introduction of typography by Gutenberg in the 1450s.

By drastically reducing labor costs, the printing press greatly increased profit margins for publishers. Even so, printed texts, including printed news products, remained quite expensive. It has been estimated that a full news account of the Ottoman seizure of Rhodes in 1522 might cost as much as a pair of children's shoes. As a result, the application of typography to news production did not immediately create a vibrant market for news. For most of the 16th century, publication was limited to isolated news pamphlets and occasional collections of news or "relations." Toward the end of the century, however, these "relations" or digests began to appear on a less haphazard basis. The first regular news digest was Michael von Aitzing's *Relatio historica* or *Messrelationen* (1588–93), a summary of political and religious news prepared for the biennial Frankfurt book fairs. Four years after the demise of Aitzing's publication, Samuel Dilbaum in Switzerland began a monthly *Historical Relation or Narrative* about the great powers in "almost the whole of Europe." During the first two decades of the 17th century, similar publications of what were increasingly called "tidings" (*Zeitung* in German, *Tydinghe* in Dutch) sprang up in various European municipalities, some on a weekly basis. In 1605, for example, Abraham Berhoeven began publishing *Nieuwe Tidinghe* on a weekly—later thrice-weekly—basis in Antwerp.[29]

It was in England, nonetheless, that the first regular and *frequent* news vehicle emerged. In 1589, seeking to satisfy demand for ongoing coverage of Elizabeth I's military support for Henry of Navarre, a group of printers led by **John Wolfe** began the production of "news quartos"—a term borrowed by Paul Voss from an anonymous newspaper story in 1930 describing some purchases by the British museum. The periodicity of these Elizabethan news quartos was closely related to the desire to keep Londoners informed of the fate of some 20,000 English soldiers fighting on behalf of Henry IV. In Voss's view, they were the first news publication with recurring protagonists and a developing story line. Their exploration of English valor, religious observation, and geographical uniqueness helped shape the imaginative writings of Shakespeare, Spenser, and Marlowe and through them fostered a new sense of national identity.

The news quartos were the first news publications governed more by commercial than power considerations. Aided by the spread of literacy, their average print run of 750 copies was marketed to a diverse audience through a variety of advertising techniques. Though sympathetic to Henry IV, they were not written at the behest of the government and cultivated at least "the appearance of objectivity: reporting the events takes priority over blatant sermonizing."[30] At the same time, however, their publication was also tied to a larger moral purpose. In contrast to contemporary poems, plays, sermons, and political tracts about the civil war, they conveyed its ghastly realities directly and forcefully through vivid images of slaughter, rape, and the devastation of Paris, where over 13,000 people died of hunger or malnutrition. The purpose of these graphic accounts of death and destruction, according to Voss, was less to attract readers through sensationalism than to warn them about the destructive consequences of civil war.

From the outset, the operation of the market principle was severely constrained by **censorship**, the granting of publishing monopolies, and other forms of control. Because of restrictions on domestic news, for example, the news quartos were limited to foreign coverage. When they came to a sudden end in 1593, the only form of regular news production in England, foreign or domestic, was that of newsletters, which were essentially a commissioned news product. In 1618, however, the outbreak of the Thirty Years War led Caspar van Hilten in the **Netherlands** to begin selling an ongoing account of events entitled *Courante uyt Italien, Duytsland &c* and the term *coranto* soon came to designate similar publications in **Spain** and **Denmark**. Late in 1620, the Dutch printer George Veseler issued a coranto consisting of one double-sided sheet of news for export to England. As these Dutch **corantos** began to multiply, a number of London printers undertook to make their own translations and, in the case of Thomas Archer, to produce a coranto of his own for sale.

Archer was temporarily imprisoned for his efforts, but after his release joined with Nathaniel Bourne and Nathaniel Butter to market the first indigenous coranto in September 1621. By 1622, it had grown from a single-sheet folio publication into a quarto pamphlet entitled *Weekely News*. Unlike the Elizabethan news quartos, however, the corantos of the 1620s were "English only in language and point of sale, not in source or content."[31] Moreover, they all died in 1632 when even news from abroad was deemed too dangerous to publish. Though free from government propaganda, their journalism was limited to what Joad Raymond has called "digestive editing." Even "the periodicity of these early corantos was irregular; they appeared at roughly weekly intervals, whenever there was enough news to fill them."[32]

CONTINUATION OF THE RESOURCES PRINCIPLE THROUGH MONOPOLIES OF NEWS

For a century and a half after the introduction of printing in France, the circulation of information and commentary about current events remained dependent on handwritten sheets or *nouvelles à la main*. In 1631, however, Théophraste Renaudot, the royal physician and a court favorite, convinced Cardinal Richelieu that a printed newspaper with a monopoly over political news could check the effects of rumor and gossip. The *Gazette de France*, which survived as the official organ of the state until the Revolution of 1848, began as a weekly two-sheet brochure with no actual material on France, but later added items on royal and noble baptisms, marriages, journeys, and deaths and eventually included scientific, cultural, and economic news. During the Fronde, Renaudot moved it (along with the court) to Saint-Germain, while his sons published the *Courrier français* for the Parlement of Paris.[33]

Because of a growing desire for timely news, the *Gazette* inadvertently served as a training ground for French journalism. Rather than wait upon the inefficient mail system, provincial printers used express couriers to obtain the *Gazette* in advance and then made counterfeit copies for impatient readers. In response, Renaudot created a faster distribution system and sold the right to reset and market the *Gazette* to printers in provincial centers. Although the reprinted *Gazette* added very little original content, its production eventually contributed to a flourishing provincial press.[34] To prevent the *Gazette* from falling under the control of a narrow clique, Colbert set up a supervisory committee that included a genealogist, poet, diplomat, novelist, and historian. But the legal dissemination of political news remained its prerogative; although the *Journal de la ville de Paris* received permission in 1676 to publish political items, it lasted only six months, probably as a result of the *Gazette*'s opposition.

Government news publications also emerged in 17th-century England, but by a more circuitous route. When Charles I lifted the restriction on publishing foreign news in 1638, Bourne and Butter renewed publication of the *Weekly News*. But it was still subject to a new system of licensing imposed by the Star Chamber a year earlier. When the Star Chamber was abolished in 1641, licensing and censorship also ceased and a new kind of publication appeared on the streets of London: a weekly periodical, eight pages in length, dated, and containing domestic news. Entitled *The Diurnall, or The Heads of all the Proceedings in Parliament*, it was the first of a series of newsbooks which tried to meet the demand for news during the English civil war. Although these newsbooks inherited a few of the characteristics of corantos (such as title pages, though these were later abandoned) and used much the same distribution network, Raymond argues that they bore a closer resemblance to non-periodical pamphlets. The publishers of corantos did not, for the most part, move into the production of newsbooks, leaving the field open for various innovations. Unlike corantos, newsbooks had consistent titles, exact periodicity, consecutive pagination, and regularity in length and they soon displaced corantos as the dominant form of news vehicle. In their fierce competition for readers, they eschewed the highbrow neutrality of tone in the corantos in favor of a colloquial style marked by passion and wit.

The early newsbooks were, as Frances Henderson has noted, "an immediate commercial success."[35] Some, such as Samuel Pecke's *A Per-*

fect Diurnall of the Passages in Parliament, which reached a circulation of 3,000 a week, presented news in a reasonably calm, sober, and objective manner. But as the civil war intensified, so too did the partisanship and rhetoric of some newsbooks. According to Raymond, newsbooks never became mere instruments of faction. Nonetheless, Sir John Berkenhead's *Mercurius Aulicus* deliberately offended the Puritans, while anti-Royalists like **John Crouch** used smutty, salacious gossip and obscenity-filled rhymes as a form of moral commentary on the Commonwealth.[36] After the execution of James I, Cromwell tried to reduce their impact through the Regulation of Printing Act of September 1649.[37] When its harsh measures failed to quell them, the legal publication of news was restricted to *Mercurius Politicus*, a newsbook edited by Marchamont Nedham[38] under the watchful eye of John Milton.[39] Although Milton had attacked licensing in his essay *Areopagitica* (1644), his commitment to the Commonwealth led to his agreement to serve as its chief licenser.[40]

The ablest journalist of his day, it was said of Nedham that he "knew how to catch the ear of the public."[41] But with the return of Charles II to the throne in 1660, his position was transferred to **Henry Muddiman**, whose newsbook, the *Parliamentary Intelligencer*, had supported the Restoration. His initial monopoly turned out to be even more short-lived. In 1662, another draconian Printing Act was passed, giving authority over news publication to a Surveyor of the Press. The first occupant of this powerful position, **Sir Roger L'Estrange**, rescinded Muddiman's monopoly and restricted printed news to his own two publications, the *Intelligencer* and the *Newes*. In 1665, however, a plague in London forced the court and Parliament to move to Oxford, where L'Estrange's enemies hired Muddiman to again provide them with news. When the king returned to the capital in 1666, L'Estrange was bought off and England's first newspaper, the *Oxford Gazette*, became the *London Gazette* with a monopoly over the licensed publication of news. Issued on Mondays and Thursdays as a folio half-sheet with each page divided into two columns, it was forced to compete briefly with non-government news publications after the Printing Act lapsed in 1679.[42] But in 1683, the Crown used its own authority to prohibit unlicensed news once again. It was not until 1695 that licensing was allowed to expire once and for all and English newspapers finally began to flourish.

THE ORIGINS OF JOURNALISM CRITICISM

Long before news was available on a daily basis, commentators worried about its impact on society.[43] In Elizabethan England, bishop **Joseph Hall** and playwright **Ben Jonson** began a long tradition of criticizing journalists for their unreliability. In works such as *News from the New World* (1620), Jonson offered "a prescient portrait of a medium just beginning to coalesce," one which "remained for at least a century the most thorough English analysis of news reporting."[44] "I have been so cheated with false revelations in my time," Jonson has an imaginary newswriter lament, "that I have found it a harder thing to correct my book than to collect it."[45]

Newsbooks were subjected to particularly scathing criticism for their debased literary quality, for being "paper bullets" leading to civil war, and for engendering a so-called **crisis of eloquence**. Contemporary historians rejected them as "speech acts with doubtful or collective authorship, questionable accuracy, seditious intent, and no vocal guarantee."[46] "A *Diurnall*," wrote the popular royalist poet John Cleveland in *Character of a London Diurnall* around 1644, "is a puny Chronicle, scarce pin feather'd with the wings of time."[47]

The underlying weakness of 17th-century news was its mechanics of truth. As Anthony Smith has reminded us, "only with a *dual* communication system, when the same news flows along more than one channel at a time, can the journalist acquire his own specialism in the telling of accurate news."[48] This requirement was recognized in the case of science reporting by John Greaves, Savilian Professor of Astronomy at Oxford. "The *credibility* of any *Reporter*," he wrote in 1645, "is to be rated (1) by his *Integrity*, or Fidelity; and (2) by his *Ability*: and a double *Ability* is to be considered; both that of *Apprehending*, what is deliver'd; and also of *Retaining* it afterwards, till it be transmitted." Greaves tried to develop a mathematical formula for assessing the reliability or "credit" of a reporter. "[I]f a single Witness should be only so far Credible, as to give me the Half of a full Certainty; a Second of the same Credibility," Greaves reasoned in part, "would (joined with the first) give me 3/4ths; a Third, 7/8ths; etc . . ."[49] The problem for newsbook publishers, however, was to get beyond a single witness. Most news, especially that received from abroad, came through an isolated source that could not easily be corroborated.

The establishment of the *London Gazette* as an official newspaper in 1666 did little to change this situation. It revealed its tenuous grasp on truth by such telling phrases as "our last letters from the frontiers advise," "we do not yet give an entire credit to it," "here is much discourse that," "several reports are spread abroad, which if true," and "it is reported here . . . which the more surprises us, for that we have all along expected."[50] Late in the century, John Aubrey noted in his unpublished *Brief Lives* that much of what was regarded as reliable news by the coffeehouse clientele turned out to be a sham.[51] In *De relationibus novellis*, a doctoral thesis submitted to the University of Leipzig in 1690, Tobias Peucer similarly complained of "collectors of news . . . indiscriminately spreading about things gleaned from other writings and even retailing suspicions and conjectures of others as history when they have no certainty about it."[52] Even in the mid-18th century, the *London Gazette*'s printer, Edward Owen, complained to Edward Weston about the difficulty of providing reliable foreign news.[53]

PROVIDENTIALISM, THE PUBLIC INTEREST, AND THE BIRTH OF MODERN JOURNALISM

During the late 17th and early 18th century, Western journalistic discourse underwent a profound transformation. Although scarcely noticeable at the time, this change amounted to the birth of modern journalism. It consisted of a major shift in the range of interpretative frames used to organize and make sense of the news. Despite repeated injunctions against prying into God's unfathomable ways, 16th- and 17th-century news accounts assumed that certain natural and human events occur in relation to God's larger plan. A common approach, therefore, was to interpret them as a form of divine judgment on the Christian community. The belief in providentialism was not abandoned in the 18th century, but it gradually disappeared as an explanatory frame in favor of secular concepts such as order, progress, nationalism, and reform. These concepts were tied to an emerging sense of society's general, common, or public interest. As this sense grew in strength, it provided a countervailing force to the resources and market principles as determinants of journalistic discourse and practices.

Alexandra Walsham provides an early 17th-century example of providentialist news. In 1623, some 90 people attending a sermon by the Jesuit priest Robert Drury in London fell to their deaths when the floor of a makeshift chapel suddenly collapsed. This disaster was "the headline news of its day." "Intent on scooping their rivals," journalists "whipped together competing accounts of the shocking accident within a matter of weeks." Referring to the event as the "fatall vesper," they were no less certain than Protestant preachers that it was "an awe-inspiring and fore-ordained act of God—a signal token of the workings of divine providence." More specifically, it was said to be God's vengeance on a group of Catholics for participating in an illegal evensong and a reproof to the recent resurgence of Catholicism in England.[54] Similarly, Mary Dyer's "monstrous" miscarriage in New England in 1637 became news not because it was sensational but because of its hermeneutic value. As David Paul Nord relates, "the governor himself conducted the investigation and wrote much of the major report of the episode. He did so because he saw in this strange birth the designing hand of God and a message for the commonwealth of Massachusetts."[55]

During the English civil war, both sides interpreted any kind of unusual event as an indication of God's support for their cause,[56] while Increase Mather explained the grievous loss of life during King Philip's War in 1675–76 as God's judgment on a sinful colonial people. Nord calls the latter war "the first great news story for the Boston press" and describes Mather's *A Brief History of the Warr With the Indians in New-England* (1676) as "the most substantial piece of journalism published up to that time . . . an instant book dashed off while the fires of the war were still smoldering."[57] Providentialism was still evident in the earliest American newspaper, *Publick Occurrences, Both Foreign and Domestick*, published in Boston for the first—and last—time on 25 September 1690 by **Benjamin Harris**. The "occurrences" in question were understood as reflections of God's judgment on the colonists' lives. As Julie Hedgepeth Williams notes, Harris intended his newspaper to be "a vehicle for readers to understand God's commentary on the local scene."[58]

By the late 17th century, political events had superseded natural occurrences as the most important examples of divine providence. According to Nord's calculations, the percentage of event-oriented publications comprised by almanacs, which focused on natural events, declined from 29 percent in 1639–74 to 13 percent in 1675–1700. At the same time, the percentage of publications consisting of histories and narratives, which dealt primarily with political developments, increased from 2 to 16 percent. The growth of newspapers not only contributed to this politicization of reality but also helped to secularize the judgments placed on political events. This secularization did not occur overnight; in a content analysis of 7,400 issues of 79 newspapers in 18th century America, David Copeland found that God still had a considerable presence in discussions of the news.[59] At the same time, however, providential intervention became steadily less important as a basic explanatory mechanism.

It was not simply a more secular approach to politics but a less partisan manner of treating political matters that marked the transition to modern journalism. Partisanship continued to prevail in many news publications. But it was now accompanied by an effort to judge matters in terms of what was taken to be the public interest. A key figure in this regard was **Daniel Defoe**, whose *Weekly Review of the Affairs of FRANCE* announced in its subtitle that it was "Purg'd from the Errors and Partiality of *News-Writers* and *Petty Statesmen*, of all Sides." Produced single-handedly by Defoe in London from February 1704 until June 1713, the **Review** tried to steer a course between the innocuous neutrality of the *London Gazette* and the scurrilous personal attacks of journalists like William Pittis in the *Whipping Post* (1705).[60] In its very first number, Defoe declared his independence from party ties and his devotion to truth and the public interest. "I am not a party man," Defoe said; "at least, I resolve this shall not be a party paper."

Defoe, who secretly spied on his fellow citizens and was accused of being a turncoat for changing his political colors with each ministerial shift, may seem an odd candidate for the honor of introducing the public interest principle. But as J. A. Downie has pointed out, "the intense conflict between Whig and Tory so prevalent throughout the reign of Queen Anne made no allowances for a paper standing outside the traditional party groupings, so the *Review* was treated as an opponent by both sides."[61] When Defoe first started writing for Robert Harley and the Tories, Harley still wanted to transcend party lines and had not yet given up on the ideal of nonparty government. Like Harley, Defoe hoped to unite the moderates of all political creeds behind the queen and her government, but this policy of moderation "angered the extremists of both sides."[62] Defoe certainly had no intention of eliminating opinion from journalism and did not always exercise the moderation he professed. He clearly wanted to reshape the social and economic world of his day. To this end, he pioneered investigative reporting, foreign news analysis, the gossip column, the obituary, and a form of editorial. But his opinion pieces were less a reflection of narrow party interests than an attempt to persuade both Whigs and Tories to serve the country better.

Defoe's new style of journalism was brought to near perfection in terms of wit and grace in **Joseph Addison** and **Richard Steele**'s jointly produced *Tatler* (1709–11) and *Spectator* (1711–12). Addison and Steele were even more concerned than Defoe to eliminate the poisonous invective of previous religious and political discussions. Although "news" was used largely as a pretext for projects of moral reform, they believed that the role of the journalist should be to hold up a reflecting mirror to society and calmly describe what it reveals, a function signified for Addison by the word *spectator*. A practical, non-ideological, and civil discussion could then proceed on the basis of actual empirical observation. As Brian Cowan has argued, their *Spectator* project "put the reform and the discipline of public sociability at the heart of its agenda."[63] It sought to encourage a moderate form of social criticism and planted the idea of the editor as a champion of the public interest.

Neither Defoe nor Addison provided any philosophical reflection on the nature of the public interest their journalism sought to promote. In an influential series of letters published in the *London Journal* between 1720 and 1723, however, two radical Whig thinkers, John Trenchard and Thomas Gordon, set forth what amounted to the first phenomenology of the public interest principle. They did so in the context of the fierce contemporary debate over the law of libel, but placed their discussion in the context of the relationship between freedom of the press and good government. Using the pseudonym "Cato" to avoid prosecution, Trenchard and Gordon argued that whether a statement is libellous should *not* be determined, as most libertarians advocated, primarily by whether it is true or false; rather, it should be decided on the basis of the public good. In developing this argument, they began by distinguishing between purely private failings on the one hand and personal faults which affect the public interest on the other. With regard to the former, they took the unconventional view that "a Libel is not the less a Libel for being true." They acknowledged that "this may seem a Contradiction," but maintained that "it is neither one in Law, or in common Sense: There are some Truths not fit to be told; where, for Example, the discovery of a small Fault may do great Mischief; or where the discovery of a great Fault can do no Good, there ought to be no Discovery at all: And to make Faults where there are none, is still worse."[64]

Where the personal failings of a government official affect the public interest, however, Trenchard and Gordon were clear that "the exposing of Publick Wickedness" is "a Duty which every Man owes to Truth and his Country" and "can never be a Libel in the Nature of Things."[65] The question of how to decide when "private Vices or Weaknesses of Governers . . . enter into their Publick Administration" has remained a difficult one. Trenchard and Gordon generally called for a wide latitude in making this determination so that the press would not be deterred from the task of exposing corrupt officials. Yet they were not prepared to give the journalist a free rein to attack public officials. Like Defoe and Addison, they recognized that certain limitations are required for healthy public debate. Rejecting the idea of society as a collection of separate orders or estates, they assumed that society has a common or general interest which it is the purpose of government to serve. But they did not believe that everything capable of selling newspapers could be justified in its name.

THE POLITICS AND ECONOMICS OF 18TH-CENTURY JOURNALISM

After the Licensing Act lapsed in 1695 and was not subsequently restored, the London press underwent an immediate growth spurt followed by a long period of slow but steady growth. By 1712, there were about 20 privately owned newspapers in London, including the first daily, the **Daily Courant**, which had begun publication a decade earlier.[66] After the turn of the century, provincial newspapers also started to proliferate.[67] By 1781, there were an estimated 76 newspapers and periodicals being published in England and Wales.[68] However, most of these publications were relatively small-scale and inconsequential. In 1780, as A. Aspinall observed, the typical English newspaper was still "a small commercial speculation designed primarily to advertise new books, quack medicines, theatre programmes, auction sales and shipping news. It contained only a few paragraphs of news and no leading articles; and its sale was measured by the hundreds."[69]

The modest growth of the 18th-century British press was a direct reflection of the continuing capacity of the resources principle to curb the operation of the market principle. Successive governments, both Whig and Tory, used three main devices to prevent the emergence of a market-driven press. The first of these was a reinterpretation of the law of seditious libel, according to which it now became a criminal offense to criticize the government. In a perverse form of logic, criticism that was demonstrably based in fact was regarded as even more seditious for bringing the government into even greater disrepute.[70] Among those prosecuted under the law was the Whig editor of the *Flying Post*, who escaped jail only by fleeing to France. To discourage newspaper publishing generally, the Tories imposed a duty on every copy of a printed half sheet, which was the standard size for newspapers at the time. The original Stamp Act in 1712 placed this duty at a halfpenny or half the price of the average paper. It also added a duty of one shilling for each advertisement. When some printers discovered that they could evade much of the tax by expanding their papers to one and a half sheets, further regulations were passed by Parliament in 1725 eliminating this loophole. That both the Whigs and the Tories supported the **stamp tax** reflected their common assumption that it would mainly hinder the radical or popular press, since they could counter its impact on themselves by subsidizing their own papers. In addition to the *London Gazette*, the Tory government under Robert Harley supported half a dozen or so London newspapers in the 1710s; it also financed the printing of numerous pamphlets and paid Jonathan Swift to oversee its propaganda efforts.[71] Later Tory publications such as the *Craftsman*, a weekly journal edited by Nicholas Amhurst under the pseudonym Caleb D'Anvers of Gray's-Inn, drew upon the talents of Lord Chesterfield and Bolingbroke to carry on a journalistic war against Robert Walpole. But Walpole now had the advantage of the power of the purse. From 1722 until his resignation in 1742, he spent over £50,000 sponsoring eight newspapers and a stable of pro-Whig essayists.[72]

Despite these restraints, journalism made a number of advances in **Great Britain** during the 18th century. In the 1770s, the ban on **parliamentary reporting** was finally lifted by both the Commons and the

Lords. An examination of late 18th-century London newspapers has found "a surprising amount of information about court proceedings," including information about "non-notorious trials at *nisi prius* and on assize" and "arguments and opinions on post-trial motions and sentencing."[73] And newspapers were by then providing increased and more penetrating coverage of social issues such as suicide. Brief reports on suicides had long been a staple of English news. But in the latter part of the 18th century, London papers began to include longer pieces by anonymous correspondents, or in some cases the editors themselves, reconstructing such deaths in detail, often including suicide notes, and depicting self-killing as "a calamity that befell ordinary people for ordinary reasons, a pathetic tragedy, not a diabolical crime." By considering the impact of suicides on families, these first-person accounts "reflected and promoted the secularization of beliefs about the causes and consequences of self-destruction. They shifted public attention away from the eschatological implications of the deed toward its social and psychological significance."[74] This coverage helped to change the law governing suicide as it affected the families of victims.

In 18th-century France, journalism continued to be mainly a product of the resources principle. But the state's resources were no longer able to exclude oppositional movements from challenging it in print. Although a few critics such as Louis-Sébastien Mercier and Etienne de Jouy restricted themselves to moderate Addisonian techniques,[75] *philosophes* like Voltaire and Diderot turned to satire and exaggeration to castigate the *ancien régime*. Even coarser methods of attack were used by the *libellistes*, a dispossessed literary rabble which vented its spleen in numerous pamphlets and newsletters. Robert Darnton depicted them as disgruntled *philosophes*—"they had knocked on the door of Voltaire's church and the door remained closed."[76] But for Jeremy Popkin, they were actually the pawns of an aspiring political elite which "had come to have too much of a stake in the use of the printing press to collaborate effectively in suppressing pamphlet journalism."[77] In the 1770s, they were joined by a group of playwright-editors who engaged in "Frondeur journalism" after having been slighted by the Comédie-Française. Though regularly censored and eventually purged by the government, their mutually supportive journals managed to engage in political criticism by disguising their attacks as criticism of the Comédie-Française. Their rhetoric on behalf of freedom of expression paralleled that of the *libellistes* and "blurred the traditional boundary between proscribed and permitted journalism."[78]

In colonial America, Addisonian wit also gave way to mockery and demonization as the chosen mode of criticism, especially as the rift with Britain began to widen. At the same time, however, the market principle made significant headway in 18th-century America and facilitated a nascent public interest principle in the process. The first printed newspapers—John Campbell's *Boston News-Letter* (1704) and William Brooker's *Boston Gazette* (1719)—were simply sidelines for the local postmaster, who had franking privileges and access to official notices. They had only a few hundred subscribers and sought government approval before publication even though licensing had expired. It was not until 1721 that James Franklin, who had been printing the *Gazette*, founded the first truly independent newspaper in America. Modeled in part on the *Tatler* and *Spectator*, which Franklin had read while apprenticing in London, the **New-England Courant** tried to combine regular news with witty commentaries, including the Silence Dogood letters of his younger half-brother Benjamin. But this combination proved to be unsustainable and the *Courant* died in 1726 or 1727. It was succeeded by two other literary papers, the *New England Weekly Journal* (1727) and *The Weekly Rehearsal* (1731), but they too were unable to attract a sufficient number of readers.[79]

A more economically viable model was the political newspaper, especially after the acquittal of **John Peter Zenger** for seditious libel in 1734. But its existence was also quite precarious in the absence of established party alignments. It was in this context that **Benjamin Franklin** wrote his "Apology for Printers" in the *Pennsylvania Gazette* on 10 June 1731. As businessmen "continually employ'd in serving all Parties," Franklin argued, printers "naturally contract an Unconcernedness as to the right or wrong Opinions contained in what they print." Franklin connected "serving all Parties" to Milton's self-righting principle in *Areopagitica* (1644). Printers, he said, were taught to present each side of a dispute to the public because "when Truth and Error have fair play, the former is always an overmatch for the latter." Even more than promoting the pursuit of truth, however, Franklin saw himself as simulating, through excerpts from London papers, the kind of polite conversation that he imagined occurring among gentlemen in a coffeehouse.[80]

Given the profitability of the *Pennsylvania Gazette*, it is not surprising that other newspaper proprietors, including Thomas Fleet Sr. and Timothy Findlay, adopted this editorial diversity as a deliberate market strategy.[81] Fleet took over the Boston *Weekly Rehearsal* around 1732 and renamed it the *Boston Evening-Post*. Despite quoting Franklin's "Apology," he was less interested in operationalizing the self-righting principle than in securing more readers. Calculating that he could have more patrons and advertising by accommodating various political viewpoints, he and his sons pursued impartiality as a business strategy and the paper became one of the most popular in Boston.[82] Though exhibiting a strong editorial voice of its own, the *South-Carolina Gazette*, edited by Peter Timothy from 1738–80, likewise presented a variety of views on controversial issues such as religious toleration, paper money, and smallpox inoculation. Even when relations with Britain worsened and most colonial newspapers abandoned even the pretense of objectivity, Timothy remained committed to the ideal of balance; during the nonimportation debates, for example, he published opinions on both sides of the issue.[83]

As with most 18th-century Anglo-American newspapers, these "opinions" were typically referred to as "paragraphs" because of their customary and intentional brevity. They were "conventionally presented as letters *to* the paper from pseudonymous correspondents signing themselves Decius or Britannicus (or, famously, Junius), who were either really or fictionally readers rather than editors or employees."[84] Moreover, when editors did write political commentaries, they generally did not present them as the voice of the paper. This detachment paralleled the 18th-century newspaper's separation from its news content, which consisted mainly of short items either cribbed from other papers or provided by local contacts. As the century progressed, the content of colonial newspapers became increasingly diverse, including stories about crime, commerce, healthcare, and race relations as well as politics. But until the early 19th century, most of the improvement in newsgathering consisted of advances in the exchange of news. In response to the threat of French and Indian warfare in the late 1750s and early 1760s, for example, colonial American newspapers developed more elaborate networks for sharing news.[85] These networks were facilitated by the decision of Benjamin Franklin and William Hunter, deputy postmasters general, in 1758 to allow printers to exchange copies of their papers without charge. But on the eve of the Revolution, there were still no paid reporters working for any of the colonies' 36 weeklies (and one thrice-weekly).[86]

ADVERTISING, THE EDITORIAL, AND THE REPORTER IN THE EARLY 19TH CENTURY

By the early 19th century, British newspapers such as the *Morning Chronicle* were not only hiring well-educated writers to produce "leading articles" or "leaders" but were also increasing the number of reporters and paying them better. These investments occurred despite increases in the stamp duty in 1797 and in 1815. They were made, moreover, in the face of increased costs of paper, printing ink, types, and journeymen's wages. Although newspapers were allowed to raise their price to 6½ pence (d) in 1809, at most only 1 d of this amount went to editorial and production costs; the rest was needed to cover the stamp duty (3½d) and to pay for the sheet of paper and the vendor (2d).[87] What accounted for the increased revenues available for news and commentary was not primarily income from greater sales but rather greater profits from advertisements. In the case of the *Chronicle* under proprietor James Perry, profits from advertising rose from £4,300 in 1800 to £12,400 in 1819. Even though the duty on advertisements went from 2 shillings (s) in 1770 to 3s 6d in 1820, the profit on each advertisement increased from 1s 11d to almost 6s 10d over the same period. At the same time, the volume of advertising steadily increased, reaching 50 percent of the *Chronicle*'s news-hole by 1820.[88]

In the **United States**, the new economics of newspaper advertising was reflected in the strange phenomenon of delinquent subscribers. During the half century after 1790, the new republic underwent an "age of reading" as Americans made a concerted effort to increase literacy. According to William J. Gilmore, this campaign was mainly premised on the need for "modern intelligence."[89] But in *The Radicalism of the American Revolution* (1992), Gordon S. Wood points to a new stream of egalitarian thinking that also fueled the desire for ready access to print. Whereas the Founding Fathers limited the role of the public to the selection of wise and virtuous leaders, prominent thinkers such as Ralph

Waldo Emerson, as well as lesser lights like Edward Everett, began to argue that ordinary citizens also have the capacity to participate in public debates, provided they have adequate information to do so. In this democratization of Milton's self-righting principle, truth was now regarded as the creation of many voices, rather than the possession of the privileged few.

The rapid growth of newspapers and newspaper reading was closely related to this enthronement of ordinary public reason. By the 1820s, there were some 600 newspapers in the United States, more than in any other country in the world, while between 1790 and 1840, the percentage of households *reading* newspapers increased from between 10 and 20 percent in 1790 to close to 70 percent by 1840. Reading newspapers did not necessarily mean subscribing to them, however, because Americans had come to regard access to news as almost a birthright. Many citizens borrowed newspapers from their neighbors, pinched them off doorsteps, or subscribed but then refused to pay. Editors tried every conceivable means of getting reimbursed—except for withholding delivery of the paper. Because their growing revenues from advertising were tied to circulation, it was more profitable for them to retain a delinquent subscriber than to refuse delivery.[90]

It was primarily these increased profits from advertising that provided Anglo-American newspapers with the financial means for better journalism. Newspapers began to change from being a printer's sideline to a viable business venture in their own right, while the tasks of reporting, editing, and printing became structurally differentiated. Although still influenced by government regulations, political subsidies, and various vested interests, the press became more responsive to market pressures and the ideal of serving the public interest. This greater responsiveness was paramount in two new developments: the emergence of the modern editorial; and the rise of reporting.

According to Dallas Liddle, what the British called "leading articles" or "leaders" arose in fits and starts between the 1790s and 1820s. In contrast to the short editorial paragraphs of 18th-century newspapers, they typically ran to about 1,500 words (or 20 to 25 column inches), occupying slightly more than one column of a six-column broadsheet. Each writer produced three or four such pieces a day for which the paper itself took credit. Whereas 18th-century papers displayed deference toward their readers, the leading article deliberately elevated itself to the status of "an authoritarian public oracle."[91] Liddle suggests that this voice of omniscience was influenced by the critical style of the *Edinburgh Review* under editor Francis Jeffrey. To a greater extent than the *Review*, however, the leading article claimed to distill the public mind, which is perhaps why it was later derided by conservative cultural critics such as Matthew Arnold.

In the United States initially, there was a clearer identification of the editor with the editorial. Although a few papers included commentaries after certain news items during the revolutionary period, it was in the mid-1790s that Noah Webster's *American Minerva* and a few other papers began placing editorials in a separate column (headed, in Webster's case, by "The Minerva"). In 1800, **Benjamin Franklin Bache**, editor of the *Aurora* in Philadelphia, moved these editorials to page two and used the editorial "we."[92] But most early 19th-century U.S. newspapers remained too partisan to limit commentary to a specific column or downplay the identity of the author. The modern American editorial is more meaningfully dated from the 1830s and credited to **James Gordon Bennett Sr.** and **Horace Greeley**. Bennett's use of the editorial "we" implied that his opinions in the *New York Herald* were the collective voice of the paper, while Greeley began making use of several writers to produce an editorial page for the *New York Tribune*. The term "editorial" itself also began to come into usage around this time: on 16 August 1836, for example, Bennett told his readers, "We rise in the morning before 5 o'-clock—write our leading editorials."

The development of the editorial was accompanied by an increased emphasis on direct reporting. According to Jean Chalaby, the rise of reporting was essentially an Anglo-American accomplishment and marks the real beginning of journalism.[93] It is important, however, not to exaggerate the speed at which this transition occurred. Active newsgathering still comprised a relatively small percentage of newspaper content. In the 1820s, American newspapers carried over four times as much "clipped news" as copy provided by reporters. Even at mid-century, they still carried more content from other papers than they gathered themselves. See the table of the percentage of news by source in U.S. newspapers, 1820–1860,[94] on the next page.

	1820–1832	1833–1846	1847–1860
Local reporter	12	13	20
Local editor	13	23	25
Correspondent	7	8	10
Letter to newspaper	10	7	6
Clipped news	54	46	30
Telegraph	0	<0.5	8
Other	4	2	2

An examination of the four main dailies in London in the 1860s (*The Times*, the *Daily News*, the *Daily Telegraph*, and the *Standard*) found that "each paper had only a handful of correspondents in the field at any one time."[95]

In the case of antebellum America, the increase in reporting indicated in this table was the result in part of the new penny papers that arose to challenge the elite six-penny press. The first of these was the **New York Sun**, established by the enterprising 23-year-old artisan **Benjamin H. Day** in 1833. It was soon followed by a host of imitators, the most important of which was Bennett's *New York Herald* (1835). As a major pioneer in reporting, Bennett established the courts as a source of news; assigned reporters to cover Wall Street, sports, high society, and the arts; and stationed correspondents in major capital cities in America and Europe. What made this investment in reporting possible was a further shift in the economics of the newspaper. Although advertising rates were tied to circulation, the growth of newspaper revenues between 1780 and 1830 came more from increases in the volume of advertising than from larger numbers of subscribers. In the case of the penny papers, however, advertising revenues accelerated largely as a result of greatly increased sales.

The most obvious factor behind the larger circulations of the penny papers was, of course, their substantially lower price. (Bennett also began insisting that readers and advertisers pay for their subscriptions and space in advance.) But these circulations were no less dependent on the altered content of the papers. Historians have generally emphasized how the *Sun* and a host of imitators downplayed politics and made use of **hoaxes** and other forms of sensationalism to capture a working-class audience.[96] But penny papers like the Philadelphia *Public Ledger* quickly earned a reputation for good news coverage and attacks on local abuses. What Helen MacGill Hughes called their **human interest stories**[97] were generally less interested in sensationalism than in providing a critical perspective on everyday life.[98] Stories by reporters like **George Wisner** about the downtrodden in police court deliberately pointed to the harsh realities of many workers' lives. In covering labor trials in particular, the penny papers "often expressed indignation against courts that convicted workingmen for trade union activities and against judges who meted out severe sentences."[99] They also attacked the morality of practices affecting lower-income Americans such as imprisonment for debt, the inequities of the militia system, and the contracting of prison labor.[100] At the same time, stories about the social activities of the elite were often implicitly critical of their effete lifestyle. Even the sensationalistic treatment of events such as the Helen Jewett murder trial was intended not only to attract readers curious about high society but to critique upper and middle-class morality.[101]

Criticism of the penny papers for their sensationalism thus stemmed in part from the challenge their reporting made to the status quo. In Britain, the so-called "pauper press" was similarly attacked for using sensationalized accounts of crime and accidents to build circulation. But papers such as Henry Hetherington's *Twopenny Dispatch*, which quickly became one of the most popular newspapers in London, led the way in using illustration as a new reporting tool. When the *Report of the Inquiry into the Employment and Conditions of Children in the Mines and Manufactures* was released in 1842, it was not the conservative *Illustrated London News* but *Bell's Penny Dispatch* that printed its sensational illustrations of coal being extracted by half-naked children crawling on all fours. As Celina Fox has noted, as a publication geared to polite Victorian society, the *Illustrated London News* did not think it was "fitting" to point to such social conditions through illustration and questioned the reliability of such depictions.[102]

THE VICTORIAN JOURNALIST
AS IDEOLOGUE AND OBSERVER

The rise of the editorial writer and reporter did not immediately increase the stature of journalists generally. During the early 19th century, British writers such as Samuel Taylor Coleridge, Thomas Babington Macaulay, and Sir Walter Scott were still decrying the distortions of news and advising their colleagues not to lose social status by descending into journalism.[103] It is "a strange anomaly," P. L. Simmonds told the Statistical Society of London on 21 June 1841, "that in England alone, newspaper writers are looked down upon as an inferior caste of literati; and that the purveyors of intelligence, whose especial business is to inform and instruct the public . . . are themselves a proscribed race."[104] Almost 80 years later, Max Weber noted similarly in **"Politics as a Vocation" (1918)** that journalists in Germany were viewed as "a sort of pariah caste, which is always estimated by 'society' in terms of its ethically lowest representative."[105] By then, however, a more positive image of the journalist had emerged in the Anglo-American world. "What is the office of journalism?" wrote J. Boyd Kinnear in the *Contemporary Review* in July 1867. "It is to inform, to advise, and to direct."[106] Others went even further and emphasized the role of the journalist as public protector. In "Government by Journalism" (1885), **William T. Stead** argued that the press constituted a "fourth estate," a term thought to have originated in Edmund Burke's comment in the Commons: "And yonder sits the Fourth Estate, more important than them all." Echoing Jeremy Bentham's writings on the press as a public opinion tribunal,[107] Stead argued that journalism helps to safeguard the interests of the people.[108]

This reassessment was based in part on a modest improvement in the tools of the reporters' trade. Although late 19th-century reporters were still overworked and underpaid and often forced to moonlight or accept payola (undercover payments for favorable coverage) to make ends meet,[109] they did acquire new techniques for gathering and presenting the news. One of the most important of these tools was interviewing. According to Stead in *The Americanization of the World* (1902), interviewing was a "distinctively American invention." Its antecedents include Bennett's questioning of one of the witnesses in the 1836 Helen Jewett murder case. By the 1860s, interviews of figures such as Brigham Young and President Andrew Johnson were considered news events in themselves. But from the outset, the interview was regarded by news editors as a valuable tool for collecting information about other events and by the 1870s increasing resources were being devoted to its use.

For many social commentators, including some journalists, interviewing was initially regarded as a "thoroughly contemptible" device and it was resisted in Britain until Stead began to popularize it through interviews with figures such as General Gordon for the *Pall Mall Gazette*. "It elevates prying into an art," complained a writer for *Galaxy* in 1874. "It is a conspiracy against the privacy of the individual . . . and it places the person who either consents or refuses to be interviewed at the mercy of his tormentor."[110] Such criticism was not without grounds; from its inception, interviewing, which was also derided as **Jenkins journalism** and disparaged by writers such as Henry James in ***The Reverberator*** (1888), was subject to various abuses, including tricking sources into speaking and the faking of interviews. But as Michael Schudson has pointed out, interviewing was also attacked because it assumed that society, as embodied in the journalist, has a right to question those in positions of authority as a matter of protecting the public interest.[111] The interview not only gave the journalist a new form of power but undermined the authority of public figures.

While journalists had always relied in part on the eyes of others to observe the world, interviewing gave them the capacity to question second-hand observations for reliability and consistency. Traditionally, they usually organized the intelligence provided to them in the form of a chronological narrative. They tended to tell their stories as they were told to them. As the amount of news being gathered directly increased, however, late 19th-century reporters began to adopt new ways of organizing it for their readers more efficiently, especially in the context of numerous competing stories. In this regard, they developed what came to be known as the inverted pyramid style of presentation, which consisted of organizing the facts or events of a story in terms of their relative importance. At the same time, they also developed the related device of the "summary lead," which involved answering the four W-questions—Who? What? When? and Where?—in the lead sentence.

The traditional explanation is that these devices were "invented" in the United States between 1850 and 1870 when the electric telegraph was still unreliable; by putting the most important information first, editors reduced the risk of not getting their message through in the event of a malfunction. An alternative explanation is that Edwin M. Stanton, President Abraham Lincoln's secretary of war, introduced the technique in his bulletins to the press during the Civil War as a means of steering public opinion; it was then adopted by journalists who used it for their own ends.[112] However, a content analysis of two leading American newspapers by Horst Pöttker suggests that the inverted pyramid style was not widely used until the 1880s and was adopted then primarily because of its advantages in terms of clear communication. Whatever the explanation, it had firmly taken hold by the 1890s. In his reporting text *Steps into Journalism: Helps and Hints for Young Writers* (1894), Edwin L. Shuman advised typically that "a well constructed story begins with its most important fact and ends with the least important."[113]

In addition to interviewing, a number of late 19th-century reporters engaged in what was called stunt journalism to help get their stories. While stunts such as **Nellie Bly**'s race around the world in 1889 had little investigative purpose or value, other stunts enabled reporters to uncover abusive conditions in asylums, prisons, and other social institutions. In Britain, where Matthew Arnold saw it as part of a New Journalism, the stunt was pioneered in the early 1880s by W. T. Stead. At the urging of the leaders of the Salvation Army, Stead exposed the "white slave" trade (child prostitution) by showing how easy it was to purchase a young girl. Though sentenced to three months in jail for abduction, his action provoked the government into passing legislation against child prostitution and contributed to international efforts to eliminate its practice. Beneficial regulations also resulted from lurid stories by British reporters about the debilitating effects of lead and phosphorous poisoning on women working in pottery and match factories.[114]

In the United States, stunt journalism was initially associated with **Joseph Pulitzer**, especially after his takeover of the *New York World* in 1883. Though well aware of the capacity of sensationalistic stunts to build circulation, Pulitzer was genuinely concerned to use the intrusive methods of reporters like Ralph Julian and Nellie Bly on behalf of social reform. As he editorialized on 11 May 1883, the goal of the *World* was to be "dedicated to the cause of the people," to "expose all fraud and sham, fight all public evils and abuse," and to "serve and battle for the people with earnest sincerity." In an attempt to match Nellie Bly, **William Randolph Hearst** hired Winifred Black ("Annie Laurie") to engage in similar stunts for the *New York Journal*. But by the late 1890s, competition between Pulitzer's *World* and Hearst's *Journal* turned much of stunt journalism's original reforming zeal into what critics such as William Cowper Brann called **yellow journalism**. Hearst's papers still sponsored projects to help the poor and afflicted, but relied increasingly on games and prizes to attract readers. More credible exposure of abuses was provided by journalists such as **Jacob Riis**, who added the new dimension of photography to reporting on the evils of industrial America.

As part of the New Journalism's attempt to reach the vast new reading public, which had arisen in conjunction with the expansion of public education, stunt journalism revealed both its novelty and its limitations in the way that it appropriated popular literary genres such as the travel adventure, the detective story, and the historical romance to reframe the news in a more exciting and entertaining manner.[115] These various genres enlivened journalistic discourse, but undermined its capacity to develop its own autonomous voice. Although writers such as **Stephen Crane** have been praised for drawing literature and journalism closer together,[116] the literary turn was generally at the expense of journalism. It reinforced the extent to which the language of Victorian reporters was tied to the discursive styles of those providing information for their stories—legal language when covering the courts, commercial language when writing about business, political language when dealing with politics, and so forth. As Donald Matheson has pointed out, the Victorian newspaper was "a medley of various public styles, voices and types of text," ranging from plain, concise, factual reports to florid, sentimental, highly descriptive prose.[117] It was not simply that the Victorian reporter was still essentially an observer. It was also that late 19th-century journalism still had not developed its own critical authority. With few exceptions, ideology drove both its search for the facts and the interpretation that it then placed upon them.

During the first decade of the 20th century, a number of American journalists took a major step beyond the empirical and interpretative shortcomings of their predecessors in the so-called muckraking journalism of the period. Though embraced by magazines such as *McClure's*, *Collier's*, *Everybody's*, and *Munsey's* primarily as a marketing strategy, muckraking was the first widespread and sustained effort at investigative journalism. It sought to generate national circulations through highly factual accounts of social abuses and corruption. Moreover, the "verifiable facts" on which the muckrakers placed a premium were "usually based on months of their own painstaking investigation" and were not generally determined by any particular "political creed."

One complaint levelled against the muckrakers was that they seldom "suggested [a] remedy for the conditions they disclosed."[118] They stuck too closely to the facts, exposing problems without offering solutions. But a study of letters from readers of the muckraking magazines found that they generally "endorsed the 'information' model of the press; they wanted 'just the facts.'"[119] It was less a case of the muckrakers wishing to confine themselves to detailed empirical research than of the public still wanting primarily this kind of service. The journalists themselves were beginning to diverge from traditional public expectations by fashioning a new professional self-image, but that image was only dimly visible in the muckraking enterprise itself. Its factual bias was simply too pronounced to constitute a norm for journalistic practice as a whole. Although there was general agreement that modern society needed better information, journalists were increasingly reluctant to see themselves as mere information providers. Instead, they began to articulate a model of the journalist as a new kind of general "expert."

THE RISE OF THE MODERN JOURNALIST AS EXPERT

Among the targets of the muckrakers was journalism itself. Will Irwin's series on "The Power of the Press" in *Collier's* in 1911 so upset Hearst that he threatened to have both Irwin and Robert Collier arrested. Irwin's concern with how advertising was influencing and even suppressing the news was shared by publications such as *Editor and Publisher*.[120] Their response, however, was often limited to urging reporters to tell the truth.[121] Only a few critics such as Upton Sinclair considered how the economics of advertising was systemically colonizing both the market and the public interest principles. In an ironic confirmation of his thesis, Sinclair had to publish *The Brass Check* (1919) himself after no commercial publisher would do so. Most newspapers even refused to review it and the few reviews that were published were almost invariably hostile. When, after selling over 150,000 copies, he tried to reprint it, he had difficulty getting sufficient paper for publication.[122] Fair coverage also eluded Sinclair when he ran for governor of California in 1934; frightened by his socialist EPIC (End Poverty in California) campaign, elements in the motion picture industry produced faked "California Election News" to discredit it.[123] Sinclair's treatment was part of the general effort of the authorities to eliminate socialist literature after the war by banning publications such as *Appeal to Reason*, published by Charles H. Kerr & Company in Chicago, from the mails.[124]

Rather than criticize press barons, lament the growth of newspaper "chains," or call for collective bargaining, even the more perceptive commentators sought refuge for journalism from commercial pressures in professional organizations, more formal education and training, and the development of codes of ethics. The latter approach culminated in the adoption of the "Canons of Journalism" by the American Society of Newspaper Editors (ASNE) in 1923. In addition to sanctifying freedom of the press, the ASNE's code called for sincerity, truthfulness, accuracy, fair play, and decency in reporting the news. It also spoke of journalism's responsibility to the general or public welfare. But what is particularly noteworthy is its emphasis on impartiality: "Sound practice," it said, "makes clear distinction between news reports and expressions of opinion. News reports should be free from opinion or bias of any kind."

More has probably been written about this ideal of "objectivity" than about any other aspect of modern journalistic practice. Its roots have been systematically pushed ever further back in time and its influence is often assumed rather than demonstrated. From the outset, it was an odd ideal. On the one hand, it was disdainful of the unscrupulous journalist portrayed in German playwright Gustav Freytag's *The Journalists* (1854), who proclaims: "I have . . . learned to write on all sides. I have written on the liberal side and again on the conservative side. I can write on any side."[125] Journalists were not hired writers; they were expected to be sincere in their views. But at the same time, they were not supposed to express these sincerely held views, at least not in the context of reporting. As the New York book publisher Jesse Haney wrote in *Haney's Guide to Authorship* (1867), an early manual for prospective reporters:

> There should be no comments. The editor should not be a partizan [*sic*] of either side. He should chronicle the facts, but not give opinions. If there be a public meeting, it should be reported fairly. It makes no difference if the editor differs with its object, or objects to its proceedings. He may comment on both with a reasonable degree of severity, if he thinks it ju-

dicious to do so; but he should report it fairly and honestly as a matter of news, giving his personal views in another portion of his paper.[126]

This kind of advice was repeated in subsequent texts such as G. A. Gaskell's *How to Write for the Press* (1884) and A. G. Nevins's *The Blue Pencil and How to Avoid It* (1890). It also became a staple in the curricula of journalism schools as they began to emerge in the early 20th century.

For at least some of the new journalism educators, however, "objectivity" meant more than impartiality or neutrality. At the Missouri School of Journalism, founded in 1908, dean Walter Williams tried to marry objectivity with battling injustice. The journalist, he said, should be "quickly indignant at injustice," "unswayed by the appeal of privilege or the clamor of the mob," and seek "to give every man . . . an equal chance."[127] Williams took this to mean that reporting the "facts" meant showing the meaning of those facts for all concerned. But the students who learned his "Journalist's Creed" did not necessarily understand it in this manner. When an African American woman attempted to enter the school's master's program in 1932, the local Williams-trained reporters who covered the story "showed contempt and anger for a woman trying to obtain the same rights as other taxpaying Missourians." In their view, she had tried to break the law and failed, and the fact that the law disenfranchised her and other African Americans was irrelevant.

Williams was not alone in rejecting this narrow conception of objectivity as a basis for modern journalism. In the same period, **Walter Lippmann**, the foremost American journalist of the 20th century, likewise tried to frame objectivity within a larger vision of journalism. During the Progressive era, American liberals argued that the United States was suffering from a "crisis in democracy." But in *Liberty and the News* (1920), Lippmann countered that the real crisis facing America was a "crisis in journalism." Disillusioned by the Wilson administration's manipulation of the press during the Versailles negotiations, Lippmann believed that most journalists were too lazy, supine, and naive to produce the rigorous, nonpartisan, and suitably skeptical accounts of events which citizens require to judge political events. Journalists needed to raise the standards by which they identified and verified their news sources. Whether they could be counted on to do so remained a matter of tension in Lippmann's thought. At the end of the day, however, the "experts" whom he thought were necessary to ensure the objective representation and assessment of events were journalists like himself. Their proximity to politics made them vulnerable to manipulation. But it also tended to breed a naturally suspicious attitude toward their information sources.

For Lippmann, the archetype of the modern journalist as expert was best seen in the new political **columnists** of the interwar years. Although Anglo-American newspapers had been using columnists of various kinds since the 1850s and 1860s, it was not until the 1920s that *political* columnists like Mark Sullivan, David Lawrence, and Frank R. Kent began to come into their own. A former muckraker, Sullivan was persuaded by his friend Arthur Krock at the *New York Times* to try his hand at a Washington political column; he began the experiment after the war at the *New York Evening Post* before settling in for two decades at the *New York Tribune*. Before founding the *United States Daily* in 1926, Lawrence wrote a national affairs column for the *Post*. Kent's long-running column, "The Great Game of Politics," which began in the *Baltimore Sun* in 1924, sought to expose the pretensions of politicians and was later syndicated to over 100 daily newspapers.

Aided by the ethos of objectivity, which sought to physically separate "straight" news from "opinion," they were initially given almost complete freedom to express their views on what became known as the "op-ed" page, which Herbert Bayard Swope pioneered at the *New York World* in the 1920s. Many acquired enormous influence through national syndication and during the late 1930s they were joined by radio news analysts like **H. V. Kaltenborn** and **Edward R. Murrow**. Their rise occurred at the expense of editors, who remained bounded by conventions of **anonymity** and worried about the displacement of their own function. "With newspaper columnists, or commentators, whichever designation one prefers, I have no particular quarrel," wrote Maurice S. Sherman of the *Hartford Courant* in 1944. "They are on the whole a most diverting lot. My quarrel is with newspapers that have found it easier and cheaper to avail themselves of columnists than to present editorials of their own having the substance and vigor of an earlier day."[128]

Lack of substance was less a concern for publishers than their own loss of influence over their papers. The new breed of columnists were not only skeptical about political authority but questioned the judgment that chief editors had traditionally exercised in tandem with owners. As the Depression and events in Europe worsened, many editors and publishers became worried about their own loss of voice. They began to see it as their own responsibility to maintain the "conscience" of their papers and to insist on greater "loyalty" from their columnists. In 1928, for example, the outspoken New York columnist **Heywood Broun** was forced to switch his column from the *World* to the *Telegram* after incurring the wrath of publisher Ralph Pulitzer for advocating clemency for Sacco and Vanzetti and attacking the *World*'s opposition to birth control. Similarly in 1940, the widely read columnist Dorothy Thompson was pressured into moving her column "On the Record" from the **New York Herald Tribune** to the *New York Post* after infuriating publisher Ogden Reid by supporting Wendell Wilkie for president. In 1947, the *Post* itself dropped the column because of her views toward Germany.[129]

The political columnist was the spearhead rather than the exclusive representative of a new type of journalism, one generally characterized by a concern to explain and make sense of the world rather than merely observe and describe it. This new emphasis depended on a different relationship between the journalist and news sources. The Victorian journalist had simply used "the voices of those in public life" and relayed information in the context in which it was provided. But the modern journalist reframed the material supplied by sources into an independent "voice of journalism." As Donald Matheson explains, "information from external texts was now severely edited, summarized, and contextualized by the newspaper and was thus translated into a single news style. The key change in practice was that it became acceptable to separate information from the style of language in which it arrived at the newspaper and to relate it in a concise and unadorned style." Although reporting lost some of its stylistic variety, journalism became a "self-sufficient form of knowledge."[130]

While Matheson emphasizes the development of a plain-speaking, colloquial style, an equally important component of this new "reportorial voice" was the attitude of the journalist toward his/her sources. The new professional authority of the journalist as expert depended on a curious and complex mixture of acceptance, neutrality, skepticism, and disbelief toward the claims, justifications, and obfuscations of sources. Working out the proper balance in this regard was a slow, difficult, and experimental process, which occurred at different rates in different parts of the newspaper. It was delayed in the case of front-page reporting by the dominant conception of objectivity as the rigorous separation of the reporter's values from what is reported. In both Britain and the United States, it proceeded more rapidly in sensational tabloids like **Lord Northcliffe**'s *Daily Mail* and William Randolph Hearst's Chicago *Herald and Examiner*. But eventually even the dignified *Times* of London and the reserved *New York Times* followed suit. In each case, it was evident first in the work of columnists, then in the inside reporting sections, and finally on the front page.

Its progress can be roughly measured by the practice of bylines. In *Discovering the News* (1978), Michael Schudson argued that bylines were first developed to make newspaper readers aware that the story they were reading was written by a specific individual with personal biases and values. It was yet another device in service of objectivity. For John Nerone and Kevin Barnhurst, on the other hand, bylines were related to the acquisition by some journalists of status and prestige as literary celebrities. "Bylines indicated that what would be followed would be a performance by a literary celebrity and that it would be inimitable . . . So writers in the sections acquired stardom because they did things that journalists on the front page weren't supposed to do. Section writers voiced opinions and expressed themselves in idiomatic fashion."[131]

Nerone and Barnhurst specifically reject the idea that bylines were essentially about indicating expertise. In their view, "experts' work was expert only because it could be replicated by any other qualified expert." However, this assessment is more appropriate in the case of the social scientist, than the journalist, as expert. Patricia Dooley has argued that by the early 20th century, most Americans believed that journalists, rather than politicians, should be providing the main interpretation of political reality.[132] The classic confrontation between Lippmann and philosopher John Dewey in the 1920s was over what form this interpretation should take. In *The Public and Its Problems* (1927), his major work on politics, Dewey proposed the creation of a "new science" for democratic communities that would have as its special province the abstract, uniform, patterned regularities governing the social and political world. Dewey thought that if the scientific generalizations discovered by this positivistic form of social enquiry could then be disseminated by the mass media, then each citizen would be able, as Timothy Kaufman-

Osborn has put it, to apprehend "the same world in the same way" and thereby come to recognize the ties that bind all citizens together.[133]

While Lippmann contemplated a similar use for social science research at points in *Public Opinion* (1922), he had a fundamentally different kind of "expertise" in mind for the ideal political journalist. Lippmann's journalist-expert is expected to provide the public with insight into political developments based on a healthy skepticism toward sources, a rich fund of personally acquired knowledge into the workings of politics, and a capacity to assess the political world from at least somewhat varying perspectives. As such, the journalist's knowledge is not of the replicable kind produced by the social sciences. During the 1970s, there were calls for journalists to include more social science research in their repertoire and become "precision journalists" by adopting techniques such as surveys and content analysis.[134] But a half century earlier, Lippmann argued that these methods are not capable of detecting the hidden political agendas behind events or interpreting political developments within a larger social and economic framework. Among his somewhat younger contemporaries, Lippmann might have regarded **I. F. Stone** as best personifying the kind of political journalism which he desired. Although Stone's investigative reporting did not provide a model that most other journalists could follow, he did exemplify Lippmann's emphasis on not taking politicians at their word, asking tougher questions, and engaging in critical journalism generally.

During the heyday of *I. F. Stone's Weekly* (1953–71), **literary journalists** such as Lillian Ross developed a number of similarly intensive approaches to their craft. As pioneered for pieces like "Portrait of Hemingway" (1950) and "Production Number 1512" (1952) on John Huston for the *New Yorker*, Ross's "wait-and-watch" method of research involved spending many months, in some cases years, with the subject of the piece, not only interviewing, but waiting and watching as the "story" unfolded. Truman Capote borrowed this technique for *In Cold Blood* (1965) and Ross herself was still using it in the 1990s.[135] In most of her writings, Ross keeps the narrator as invisible as possible. But other literary journalists have combined the waiting-and-watching with a participant-observation method in which the journalist becomes part of the story. These approaches have produced numerous works of rich, insightful journalism. But like the muckraking of the Progressives, they do not provide an appropriate model for a journalism that aspires to provide a regular discerning filter between politics and the public; they do not constitute a sufficiently active or pragmatic ideal for mainstream journalism to emulate. Epistemologically, they tend to turn the journalist into a neutral, social scientific observer whose skill at passive witnessing is more important than the intellectual framework used to understand what has been seen. But as journalism scholar **James Carey** emphasized, the journalist is part of a cultural process that necessarily influences, in accordance with its own level of operation, a society's capacity for democracy. The task is not to suppress this effect by reducing the journalist to a cipher, but to refine and uplift it through the standards set for journalism.

The long delay in giving bylines to front-page reporters, especially in the case of elite newspapers like the *New York Times*[136] and *The Times* of London (I could find no bylines for its main reporters until January 1967, when they suddenly became the norm),[137] was mainly the result of objectivity's continuing diminution of the idea of the journalist as a special kind of expert. It still assumed that the front-page reporter only needed training in gathering and presenting the facts in accordance with prescribed techniques such as the inverted pyramid. This dictum played into the hands of demagogues like Senator Joseph McCarthy in his witch hunt against alleged communists in America. Reporters uncritically relayed McCarthy's unsubstantiated charges verbatim as being newsworthy in themselves, without commentary on their possible motivation or reliability. Even after Edward R. Murrow's famous exposure of McCarthy on *See It Now* on 9 March 1954, editors were slow to blame themselves or their restricted sense of objectivity for helping to make McCarthy powerful.[138] The cult of objectivity continued to exercise control over major news stories and facilitated the further development of **news management**.

During the past quarter century, however, there has been a significant erosion of the traditional way of understanding objectivity. Studies have found a steady shift from a neutral, descriptive journalism to a more analytical and interpretative journalism.[139] Even on the front pages of elite newspapers, the barrier between news and opinion has become increasingly permeable. Many of the original semiotic indicators separating the two have been thrown into a state of disarray. Viewpoints are now making their way into hard news stories and front-page commentaries and are no longer exceptional. Taken overall, this trend represents the rise of the journalist as a professional expert on making sense of the world. As Nerone and Barnhurst explain, "mapping the social . . . required authority of the sort claimed by professionals—that is, authority supposedly derived from superior expertise."[140]

The nature of this new authority is a product of the competitive interaction of the resources, market, and public interest principles. It is also affected by the contradictory internal dynamics of the resources principle. In the Roman Empire, where the *acta diurna* marked the beginning of journalism, communication was governed entirely by the operation of the resources principle and the state held a virtual monopoly of *consolidated* resources. But despite its direct challenge to the prevailing paganism, the Roman authorities were not able, through persecution or other means, to prevent the long, slow rise of Christianity, culminating in its toleration by the Emperor Constantine in 313 A.D. As Rodney Stark has shown, the capacity of a small group of Christians to make a modest addition to their number through only a small expenditure of personal resources was sufficient, given enough time, for Christianity to grow from hundreds to tens of thousands and eventually to many millions of converts.[141] Similarly, the continuing growth of large media empires, often controlled by non-media interests, is counterbalanced by the capacity of bloggers on the Internet to enter the public sphere with a relatively small outlay of resources.

Both media conglomeration and blogging threaten the role of the journalist through their pressure toward less professional and more ideological forms of discourse. Though variously defined, an ideology is essentially a rigid set of ideas used to promote a class, religion, ethnic group, lifestyle, or social practice to the specific exclusion, and at the expense, of an alternative one. Even without any form of organizational pressure or competition from **blogs**, the journalist would be drawn toward ideology by the perceived need to take a clear, strong stand on any issue, as opposed to probing for compromises that might serve everybody's interests. In this case, the market principle works to reinforce the resources principle by suggesting that what the public wants are instant experts.

The market principle has also combined with the resources principle to produce reduced levels of restraint in reporting on the private failings of officials and other public figures. According to John Summers, coverage of the sexual improprieties of American politicians was a regular feature of reporting during the 19th century, but declined noticeably during the administrations of Harding, Roosevelt, and Kennedy as a result of changes in "the ideology and practices of professional journalism." Since then, however, there has been a "repeal of reticence" in this area and in the treatment of politicians' private failings generally.[142] Most segments of the press not only provide ready coverage of the personal attacks of politicians on each other but engage in such sniping themselves when it serves their own political agenda. At the same time, the market principle ensures that the press is always on the lookout for a ripe scandal. Even reporters with a strong commitment to serving the public interest have in recent decades often overlooked the long-term effect of indiscriminately exposing private faults.

In the early 1990s, a number of journalists and academics responded to these pressures by advocating a new civic or **public journalism**. Based on a belief that traditional objective journalism was contributing to the increasing alienation of the public from politics, Jay Rosen, W. J. "Buzz" Merritt, and others called upon journalists to become more active in community life. Instead of simply providing citizens with factual news, they proposed, among other things, that journalists organize forums and debates at which citizens could work out possible solutions to specific community problems. Insofar as journalists would not be advocating solutions themselves and would be providing information to assist the process of public discussion, public journalism does not entirely abandon conventional journalistic values. But it prioritizes the active and concrete participation of journalists in the democratic process.

Like muckraking, investigative journalism, and literary journalism, public journalism is better conceived as ancillary to journalism's role than as its main *raison d'être*. In addition to dealing with community problems, citizens need to be able to engage constructively in the discussion of regional, national, and international problems; these broader problems, which often involve intense conflicts over values, cannot be left to politicians and special interests to interpret and handle in isolation from public input. For meaningful public participation at these levels, the journalist as flexible expert remains indispensable. Interestingly, the main advocate for this journalistic enterprise has been the well-educated editorial writer, whose public stature has been steadily reduced in favor of columnists and star reporters. G. Cleveland Wilhoit and Dan

G. Drew have found that "on most newspapers" editors continue to be "the preeminent 'idea-mongers' . . . through whom the papers, as institutions, speak directly to their readers."[143] In various surveys, editors have not only reported a continuing high level of job satisfaction but have seen themselves, more than news reporters, as autonomous professionals serving the public good. Their skeptical attitude toward sources and broad knowledge of the political and social world remain vital in this regard. But their most important contribution lies in their capacity to think perceptively and sensitively about the common bonds that supersede the vested interests of particular constituencies. It is this ability that distinguishes the journalist from the propagandist, the public relations practitioner, the politician, the blogger, and even the narrowly trained social scientist, and constitutes modern journalism's main form of service to society. It is a fragile capacity, but one with deep wellsprings in the history of journalism.

Is the Lippmannesque ideal, practiced more in his own journalism than preached in his books, a *feasible* one in the "real world" of journalism? Since the 1950s, the total number of daily newspapers sold in the United States has remained more or less constant, but during the same time period total population increased by about two-thirds. The result has been a decline in newspaper penetration rates of more than 50 percent. According to the Newspaper Association of America, only 48.4 percent of the adult population now read a newspaper on a daily basis (other sources place it even lower). American newspapers have responded to these trends in a variety of ways, but their general strategy has been to increase local news and features such as lifestyle coverage. In a survey of 1,300 newspapers between 1979 and 1983, Leo Bogart found both an increasing ratio of features to hard news and an increasing ratio of local to national and world news.[144] While this pattern cannot be assumed to apply equally to other countries, it is certainly not unique to the United States, where it has been studied with particular intensity by social scientists as well as by the newspaper industry itself. Does this research indicate that the journalist-as-expert is an antiquated or irrelevant ideal? From the vast literature on newspaper readership and news content, two studies—one published in 1991, the other in 2005—suggest that it does not.

In a 1984 survey of 114 U.S. newspapers, Stephen Lacy and Frederick Fico studied whether newspapers that cut "quality" improve or further erode their circulation. Recognizing the difficulty of operationalizing quality, they surveyed editors to find out what they consider to be the main indicators of quality. Among these indicators are: a high ratio of staff-written copy to wire service copy; a high ratio of non-advertising to advertising content in the news sections; the average length of news stories in the news sections; and the ratio of series, news analysis, and interpretative stories to hard news copy. In general, the editors' "quality" indicators are the requirements for the journalist-as-expert to operate; but they are also the factors that have been in steady decline. Lacy and Fico found, however, that the strategy of reducing quality was not working. They found "strong support" for the relationship between high news quality and high circulation and concluded that there is a significant connection between journalists' perceptions of quality and those of their readers. In short, newspapers that cut quality eventually ended up losing circulation.[145]

While this conclusion may be music to many journalists' ears, it would appear to overstate the connection between quality of content and circulation. A recent study by Jack Rosenberry of 41 newspapers, with an average penetration virtually identical to the national rate, found that the type of content that composes a newspaper does not have nearly as significant a relationship to circulation variance as demographics, competition, and other market characteristics. To put this in perspective, however, two points need to be emphasized. First, it means that there is actually little support as well for the conventional wisdom that local news and lifestyle coverage are better suited to maintaining circulation than quality journalism. Secondly, Rosenberry allowed that his coding of "quality" was imperfect and may not have captured its entire effect. He concluded, therefore, that "while the results of this study don't provide unqualified support for the idea that quality of coverage is related to circulation success, it's not certain that they contradict it either."[146]

It would be premature and unwise, therefore, to conclude that the dynamics of circulation provide any basis for compromising the journalistic ideal of helping the public to discern its common interest. Moreover, recent elections in Canada, the United States, and elsewhere have accentuated the growing need for quality journalism that rises above the excessive rhetoric, attack ads, and outright trickery used in many campaigns and enables voters to judge the competing parties on their own merits. At the end of the day, the survival of print journalism will depend on the standards that it sets for itself and the capacity of journalists to meet those standards.

REFERENCES

1. Dallas Liddle, "Salesmen, Sportsmen, Mentors: Anonymity and Mid-Victorian Theories of Journalism," *Victorian Studies* 41, no. 1 (1997), 31–68.
2. George H. Mead, "The Nature of Aesthetic Experience," *International Journal of Ethics* 36, no. 4 (1926), 389–90.
3. Lynette Sheridan Burns, *Understanding Journalism* (London: Sage, 2002), 28. Emphasis in original.
4. Sian Lewis, *News and Society in the Greek Polis* (Chapel Hill: University of North Carolina Press, 1996).
5. C. A. Giffard, "Ancient Rome's Daily Gazette," *Journalism History* 2, no. 4 (1975–76), 107.
6. Chul Heo, Ki-Yul Uhm, and Jeong-Heon Chang, "South Korea," in Shelton A. Gunaratne, ed., *Handbook of the Media in Asia* (New Delhi: Sage, 2000), 612.
7. Frederick H. Cramer, "Bookburning and Censorship in Ancient Rome: A Chapter from the History of Freedom of Speech," *Journal of the History of Ideas* 6, no. 2 (1945), 161.
8. Michael H. Fisher, "The Office of Akhbār Nawīs: The Transition from Mughal to British Forms," *Modern Asian Studies* 27, no. 1 (1993), 45–82.
9. James A. Doig, "Political Propaganda and Royal Proclamations in Late Medieval England," *Historical Research* 71, no. 176 (1998), 275.
10. C. A. J. Armstrong, "Some Examples of the Distribution and Speed of News in England at the Time of the Wars of the Roses," in R. W. Hunt, W. A. Pantin, and R. W. Southern, eds., *Studies in Medieval History: Presented to Frederick Maurice Powicke* (Oxford: Clarendon Press, 1948), 433.
11. John C. Baldwin, "The Image of the Jongleur in Northern France Around 1200," *Speculum* 72, no. 3 (1997), 635–63.
12. Hyder E. Rollins, "The Black-Letter Broadside Ballad," *PMLA* 34, no. 2 (1919), 267–70.
13. Adam Fox, "Ballads, Libels and Popular Ridicule in Jacobean England," *Past and Present* no. 145 (1994), 597–620.
14. D. R. Woolf, "Genre into Artifact: The Decline of the English Chronicle in the Sixteenth Century," *Sixteenth Century Journal* 19, no. 3 (1988), 334.
15. Mariane Ailes, "Early French Chronicle—History or Literature?" *Journal of Medieval Literature* 26, no. 3 (2000), 302.
16. William J. Brandt, *The Shape of Medieval History: Studies in Modes of Perception* (New York: Schocken Books, 1973), 65.

17. John Timpane, book review in *Renaissance Quarterly* 36, no. 4 (1983), 639–40.

18. Brian Winston, *Messages: Free Expression, Media and the West from Gutenberg to Google* (London: Routledge, 2005), 34.

19. M. A. Shaaber, *Some Forerunners of the Newspaper in England, 1476–1622* (New York: Octagon Books, 1966 [1929]), 5, 65.

20. Brendan Dooley, *The Social History of Skepticism: Experience and Doubt in Early Modern Culture* (Baltimore, Md.: Johns Hopkins University Press, 1999).

21. Raymond B. Waddington, "A Satirist's *Impressa*: The Medals of Pietro Aretino," *Renaissance Quarterly* 42, no. 4 (1989), 655.

22. Paul F. Grendler, "The Rejection of Learning in Mid-Cinquecento Italy," *Studies in the Renaissance* 13 (1966), 230, 249.

23. Mitchell Stephens, "Sensationalism and Moralizing in 16th and 17th-Century Newsbooks and News Ballads," *Journalism History* 12, nos. 3–4 (1985), 92–5.

24. Quoted from the cover as printed in Thomas Cragin, "Journalism," *Encyclopedia of European Social History: From 1350 to 2000*, vol. 5 (Detroit, Mich.: Charles Scribner's, 2001), 422.

25. Joy Wiltenburg, "True Crime: The Origins of Modern Sensationalism," *American Historical Review* 109, no. 5 (2004), 1377–1404.

26. Bernard S. Chandler, "A Renaissance News Correspondent," *Italica* 29, no. 3 (1952), 158–63.

27. Elizabeth L. Eisenstein, *The Printing Press as an Agent of Change: Communications and Cultural Transformation in Early-Modern Europe*, 2 vols. (Cambridge: Cambridge University Press, 1979), vol. 1.

28. Derek Pearsall, "Introduction" to Jeremy Griffiths and D. Pearsall, eds., *Book Production and Publishing in England, 1375–1475* (Cambridge: Cambridge University Press, 1989), 2–3.

29. Winston, *Messages*, 38–39.

30. Paul J. Voss, *Elizabethan News Pamphlets: Shakespeare, Marlowe and the Birth of Journalism* (Pittsburgh, Pa.: Duquesne University Press, 2001), 24.

31. Joseph Frank, *The Beginnings of the English Newspaper, 1620–1660* (Cambridge, Mass.: Harvard University Press, 1961), 6.

32. Joad Raymond, *The Invention of the Newspaper: English Newsbooks, 1641–1649* (Oxford: Oxford University Press, 1996), 8–9.

33. Howard M. Solomon, *Public Welfare, Science, and Propaganda in Seventeenth Century France: The Innovations of Théophraste Renaudot* (Princeton, N.J.: Princeton University Press, 1972).

34. Gilles Feyel, *La "Gazette" en province à travers ses réimpressions, 1631–1752* (Amsterdam: APA-Holland University Press, 1982).

35. Frances Henderson, book review in *English Historical Review* 114, no. 457 (1999), 714.

36. Jason McElligott, "John Crouch: A Royalist Journalist in Cromwellian England," *Media History* 10, no. 3 (2004), 139–55.

37. Jason McElligott, "'A Couple of Hundred Squabbling Small Tradesmen'? Censorship, the Stationers' Company, and the State in Early Modern England," *Media History* 11, nos. 1–2 (2005), 87–104.

38. Joseph Frank, *Cromwell's Press Agent: A Critical Biography of Marchamont Nedham, 1620–1678* (Washington, D.C.: University Press of America, 1980).

39. Sylvia H. Anthony, "*Mercurius Politicus* under Milton," *Journal of the History of Ideas* 27, no. 4 (1966), 593–609.

40. Mark Fackler and Clifford G. Christians, "John Milton's Place in Journalism History: Champion or Turncoat?" *Journalism Quarterly* 57, no. 4 (1980), 563–70.

41. C. H. Firth, book review in *English Historical Review* 24, no. 95 (1909), 573.

42. John Childs, "The Sales of Government Gazettes During the Exclusion Crisis, 1678–81," *English Historical Review* 102, no. 402 (1987), 103–6.

43. C. Edward Wilson, "Egregious Lies from Idle Brains: Critical Views of Early Journalism," *Journalism Quarterly* 59, no. 2 (1982), 260–64.

44. Mark Muggli, "Ben Jonson and the Business of News," *Studies in English Literature, 1500–1900* 32, no. 2 (1992), 336.

45. As quoted in Woolf, "Genre into Artifact," 331.

46. Raymond, *The Invention of the Newspaper*, 287.

47. As quoted in Raymond, 276.

48. Anthony Smith, "The Long Road to Objectivity and Back Again: The Kinds of Truth We Get in Journalism," in George Boyce, James Curran, and Pauline Wingate, eds., *Newspaper History: From the Seventeenth Century to the Present Day* (London: Constable, 1978), 155.

49. John Greaves, "A Calculation of the Credibility of Human Testimony," *Philosophical Transactions (1683–1775)* 21 (1699), 359, 362.

50. Extracted from numbers included in Electronic Historical Publications, http://www.history.rochester.edu/London_Gazette/. Accessed on 3/25/06.

51. Kate Bennett, "John Aubrey, Joseph Barnes's Print-shop and a Sham Newsletter," *Library* 21, no. 1 (1999), 50–58.

52. As quoted in Roy A. Atwood and Arnold S. De Beer, "The Roots of Academic News Research: Tobias Peucer's 'De relationibus novellis,'" *Journalism Studies* 2, no. 4 (2001), 489.

53. Jeremy Black, "Conducting the *Gazette*. Comments by the Printer in 1757," *Publishing History* 21 (1987), 93–8.

54. Alexandra Walsham, "'The Fatal Vesper': Providentialism and Anti-Popery in Late Jacobean London," *Past and Present* no. 144 (1994), 39–41.

55. David Paul Nord, "Teleology and News: The Religious Roots of American Journalism, 1630–1730," *Journal of American History* 77, no. 1 (1990), 11.

56. Jerome Friedman, *The Battle of the Frogs and Fairford's Flies: Miracles and the Pulp Press During the English Revolution* (New York: St. Martin's Press, 1993).

57. Nord, "Teleology and News," 30, 22.

58. Julie Hedgepeth Williams, "The Purposes of Journalism," in W. David Sloan and Lisa Mullikan Parcell, eds., *American Journalism: History, Principles, Practices* (Jefferson, N.C.: McFarland, 2003), 3.

59. David Copeland, *Colonial American Newspapers: Character and Content* (Newark: University of Delaware Press, 1997).

60. Theodore F. M. Newton, "William Pittis and Queen Anne Journalism," *Modern Philology* 33, no. 2 (1939), 169–86.

61. J. A. Downie, "Mr. Review and His Scribbling Friends: Defoe and the Critics, 1705–1796," *Huntingdon Library Quarterly* 41, no. 4 (August 1978), 352.

62. James Sutherland, *Daniel Defoe: A Critical Study* (Cambridge, Mass.: Harvard University Press, 1971), 9.

63. Brian Cowan, "Mr. Spectator and the Coffeehouse Public Sphere," *Eighteenth-Century Studies* 37, no. 3 (2004), 346.

64. As quoted from David L. Jacobson, ed., *The English Libertarian Heritage: From the Writings of John Trenchard and Thomas Gordon in "The Independent Whig" and "Cato's Letters"* (New York: Macmillan, 1965), 73.

65. Ibid., 74.

66. Michael Harris, "The Structure, Ownership and Control of the Press, 1620–1780," in Boyce, Curran, and Wingate, eds., *Newspaper History*, 83.

67. Geoffrey A. Cranfield, *The Development of the Provincial Newspaper, 1700–1760* (Oxford: Clarendon Press, 1962).

68. Ivon Asquith, "The Structure, Ownership and Control of the Press, 1780–1855," in Boyce, Curran, and Wingate, eds., *Newspaper History*, 99.

69. A. Aspinall, *Politics and the Press, c. 1780–1850* (London: Horne & Van Thal, 1949), 379.

70. Philip Hamburger, "The Development of the Law of Seditious Libel and Control of the Press," *Stanford Law Review* 37 (February 1985), 666–73.

71. J. A. Downie, *Robert Harley and the Press: Propaganda and Public Opinion in the Age of Swift and Defoe* (New York: Cambridge University Press, 1979).

72. Simon Targett, "Government and Ideology during the Age of Whig Supremacy: The Political Argument of Sir Robert Walpole's Newspaper Propagandists," *Historical Journal* 37, no. 2 (June 1994), 290.

73. James Oldham, "Law Reporting in the London Newspapers, 1756–1786," *American Journal of Legal History* 31, no. 3 (1987), 177.

74. Michael MacDonald, "Suicide and the Rise of the Popular Press in England," *Representations* no. 22 (1988), 42–3.

75. Ralph A. Nablow, *The Addisonian Tradition in France: Passion and Objectivity in Social Observation* (Rutherford: Fairleigh Dickinson University Press, 1990). See also Claire Boulard, "The Spectator's Curtailed Legacy: The Periodical Press between England and France in the Eighteenth Century" in Frédéric Ogée, ed., *"Better in France?" The Circulation of Ideas Across the Channel in the Eighteenth Century* (Lewisburg, Pa.: Bucknell University Press, 2005).

76. Robert Darnton, "The High Enlightenment and the Low Life of Literature in Pre-Revolutionary France," *Past and Present* 51 (May 1971), 100.

77. Jeremy D. Popkin, "Pamphlet Literature at the End of the Old Regime," *Eighteenth-Century Studies* 22, no. 3 (Spring 1989), 356.

78. Nina Gelbart, "'Frondeur' Journalism in the 1770s: Theater Criticism and Radical Politics in the Prerevolutionary French Press," *Eighteenth-Century Studies* 17, no. 4 (Summer 1984), 494.

79. Sheila McIntyre, "'I Heard It So Variously Reported': News-Letters, Newspapers, and the Ministerial Network in New England, 1670–1730," *New England Quarterly* 71, no. 4 (1998), 593–614.

80. John Nerone and Kevin G. Barnhurst, "U.S. Newspaper Types, the Newsroom, and the Division of Labor, 1750–2000," *Journalism Studies* 4, no. 4 (2003), 436–37.

81. Stephen Botean, "'Moor Mechanics' and an Open Press: The Business and Political Strategies of Colonial American Printers," *Perspectives in American History* 9 (1975), 127–225.

82. James L. Moses, "Journalistic Impartiality on the Eve of Revolution: The *Boston Evening Post*, 1770–1775," *Journalism History* 20, nos. 3/4 (1994), 125.

83. Jeffery A. Smith, "Impartiality and Revolutionary Ideology: Editorial Policies of the *South-Carolina Gazette*, 1732–1775," *Journal of Southern History* 49, no. 4 (1983), 511–26.

84. Dallas Liddle, "Who Invented the 'Leading Article'? Reconstructing the History and Prehistory of a Victorian Newspaper Genre," *Media History* 5, no. 1 (1999), 5.

85. David Copeland, "'Join or Die': America's Newspapers in the French and Indian War," *Journalism History* 24, no. 3 (1998), 113.

86. Frank Luther Mott, "The Newspaper Coverage of Lexington and Concord," *New England Quarterly* 17, no. 4 (1944), 490–91.

87. Ivon Asquith, "Advertising and the Press in the Late Eighteenth and Early Nineteenth Centuries: James Perry and the *Morning Chronicle*, 1790–1821," *Historical Journal* 18, no. 4 (1975), 704–5.

88. Ibid., 706–7.

89. William J. Gilmore, *Reading Becomes a Necessity of Life: Material and Cultural Life in Rural New England, 1780–1835* (Knoxville: University of Tennessee Press, 1989).

90. Charles G. Steffen, "Newspapers for Free: The Economies of Newspaper Circulation in the Early Republic," *Journal of the Early Republic* 23, no. 3 (2003), 381–419.

91. Liddle, "Who Invented the 'Leading Article'?" 6.

92. Frank Luther Mott, *American Journalism* (New York: Macmillan, 1962), 153.

93. Jean K. Chalaby, *The Invention of Journalism* (Houndmills, Basingstoke, Hampshire: Macmillan Press, 1998).

94. Donald Lewis Shaw, "At the Crossroads: Change and Continuity in American Press News 1820–1860," *Journalism History* 8, no. 2 (1981), 38–50. Condensed version of Shaw's table, p. 39. Shaw did a content analysis of 67 U.S. newspapers, 38 dailies and 29 non-dailies.

95. Lucy Brown, "The Treatment of News in Mid-Victorian Newspapers," *Transactions of the Royal Historical Society*, Fifth Series 27 (1977), 38.

96. James L. Crouthamel, "James Gordon Bennett, The New York *Herald*, and the Development of Newspaper Sensationalism," *New York History* 54, no. 3 (1973), 294–316; and Warren Francke, "Sensationalism and the Development of 19th-Century Reporting: The Broom Sweeps Sensory Details," *Journalism History* 12, nos. 3–4 (1985), 80–85.

97. Helen MacGill Hughes, *News and the Human Interest Story* (Chicago: University of Chicago Press, 1940).

98. Donald L. Shaw and John W. Slater, "In the Eye of the Beholder? Sensationalism in American Press News, 1820–1860," *Journalism History* 12, no. 3–4 (1985), 86–91.

99. Alexander Saxton, "Problems of Class and Race in the Origins of the Mass Circulation Press," *American Quarterly* 36, no. 2 (1984), 224.

100. Ibid., 226.

101. David Anthony, "The Helen Jewett Panic: Tabloids, Men, and the Sensational Public Sphere in Antebellum New York," *American Literature* 69, no. 3 (1997), 487–514.

102. Celina Fox, "The Development of Social Reportage in English Periodical Illustration during the 1840s and Early 1850s," *Past and Present* no. 74 (1977), 91. See also Peter W. Sinnema, *Dynamics of the Pictured Page: Representing the Nation in the Illustrated London News* (Aldershot and Brookfield, Vt.: Ashgate, 1998).

103. Lenore O'Boyle, "The Image of the Journalist in France, Germany, and England, 1815–1848," *Comparative Studies in Society and History* 10, no. 3 (1968), 290–317.

104. P. L. Simmonds, "Statistics of Newspapers in Various Countries," *Journal of the Statistical Society of London* 4, no. 2 (1841), 111.

105. "Politics as a Vocation" is contained in H. H. Gerth and C. Wright Mills, eds., *From Max Weber: Essays in Sociology* (New York: Oxford University Press, 1946), 77–128.

106. As quoted in Liddle, "Salesmen, Sportsmen, Mentors," 31–68.

107. Fred Cutler, "Jeremy Bentham and the Public Opinion Tribunal," *Public Opinion Quarterly* 63, no. 3 (1999), 321–46.

108. George Boyce, "The Fourth Estate: The Reappraisal of a Concept," in Boyce, Curran, and Wingate, eds., *Newspaper History*, 19–40.

109. Ted Curtis Smythe, "The Reporter, 1880–1900: Working Conditions and Their Influence on the News," *Journalism History* 7, no. 1 (1980), 1–10.

110. As quoted in Andie Tucher, "In Search of Jenkins: Taste, Style, and Credibility in Gilded-Age Journalism," *Journalism History* 27, no. 2 (2001), 52.

111. Michael Schudson, "Question Authority: A History of the News Interview in American Journalism, 1860s–1930s," *Media, Culture & Society* 16, no. 4 (1994), 565–87.

112. David T. Z. Mindich, "Edwin M. Stanton, the Inverted Pyramid, and Information Control," *Journalism Monographs* no. 140 (1993), 1–31.

113. Horst Pöttker, "News and Its Communicative Quality: The Inverted Pyramid—When and Why Did It Appear?" *Journalism Studies* 4, no. 4 (2003), 508.

114. Carolyn Malone, "Sensational Stories, Endangered Bodies: Women's Work and the New Journalism in England in the 1890s," *Albion* 31, no. 1 (1999), 49–71.

115. Karen Hartmann Roggenkamp, "Narrating the News: New Journalism and Literary Genre in Late Nineteenth-Century American Newspapers and Fiction" (Ph.D. thesis: University of Minnesota, 2001).

116. Michael Robertson, *Stephen Crane, Journalism, and the Making of Modern American Literature* (New York: Columbia University Press, 1997).

117. Donald Matheson, "The Birth of News Discourse: Changes in News Language in British Newspapers, 1880–1930," *Media, Culture and Society* 22, no. 5 (2000), 564.

118. Richard C. Brown, "The Muckrakers: Honest Craftsmen," *History Teacher* 2, no. 2 (1969), 52.

119. Brian Thornton, "Muckraking Journalists and Their Readers: Perceptions of Professionalism," *Journalism History* 21, no. 1 (1995), 29–41.

120. Ronald R. Rodgers, "An Untamed Force: Magazine and Trade Journal Criticism of the New Journalism and the Rise of Professional Standards" (Ph.D. thesis: Ohio University, 2005).

121. Ronald R. Rodgers, "The Problems of Journalism: An Annotated Bibliography of Press Criticism in *Editor and Publisher*, 1901–1923," *Media History Monographs* 9, no. 2 (2006–07), 40 pp.

122. Robert W. McChesney and Ben Scott, "Upton Sinclair and the Contradictions of Capitalist Journalism," *Monthly Review* 54, no. 1 (2002), 1–14.

123. Greg Mitchell, *The Campaign of the Century: Upton Sinclair's Race for Governor of California and the Birth of Media Politics* (New York: Random House, 1992).

124. Ruff, Allen. *"We Called Each Other Comrade": Charles H. Kerr & Company, Radical Publishers*. Urbana: University of Illinois Press, 1997.

125. As quoted in Siegfried Mews, "'The Evil Spirit of Journalism': The Press in the Context of Literature," *South Atlantic Bulletin* 43, no. 4 (1978), 11.

126. As quoted in Joseph A. Mirando, "Embracing Objectivity Early On: Journalism Textbooks of the 1800s," *Journal of Mass Media Ethics* 16, no. 1 (2001), 25.

127. As quoted in Aimee Edmondson and Earnest L. Perry Jr., "Objectivity and 'The Journalist's Creed,'" *Journalism History* 33, no. 4 (Winter 2008), 233–40.

128. Maurice S. Sherman, "The Editor and the Columnist," *Public Opinion Quarterly* 9, no. 3 (1945), 279.

129. Lynn D. Gordon, "Why Dorothy Thompson Lost Her Job: Political Columnists and the Press Wars of the 1930s and 1940s," *History of Education Quarterly* 34, no. 3 (1994), 281–303.

130. Matheson, "The Birth of News Discourse," 561.

131. John Nerone and Kevin Barnhurst, "Visual Mapping and Cultural Authority: Design Changes in U.S. Newspapers, 1920–1940," *Journal of Communication* 45, no. 2 (Spring 1995), 28.

132. Patricia L. Dooley, Taking *Their Political Place: Journalists and the Making of an Occupation* (Westport, Conn.: Greenwood Press, 1997).

133. Timothy V. Kaufman-Osborn, "John Dewey and the Liberal Science of Community," *Journal of Politics* 46, no. 4 (1984), 1153. For a "postpositivist" interpretation of what Dewey had in mind, see Debra Morris, "'How Shall We Read What We Call Reality?': Dewey's New Science of Democracy," *American Journal of Political Science* 43, no. 2 (1999), 608–28.

134. Maxwell E. McCombs, Richard R. Cole, Robert L. Stevenson, and Donald M. Shaw, "Precision Journalism: An Emerging Theory and Technique of News Reporting," *Gazette* 27, no. 1 (1981), 21–34.

135. Helen Benedict, "Literary Journalism and the Media," in Donald H. Johnston, ed., *Encyclopedia of International Media and Communication*, vol. 3 (San Diego, Calif.: Academic Press, 2003), 76.

136. Christine Ogan, Ida Plymale, D. Lynn Smith, William H. Turpin, and Donald Lewis Shaw, "The Changing Front Page of the *New York Times*, 1900–1970," *Journalism Quarterly* 52, no. 2 (1975), 340–44.

137. Before then, *The Times* was still referring to stories "From Our Political Correspondent," "From Our Estates Correspondent," "From Our Acronautical Correspondent," or simply "From Our Correspondent" with no attribution. On Saturday, 21 January 1967, a cover story was attributed to John Woodcock, but he was the paper's "Cricket Correspondent." On June 23, city editor George Pulay was identified, though not the next day in a shorter piece. Then on June 25, Charles Hargrove and Richard Wigg were identified as Paris and Washington correspondents respectively. Thereafter, the number of attributions increased fairly steadily.

138. Brian Thornton, "Published Reaction When Murrow Battled McCarthy," *Journalism History* 29, no. 3 (2003), 133–46.

139. Hoon Shim, "The Professional Role of Journalism Reflected in United States Press Reportage from 1950 to 2000" (Ph.D. thesis: University of Texas at Austin, 2003).

140. Nerone and Barnhurst, "Visual Mapping and Cultural Authority," 11.

141. Rodney Stark, *The Rise of Christianity: A Sociologist Reconsiders History* (Princeton, N.J.: Princeton University Press, 1996).

142. John H. Summers, "What Happened to Sex Scandals? Politics and Peccadilloes, Jefferson to Kennedy," *Journal of American History* 87, no. 3 (2000), 825–26.

143. G. Cleveland Wilhoit and Dan G. Drew, "Editorial Writers on American Daily Newspapers," *Journalism Monographs* no. 129 (October 1991), 1.

144. Leo Bogart, "How U.S. Newspaper Content is Changing," *Journal of Communication* 35, no 2 (1985), 82–90.

145. Stephen Lacy and Frederick Fico, "The Link Between Newspaper Content Quality and Circulation," *Newspaper Research Journal* 12, no. 2 (1991), 46–57.

146. Jack Rosenberry, "The Effect of Content Mix on Circulation Penetration for U.S. Daily Newspapers," *Journalism and Mass Communication Quarterly* 82, no. 2 (2005), 389.

The Dictionary

– A –

ABBOTT, LYMAN (1835–1922). American Congregational minister, editor, and author who was among those who responded to Darwin by trying to reconcile science and religion. After abandoning law for religion and then his pastorship for literature, he was associate editor of *Harper's*, editor of the *Illustrated Christian Weekly*, and coeditor (with Henry Ward Beecher) and later editor of *The Christian Union*, a family oriented religious magazine, which he renamed *The Outlook* in 1893, turned into a progressive journal of opinion, and edited until his death. Through its weekly columns, he exerted a powerful influence on Protestant opinion in the **United States**. In addition to numerous works on theology, he also wrote about current social problems. Although vague and superficial, his Christian evolutionism generally encouraged a more humane social outlook, but not one that extended to the rights of African Americans or women.

ABC. One of the three leading national circulation newspapers in **Spain** (the others being *El País* and *El Mundo*). It was founded in Madrid as a weekly by Ignacio Luca de Tena on 1 January 1903 and became a daily two and a half years later. It developed into the country's leading conservative paper, with strong sympathies for the monarchy and the Catholic Church. Among its early reporters was the poet and author Sofia Casanova (1861–1958), Spain's first war correspondent. She contributed more than 850 articles to *ABC* and was widely praised for her coverage of events on the Eastern Front during **World War I**; she also covered the Russian Revolution.

During the five years of the Second Republic, *ABC* was highly critical of its political reformism and sympathetic attitude toward

Catalonian nationalism. It published two editions during the Spanish Civil War, one supportive of each side. In line with its postwar support of the regime of Francisco Franco, the paper represented the 1961 hijacking of the transatlantic liner *Santa Maria* by the Revolutionary Iberian Directory of Liberation (DRIL) as an act of piracy and terrorism rather than as a platform for denouncing dictatorship. In recent years, it has adopted a more moderate, conservative approach.

ACCURACY IN MEDIA (AIM). Watchdog organization created in Washington, D.C., in 1969 to expose what founder Reed J. Irvine believed was the persistent left-wing slant of the major news outlets in the **United States**. In addition to a twice-monthly newsletter, AIM has made use of radio and television to publicize its complaints. In 1985, PBS agreed to broadcast an hour-long AIM documentary criticizing its own acclaimed 13-part series *Viet Nam: A Television Documentary.* In recent years, AIM has criticized coverage of the United Nations, the former career of Senator Joseph McCarthy, and global warming.

ACTA DIURNA. A news vehicle (meaning daily acts or public record) in ancient Rome that provided citizens with timely information about the senate's debates and decrees. Previously, the senate's business had been secretly recorded in the *acta senatus* for its own consultation. But in 59 B.C.E., Julius Caesar, as leader of the popular party, broadened its content and made it public. Apart from being written on papyrus, the capacity of the *acta diurna*—or, in the words of Suetonius, *populi diurna acta*—to keep up with the debates likely benefited from the earlier development of a primitive system of shorthand. Posted in a public place where it could be copied for further distribution, it continued, with some interruption during the reign of Augustus, for almost 300 years. Though later censored, it functioned at least in part as a source of public information.

ADAMS, FRANKLIN P. (1881–1960). General-interest **columnist** for various New York City newspapers, who signed himself "F.P.A." and, though now largely forgotten, gained a national reputation between the wars. He began his columns with "Always in Good Humor" while working for the *New York Evening Mail* from 1904 to 1913. Except for a brief stint writing columns for *Stars and Stripes*, he wrote "The Conning Tower" (named after the raised navigational structure on a submarine) from 1914 to 1941 for, in succession, the **New York Tribune**, the **New York World**, the **New York Herald Tribune**, and finally the **New York Post**. In addition to his own views (and occasional poetry) on the arts, culture, and society, he presented contributions from budding writers such as Eugene O'Neill and James Thurber. He also wrote the Foreword for Finley Peter Dunne's **Mr. Dooley at His Best** (1938) and was a panelist on the popular radio program "Information, Please!" from 1938 to 1948.

ADAMS, HENRY (1838–1918). Major American writer who, despite being descended from presidents, began his career as a special correspondent from Washington for the **Boston Daily Advertiser**. He later sent dispatches from abroad to the **Boston Courier** and **New York Times** while his father, Charles Francis Adams, was the U.S. minister to **Great Britain**. From 1870 to 1876, he served as editor of the **North American Review**. After completing a nine-volume history of the early American republic, he became interested in the philosophy of history. In **Mont-Saint-Michel and Chartres** (1913) and his tour-de-force autobiography **The Education of Henry Adams** (1918), he explored man's quest for inner unity through the symbols of the Virgin and the dynamo.

ADAMS, SAMUEL (1722–1803). American political journalist and statesman. At Harvard College, he answered "Yes" to the commencement thesis: "Is it Lawful to resist the Supreme Magistrate if the Commonwealth cannot otherwise be preserved?" In addition to writing **pamphlets**, he helped to found the weekly **Public Advertiser** (1748–75) and contributed essays under a variety of pen names to other newspapers. A Freemason, he organized opposition to the Stamp Act, orchestrated the Boston Tea Party, signed the Declaration of Independence, and later served as lieutenant governor and governor of Massachusetts. John C. Miller called him a "pioneer of propaganda" in his 1936 study by that name, while John C. Irvin suggests in a 2002 biography that he did more than anyone else "to make the revolution happen." Toward the end of his life, he apparently lost faith in what the revolution had accomplished as America seemed to move away from his republican ideals.

ADAMS, SAMUEL HOPKINS (1871–1958). Prolific American writer who began his career as a **muckraker**. Together with the efforts of officials such as Harvey Wiley and other writers such as Upton Sinclair, his series of 11 articles on patent medicines, published in *Collier's* as "The Great American Fraud" in 1905, contributed to passage of the Pure Food and Drug Act in 1906. Adams began his career as a reporter at the *New York Sun*, covering the murder trial of Harry Thaw, before joining *McClure's* in 1900 to write about the state of public health in the **United States**. The American Medical Association, which published his series as a book, honored him as a lay associate member. After the U.S. Supreme Court ruled in 1911 that the prohibition of false advertising pertained only to the ingredients of medicines, Adams used a consumer advocacy column to expose false claims about products. In *The Clarion* (1914), a fictionalized account of the fight against patent medicines, he described how the press generally supported the industry during the campaign for reform. In response, various newspapers rejected Houghton Mifflin's advertisements for the novel and in Binghamton, New York, where the Swamproot company operated, the local bookstore and library refused to order it. Adams later fictionalized the scandals of the Warren G. Harding administration and penned the story that became the 1935 Academy Award-winning film *It Happened One Night*. In addition to hundreds of magazine articles, he wrote over 50 popular books.

ADDISON, JOSEPH (1672–1719). English statesman and coauthor with **Richard Steele** of *The Tatler* and the *Spectator*. Along with **Daniel Defoe**, he is generally considered to be the finest of the early newspaper journalists. Born in Wiltshire, Addison was educated at Charterhouse in London, where he first met Steele, and then attended Oxford, later becoming a don with a reputation for verse. With the patronage of several Whig statesmen, he prepared for a diplomatic career by making a grand tour of Europe and secured an appointment as an undersecretary of state. In 1705, he helped revise Steele's comedy *The Tender Husband* and continued this collaboration when Steele became Gazetteer. Though serving in **Ireland** when Steele began *The Tatler* in April 1709, he sent material for several numbers and began contributing directly upon his return in September. Of *The*

Tatler's 271 issues, Addison wrote only 42 on his own, but in the case of its successor, the *Spectator*, produced 274 of 555 issues. In recent years, his famous "moderation" has not only been praised for dampening the incendiary politics of Augustan England but also criticized as a strategy for facilitating the upward mobility of the more affluent members of the middle class while keeping his own political options open.

ADVERTISING, NEWSPAPER. The use of advertising to help support the publication of news began with English newsbooks in the mid-17th century. One such advertisement appeared as early as 1626. In the early 18th century, both **Daniel Defoe** and **Joseph Addison** used advertising in their literary newspapers, but buried it on the back page. In colonial America, printer-editors were initially skeptical about advertising, but gradually reduced their dependence on political patronage through its use. In addition to announcing slave sales, newspaper ads were used to solicit information about deserters, runaways, and other missing persons. As competition for ads increased, especially after 1750, newspapers were forced to cut their rates.

The growth of advertising after 1800 increased the commercial value and profitability of newspapers and contributed to the somewhat improved social status of journalists. But it was not until after 1860 that advertising became the predominant source of revenue for newspapers in **Great Britain** and the **United States**. In the United States, for example, total expenditures on advertising were still only $7.5 million in 1865, whereas by 1919 this figure had increased to over $2 billion. By 1910, advertising accounted for almost 60 percent of total newspaper revenue. This rapid growth benefited from the founding of the *American Newspaper Directory* by George P. Rowell in New York City in 1869; it was the first such directory to include estimates of newspaper circulation. In 1883, the first international advertising agency (Dorland) was also founded in the United States. Elsewhere growth of newspaper advertising proceeded more slowly. In **Russia**, for example, there was little paid advertising in the bourgeois press until the 1890s, when banks, private railways, and heavy industries began to advertise. It was soon followed by the creation of advertising agencies such as Mettsel and Co., which controlled over half of the newspaper ad market by **World War I**.

By the late 19th century, American editors and journalists were becoming increasingly suspicious of the influence of advertising on the content of newspapers and began to insist on a strict separation of the business and editorial sides of the press. However, reliance of newspapers on advertising continued to grow. One beneficial side effect was a campaign against publicists and press agents seeking free publicity. By 1925, income from subscriptions and sales of single copies was less than 25 percent of total newspaper revenues. Dependency on advertising made American newspapers particularly vulnerable during the Great Depression, when total advertising linage dropped from 1.9 billion agate lines in 1929 to 1.05 billion lines in 1933. As a result of this decline, American newspapers began to place more emphasis on subscriptions and sales, so that by 1940 these constituted one third of total revenue.

At the end of **World War II**, most U.S. newspapers still carried more news and editorials than advertising. But between the late 1940s and early 1970s, the traditional 60/40 news-to-advertising ratio was reversed. Advertising now constitutes close to 75 percent of newspaper content, even though studies have found that about half of newspaper readers deliberately avoid the advertising pages. Although community access groups have drawn up budgets that suggest that a much smaller percentage of advertising is compatible with newspaper profitability, advertising remains the dominant source of newspaper revenue. The preponderance of advertising in newspapers is reflected in language: journalists refer to the space between advertisements as the *hole* which is to be filled with what they produce as news.

ADVICE COLUMN, ORIGINAL. Syndicated advice columns such as "Dear Abby" and "Ann Landers," which are a popular element in most newspapers, have a long history. By the late 18th century, American newspapers were trying to appeal to the young by including romantic poetry, appeals for courtship, and advice about courtship. Even earlier in the century, **Daniel Defoe** tried his hand as an advice columnist. After the ***Review***'s Scandalous Club feature began eliciting letters asking for advice, Defoe published the *Little Review* for a year or so until illness forced him to give it up. The first newspaper advice seems to have originated in 1691, however, when the London bookseller John Dunton began publishing *The Athenian Mercury*, a weekly journal which promised that "all Persons whatever may be resolved *gratis* in any Question that their own satisfaction or Curiosity shall prompt 'em to, if they send their Questions by a Penny Post Letter . . ." Dunton hired a few authorities (and invented others) to answer the nearly 6,000 questions sent his way over the next decade. Over this time span, the emphasis gradually shifted from natural science to love and marriage. Sometime after he was forced to fold the *Mercury* because of personal problems, Dunton tried to revive the concept of a journal devoted solely to the questions of readers, but did not meet with much success.

AFGHANISTAN. The development of journalism in Afghanistan has suffered not only from warfare, poverty, and extremely low literacy rates but from an ongoing seesaw between freedom and repression of the press. The first reasonably permanent indigenous newspaper was the oppositional *Seraj al-Akhbar Afghaniya* [Beacon of Afghan News], founded by Mahmud Tarzi, the "father of Afghan journalism." It began in 1911 while the country was still under British rule and provided both domestic and foreign news until 1918. It was initially lithographed from a handwritten copy, but later issues were typeset and illustrated. Tarzi's "Young Afghans" criticized the decline of Afghanistan in the Islamic world and sought to restore its place through a combination of nationalism and modernization. His editorials discussed topics such as education, ethnic relations, public health, railroads, and neutrality in **World War I**. Following independence in 1919, the weekly *Aman-I Afghan* [Afghan Peace] carried on Tarzi's reformist and nationalistic emphasis. In 1927, however, the government founded *Anis* [Companion or Friendship] as an instrument of propaganda, and it soon dominated the news system.

After **World War II**, the government of Prime Minister Shah Mahmud passed a press law encouraging the growth of independent newspapers. But in 1953, Prime Minister Mohammad Daud ordered their closure. In 1964, King Mohammad Zaher promulgated a new constitution that included a guarantee of freedom of the press. The result was a "decade of democracy" during which independent journalism flourished once again. In 1973, however, Daud led a coup d'état eliminating the monarchy and shutting down 19 newspapers.

From then until the overthrow of the Taliban in 2001, the press was subjected to increasingly harsh controls and the circulation of newspapers plummeted. Although the new constitution of 2004 declares freedom of expression to be "inviolable," it also stipulates that "no law can be contrary to the beliefs and provisions of the sacred religion of Islam."

AFRICA. The first newspapers in Africa were founded by colonial regimes for the purposes of replicating European culture and controlling public opinion. However, their employees gradually included African journalists, who in some cases later used their experience to found indigenous newspapers in many African countries. The indigenous newspapers were initially concerned mainly with local grievances, but most soon became nationalist in nature and played a major role in the promotion of independence throughout most of the African continent. After independence was eventually achieved, they generally sought to assist the new governments with the difficult task of creating legitimate, stable, and economically viable societies, using the concept of development journalism to justify their playing this role. In recent years, its continued application has become more problematic.

In Freetown, Sierra Leone, the career of James Bright Davies (1848–1920), who was of Ibo origins, illustrates the transition from colonial employee to African ownership. Bright Davies began contributing to newspapers in his mid-twenties while also working for the government. His journalism was so good that in 1876 he was hired as editor of the influential *West African Reporter*, just a year after its creation by William Grant. He later resumed his administrative career in the Gold Coast (present-day Ghana), only to return to journalism by helping to found the Gold Coast Printing and Publishing Co. and becoming editor and manager of its new newspaper, the *Gold Coast Independent*, in 1895. After yet another lengthy absence from journalism, he went to Lagos in 1910 and founded the *Nigerian Times* in 1910, becoming the first Nigerian journalist to be sent to prison for criticizing British rule in a time of war. The Methodist churchman Attoh Ahuma (1863–1921) also worked first for a colonial newspaper in the Gold Coast before eventually founding one of his own. During the 1890s, Attoh worked his way up to the editorial staff at the *Gold Coast Methodist Times* before leaving to help found the Aboriginal Rights Protection Society (ARPS). After his article "Colony or Protectorate, Which?" led to his expulsion from the Methodist ministry, he wrote for the ARPS paper *The Gold Coast Aborigines* and in 1912 founded a new nationalist newspaper, *The Gold Coast Nation.*

Building on colonial journalism experience was not the only route to establishing an indigenous newspaper; others went abroad to acquire skills related to journalism. In 1888, John Langalibalele Dube (1871–1946), who was of royal Zulu lineage in Natal and became the founding president of the African National Congress, went to the United States to study at Oberlin Preparatory Academy; while there he worked for a printing firm and later used the skills he acquired to help cofound and produce *Ilanga Lase Natal,* the first Zulu-language newspaper. Still other Africans used careers in law or other professions as a springboard into journalism. After studying law in London, Kitoyi Ajasa (1866–1937), the son of a Sierra Leone "recaptive" (a slave freed from a slave ship), set up a practice in Nigeria before helping to found *The Lagos Standard* in 1894. Later, after breaking with the *Standard* over its confrontational approach, he founded the *Nigerian Pioneer* in partnership with European business interests. Having secondary careers was essential in many cases for involvement in journalism. J. E. Casely Hayford (1866–1930), an early advocate of pan-African nationalism, maintained a law practice while editing the *Gold Coast Leader.*

The first African-owned newspaper in East Africa was *Sekanyolya,* a Luganda-language monthly founded in 1920 by Sefanio K. Sentongo in the British protectorate of Uganda, though printed in Nairobi to avoid prosecution. Named after a bird, it was critical of the ruling Baganda chiefs and Buganda society in general, especially its Indian businessmen, mission education system, and inequitable distribution of land. Two years later, the Bataka in Kampala began publishing the Luganda-language *Munyonyyozi* under editor Daudi Bassade to plead the case for land reform. In 1923, Bassade and publisher Joswa Kate were found guilty of defaming the Buganda treasurer and fined. During their appeal to the Uganda High Court, Justice Smith declared that truthful criticism of public policy and public officials is "entirely legitimate" and "an advantage to the community," but upheld the conviction.

As the indigenous newspapers gradually shifted their focus from local injustices to the larger question of national independence, they rejected what they regarded as a Eurocentric approach to journalism in favor of an Afrocentric one. To best serve the community, they argued in part, the African press should concentrate on getting its political message across without worrying about profitability. Given the low level of commercialization, this philosophy was partly a matter of making a virtue of necessity. But it also made it easier for the colonial authorities to restrict the growth of the indigenous press through various bonding requirements and for the commercial colonial newspapers to draw away its target audience through more popular content.

The most successful African papers tended to be those which tried to balance Afrocentric values with Western commercialism. In 1937, for example, Nnamdi Azikiwe (1904–1996), founded the *West African Pilot*, the first of a chain of Nigerian papers. It not only challenged the exclusion of the Nigerian elite from participation in government but gradually aroused national consciousness among the Nigerian masses. But the *Pilot*'s effectiveness as a vehicle for nationalism was tied to its combination of traditional African symbols and myths with modern journalistic elements. The retention of indigenous forms of cultural representation reduced the capacity of British rulers to understand its discussions, while the use of photographs, wire service copy, and American news formats increased circulation and helped it to succeed as a business venture.

In the Gold Coast, the indigenous *Ashanti Pioneer* went even further in trying to attract readers. Founded by John S. Tsiboe in 1939, it mixed anti-British editorials with stories about crime and sensational items such as the banner-headlined page-one story "Girl Gives Birth to Reptiloid Monster" (21 February 1946). On the other side of the continent, higher levels of colonial confrontation led Africans to place greater reliance on traditional modes of political pressure, such as secret societies, than on the modern media. But the indigenous press still played a role in obtaining support for the nationalist cause. In general, it was most successful in promoting national independence in the British colonies, much less effective in the French colonies, and least influential in the Portuguese and Belgian colonies.

By the early 1950s, the die was cast in most African colonies for eventual independence and the only remaining debate was over the timing of the transition. Between 1956 and 1972, 35 new nations emerged in Africa. In many cases, their leaders were former pioneers of African journalism: Nnamdi Azikiwe in Nigeria, Jomo Kenyatta in Kenya, Julius Nyerere in Tanzania, and Kwame Nkrumah in Ghana. After graduating from Lincoln University in Pennsylvania in 1939, Nkrumah edited the *Accra Evening News* in the Gold Coast. Upon Ghana's independence from Britain in 1957, he served as prime minister for three years and then as president from 1960–66 until he was toppled by a military coup.

During the pre-independence period, the African-owned press was regarded by nationalist leaders as a legitimate instrument for promoting change in both government policies and the form of government itself. After independence, however, this concept gave way to what came to be known as development journalism. It was argued that before independence, the press had served traditional collectivist values in Africa by helping to achieve national autonomy. But given the monumental problems facing the fragile and ethnically volatile new states, it was now essential for the press to assist governments in establishing the economic, social, and cultural infrastructure necessary for successful nationhood.

For the early advocates of this philosophy, including the United Nations Educational, Scientific and Cultural Organization (UNESCO) at its 1976 General Conference in Nairobi, development journalism meant essentially responsible and constructive journalism. It was not seen as a threat to freedom of the press, because reporting the news in the Western sense was not what most African journalists aspired to do; their role was to help forge new nations in a particularly difficult set of circumstances. Because of the continuing lack of an economic base for private media ownership, most of the new African governments created their own media outlets, especially in radio and television, where development journalism was initially a good fit.

By the mid-1980s, development journalism was making a significant contribution to rural development in countries such as Nigeria. In a growing number of African countries, however, governments also began to use control of the media for their own political purposes.

Journalists in Gabon, Central African Republic, Congo, Malawi, and elsewhere became subject to dismissal, arrest, and even torture for criticizing government policy. In Kenya, for example, the well-known Kikuyu journalist George Githi was dismissed as editor-in-chief of the *Standard* in 1982 after the government apparently took exception to his criticism of the policy of detaining people without trial. Even in Nigeria, journalists like **Oladele Giwa** were subject to intimidation and death once their journalism threatened the government. Development journalism was also compromised in some cases by the emergence of wealthy elites, which used their resources to either buy space and time in various media outlets or purchase them outright as personal political instruments. Despite this perversion of their original vision, advocates of development journalism had difficulty embracing rhetoric about the free flow of information because of its association with Western media imperialism.

By the 1990s, nonetheless, the development paradigm was being criticized by African journalists themselves for encouraging self-censorship and a style of journalism known disparagingly as "the Minister said." At the same time, however, it was recognized that greater press freedom alone would not lead to better journalism. There needed to be better training for journalists and media managers; better equipment in newsrooms ("Entering some newsrooms in Africa is like entering a museum," wrote Canadian professor Robert Martin after the Windoek seminar in Namibia in 1991); and a better financial and regulatory environment for independent newspaper operations. There also needed to be more emphasis on professional behavior and responsibility in the development journalism tradition.

For some commentators, the behavior of the press following the reduction of controls in multiparty states in the 1990s was particularly worrisome; its highly confrontational approach would, they feared, lead to **censorship** once again. The task remains for the African press to find a mode of criticism that does not invariably erode its freedom, while still enabling it to play an influential and constructive role in African society.

AGEE, JAMES (1909–1955). Harvard-educated journalist who wrote for *Fortune* magazine from 1932–39. The son of a backwoods Tennessee farmer, Agee's portrayal of Alabama tenant farmers was rejected by **Henry Luce** as too stark, but was later published as *Let Us Now Praise Famous Men* (1941). His work also included film criticism, screenwriting, and novels. He was a film critic for *Time* magazine and *The Nation* in the 1940s; coauthored the film script for *The African Queen* (1951) with director John Huston; and won a **Pulitzer Prize** for his novel *A Death in the Family*, published posthumously in 1957. According to critic Kenneth Seib, his writing was unsurpassed by any of his contemporaries.

AGENCE FRANCE-PRESSE (AFP). The leading French news agency, established in 1944 but with strong roots to the **Havas** news agency founded in 1835. Following its establishment in July 1940, the Vichy government or regime, which collaborated with the German occupation of **France** until August 1944, turned Havas into Agence Havas and had it function as the Office français d'information. Havas had always had close ties to the state, accepting subsidies, for example, in return for maintaining an international network of bureaus. In 1944, Agence Havas was renamed Agence France-presse and remained under direct government control. It was not until 1957, when members of the daily press became a majority of its board of directors, that it began to reclaim a measure of independence. Even then, successive French governments tried to influence its operations by financial means. Under Jean Marin (who was eventually pressured to step aside by president Valéry Giscard d'Estaing) and his successors, however, it was able to maintain its political independence and develop a worldwide presence. It is generally credited with raising the standards of news reporting in France.

AGENDA-SETTING. The idea that, while the press does not exert much influence over what people think, it does play a major role in what they think *about*. The term *agenda setting* was first used by Bernard Cohen in *The Press and Foreign Policy* (1963) at a time when mass communication research seemed to have demonstrated that the mass media were not as powerful as previously believed. The first attempt to document this effect using quantitative research methods was conducted by Maxwell McCombs and Donald Shaw in 1968 and published four years later in the *Public Opinion Quarterly*. McCombs spent almost four decades refining his initial hypothesis into a theory of how the news media create issue salience. Ironically, the 400-odd studies inspired by his work have tended to return to the initial view that the media also shape *how* we think about the issues they have rendered salient.

AKHBĀR NAWĪS. "Newswriters" in Mughal **India** who recorded the formal acts and words of the emperor and the events of his reign. Their preliminary accounts were then synthesized and scrutinized by higher-level officials and even the emperor himself. The final polished product was placed in the imperial archives for subsequent use by official historians, but was not otherwise available to the public. In addition to newswriters in his own court, Emperor Akbar established correspondents in the courts of regional rulers, who later used a similar system of information control to expand their power at his expense. When the East India Company began placing Mughal territories under its direct rule, it took over their news systems and tried to adapt them to its own purposes. Because of the prejudice against trusting Indian officials to gather intelligence on its behalf, however, the company came to rely on its commercial and political residents for information.

ALBANIA. The first daily newspaper in Albania, *Taraboshi*, began publication in Scutari in 1913, the year the London Conference on the Balkans granted Albania full independence from the Ottoman Empire. Together with various provincial weeklies, it disappeared during **World War I**, when the Allies allowed Albania's neighbors to carve up its territory in return for military assistance. After the war, the Albanian clan leader Ahmed Zog was able—with American, and later Italian, support—to reestablish a measure of independence and a number of newspapers reappeared. As president and then king of Albania, Zog initially allowed a degree of press freedom. But during the 1930s, his regime became increasingly repressive and the only newspapers allowed were three government dailies and a few weeklies. From 1925 to 1936, *Liria Kombëtar*, the newspaper of the Albanian National Revolutionary Committee (later the Committee of National Liberation), was published in Geneva. With financial support from the Comintern and the Communist Balkan Confederation, it attacked the policies of the Zog regime.

After Zog was overthrown by the Italian military in 1939, the government papers were suppressed and replaced by Italian publications. Following the defeat of **Italy** in 1944, a Communist government under Enver Hoxha assumed control of Albania and took over the media, establishing *Zeri i Puppulit* [People's Voice] as the Communist Party's mouthpiece and *Baskimi* [Unity] as voice of the government. Both had very low circulations and were dependent for foreign news on the Albanian Telegraph Agency (ATA), which received its news by shortwave from Beijing. After Hoxha's death in 1985, the press was liberalized to some degree and a number of papers representing opposition parties were able to emerge. This process was extended with the adoption of a new constitution in 1998. Despite financial difficulties, lingering clan rivalries, and limited educational programs in journalism, Albanian journalists have become steadily more professional in recent years. However, the press remains largely at the service of political parties.

ALGERIA. Journalism was slow to develop in Algeria following the French occupation in 1830. In 1900, the League of the Rights of Man sent Victor Barrucand (1864–1934) to combat the anti-Semitic movement in the colony. In 1902, he established the review *Akhbar* and for more than 30 years tried to promote reconciliation between the French and Arab populations. French journalists such as Yves Courrière depicted the war of independence as one of the most sordid and shameful periods of French history.

Following independence in 1962, newspapers were edited by intellectuals from the National Liberation Front (FLN), the country's only recognized political party. By 1965, however, the military Council of the Revolution under Houari Boudmedienne was effectively running the government and editorial control of the press shifted to the bureaucracy. The two main government dailies papers were *El-Moudjahid* [The Freedom Fighter] in French and *Ech-Chaab* [The People] in Arabic. Following the uprising of 1988, the military retained power but allowed the formation of political parties other than the FLN and provided for a measure of press freedom. In this environment, a number of new papers emerged.

In 1992, however, the army nullified the pending electoral victory of the Islamic Salvation Front (FIS), banned the formation of parties other than the FLN, and once again curtailed freedom of the press. During the bloody civil war that followed, numerous journalists were assassinated, likely by forces on both sides of the conflict. Since 2000, the Algerian press has gradually regained a measure of safety and autonomy. While papers such *L'Expression* generally support the government, criticism of its actions can be found in *Le Matin* and *Le Soir d'Algérie*. Some of the best journalism is to be found in *Le Quotidian d'Oran*, *El Khaber* [The News], and *El Youm* [Today]. Because of continuing low rates of literacy, readership is largely restricted to the elite.

AL JAZEERA. A 24-hour news channel that serves the Arab world. It was founded in 1996 by Sheik Hamad bin-Khalifa al-Thani, the emir of the small Gulf state of Qatar, and initially recruited many of its staff from the BBC. Though funded by the Qatari government, al-Jazeera (meaning "the island" and referring to the Arabian Peninsula) has been permitted considerable editorial freedom. Western assessments range from seeing it as little more than a mouthpiece for terrorists to acknowledging its contribution to the free flow of information in the Middle East. It currently has more than 30 million viewers in some two dozen countries.

ALSOP, JOSEPH W., JR. (1910–1989). American Cold War journalist who used his syndicated columns to influence the decision-making process. He began his career in 1932 as a reporter for the *New York Herald Tribune*. Following his strong coverage of the 1935 trial of the accused killer of the Lindbergh baby, he was assigned to the paper's Washington bureau and began to develop a passion for foreign affairs. In 1937, he and Robert E. Kintner were hired by the North American Newspaper Alliance to write a syndicated column called "The Capital Parade," which dealt with national and international affairs. After serving in **World War II**, he and his brother Stewart Alsop (1914–1974) began the syndicated column "Matter of Fact," which won the Overseas Press Club Award in 1950 and 1952 for the "best interpretation of foreign news." After Stewart left for the *Saturday Evening Post* in 1958, Joseph continued it on his own until his retirement in 1974. Although militant anti-Communists, the two brothers condemned the treatment of Robert Oppenheimer in *We Accuse* (1954) and also coauthored *The Reporter's Trade* (1958).

AMERICAN MINERVA. New York City's first daily newspaper. It was founded in 1793 by Noah Webster (1758–1843) to provide support for the Federalists and combat French influences. A Connecticut-born, Yale-educated lexicographer, Webster had produced a best-selling *Spelling Book* in the early 1780s. In 1787, he began editing the monthly *American Magazine,* a staunchly Federalist publication which included articles on education and subjects of interest to women but lasted less than a year. Webster then founded *American Minerva* (renamed the *Commercial Advertiser* in 1797), which he edited until 1803 when he abandoned journalism to work on *An American Dictionary of the English Language* (1828). Later editors of the paper included, among others, Thurlow Weed. In 1905, it merged with the *New York Globe* to become the *Globe and Commercial Advertiser,* which was purchased by the *New York Sun* in 1923.

AMERICA'S TOWN MEETING OF THE AIR. Popular and influential town-hall-style public affairs program which featured a variety of experts discussing a controversial topic on each show. It began on the NBC-Blue radio network in 1935, but switched to ABC in the mid-1940s when NBC was forced to divest itself of one of its networks. It was discontinued on radio in 1948, but was carried on ABC television in 1948–49 and 1952. Founded and moderated by professional actor George V. Denny Jr., it achieved large audiences for a public affairs program through its lively and entertaining format and the use of promotional devices such as on-air testimonials and listening groups. Though based in New York, it spent part of each season traveling to cities across the nation. It was the first public affairs program to tackle the subject of racial inequality.

ANDERSON, JACK (1922–2005). America's leading investigative reporter and its most widely read political columnist for much of the postwar period. He worked as a newspaper correspondent for the *Deseret News* in Utah before being inducted into the army in 1945. After two years of service, he went to work for **Drew Pearson**'s syndicated "Washington Merry-Go-Round" column. Though initially receiving little recognition for his contribution, he was eventually given credit as an equal partner. He took over the column entirely when Pearson died in 1969 and continued it until his retirement in

2004. His sworn enemies included J. Edgar Hoover, chief of the **Federal Bureau of Investigation (FBI)**, and President Richard Nixon, who felt Anderson had cost him the 1960 election and was infuriated by his revelation of how the Justice Department had dropped an antitrust suit against IT&T after the latter made a $400,000 pledge to the Republican Party. After several nominations, Anderson finally won the **Pulitzer Prize** for National Reporting in 1972 for showing how the Nixon administration, despite proclaiming its neutrality, had actually supported Pakistan during its war with India in 1971. In addition to his column, he authored or coauthored more than a dozen books, including the memoir *Confessions of a Muckraker* (1979). He also appeared regularly on radio and television. *See also* INVESTIGATIVE JOURNALISM.

ANGOLA. For most of the 19th century, printed news in the Portuguese colony of Angola was restricted to the *Boletim oficial do governo geral de província de Angola*. By the turn of the century, there were a few small commercial newspapers such as *O Mercantil* in Luanda. But it was not until the 1930s and 1940s that a large number of indigenous journals such as Liceu Salvador Correia's *O Estudante* (1933) sprang into existence in response to Portuguese attempts to exert greater political and economic control over Angola. Following independence from **Portugal** in 1975, both the print and broadcast media were nationalized by the government. At the same time, the country was plunged into a prolonged and devastating civil war between the ruling Popular Movement for the Liberation of Angola (MPLA) and the National Union for the Total Independence of Angola (UNITA). Throughout this period, both sides were extremely hostile to journalists. Following the death of UNITA leader Jonas Savimbi in 2002, the MPLA gained ascendancy but continued to stifle freedom of the press by retaining control over the only daily paper (*Jornal de Angola*) and the only news agency (ANGOP). The only independent papers are weeklies like *Folha 8, Actual*, and *Agora*, and their journalists have been subjected to threats and harassment. *See also* AFRICA.

ANNENBERG, WALTER H. (1908–2002). American media magnate and benefactor of the arts, public television, and the Annenberg

Schools for Communication at the University of Pennsylvania and the University of Southern California. His media empire encompassed newspapers, magazines (including *TV Guide*, which he founded in 1956), and radio, television, and cable operations. In 1988, he sold *TV Guide* and Triangle Publications to **Rupert Murdoch**'s News Corporation for some $3 billion.

ANONYMITY. Until the mid-19th century, most writers in **Great Britain**, especially the less well known, did not sign their names to their work in newspapers, magazines, and reviews. After a fervent debate among critics and journalists during the 1860s, this practice was largely abandoned in the case of magazine articles and reviews. However, unsigned editorials and political articles remained the norm in British newspapers. In **France**, on the other hand, most newspaper articles were attributed to particular writers. In 1889, the *New Review* in London revived discussion of the practice of anonymity in the newspaper. Disparaging the French practice of systematic attribution, those in favor of anonymity continued to argue that it provided a safe haven from which to engage in social criticism. They also suggested that anonymity gave journalism a transcendental relation to personal testimony. In response, a number of contributors to the debate countered that too much authority had shifted to the "mysterious power" of the anonymous article. During the official inquiries into the Titanic disaster in 1912, the British writer Joseph Conrad wrote two articles in the *English Review* lamenting how the practice of anonymity was used to absolve the commercial and industrial interests of responsibility. The current practice in Britain and North America is to restrict anonymity to editorial writing.

AREOPAGITICA. Work by John Milton (1608–1674) in which freedom of the press is defended in terms of an alleged self-righting principle. Issued anonymously in 1644, *Areopagitica* maintained that prohibiting the publication of certain books or **pamphlets** not only serves to increase their circulation but hinders truth from defeating falsehood in the intellectual arena. "Though the winds of doctrine were let loose to play upon the earth," Milton wrote, "so Truth be in the field, we do injuriously by licensing and prohibiting to misdoubt her strength. Let her and Falsehood grapple; who ever knew Truth put to the worse, in a free and open encounter. Her confuting is the best and surest suppressing."

Despite wanting to eliminate prepublication controls over the press, however, Milton still accepted the need for postpublication controls. As Willmoore Kendall has pointed out, he believed that English society was founded upon revealed religion and especially favored by God. As such it had an obligation to protect and propagate a body of religious doctrine and to work out its full implications for other societies. England was thought to be blessed with a greater degree of religious truth than other nations, but did not yet have the whole truth. "For such is the order of God's enlightening his Church, to dispense and deal out by degrees his beam, so as our earthly eyes may best sustain it."

For Milton, therefore, there remained a kind of grey zone between the black and white areas of revealed truth and demonstrated falsehood. He wanted freedom for men like himself to roll back this area, not freedom to disseminate known falsehoods as if they were true. He was prepared to tolerate "neighbouring differences" among Protestant sects, but not "open superstition" or "popery." For works that are "found mischievous and libelous," he wrote, "the fire and the executioner will be the timeliest and the most effectual remedy, that man's prevention can use."

ARGENTINA. As in many other **Latin American** countries, Argentine journalism has had a close connection with literature, the struggle for independence, and opposition to authoritarian regimes. The first newspaper in Argentina was the *Telégrafo mercantil, rural, político, ecónomico e historiógrafo del Río de la Plata*, founded by the Literary Society in Buenos Aires in April 1801. As its meandering title suggests, it was less interested in providing breaking news than relating detailed information about current developments and resources in the Argentine provinces. The spreading of useful knowledge was also the underlying purpose of the *Semanario de agricultura*, which began publishing the following year. Although the British started a newspaper during their invasion in 1807, the first Argentine papers concentrating on current events were the *Correo de comercio* and the *Gaceta de Buenos Aires*, both established in 1810 in connection with the movement for independence. Despite their contribution in this regard, newspapers were subsequently censored and harassed under Governor Roas and his successors. During a period of relative peace after 1870, contemporary papers such as *La Nación* and *La Prensa* were established. After 1900, provincial newspapers such as *La Confederación* in Santa Fe also began to emerge in reaction to conservative papers such as *El Cronista* and *Noticias Gráficas* in Buenos Aires.

During the presidency of Juan Peron after **World War II**, popular papers such as *Clarín* were founded. But Peron also established press censorship and suppressed the opposition paper *La Prensa*. After he was deposed, the newspapers that had supported him were repressed and in 1959 the state news agency *Telam* was created. In the 1960s, controls over the press were temporarily relaxed and left-wing publications such as the magazine *Panorama* and the newspaper *Crítica* were able to commence; by 1968, there were some 200 dailies with a circulation of over 3 million. But following a military coup in 1976, the government closed or took over newspapers *La Opinión*, reinstituted tight **censorship**, and likely murdered dozens of journalists. Among the persecuted was the Ukrainian-born journalist Jacobo Timerman (1923–1999), who founded the liberal newspaper *La Opinión* in 1971. In 1977, he was arrested and tortured for his investigation of people who had disappeared without a trace. Despite being cleared by the judiciary, he was stripped of his citizenship and exiled two years later. He wrote of his ordeal in the best-selling *Prisoner Without a Name, Cell Without a Number* (1981). After democracy was restored in 1983, he returned to Argentina, testified against his torturers, and won compensation. However, the intimidation and even the killing of journalists did not entirely disappear. In this context, press organizations such as PERIODISTAS and COMICADORES have played an important role in defending press freedom.

Although a journalism degree is not a formal requirement to practice journalism in Argentina, programs in journalism education are now widespread. Traditionally, the most prestigious schools were those associated with the national universities of La Plata and Córdoba. More recently, however, the two largest newspapers in Argentina, *Clarín* and *La Natión*, have established their own Masters degrees (in association with particular universities) in which students apprentice at the papers themselves; as these Buenos Aires-based papers are also the most sought-after destinations for print journalists, these programs have quickly risen is stature. *La Natión* has played an influential role in Argentine history, while *Clarín* is currently the most widely read newspaper in Spanish-speaking **Latin America**. Both have about double the circulation of sensationalist papers like *Diario popular* and *Crónica*. They also partly own the national news agency DYN.

ARMENIA. Armenian journalism had its inception outside the homeland, beginning with a newspaper published in Madras, **India**, in 1794. For the next half century, its development was hindered by the lack of a suitable vernacular medium of expression. With the development of Ashkharabar in the mid-19th century, the number of periodicals expanded rapidly; the first journal using the new vernacular was *Ararat* [Morning], established in Tiflis in 1849. Beginning in the late 1850s, journalists such as Mikayel Nalbandyan (1829–1866), editor of *Hyussissapayl* in Moscow, and Stepan Voskanian (1825–1901), editor of *Arevelk* and *Arevmoutk* in Paris, began to promote a nonterritorial Armenian nationalism. Both were inspired by the writings of Shakespeare, Voltaire, and Rousseau and experienced exile and imprisonment for using the press as an instrument of social criticism.

During the half century before the **World War I**, most Armenian newspapers were mouthpieces of political parties. After obtaining independence in May 1918, Armenia suffered the loss of one million of its citizens, for which it justifiably believes **Turkey** was responsible, before being forced along with Azerbaijan and Georgia into the Transcaucasian Soviet Federated Socialist Republic. Moscow installed a Communist-controlled government and imposed the Russian language. In the 1920s and early 1930s, when the Armenian Bolsheviks wanted to give the impression of Soviet Armenia's cultural autonomy, a few prominent Armenian writers such as Vahan Totovents (1893–1938) were able to engage in nationalist journalism. However, the Stalinist purges ended this kind of accommodation of Armenian national culture.

During *perestroika* and *glasnost* in the 1980s, controls over the press were relaxed somewhat, dozens of new newspapers were created, and journalists were allowed to use Armenian once again. However, even after Armenia gained independence from the **Soviet Union** in 1991, journalists were still subject to a number of constraints on their professional development, including compulsory registration, a strict law of libel, and a legal requirement to reveal their sources in court cases. Following the 1999 terrorist attack on the Armenian Parliament, these controls were tightened further. Although membership in the Council of Europe since 2001 has acted as a countervailing force against episodes such as the beating of journalist Vahang Gnukasian by the Interior Ministry a year earlier, Armenian journalism is still compromised by bribery, self-censorship, and uncertain professional norms.

ASAHI PAPERS. Serial publication in 1971 of **Japanese** journalist Honda Katsuichi's graphic account of the Imperial Army's massacre of Nanking (now Nanjing) in December 1937. Although subjected to harassment for his investigations, Honda helped to bring about greater acceptance of responsibility for Japan's wartime acts among its current intellectual and political leaders.

ASIA. Freedom House has repeatedly classified most Asian countries as lacking what it considers to be true press freedom. However, a few scholars, most notably Shelton A. Gunaratne, have suggested that its ranking system is biased toward a Western conception of freedom that focuses on government controls and ignores media ownership as a possible restraint on freedom. For Gunaratne, the main Asian philosophies, Buddhism, Confucianism, and Hinduism, do not entail or endorse an authoritarian approach to the press but are more consistent with a socially responsible press. In his view, the authoritarian controls over the press in most Asian countries are the result of ongoing economic instability after centuries of Western exploitation; the traditional subjugation of the indigenous press by Dutch, French, and British colonial regimes; and Orientalist denigration of Asian philosophies supportive of responsible press freedom.

For advocates of an "Asian model of journalism" such as Lee Kuan Yew, the idea of a cooperative media-government partnership is more compatible with Asian values and economic interests than the liberal concept of an independent press as a watchdog over government. However, the control of the press in some Asian countries has exceeded what could be explained by Gunaratne's factors and can hardly be called a partnership. While it is reasonable to argue that the press should not disrupt legitimate government efforts to promote development, fair coverage of government initiatives does not entail ignoring cases of blatant mismanagement or corruption. A study by Kokkeong Wong of press coverage of the 1999 general elections in **Malaysia** found that the English-language papers *The New Strait Times*, *The Star*, and *The Sun* acted largely as mouthpieces for the party in power. Moreover, this sort of behavior is fairly widespread in Asia, with the exception of **India**, Sri Lanka, **Japan**, the **Philippines**, and recently South **Korea** and Taiwan. In Communist-controlled countries such as the People's Republic of **China** and Vietnam, newspapers remain under party control. In countries like **Burma** (Myanmar), there is no press freedom in any meaningful sense of the term.

Asian countries have generally undergone what John A. Lent once called a "perpetual see-saw" between some degree of press freedom and harsh repression of the press. Overall, however, Asian journalists have experienced much less autonomy than their Western counterparts. One explanation of this fact is that Asian journalists have tended to treat freedom as license and have thus had to have their freedom curtailed. Theoretically, however, the existence of an undisciplined **public sphere** cannot be cured through government controls but only through the balanced interaction of power, market, and public interest considerations. *See also* BANGLADESH; CAMBODIA.

ASSOCIATED PRESS (AP). One of the world's main news agencies. It originated in 1827 as an outgrowth of the New York Associated Press. Before **telegraphy**, its reporters would row to incoming ships and relay news to shore by semaphore or carrier pigeons. By 1860, it had absorbed most of the competing news services and had entered into an arrangement of convenience with Western Union. In return for Western Union refusing to provide wire service to newspapers that were not affiliated with the Associated Press, AP and its subscribers supported Western Union's opposition to any form of public ownership of telegraphy or the railroads. It was eventually forced by Congress to dissolve its monopoly, but had little domestic competition until 1907 when Edward W. Scripps and Milton R. McRae organized the forerunner of United Press International (UPI). *See also* NEWS MANAGEMENT.

ATKINSON, JOSEPH E. (1865–1948). Pious Methodist editor (known as "Holy Joe") of the *Toronto Daily Star* (as of 1971 the *Toronto Star*) from 1899 to 1948. He began his career in journalism as a reporter for the *Port Hope Times*, became the Ottawa correspondent for the Toronto *Globe* in 1890, and was hired as managing editor of the *Montreal Herald* in 1897. In 1899, the Liberal proprietors of the struggling *Toronto Evening Star* (1892) invited him to serve as editor. With the support of Prime Minister Wilfrid Laurier, he persuaded the group to let him edit the paper as an independent voice of liberalism rather than as a party paper as such. He also acquired the opportunity to eventually become the paper's controlling shareholder. He combined sensationalism and crusading journalism to make the *Star* one of the largest and most influential newspapers in **Canada**. During the Winnipeg General Strike in 1919, he sent two of his most experienced reporters to Winnipeg to find out firsthand what was happening. As a result of their impartial coverage, the *Star* was able to provide an alternative to the hostile editorials of most other Canadian newspapers, which saw the strike as a Bolshevik plot. During the 1920s and early 1930s, he called upon wealthy Torontonians to do their Christian duty and help those less fortunate than themselves. But he gradually became convinced of the need for state-based social welfare measures such as unemployment insurance, health care, and old age pensions. As a friend of Liberal prime minister Mackenzie King, he was able to exert considerable influence over social policy in Canada. His progressive editorial philosophy, which continues to motivate the *Star* today, has been codified in terms of six precepts known as the Atkinson Principles: a strong, united, and independent Canada; social justice; individual and civil liberties; community and civic engagement; the rights of working people; and the necessary role of government.

ATLANTIC CABLE. The first underwater **telegraph** was laid between **Great Britain** and **France** in 1850, but it took several efforts to complete a transatlantic cable. In February 1857, Cyrus W. Field began laying a cable from Valencia Bay, **Ireland**, to Trinity Bay,

Newfoundland, with the help of ships loaned by the British and American governments. After three attempts, a temporary link was established in the summer of 1858. Although this connection later failed, Field managed to establish a permanent link in 1866, covering a distance of 1,852 nautical miles (3,432 kilometers). By 1900, there were a dozen or more submarine cables spanning the Atlantic and several others across the Pacific. In 1903, President Theodore Roosevelt sent the first telegraph message around the world—in a time of nine minutes.

ATOMIC BOMB. The decision to drop atomic bombs on Hiroshima and Nagasaki on 6 and 9 August 1945 was justified by President Harry S. Truman in terms of the need to save American lives. In countries such as **Australia**, the media withheld unequivocal approval of Truman's decision, despite strong feelings against the Japanese. In **Mexico**, newspapers compared the horror of the bomb to Nazi concentration camps. In the **United States**, however, Truman's explanation was accepted by most journalists and commentators at the time, even though there had been some press discussion previously of the growing prospect of a Japanese surrender. In contrast, employees at the Los Alamos laboratory who had helped to build the bomb were horrified by its destructive powers and tried to express their concern through **newsletters** and activist organizations.

During the 1960s, a number of revisionist American historians began to question Truman's explanation of his decision, but the American media continued to accept the traditional account. While John Hersey's "Hiroshima" article in *The New Yorker* helped to undermine American stereotypes of the Japanese, postwar Americans were prevented from witnessing film footage of the bomb's horrific effects on civilians. Immediately after the attacks, the Japanese filmmaker Akira Iwasaki had shot footage of the destruction, but this was confiscated by the occupation censors. After managing to get Iwasaki and his crew released from military custody, Daniel McGovern, a lieutenant with the U.S. Strategic Bombing Survey, had them shoot additional footage, showing the effects of the bomb on human bodies. McGovern later used this footage in a one-hour documentary entitled *The Effects of the Atomic Bombs Against Hiroshima and Nagasaki*. However, the documentary was labeled "Top Secret" by the Pentagon and embargoed for the next 22 years. Some insight into the experience of survivors was provided by heavy media coverage of the so-called "Hiroshima maidens," 25 young Japanese women who were flown to a New York City hospital in 1955–56 for reconstructive surgery.

In general, however, the attitude of the American public has remained one of sympathy for Japanese victims of the bomb rather than guilt over its use. The Japanese argument that Hiroshima and Pearl Harbor should be seen as moral equivalents is thought to ignore a critical distinction between a just and unjust war. The public's assessment is based on the continuing belief that up to half a million U.S. (and many more Japanese) lives would have been lost had the bomb not been used. It largely ignores the extent to which the mass media, with the compliance of Western leaders, created a climate of hatred of the Japanese that prevented the full consideration of other options. On the other hand, the fact that the bomb was used, and its full effects gradually revealed by the media, may have served to deter its use in subsequent Cold War confrontations. *See also* BURCHETT, WILFRED; JAPAN.

AUSTRALIA. The first newspaper in Australia was the *Sydney Gazette and NSW Advertiser*, a government-controlled weekly which began publication on 5 March 1803. It was edited by the former convict George Howe, but many of the earliest Australian and New South Wales newspapers were founded and run by ministers and missionaries, including the *Australian* (1824), the *Monitor* (1826), the *Gleaner* (1827), the *Sydney Herald* (1831), and the *Colonist* (1835). In addition to press freedom and self-government, they wanted to end the use of convict labor on the grounds that it was undermining the development of a respectable, bourgeois society.

Nineteenth-century Australian newspapers were generally cheap, widely read, and intensely ideological, promoting not only British imperialism but also a separate national identity. For most of the century, however, they had restricted access to outside news. In 1863, the British news agency Reuters began supplying news using a cable line from Bombay. But until 1910, when Australia finally acquired a cable connection with its own Pacific region, Reuters was largely able to dictate its own syndication practices. At the same time, poor communications within Australia resulted in a plethora of local newspapers.

Their provincialism caused many Australian journalists to leave for London in pursuit of greater opportunities and excitement on Fleet Street.

During the 20th century, Australian newspaper ownership became steadily more concentrated. By the 1990s, the Australian press had become one of the most monopolized in the English-speaking world, with **Rupert Murdoch** selling two out of every three newspapers in Australia's capital cities. A recent survey of Australian journalists found that they are generally somewhat younger and less formally educated than journalists in **Great Britain** and also less likely to adopt an adversarial role or use subterfuge to get information for a story. Unlike their British counterparts, Australian journalists tend to place less emphasis on providing entertainment than on developing the intellectual and cultural interests of the public. Some feminist critics have suggested that the gendered nature of Australian news coverage continues to reflect anxieties related to the country's colonial past.

AUSTRIA. A variety of news publications developed within the Austro-Hungarian Empire following the introduction of printing in 1483. By the early 18th century, these included twice-weekly newspapers such as *Der postalische Mercurius*. It was not until the second half of the 19th century, however, that increased literacy, rapid urban growth, and the abolition of press **censorship** (1862) provided the basis for a mass-circulation newspaper industry, ranging from quality papers such as *Die Presse*, founded during the Revolution of 1848, to **tabloids** like *Neue Kronen Zeitung*, currently Austria's largest newspaper. Tabloids received a further boost in 1922 when the ban on street sales was lifted.

Following the Nazi takeover in 1938, most of Austria's dailies were forced out of operation. After the war, many papers temporarily affiliated with political parties as a safeguard against future government controls. In 1961, the Association of Austrian Newspapers and the Austrian Journalists Association established the Austrian Press Council as an independent watchdog agency. In recent years, the diversity and objectivity of the press has been as much a concern as freedom of the press. In 1975, the state began subsidizing newspapers and magazines in an attempt to maintain a broad spectrum of viewpoints; the Media Act of 1981 included further measures to ensure balanced and impartial reporting; and antitrust legislation was introduced in 1993 to prevent excessive media concentration. For graduates of journalism programs at the universities of Vienna and Salzburger, the three most prestigious newspapers in Austria are *Die Presse*, *Der Standard*, and *Salzburger Nachrichten*.

– B –

BACHE, BENJAMIN FRANKLIN (1769–1798). Philadelphia printer who, like his grandfather **Benjamin Franklin**, used his press to promote the ideas of the Enlightenment and a broad range of political and social reforms in America. In 1790, he founded the Philadelphia *General Advertiser* (later renamed the *Aurora*) to promote Jeffersonian republicanism. Its scurrilous attacks on the Federalists and President George Washington, including the use of forged letters, led veterans of Washington's army to wreck its offices and throw its type into the street. As the 1790s progressed, Bache engaged in increasingly personal attacks on national leaders such as Washington. In response to Noah Webster's declaration in the *American Minerva* that it was treacherous to refuse to toast President Washington, Bache replied in the *Aurora* that "if want of respect for Mr. WASHINGTON is to constitute *treason*, the United States will be found to contain very many *traitors*." Arrested under the Sedition Act of 1798, Bache died of yellow fever shortly after being released on parole.

BAKER, RAY STANNARD (1870–1946). American **muckraker** who focused on railroad and financial abuses. One of his stories led to a libel suit that cost *McClure's* $150,000 in damages. A close friend of President Woodrow Wilson, he directed the press bureau at Versailles in 1919. In addition to multi-volume works on Wilson, he produced seven volumes of essays under the pen name David Grayson. In later life, he wrote the autobiographical *Native American* (1941) and *American Chronicle* (1945).

BANGLADESH. Along with other **Indian** states, present-day Bangladesh was governed by the East India Company until 1858 when it came under direct British rule. During the 19th century, most of the newspapers and magazines published in the area were concentrated in Dhaka, although the prestigious paper *Amrit Bazar Patrika* (1868) was based in Jessore. In the early 20th century, the Bengali Muslim press played an important role in the development of modern Muslim society, stressing the role of education in particular. Following independence from **Great Britain** and the separation of Pakistan in 1947 into two partitions, new dailies such as *Purba Pakistan*, *Azad*, and the *Pakistan Observer* in English were established in the eastern half. In the early 1950s, the important present-day papers, the *Sangbad* and the *Ittefaq*, also began publication in East Pakistan. A further expansion of the press occurred in connection with the birth of Bangladesh in 1971. In 1972, however, the government of Mujibur Rahman took control of four dailies and imposed severe restrictions on the rest. These controls were relaxed when the Awami League Party returned to power in 1997, but many were reinstated after a military coup in 2007.

BANKS, ELIZABETH L. (1872–1938). American-born stunt reporter who followed in the footsteps of **Nellie Bly**. Hoping to overcome the limited opportunities for women journalists in the **United States**, she went to **Great Britain** in the early 1890s only to find it equally problematic to break into Fleet Street. Her solution was to go undercover in such guises as a housemaid, flower girl, and laundress in order to expose the working conditions of women in London. Her newspaper series entitled "Campaigns of Curiosity" gave her instant notoriety and celebrity status and was followed in 1894 by an autobiography with the same title. To her dismay, however, she became typecast as a stunt journalist. Her intrusive reporting contributed to later debate about the ethics of **investigative journalism**.

BEALS, CARLETON (1893–1979). American journalist who wrote about **Latin America** from an anti-imperialist standpoint for magazines such as *The Nation* and the *New Republic*. Many of his articles emphasized the social problems resulting from American support for free trade and anti-Communist dictators such as the Somozas in Nicaragua. As a result, he not only had difficulty getting some of his material published but was also harassed by the **Federal Bureau of**

Investigation (FBI) and the State Department. He was one of the first journalists to use some of the new tools being developed in the social sciences. In addition to numerous articles, he wrote over 40 books.

BEAVERBROOK, MAX (1879–1964). Wartime propagandist and media baron. Born in **Canada** as William Maxwell Aitken, the first Baron Beaverbrook moved to **Great Britain** after making a fortune in business and entered politics. Toward the end of **World War I**, he reinvigorated British propaganda as minister of information. In 1919, he purchased the London *Daily Express* and turned it into the highest circulation daily in the world. According to A. J. P. Taylor in *Beaverbrook* (1972), his methods of shaping the character of the paper were "elusive." "He hardly ever wrote letters of detailed instruction as **Northcliffe** did. For most of his life he did not go to the office. Sometimes he told his editors by telephone what to say. More often he harassed them from afar. It was fear of his telephone calls . . . that kept editors and journalists up to the mark." During **World War II**, he again made effective use of propaganda as minister of aircraft production and later as minister of supply.

BELARUS. The first newspaper in the present-day territory of Belarus, the two-page *Gazeta Grodzen'ska* (1776) was published in Polish. During the 19th century, however, official newspapers such as *Vitebskie gubernskie novosti* [Vitebsk Provincial News] (1838) were published in Russian, the official language of the Empire. In 1862, an underground newspaper called *Muzhytskaia prauda* [Peasant Truth] was issued in Belo Russian language, but at the time of the 1917 Revolution the vast majority of publications were in Russian. Following independence in 1991, the main newspapers and magazines underwent little immediate change, retaining their former names, government subsidy, and readership. Over the next decade, however, the number of publications increased significantly, with a moderate increase in the percentage using Belo Russian. The only nongovernment daily in the capital of Minsk is *Narodnaia Volia*.

BELGIUM. Early Belgian newspapers were created to promote the fortunes of political parties, ideological camps, or the Catholic

Church. In 1795, a local revolutionary committee in Ghent went so far as to create a direct imitation of the existing *Gazette de Gend* in an attempt to steal readers for its own ideas. After Belgium achieved independence from the **Netherlands** in 1830, some of its newspapers began to downplay politics. In the 1840s, *feuilletons* such as the *Messager de Gand* took to serializing popular Parisian novels, but also carried political messages in their poetry and **caricatures**. For example, the *Deutsche-Brüsseler-Zeitung* (1847–48), a twice-weekly newspaper in Brussels edited by the exiled German socialist Adalbert von Bornstedt, called for revolution and unification.

Beginning in the 20th century, newspaper ownership gradually shifted from the Catholic Church and political parties to large conglomerates primarily interested in enhancing their market share. In recent years, the Belgian press has gravitated toward nonpolitical "tabloid" content in an effort to attract readers in a country where, given its high rate of literacy, daily newspaper subscriptions have been surprisingly low (about 36 percent). Most Belgian journalists are graduates of university programs and belong to organizations such as the Belgian Association of Professional Journalists. The most popular newspapers in Flemish date back to the late 19th and early 20th century: *De Gentenaar* (1879), *Het Laatste Nieuws* (1888), and *De Standaard/Het Nieuwsblad/De Dentenaar* (1914). The French-language newspaper with the highest circulation is *Le Soir*, founded in 1887.

BENGAL GAZETTE. The first newspaper in **India**, also known as the *Calcutta General Advertiser* or *Hicky's Bengal Gazette*. It was founded on 29 January 1780 by James Augustus Hicky, an expatriate Irishman and disgruntled employee of the East India Company. Described by Hicky as "a weekly political and commercial paper open to all parties, but influenced by none," its scandalous accounts of the East India Company soon brought the wrath of Company officials down upon it. Warren Hastings launched several cases against the paper, including a suit for defamation after being called "the Great Moghul." On 5 January 1782, Hastings seized the paper's press and forced its closure. Hicky died a pauper, but not before contributing to the eventual downfall of the East India Company and its replacement by a colonial government.

BENJAMIN, ANNA (1874–1902). The first female photojournalist to cover a war. She began her brief career in 1898 by covering the Cuban phase of the Spanish–American War for *Leslie's Illustrated Newspaper* and then reported on its continuation in the **Philippines** for the *New York Tribune* and *San Francisco Chronicle*. Resented by the male correspondents, she provided an unsentimental portrait of the war. After a trip around the world, she returned to Europe in 1901 to write about peasant life in **Russia**, where she died from a tumor the following year.

BENJAMIN, WALTER (1892–1940). Marxist literary critic and philosopher. He and fellow German journalist Arthur Holitscher covered the Russian Revolution of 1917 and **V. I. Lenin**'s New Economic Plan, providing insightful views of the **Soviet Union** in its formative years. During the Weimar Republic (1919–33), Benjamin worked in radio and tried to establish a dialogue with listeners instead of treating them as a mass audience of consumers. In his posthumous *Illuminations* (1969), he theorized that advanced capitalism has reduced the storytelling dimension of news in favor of conveying information that is comprehensible in its own terms.

BENNETT, JAMES GORDON, SR. (1795–1872). Newspaper publisher and editor who helped to modernize American journalism in the mid-19th century through the use of timelier news, livelier writing, and **human interest stories**. Born in **Scotland**, Bennett emigrated to **Canada** in 1819 and then moved to the **United States**, where he eventually settled in New York City. After freelancing for a few years, he was hired in 1826 as a political correspondent for Mordecai Noah's *New York Enquirer*. In 1829, the *Enquirer* merged with James Watson Webb's *New York Courier* to become the highest circulation paper in the country. Bennett became the associate editor and editorialized on behalf of President Andrew Jackson's attack on the National Bank. When the *Courier and Enquirer* began supporting the Whigs, he quit and founded the Philadelphia *Pennsylvanian* as a Democratic daily. After it ran into financial difficulties, he returned to New York City where he witnessed the success of **Benjamin Day**'s **penny paper**, the *New York Sun*. In May 1835, he established his own four-page equivalent, the politically independent *New York*

Herald, which soon became the most popular paper in New York with a circulation of 100,000 by the time of the Civil War.

In addition to sensational coverage of **crimes** and disasters, Bennett sought to provide better national and international coverage. He led the way in using **telegraphy** to gather news, conducted what some historians consider to be the first news interview, and began the practice of foreign correspondence when he reported on Queen Victoria's coronation from London. He was also the first editor to employ foreign correspondents such as **Januarius MacGahan**. Like most 19th-century editors, he treated his reporters poorly, paying low wages and providing no guarantees from one assignment to the next. In retaliation for his attacks on them, rival editors organized a boycott of the *Herald* during the "Great Moral War" in 1840. Though opposed to the expansion of slavery, Bennett did not criticize the "peculiar institution" itself.

His son, James Gordon Bennett Jr. (1841–1918), succeeded him as editor in 1867. It was the younger Bennett who sent Stanley to Africa to find Livingston and supported other expeditions to Africa and the Arctic. In 1887, he founded the *Paris Herald*, which later became the ***International Herald Tribune***.

BESANT, ANNIE (1847–1933). English journalist (whose last name rhymes with "peasant") who championed social reform and the independence of **India**. While in her twenties, she wrote articles on women's issues for Charles Bradlaugh's *National Reformer*. In 1877, both were found guilty of an obscene libel for publishing Charles Knowlton's book on birth control. After successfully appealing her six-month sentence, Besant wrote her own book entitled *The Laws of Population*, which *The Times* described as "indecent, lewd, filthy, bawdy and obscene." In the 1880s, she began a newspaper called *The Link* and wrote "White Slavery in London" (1888), which exposed the poor working conditions and wages of women at the Bryant & May match factory. When her sources were then fired, she helped to organize a union and conduct a successful strike. Influenced by Bradlaugh, who was known as the MP for India, she wrote *England, India and Afghanistan* (1879), subtitled in part "Why the Tory government gags the Indian press."

In 1893, following her conversion from Free Thinking to Madame Blavatsky's Hindu-based Theosophy movement, Besant moved to India and began to promote social reform based on her understanding of Hindu morality. In 1907, she was elected president of the Theosophical Society, which had its international headquarters in India. After the granting of Irish Home Rule in 1913, Besant (who was three-quarters Irish) began applying the term to India, but also argued that religious, educational, and social reform should be part of the struggle for political freedom. When the Indian National Congress rejected this linkage, she created the weekly publication *Commonweal* to promote her program. The following year, however, she bought the *Madras Standard*, renamed it *New India*, and began to argue that Home Rule should be the immediate goal since it would eventually be followed by reform. She then joined the Indian National Congress, wrote a series of articles on its history, and in 1917 was elected its president.

BLEYER, WILLARD G. (1873–1935). Journalist and educator who helped found the department (1912) and later the school of journalism (1927) at the University of Wisconsin. He began his teaching with a single noncredit course on the law of the press in 1905. To increase its credibility, Bleyer sought to link journalism **education** to the social sciences rather than English. He also promoted cooperative efforts between journalists and universities through the establishment of educational programs and **professional organizations**. His textbook *Main Currents in the History of American Journalism* (1927) traced the early growth of journalism as a profession.

BLOGS. A blog is an Internet Web site used to maintain an ongoing and interactive journal or log of some sort. The term "blog," which is used as both a noun and a verb, came quickly into use in the late 1990s out of the term "weblog," used to designate such sites, and the subsequent play on words, "we blog." Jorn Barger and Peter Merholz are credited with its genesis. Blogs themselves vary greatly in content, sophistication, and endurance. Of the 100 million or more blogs created by 2008, perhaps only about 15 percent were actively operating. Collectively, they are thought to be ushering in yet another "information revolution," transforming not only business through mass product complaint campaigns but also politics by creating a new, purportedly more democratic **public sphere**. They have been called the new Fifth Estate, but their impact on journalism to date has been a mixed blessing. Most newspapers and magazines have some of their journalists blogging, creating a more interactive relationship with their readers. But journalists are also among the favorite targets of bloggers. In 2004, bloggers' questionable attacks on Dan Rather's account of President George W. Bush's military career on *60 Minutes II* led to his dismissal from CBS. Critics of journalism have long played an important role in helping to maintain standards, but the qualifications of the bloggers "watching the watchdog" vary considerably. One benefit of blogging may be that politicians become more aware of the need for fair, accurate, and well researched reporting about their policies and debates, while journalists may begin to reassert the importance of their own professional qualifications.

BLY, NELLIE (1864–1922). Pen name of American journalist Elizabeth Cochrane Seaman. She took it from a character in the 1882 Grundy and Solomon operetta *The Vicar of Bray* when she began writing for the *Pittsburgh Dispatch* in her native Pennsylvania. After moving to New York in 1887, she feigned madness to get herself committed to Blackwell's Island, the city's insane asylum for women, and exposed its terrible conditions in *Ten Days in a Mad House*. The stunt resulted in $3 million being spent on improvements and convinced **Joseph Pulitzer** to hire her as a reporter for the *New York World*. As the most famous journalist of her day, she continued to go undercover in order to target lobbyists, the recruitment of prostitutes, and conditions in prisons, factories, and nursing homes. In 1889, she set off from New York to see if she could beat the time taken by the fictional character Phileas Fogg in Jules Verne's *Around the World in Eighty Days* (1873). She accomplished the trip in 72 days, 6 hours, and 11 minutes, beating Fogg's fictional time and finishing ahead of a rival female reporter from a Hearst paper.

BOK, EDWARD W. (1863–1930). Progressive editor of the *Ladies' Home Journal* during its formative years. Born in the **Netherlands**, Bok worked for the Brooklyn *Eagle* and founded his own magazine syndicate before Cyrus Curtis, whose daughter he married, offered him the editorship of the *Journal* in 1889. Aimed primarily at women readers from the urban middle class, the *Journal* combined a mild form of reform journalism with mass advertising. During Bok's editorship, the causes it embraced ranged from wildlife conservation and cleaner cities to sleeping-car improvements and sex education. Bok's reformism did not, however, extend to women's liberation; for Bok and the Progressive-era *Ladies' Home Journal*, a woman's place remained in the home. Following disagreements with Curtis, Bok resigned from the *Journal* in 1919 and wrote about his magazine experiences in *The Americanization of Edward Bok* (1920).

BOWLES, SAMUEL, II (1826–1878). American newspaper publisher known for his vigorous but balanced editorials. At the age of 17, he began working for the *Springfield* (Mass.) *Republican*, which his father, Samuel Bowles (1797–1851), had established as a country weekly in 1824. The following year, he persuaded his father to turn it into a daily and, after his death, took over as publisher and editor-in-chief. Over the next quarter century, the *Republican* became one of the most influential political newspapers in the **United States**. Following the passage of the Kansas-Nebraska Act in 1854, Bowles's call for antislavery groups to form a single national party contributed to the formation of the Republican Party. He was succeeded by his son, Samuel Bowles III (1851–1915), who maintained the paper's reputation but did little editorial writing himself.

BRAZIL. During the 17th and 18th centuries, the Portuguese colonizers of Brazil prohibited the operation of a **printing press**, limiting the reading material of officials and intellectuals to books and journals brought into the country illegally. It was not until 1808, when the Portuguese royal family was forced to settle in Rio de Janeiro to escape the army of Napoleon, that the first newspaper in Brazil, the weekly *Gazeta do Rio de Janeiro*, was published as an official organ. It was followed by the establishment of a number of other semi-official periodicals representing the interests of the political elite. With the support of the anti-mercantilist commercial elite, however, a counter-hegemonic press espousing independence also emerged and succeeded in uniting the two groups. Among the most significant of these rebel papers was the *Echo*, edited by Joaquim Goncalves Ledo (1781–1847).

Following independence from **Portugal** in 1822, Brazil developed a party press not unlike that in the **United States**, while publications such as the *Jornal de sociedade de agricultura, commercio et industria da provincia da Bahia* (1832–36) and its successors made an important contribution to the economic development of Brazil. However, limited education, low literacy, and widespread poverty delayed the subsequent emergence of mass-circulation newspapers. During both the First and Second Empires (1822–1889) and the Old Republic (1889–1930), newspapers remained mainly a forum for debates among the educated political elite. A large number of those who rose to political prominence were aided by their participation in journalism, while editorial writers who did not go into politics still exercised considerable influence over decisions made by the ruling class. But by doing little to solidify the republic through the education and enfranchisement of the masses, the journalistic elite failed to help stave off the subsequent dictatorship of President Getúlio Vargas.

During the Vargas era from 1930 to 1945, freedom of the press was curtailed and journalists were **censored**, harassed, and jailed. After **World War II**, press freedom was restored and Brazil underwent a remarkable period of democracy and economic growth. In the 1950s, the American model of journalism began to take root in the Brazilian press, leading to the modernization of publishing and greater professionalization among journalists. Since the 1990s, Brazilian journalists have helped to reform the country's political and economic structures by exposing problems such as corruption, homelessness, and environmental degradation. *See also* LATIN AMERICA.

BRISBANE, ALBERT (1809–1890). American communitarian thinker who popularized his ideas through a column in **Horace Greeley**'s *New York Tribune* (1842–44). After studying under Charles Fourier in Paris, he wrote *Social Destiny of Man* (1840), which contributed to the formation of over 40 cooperative communities in America. Brook Farm, which had been established in 1841 by the Transcendental Club under George Ripley, was transformed under Brisbane's influence into the phalanx of American Fourierism, producing *The Phalanx* (1843–45) and *The Harbinger* (1845) until its demise in 1847. After the Civil War, Brisbane worked as a reporter for **Charles A. Dana**'s *New York Sun* and further defended Fourierism in his *General Introduction to the Social Sciences* (1876). His son, Arthur Brisbane (1864–1936), was editor of **William Randolph Hearst**'s *New York Evening Journal* from 1897–1921 and wrote two popular columns, "Today" and "This Week."

BRITAIN. *See* GREAT BRITAIN.

BROUN, HEYWOOD (1888–1939). Political columnist for the *New York World* (1921–28) and the first president of the American Newspaper Guild. After graduating from Harvard, he worked as a reporter for the *New York Tribune* (1912–21), including a stint as correspondent with the American forces in **France** during **World War I**. He used his *World* column "It Seems to Me" to promote social justice and also wrote for *The Nation* and the *New Republic* as well as numerous books. He became president of the Guild in 1933. After his death, John Llewellyn Lewis, **Franklin P. Adams**, Herbert Bayard Swope, and other members of the Newspaper Guild of New York produced *Heywod Broun as He Seemed to Us* (1940). Some of his best writing was published posthumously as *A Collected Edition* (1941).

BROWN, GEORGE (1818–1880). Canadian journalist and statesman. After emigrating with his father from **Scotland** to the **United States** in 1837, he began contributing to the *Albion*, the weekly paper of British émigrés in New York City. In 1842, he helped his father establish the weekly *British Chronicle*, renamed the *Banner* and moved to Toronto a year later to support the new Free Church of Scotland. As editor of the paper's "Secular Department," he threw his weight behind the movement for responsible government in Canada West (present-day Ontario). In 1844, a group of Reformers in Toronto provided Brown with the financial means (£250) to begin publication of the *Globe* as a weekly party paper. Brown soon made it the most influential newspaper in British North America through its strong editorials and emphasis on the latest and most detailed news. The *Globe* became a daily in 1853, a year after Brown was first elected to parliament, and later provided crucial support for Canadian Confederation. In March 1880, Brown was shot during an argument with an employee and died from an ensuing infection a month and a half later. *See also* CANADA.

BUCKLEY, WILLIAM F., JR. (1925–2008). Articulate editor of *The National Review* from 1955 to 1990. Educated at Yale, Buckley defended conservative principles and values through what he called "right reason" rather than by demonizing liberalism. A frequent television commentator, his books ranged from *Up from Liberalism* (1959) to *Happy Days Were Here Again: Reflections of a Libertarian Journalist* (1993).

BULGARIA. The first Bulgarian newspaper to be published on a sustained basis was the *Tsarigradski Vestnik* [Istanbul Herald], edited by Ivan Bogarov from 1846 to 1862. During the period before liberation in 1878, Bulgarian writers made extensive use of the press to promote national revival. By the end of the 19th century, the major newspapers were closely associated with political groups: for example, *Svoboda* [Freedom], *Narodni prava* [People's Rights], and *Mir* [Peace] represented the National Party (NP), while *Rabotnicheski vestnik* [Workers' Daily] was the organ of the Bulgarian Communist Party (BCP). The Democratic Party and the Bulgarian Agrarian National Union also had their own newspapers.

Following the Communist takeover in 1944, all of these publications were taken over by the BCP and edited by tightly controlled party members. With the fall of the Communist regime in 1989, there was an explosion of new papers and journals, including a number of popular **tabloids**. At the same time, however, the government reestablished a degree of state control through the centuries-old mechanism of taxation, introducing a value-added tax first on printed matter and then on all goods.

BURCHETT, WILFRED (1911–1983). Highly controversial war correspondent from **Australia** who was vilified in the mainstream press for his systematically anti-Western coverage. During **World War II**, Burchett covered eastern **Asia** for the London *Daily Express* and was the first Western reporter to observe Hiroshima in the aftermath of the **atomic bomb**. His report on the effects of radiation and nuclear fallout in "The Atomic Plague" (5 September 1945) was rejected as pro-

Japanese propaganda by the U.S. military as well as by *New York Times'* correspondent William L. Laurence, who won a **Pulitzer Prize** for his awestruck approach to the bomb. After the war, Burchett covered eastern Europe for the *Daily Express* and later for *The Times* of London. His treatment of the Stalinist show trials began a pattern of reporting, extending through the Korean and Vietnam Wars, which opened the door to accusations that he was a Communist propagandist, agent, or **spy**. The most charitable characterization of much of this reporting, which generally took the Communist side at face value, is that it was gullible and naive. In 1974, Burchett launched a libel suit against one of his critics. Although the charge of libel was dismissed, an appeals court later ruled that he had been defamed. A prolific writer, Burchett told his side of the story in his autobiography *At the Barricades* (1981). A definitive assessment of his career as a self-styled "rebel journalist" remains to be written.

BURMA. The first newspaper in what was then the British colony of Burma was *The Maulmain Chronicle*, an English-language weekly founded in Mawlamyine in 1836. It was gradually joined by vernacular papers, beginning with the *Yadanaopon*. In 1874, *Yadana Neipyidaw* was founded in Mandalay, which was still under the rule of Myanmar kings. The vernacular press later facilitated opposition to British rule and helped Burma to gain independence in 1948. During the decade after independence, there was a rapid increase in the number of newspapers and papers such as *Kyemon* [The Mirror Daily], founded by U Thaung in 1957, enjoyed relative freedom.

In 1962, however, General Ne Win seized control through a military coup and undertook to determine which newspapers could be relied upon to support his socialist agenda. These papers were then nationalized and the rest eliminated. The remaining papers were subjected to strict **censorship** by a Press Scrutiny Board, while foreign (as well as a number of Burmese) reporters were forced to leave the country. Within a few years, virtually the entire media had been dragooned into supporting Win's socialist revolution. To supply its own press, the military government also created the News Agency of Myanmar (NAM) in Yangon in 1963. The Committee to Protect Journalists (CPJ) has repeatedly identified Burma as one of the most hostile **Asian** environments for journalism. The only anomaly is *The*

Myanmar Times, which the **Australian** journalist Ross Dunkley began publishing in 2000 in Rangoon. But its relative freedom has been used largely to promote the ruling junta among international readers.

BUSINESS JOURNALISM. According to John J. McCusker, the first newspapers were commercial or business newspapers. Beginning in Antwerp around 1540 (possibly earlier in Venice), the licensed brokers of the city organized the publication by one of their guild of what were called commodity price currents and exchange rate currents. Similar publications were later developed in other European commercial centers as the locus of financial power shifted from Antwerp in the 16th century to Amsterdam in the 17th century and then to London in the 18th century. In the case of **Great Britain**'s American colonies, the London business press served as the main source of information about prices and markets until the achievement of independence, at which point business publications emerged in Philadelphia and later in New York City.

During the 19th century, accuracy and general reporting standards remained a problem in many business newspapers. In the **United States**, William Buck Dana's weekly *Commercial and Financial Chronicle*, founded in 1866, eventually became "the Bible of Wall Street." In Britain, Charles Duguid helped to establish a professional code for financial editors through an article published in the *Journal of Finance* in 1897. At the same time, business newspapers continued to emphasize stock market quotations, company earnings, and stodgy, ghostwritten public relations profiles of business leaders and their firms. The first publication to counter this approach was *Fortune*, a cosmopolitan monthly business and financial magazine founded in 1930 by the publishers of *Time* magazine. Its young, well-educated writers adopted a somewhat more critical posture toward their subjects, but also gave them a modern self-image through the use of photojournalism and a more literary style of writing. However, it was not until after **World War II** that business publications, led in America by the *Wall Street Journal*, began to report on general economic trends and their significance for the average citizen. The adoption of a broader economic approach not only increased the circulation of business publications but also led to more comprehensive coverage of business and finance in the mainstream press.

– C –

CAMBODIA. For most of the colonial period in Cambodia, printed news was limited to the French government's own *Journal officiel de Cambodge* and the semi-official, bilingual newspaper *Cambodge*. It was not until 1936 that Pach Chhoeun and two associates created the small, Khmer-language newspaper *Nagaravatta* for the emerging Cambodian intelligentsia. It called for improvements in health and education, advocated that Vietnamese clerks be replaced by native Khmers in the French administration, and promoted a modern sense of national identity. It was banned in 1942, however, after Chhouen was arrested for participating in a demonstration. During the final years of the Protectorate, a myriad of new newspapers were founded in both French and Khmer in conjunction with the formation of political parties. Aided by new laws proclaiming freedom of the press, their number soon included pro-Communist publications and the level of debate began to deteriorate. In September 1967, Prince Sihanouk banned all privately owned papers and subjected the state-owned ones to tighter control. Following Sihanouk's overthrow, Lon Nol gradually restored press freedom and a host of independent papers emerged again. After an attempt on his life in March 1973, however, a state of emergency was declared and most of the new papers were shut down again. During the final days of the Khmer Republic, the press began to revive again, only to be terminated once more when the Communist Democratic Kampuchea regime seized power in April 1975. It was not until the United Nations interregnum that private newspapers reappeared and their operations have continued to suffer from various controls. *See also* ASIA.

CANADA. The first newspaper in Canada was the *Halifax Gazette*, founded by printer-editor John Bushell from Boston on 23 March 1752. In addition to subscriptions, it relied on local advertising and government printing to make ends meet. In New France, the settlers had not been allowed a **printing press**, but in 1764 William Brown and Thomas Gilmore established the *Quebec Gazette* to assist in the transition to British rule. In New Brunswick and Prince Edward Island, newspapers also facilitated the creation of stable new communities. In Upper Canada (present-day Ontario), John Graves Simcoe, the lieutenant governor, brought Louis Roy from Quebec City to serve as King's Printer. On 18 April 1793, Roy began publishing the *Upper Canada Gazette* or *American Oracle*. It remained the only newspaper west of Montreal until after the War of 1812, but thereafter the press began to expand rapidly in response to the growing need for commercial information.

By 1857, there were 159 newspapers in what was then called Canada West, or over half of the 291 newspapers in British North America as a whole. Most were instruments of particular politicians or parties and many were short-lived, owing to the fact that even a party paper needed a good circulation, a good subscription collection rate, considerable advertising, some government printing contracts, and often a few other sources of revenue as well. These factors limited the range of content and debate, which was already hampered by a strict law of libel. Despite the outcome of the trial of **Joseph Howe** in 1835, it remained libelous to publish any matter calculated to degrade individuals or disturb the public peace, regardless of its truthfulness. In Upper Canada, nonetheless, **William Lyon Mackenzie** founded the *Constitution* in 1836 with the specific intention of attacking what he called the "Family Compact." Mackenzie was forced to flee to the **United States** after an unsuccessful attempt to foment rebellion in 1837. In his *Report on the Affairs of British North America* (1839), Lord Durham noted that "rumours are diligently circulated by the Canadian press; and every friendly act of the American people or government appears to be systematically subjected to the most unfavourable construction." At the same time, however, he suggested that newspapers were helping to bring the inhabitants of British North America closer together as "men discover [through them] that their welfare is frequently as much involved in the political condition of their neighbours as of their own countrymen."

Although the press played a role in the achievement of Confederation in 1867, it was not until the 1870s that market forces helped to create a more popular press. At the same time that higher costs of newsprint, printing, and labor were increasing the capital requirements for running a newspaper, growing numbers of workingmen and clerks in central Canadian cities were creating a market for papers prepared to serve their interests. Hugh Graham, John Ross Robertson, and a number of other young, flamboyant entrepreneurs responded by founding newspapers such as the *Montreal Star* (1869), the *Toronto Telegram* (1876), the *Toronto World* (1880), *La Presse* (1884), the *Ottawa Journal* (1885), the *Hamilton Herald* (1889), and the *Toronto Star* (1892). These new "people's journals," as Paul Rutherford has called them, discarded party identities, reduced political editorials, and introduced a more varied and popular selection of news, features, and commentaries, all for a lower price than the traditional party papers. They also encouraged their reporters to use a simpler prose style and tried to make their publications more visually appealing. Following the lead of Trefflé Berthiaume's *La Presse* in Montreal, they drew a sharper distinction between fact and opinion and elevated "facts" in status by clearing the front page for news alone. While most championed manhood suffrage and a few gave credence to ideas such as Henry George's proposal for a single tax, their popularity effectively killed the nascent Canadian labor press.

By **World War I**, most of the original "people's journals" had taken on party affiliations again as a further marketing technique; only the *Ottawa Journal* remained free of political labels and associations. After the war, however, most of the larger Canadian dailies discarded party identities entirely as the growth of chains and single-newspaper cities made it imperative to attract readers with diverse political beliefs. Though no longer constrained by party politics, many Canadian journalists now had to navigate within the new order of corporate media. In Canada as elsewhere, they adopted the professional ideal of objectivity or balanced coverage as a means of preserving a measure of autonomy in the newsroom. This ideal was bolstered by the emergence of The Canadian Press (CP) news agency in 1923 with member newspapers from across the country.

During the 1930s, CP worked hard on behalf of its members to maintain a monopoly over the distribution of news. Following its creation in 1932, the publicly owned Canadian Radio Broadcasting Commission (CRBC) contemplated providing news twice daily to remote areas in Canada without ready access to newspapers. Alarmed by this possibility, CP proposed that it provide the CRBC with news bulletins free of charge; in return, CP would control the content of the bulletins and determine their time of broadcast. The financially strapped CRBC agreed to this proposal and also undertook to regulate the news broadcasts of privately owned radio stations in line with CP's interests.

Following its replacement of the CRBC in November 1936, the Canadian Broadcasting Corporation (CBC) continued the arrangement for free daily news bulletins, despite growing criticism of their staleness and unsuitability for radio.

With Canada's entry into **World War II**, however, the CBC board of governors decided that the Corporation needed its own news service to ensure that Canadians received a uniform and unifying account of the war. On New Year's Day 1941, the CBC News Service began operations in English (one day later in French). But its two dozen news editors initially did little more than rewrite copy provided by wire services like CP, a practice which continued throughout the 1940s. The News Service also adopted a strict code of objectivity as a means of establishing its independence from the government. Chief editor Dan McArthur instructed newswriters to be "faithful to source material in facts, emphasis and general purport" and "not editorialize, speculate or predict into factual news items. Speculative comment should be used only if it comes into the body of a news story and is quoted from an authoritative source." This philosophy remained entrenched at the CBC for the next two decades. As Robert Fulford wrote in the Toronto *Sunday Telegram* on 19 May 1957, "no hint of opinion, no trace of analysis, ever passes through the pristine **typewriters** of the men who write news" at CBC. Its newswriters are little more than "faceless, nameless robots stripped of all personality and opinion."

The purpose of such objectivity was not to eliminate controversial commentary, but to segregate it institutionally. Initially, the CBC tried to accommodate "talks" and public affairs by treating the airwaves as a soapbox or concert hall available for hire. But this laissez-faire approach led to complaints of abuse as certain religious and other groups purchased time to attack other groups or disseminate ideas on controversial topics such as eugenics. In 1939, therefore, the CBC board of governors adopted a "White Paper" on "controversial broadcasting" setting forth an explicit set of rules governing discourse in the broadcast **public sphere**. Neither individuals nor groups would be allowed to purchase airtime; instead the public broadcaster would orchestrate the discussion of public issues so as to ensure balance and fairness. With the outbreak of World War II, this policy was temporarily shelved as CBC management feared that any public affairs programming might undermine the war effort. By 1943, however, there was growing concern that anti-Nazi propaganda was no longer working as a motivating force and a sense that Canadians needed the hope of a new postwar world to continue fighting effectively. Working in conjunction with the Canadian Association for Adult Education (CAAE), advocates of public affairs programming such as Neil Morrison were allowed to develop programs such as *Farm Radio Forum* and *Citizen's Forum* based on the White Paper's philosophy of balanced discussion.

The difficulties faced by such programs were illustrated in June 1959 when acting CBC president Ernie Bushnell decided to cancel the English radio network program *Preview Commentary*. A five-minute, early-morning opinion piece on political events, the program had been on the air since 1957 and had seldom occasioned any complaints. When Parliament was in session, four of the program's five commentaries were by members of the press gallery and, in the interest of maintaining healthy debate, some of those who generally supported the Progressive Conservative government, which had a massive majority, had taken to criticizing certain aspects of its performance. Although both Bushnell and the minister responsible for the CBC, George Nowlan, later denied that any political pressure had been brought to bear on CBC management, broadcasting historians have not been convinced by Bushnell's claim that he simply pulled the plug on a substandard program. Despite protests from several senior program staff, including chief news editor Bill Hogg, the CBC board of directors confirmed Bushnell's decision. As a result, public affairs supervisor Frank Peers and three assistants resigned, followed by 30 other producers in Toronto and Montreal. The following day, the CBC board reversed its decision and reinstated the program, but reduced its length to three minutes. A Commons committee on broadcasting later investigated the incident, but failed to determine whether political pressure had been involved.

As radio and TV news and public affairs cut into their markets, newspapers began to modify their own commitment to objectivity in order to differentiate their product. During the pipeline debate in 1956, **columnists** like Douglas Fisher, Charles Lynch, and Bruce Phillips adopted a more critical stance toward government and newspapers generally began to assume more of a watchdog role. On the eve of the introduction of television in 1952, there were only 94 dailies in Canada, compared to 121 a half century earlier. Although the number of Canadian cities with two or more dailies continued to decline thereafter, a more critical and investigative journalism helped to stabilize the total number of daily newspapers. During the 1960s, television began to respond in kind with adversarial public affairs programs such as the CBC's *This Hour Has Seven Days* (1964–66) and CTV's *W5* (1966–present). Both programs contributed to the rise of journalists as personalities, a trend which soon embraced newspapers as well. At the same time, Canadian journalists continued to pursue professionalization through unionization, university education, and organizations such as the Fédération professionelle des journalistes du Québec and the Centre for Investigative Journalism (CIJ). Founded in 1978 with a home at Carleton University's school of journalism, long regarded as the country's premier journalism program, the CIJ became the Canadian Association of Journalists (CAJ) in 1990. A comparative study of journalists in Canada and the United States by Vernon Keel concluded that Canadian journalists, especially those in Quebec, are more likely than American journalists to temper their belief in the right of free speech with elements of social responsibility and community values. *See also* BROWN, GEORGE; COLEMAN, KIT; FARRER, EDWARD.

CAREY, JAMES (1934–2006). Major American communications scholar who helped to raise the level of journalism history by placing it within a broad cultural framework. Most of his academic career was spent at the College of Communications at the University of Illinois, but in 1992 he joined Columbia University as CBS professor of international journalism. In "The Problem of Journalism History" (1974), he lamented the narrow "range of problems" studied by journalism historians and tried to rectify this shortcoming through works such as *Television and the Press* (1988), *Communication as Culture* (1989), and *James Carey: A Critical Reader* (1997). His sense of journalism as a cultural formation and the life-blood of democracy was shaped by John Dewey, whose own writings on communication he helped to resuscitate.

CARICATURE. The exaggerated graphic representation, sometimes to the point of being grotesque or ludicrous, of the most characteristic features of persons or things for the purposes of satire or ridicule. The terms *caricature* and *cartoon* have often been used interchangeably and caricaturists are often referred to as cartoonists. However, while cartoons can sometimes be value-neutral, caricatures are invariably negative, though their indignation can also vary in accordance with social and historical circumstances.

In **Great Britain**, where visual materials were not subject to government **censorship**, satirical images were first published during the English civil war (1642–51) and were later used to attack the administration of Sir Robert Walpole. But it was only after British painters began going to **Italy** for inspiration, and came in contact with the innovative caricature techniques being developed by Italian painters such as Pier Leone Ghezzi, that the "Golden Age of British caricature" occurred during the reign of George III. Among those who exploited the new skills of caricaturists like James Gillray was **John Wilkes**, establishing what would continue to be close ties between journalism and caricature. Following the death in 1815 of Gillray, whose mantle was taken up by George Cruikshank, British caricature fluctuated in virulence, but slowly became milder and more decorous, culminating in the softened, frolicking style of *Punch* magazine, which debuted in 1841. During the 1820s and 1830s, scurrilous caricatures were used by both working-class agitators and political reformers to push their respective causes. But following the passage of the Reform bill, agitation waned and caricature lost much of its previous intensity and became domesticated.

In 19th-century **France**, where caricature contributed to the downfall of both Louis-Philippe and Napoleon III, the authorities had an intense fear of its capacity to disseminate dangerous political ideas to the poor and illiterate. Adding to its power after 1850 was the competing medium of photography, which enabled caricaturists like Nadar (pseudonym of Gaspard-Félix Tournachon) and his rival Etienne Carjat to make hundreds of inexpensive prints of a single caricature. For much of the century, therefore, caricaturists were subjected to an ongoing cycle of liberation and repression: after helping to bring down one regime, they would be given a measure of freedom; but once they turned their artistic guns on the new government, censorship would be reimposed. Even then, damaging caricatures were able to slip by the censors, who made no effort to censor scathing caricatures of either the institution of censorship or themselves as censors (perhaps they appreciated a little humor in the midst of their thankless job). Ironically, French caricature seems to have gone into decline after censorship was formally abolished in 1881; it is as if caricature needs repression to operate best.

In the **United States**, the use of caricature did not become common in newspapers until after the Civil War and was used initially by editors to attack their competitors more than politicians. Beneath an image of various editors at their editorial washboards using **Horace Greeley**'s "U-Lye-Soap," the leading cartoon weekly *Punchinello* expressed hope they might switch to something with a milder fragrance. In 1870–71, however, the full power of caricature to exact political damage was first demonstrated by Thomas Nast (1840–1902). A German-born artist, Nast began drawing caricatures for *Frank Leslie's Illustrated Newspaper* in 1852, joined the New York *Illustrated News* in 1860, and became a staff artist for *Harper's* in 1862. President Abraham Lincoln called him "our best recruiting sergeant" for his cartoons attacking northern defeatists. His representations of the Draft Riots in New York City in 1863 tried to counter images of uncontrolled class conflict with a soothing vision of middle-class order. In a brilliant series of cartoons in *Harper's* in 1869–71, he helped to defeat the corrupt "Boss" Tweed and his ring in New York City. His cartoon "The Tammany Tiger Loose—'What are you going to do about it?'" popularized the tiger, donkey, and elephant as symbols for Tammany Hall and the Democratic and Republican Parties, respectively. When Tweed fled to **Spain**, he was identified by the authorities from a Nast cartoon and sent back to the United States.

A year after taking over the *New York World* in 1883, **Joseph Pulitzer** began publishing editorial cartoons, including a blistering caricature of the Republican presidential candidate James G. Blaine entitled "Belshazzar's Feast." During the heyday of **yellow journalism**, the California state legislature passed a law prohibiting caricatures that attacked character, but it was never enforced. During **World War I**, caricature was used by both sides and tended to become increasingly grotesque. The German government was so upset with the cartoons of the Flemish artist Louis Raemaekers (1869–1956) that it placed a bounty on his head. The son of a small newspaper proprietor in the **Netherlands**, Raemaekers began cartooning for the weekly magazine *Algemeen Handelsblad* in 1906.

Upon the outbreak of war, he went to **Belgium** to determine for himself whether reports of German atrocities were true. Outraged by what he saw, he depicted the Germans as bloated, subhuman aggressors in a series of cartoons for the Dutch newspaper *Telegraaf.* Yielding to German pressure, the Dutch government tried him for endangering its neutrality; when the jury cleared him, the Germans offered 12,000 guilders ($3,000) for his capture, dead or alive. In the meantime, the British and American media made extensive use of his cartoons for propaganda purposes.

For much of its history, caricature has functioned primarily as a tool with which the weak and the dispossessed, or their self-styled representatives, have been able to attack their perceived oppressors. More recently, however, the alternative use of caricature by established groups feeling threatened by lower or culturally different elements of society seems to have become more prevalent. This trend is arguably reflected in the **Danish cartoon controversy**, which emerged in the context of growing tensions over Muslim laborers in **Denmark**, as well as in a *New Yorker* caricature at the outset of the 2008 U.S. presidential campaign depicting Democratic candidate Barack Obama as a terrorist and his wife as a gun-toting hippie.

CARLILE, RICHARD (1790–1843). English journalist and reformer. While struggling to make a living in his twenties, Carlile became interested in parliamentary reform and began issuing the suppressed works of **Thomas Paine**, William Hone, and others in a more accessible pamphlet form. He also founded a radical weekly newspaper called *The Republican* (1819–26), which not only promoted reform but proved to be very profitable. In October 1819, he was convicted of seditious libel and sentenced to three years in prison for an article criticizing the government for its role in the Peterloo massacre at which he had been present as an invited speaker. While in jail, his wife and sister tried to keep *The Republican* going, but they were also imprisoned for seditious libel. Upon his release in 1825, Carlile began to champion women's rights, including sexual as well as political emancipation. He also used his paper to begin a campaign against child labor and support agricultural workers suffering from wage cuts. After further imprisonment and fines, however, he was too impoverished to continue publishing.

CARY, MARY ANN SHADD (1823–1893). Educator, abolitionist, suffragist, and the first African American woman to edit a newspaper in North America. The daughter of Abraham Shadd, who worked for **William Lloyd Garrison**'s *Liberator*, she was part of the exodus to **Canada** after the passage of the Fugitive Slave Law in 1850. In 1853, she began publishing the *Provincial Freeman*, which attacked slavery and advocated Canadian emigration, school integration, and women's rights. Plagued by financial difficulties, the Canadian-based paper closed in 1860 following the death of her husband, Thomas Cary of Toronto. After returning to Washington, D.C. in 1863, Cary became the first female African American lawyer in the **United States** and organized the Colored Women's Progressive Franchise in 1880.

CENSORSHIP. Censorship consists, most generally, of any form of control over access to, or the dissemination of, information or ideas. In this sense, it includes secrecy or the withholding of information by governments from the public as well as the expurgaton of words (written or oral) or visual representations from texts intended for public consumption. In a narrower, more customary sense, however, it refers to prior control over the content of print, audio, or visual materials. As such, censorship is not the only way of controlling content; threats of certain consequences for making public certain kinds of content can also deter the dissemination of texts, but is not usually regarded as censorship *per se*. In both senses, censorship has a long history and has existed in all societies. In ancient Rome, the censor occupied an office of high prestige and was expected to have strong individual merit. By the 6th century, the Catholic Church was issuing lists of prohibited (hand-copied) books, a practice which was not discontinued until 1966.

During the 17th century, the European press was widely (but not universally) subject to prepublication controls. In recent years, however, the severity and effectiveness of early modern censorship has been a matter of considerable debate, especially in the case of Tudor and Stuart England. The traditional view, first developed by Fred Siebert and later espoused by Christopher Hill, was that, except for a lapse during the Civil War in the 1640s, the English state exerted an all-pervasive, draconian control over printed materials. Subsequently, however, scholars such as Sheila Lambert, Don McKenzie, and Cynthia Clegg argued that this assessment greatly exaggerates the capacity and the desire of the Stationers' Company, the state's main tool for suppressing oppositional publications, to enforce its will on the press. In an attempt to navigate between these extremes, Jason McElligott has recently suggested that a better characterization for early modern England as a whole would be that prepublication censorship was conceived, not as a Berlin Wall designed to prevent the publication of any offensive materials, but rather as a "Keep off the Grass" sign meant to deter most transgressors. For McElligott, the fact that only 0.4 percent of titles (according to McKenzie's calculations) were ever even mentioned by the Stationers' Company (and a smaller percentage still actually charged and convicted) does not point to ineffectiveness, but rather to a strategy of selective punishment of the most flagrantly dangerous works.

Although prepublication controls were eliminated in England in 1695, censorship of the press remained operative in continental Europe until the late 19th century. In **France**, numerous newspapers were shut down and thousands of journalists imprisoned before the press law of 1881 liberalized controls over freedom of expression. From the outset, however, evasive measures were used in France and elsewhere to outwit censors. In December 1633, for example, Théophraste Renaudot introduced readers of the official *Gazette de France* to the heretical Copernican view of a sun-centered cosmos by publishing the Inquisition's condemnation of Galileo and apologizing for organizing a conference at which the doctrine had been discussed. Beginning in the late 17th century, censorship was also evaded through the publication of international newspapers in the **Netherlands**; written in French by correspondents in the major cities of Europe, these gazettes were distributed in France and other European countries where domestic news was censored. In restoration France, where **caricature** was regarded as even more dangerous than words, all images of pears were subject to censorship after the portly Louis-Philippe was sketched as a pear; but by then the symbol had already impressed itself on the public mind and could easily be drawn on Paris walls. Elsewhere, creative journalists used Aesopian language and code phrases to camouflage political criticism. Even in Nazi **Germany**, Arnold Mayer was able to engage in criticism of Hitler's foreign policy by couching it in terms of praise for the limited objectives of Otto von Bismarck.

Insofar as censorship takes the decision about what to include in a story out of the journalist's hands, it undermines the capacity of the journalist to reconstruct and judge events as accurately and fairly as possible. But journalists themselves have often been involved in, or supported, censorship operations, especially in times of war. In the **United States**, for example, journalist George Creel headed the **Committee on Public Information (CPI)** during **World War I**, while the main strategy of the Office of Information under Byron Price in **World War II** was to develop a system of voluntary censorship by journalists themselves. It is not only in times of war, however, that journalists have been complicit in censorship. During the Stalinist regime, the Soviet government censored not only its own journalists but those from other countries stationed in Moscow. By refusing to inform their readers that their stories were heavily censored and accepting Soviet propaganda, journalists like **Walter Duranty** engaged in what Morris Wayne calls a "conspiracy of silence" about events such as the famine of 1932–33. The occasional defection of censors from authoritarian regimes makes clear the extent to which gullible journalists can be deceived. In the mid-1970s, for example, a Polish censor defected to the West with 700 pages of classified censors' documents. The smuggled documents revealed, among other things, how Soviet-controlled Polish censors shifted the blame for the massacre of 8,000 Polish army officers in the Katyn Forest in 1940 from the Soviet army to the Nazis.

CENTRAL INTELLIGENCE AGENCY (CIA). In 1976, the director of the CIA, George Bush, announced that the agency would no longer enter into any "paid or contractual" relationships with employees of American news organizations. Previously, the CIA had not only made secret arrangements with individual journalists to supply it with intelligence, disseminate disinformation on its behalf, and even help recruit agents, but had also purchased or subsidized radio stations, newspapers, and various periodicals. It had also placed some of its own agents undercover abroad as journalists. These practices were partially revealed in a House committee report the same year as Bush's announcement and were later investigated by journalists such as Carl Bernstein. However, the extent to which American journalists have continued to assist CIA intelligence operations is unclear. It has probably been camouflaged by the extent to which the CIA has also had an adversarial relationship with the American press, especially in terms of the release of "sensitive" information. In their attempts to circumvent indirect CIA **censorship**, journalists have generally fared better when another branch of government has favored the publication of such information. *See also* FEDERAL BUREAU OF INVESTIGATION (FBI).

CHAPELLE, DICKEY (1918–1965). American photojournalist who developed a highly interpretive documentary style. Born Georgette Louise Meyer, she covered Iwo Jima and Okinawa for *National Geographic*. During the Algerian War of 1957, she went against her colleagues' sympathies for the French by portraying the rebels as brave freedom fighters. Her engagement with her subjects anticipated the New Journalism of the 1960s and won her numerous awards. She was the first war correspondent to be killed in Vietnam and the first female American reporter to die during battle.

CHECKBOOK JOURNALISM. The practice of paying sources for their stories. Newspapers and magazines competing for readers were the first media to consider it expedient to pay for information or pictures. But such payments have become particularly widespread in television where networks now reimburse political figures for taped memoirs and often purchase amateur videos from individuals witnessing a news event. Apart from raising a variety of ethical issues, checkbook journalism undermines the reportorial voice of journalism by reducing editorial control. For example, the memoirs which former president Gerald Ford sold to NBC for $1.5 million omitted his controversial pardoning of Richard Nixon.

CHENG SHEWO (1898–1991). Chinese newspaper entrepreneur who took **William Randolph Hearst** as his model in creating commercially successful papers in Beijing and Nanjing during the 1920s. In 1935, after a lengthy tour of American institutions, he founded the *Libao* in Shanghai, a small, cheaply priced **tabloid** aimed at a mass audience. In contrast to the satirical gossip of the "small papers" in the late Qing, the *Libao* concentrated on short, simply worded news stories on matters of human interest and achieved a circulation of over 200,000. Cheng also established schools of journalism in Shanghai and Taiwan. *See also* CHINA.

CHICAGO DEFENDER. Militant African American newspaper which initially styled itself as "the World's Greatest Weekly" and later became the largest black-owned daily in the world. It was founded on a shoestring in 1905 by Robert S. Abbott (1868–1940), the child of former slaves in Georgia who had been educated as a printer and worked in several Chicago printshops. A four-page paper the size of a handbill, it carried the motto "American race prejudice must be destroyed!" on its masthead. It was distributed nationally by Pullman railroad porters and used bold red headlines, sensational **crime** stories, and special features such as a health column to achieve a national circulation of 250,000 by the 1920s. During both world wars, the federal government attempted to prosecute it for sedition. In 1940, Abbott was succeeded by his nephew and heir, John H. Sengstacke, who continued as publisher until his death in 1997. In 1956, the *Defender* became the *Chicago Daily Defender*. By the 1990s, it was one of only two African American dailies.

CHILE. Following its colonization by Spanish conquistadors in the 1540s, Chile remained an isolated frontier society with few of the requirements for indigenous journalism. Although printing was introduced in the late 18th century by José de Rezabal y Ugarte, the senior judge of the Royal Audiencia of Cuzco, the only newspapers, magazines, and books in the colony were those brought from Europe. The first indigenous newspaper in Chile was the *Aurora de Chile*, a weekly founded in 1812 in Santiago by Juan Egaña Risco. Printed on a press specially imported from the **United States**, its purpose was to promote independence from **Spain** and it came to an end (as the *Monitor araucano*) two and a half years later when the royalists triumphed at the battle of Rancagua. During the Reconquista española (1814–17), the royalists established the official *Gaceta ministerial del gobierno de Chile*. After the civil war in 1823, journalism began to flourish; by 1830, over a hundred newspapers had been launched. Most were short-lived, but *El Mercurio*, founded in 1827 and circulated daily beginning in 1829, became the country's most prestigious paper.

In the 1850s, the government began subsidizing a number of papers to help promote its policies. By the 1860s, each of the main parties had its own organ: *El Independiente* (1864–91) for the Conservatives and *La República* (1866–78) for the Liberals. Cobo Gutiérrez, a lawyer, poet, and editor of *La República*, served in the governments of Liberals such as Federico Errázuriz. In the late 19th and early 20th century, members of the liberal intellectual elite continued to move freely between academia, journalism, and politics, enabling them to exert considerable influence over public opinion. After 1900, the promotion of education and literacy increased the market for newspapers, especially in the provinces where nearly every town developed its own newspaper. Urban dailies such as *Zig-Zag* in Santiago diversified their content to attract even more readers. In an environment of relative freedom, both print and broadcast media flourished and came to represent a broad spectrum of political viewpoints.

Following the election of Salvador Allende in 1970, however, the U.S. **Central Intelligence Agency (CIA)** began plotting a right-wing military coup d'état. On 11 September 1973, Allende was overthrown by General Augusto Pinochet and press freedom came to an end. A government office was set up to censor the news. Laws were passed severely restricting political commentary. The media were also used as agents of government propaganda. And in universities, the teaching of Marxism became taboo, libraries and even dictionaries were censored, and a number of subjects, most notably journalism, were removed from the curriculum. Many of these repressive measures remained in place after Pinochet stepped down in 1989. It was not until 2001 that President Ricardo Lagos approved new laws allowing journalists to criticize the government and its policies. *See also* LATIN AMERICA.

CHINA. The development of modern Chinese journalism began in 1815 when William Milne and Robert Morrison founded the first missionary periodical. By the end of the century, there were over 80 British and American missionary publications in China, including the popular weekly, *Wanguo gongbao* [Review of the Times or, literally, "A Public Newspaper about Ten Thousand Nations"], begun by

Young J. Allen and Timothy Richard in 1868. Though mainly intended to help propagate Christianity, these newspapers and magazines also disseminated Western ideas about modernization.

Beginning in the 1860s, these proselytizing organs were joined by foreign-owned commercial newspapers in treaty ports such as Shanghai and Hong Kong. The treaty port papers provided the initial model for a Chinese press; by the late Qing period, about one-third of the 200 newspapers in the treaty ports were indigenous commercial publications. During the same period, a reform movement aimed at modernizing Chinese society also established a number of newspapers in the concessions. After China's humiliating defeat in the Sino–Japanese War of 1895, the reformers increased their efforts and founded a number of newspapers in the hinterland as well. In 1898, however, the imperial government banned the reform papers, curtailed the inland distribution of treaty port papers, and stepped up publication of its own official papers. It also attacked journalists generally as "the dregs of literary classes" (*siwen balei*).

In addition to organizing their own clubs, journalists such as **Liang Qichao** tried to preserve their role as reformers by fashioning a new professional image and identity. Other journalists responded by seemingly abandoning politics in favor of mass entertainment. But along with sensational news and gossip, the so-called "small papers" such as *Youxi bao*, founded by Li Boyuan in 1897, included cynical political jokes and satire intended to expose the follies of bureaucrats and socialites. Over the next decade, more than a hundred of these cheap populist papers (Liang called them "mosquito papers") appeared in China's coastal cities. While declaring their devotion to truth, they blurred the distinction between news and opinion and drew upon various literary forms in contrast to their Western **tabloid** counterparts. Along with the reform papers, they contributed to the emergence of an oppositional public space that several scholars have argued made possible the successful Republican Revolution of 1911.

Following the Revolution, a number of Chinese students went abroad to study journalism and returned with visions of objectivity in their heads. Although the new Republican authorities showed little interest in nurturing a free and objective press, the 1919 protests against the Versailles treaty gave rise to the politically independent **"May Fourth" journals** as well as the first Chinese texts on reporting. After gaining control of China in 1927, however, the Kuomintang (KMT) used its own newspapers for political propaganda while subjecting opposition papers to various forms of intimidation. Outside of Shanghai's concession zones, almost all newspapers soon required political patronage to survive and had to submit to regular **censorship** to obtain it.

Only a few papers managed to maintain a degree of independence. The most importance of these was the ***Dagong bao*** [Impartial Daily] under editor-in-chief Zhang Jiluan; it hired reporters on the basis of professional competence, avoiding anyone with a party affiliation, and turned itself into a public forum by opening its pages to its readers. By treating the nation as a large family of which he was a devoted member concerned only with the family's good, Zhang was able to engage in a degree of criticism of Chiang Kai-sheck's regime, including its nonresistance policy toward **Japan**. Other editors survived by linking the concept of professionalism to the development of non-elitist news forms rather than public discourse. In addition to establishing journalism schools, societies, and scholarly publications, journalists such as **Cheng Shewo** began to incorporate elements of popular Western journalism into their content and style.

With the Communist takeover in 1949, Chinese journalism underwent a further series of shock waves. The Chinese Communist Party (CCP) had always attached great importance to the role of the press. Soon after its founding in 1921, it established newspapers in major Chinese cities, principally the *Laodong zhoukan* [Labor Weekly] in Shanghai and *Gongren zhoukan* [Worker's Weekly] in Beijing. In 1931, it set up its first news agency, the Red China News Press. After 1949, it turned the entire press into an instrument of the Communist revolution. The private ownership of newspapers was abolished and the party papers were subjected to increasingly centralized control. The result was a sometimes disastrous loss of purchase on reality; by exaggerating crop production figures, for example, the Communist-manipulated press contributed to the starvation of millions of peasants.

During the Cultural Revolution from 1966 to 1978, the disengagement of news from the real world became almost complete, as numerous party papers disappeared and the few that remained were little more than reproductions of the *People's Daily*. During the 1980s, the reforms of Deng Xiaoping facilitated the revival of a more independent press, but its freedom came to end after the brutal repression of the student uprising in Tiananmen Square in 1989. While growing commercial revenues have provided the post-Tiananmen media with a degree of economic independence, their freedom to engage in critical political analysis and Western-style **investigative journalism** has remained limited. *See also DAGONG BAO.*

CNN. The first 24-hour television news network, CNN (Cable News Network) was launched in the **United States** by Robert Edward (Ted) Turner with limited resources on 1 June 1980. After a rough start, it surprised its critics and forced the major American networks to increase their live event coverage and provide more frequent news updates. Turner's hope was that the live reporting of events around the world would contribute to international understanding. But as William E. Huntzicker has pointed out, it also provides international terrorists with a ready audience for hostage takings and other acts of violence. Moreover, the reduced time for reflection on the meaning of events inherent in journalism as a form of discourse is almost completely eliminated in live news coverage, forcing journalists to rely on a narrow range of preconceived frames for making sense of events.

COBBETT, WILLIAM (c. 1763–1835). British journalist and social reformer. In 1792, he fled to **France** and then to the **United States** to escape a lawsuit resulting from his attempt, based on his own experience, to expose army fraud. After opening a bookstore in Philadelphia, he published *Porcupine's Gazette* (1797–99), praising the British monarchy and attacking French Jacobinism. He also wrote several vituperative **pamphlets** on the Federalists' behalf. He returned to **Great Britain** after a judge found him guilty of libel for claiming that Dr. Benjamin Rush had killed former President George Washington through poor medical care. As the threat of French Jacobinism declined, Cobbett became increasingly concerned about social injustice and the plight of the working poor. In his *Political Register*, which he began in 1802, and its cheaper counterpart, *Two-Penny Trash*, he developed what one writer has called a "journalism for the lower orders." He also wrote *Rural Rides* (1830), a collection of essays about the negative impact of the Industrial Revolution on rural life.

COLEMAN, KIT (1864–1915). Canadian journalist and war correspondent. Born Catherine Ferguson but taking the name Kathleen, she emigrated from **Ireland** in 1884 after being disinherited by the family of her late husband. In 1889, she was hired by **Edward Farrer** as the women's page editor of the *Toronto Daily Mail*. The same year she began writing a weekly **advice column** as "Kit" (later Kit Coleman, after her third husband), which grew into the "Woman's Kingdom" page and included serious topics outside the domestic sphere. She continued the page after the *Mail* merged with the *Empire* in 1895, but also began to travel widely in pursuit of stories. She helped to found the Canadian Women's Press Club in 1904 and served as its first president. *See also* CANADA.

COLLIER'S. Weekly magazine founded by Peter F. Collier in 1888 to promote his installment plan for selling books. It soon became an illustrated literary and critical journal. Under editors Norman Hapgood (1903–12) and Mark Sullivan (1914–17), it became a leading publication for the **muckrakers**, but later shifted its focus to light fiction, cartoons, and popular articles. Its circulation reached 2.5 million before the market for general entertainment magazines weakened and it died in 1957.

COLUMBIA SCHOOL OF JOURNALISM. Pulitzer-endowed graduate school of journalism. In 1903, **Joseph Pulitzer** instructed his personal secretary, George W. Hosmer, to dangle the possibility of a large donation for a school of journalism before the eyes of both Columbia and Harvard University, despite Columbia's having rejected a proposal to add journalism to its offerings a decade earlier. Each institution was asked to comment on a pamphlet entitled "The Making of a Journalist," written by Hosmer at Pulitzer's request. Columbia's quicker response enabled it to secure a huge $2 million endowment. The school did not actually begin operations until 1912.

COLUMNISTS. With the decline in influence of the heavy, serious editorial, the column has become one of the prominent features of contemporary journalism. It is difficult to determine who would best qualify as the first modern columnist in the sense of providing personal commentary on a regular basis. From 1836 to 1839, Delphine de Girardin, writing as the vicomte de Launay, produced a series of contemporary sketches for her husband's newspaper *La Presse* that have been called a column. A better candidate is the long-forgotten Irish writer Fitz-James O'Brien, who, after squandering his patrimony in London by the age of 24, arrived in New York City in the early 1850s and became an overnight literary sensation. Before disappearing from sight by the end of the decade, O'Brien produced dozens of short stories, eight plays, and a piece of satirical prose or poetry for every issue of *Harper's* magazine for some six years. He also contributed a column for eight months to the newly established *Harper's Weekly* called "The Man About Town." According to biographer Francis Wolle, this makes O'Brien "America's first columnist in the modern sense."

Whatever the merits of this claim, it is clear that columnists were becoming a fixture in journalism by the pre-Civil War decade. Their numbers included Karl Marx, whom the *New York Tribune* paid £2 apiece for a regular twice-weekly column on European affairs, though almost half of the 500 or so columns submitted were actually ghostwritten by Friedrich Engels.

At a time when women were still largely excluded from the ranks of reporters, writing a column opened a door to mainstream journalism for women with sufficient talent and ideas to hold an audience. Among the publications preparing them for this transition was *Godey's Lady's Book*, which, though ostensibly a fashion magazine, had expanded its content to include articles on education and financial independence and later served as a model for both the *Ladies' Home Journal* and the first women's pages. One of the first women to make the leap was Sara Willis Parton (1811–1872), who began writing a long-running column for the weekly *New York Ledger* in 1851 using the alliterative pen name "Fanny Fern," a practice imitated by later women columnists such as Sally Joy White ("Penelope Penfeather"). Parton used her caustic wit to promote women's issues through the reform of social values generally; it has been suggested that her "performative incivilities" are similar in their defiance to modern rap music. She also wrote a best-selling novel, *Ruth Hall* (1855), about the life of a famous columnist. In the 1860s, she was joined in the ranks of women columnists by Mary Clemmer Ames (1839–1884), a nationally recognized Washington correspondent for the *New York Independent* and *Brooklyn Daily*. From 1866 to 1884, Ames wrote a public affairs column entitled "A Woman's Letter from Washington" in which she tried to elevate the standards of public life. Along the way she wrote *Ten Years in Washington: Life and Scenes in the National Capital, as a Woman Sees Them* (1874).

The combination of public affairs commentary with humor is usually associated with 20th-century political satirists like Will Rogers, who used homespun philosophy to poke fun at current affairs. But this type of column also has 19th-century origins. Although James M. Bailey is sometimes credited with writing the first humorous newspaper column for the *Danbury* (Conn.) *News* beginning in 1873, the main pioneer of the genre was Finley Peter Dunne (1867–1936). Dunne began his career in journalism as a reporter for the *Chicago Evening Telegram* in 1884, became city editor of the *Chicago Times* in 1888, and was writing lead editorials for the *Chicago Evening Post* by 1892. The following year, he created the fictional character Martin Dooley, a Chicago bartender who ruminated in Irish brogue about politics and social morality. Mr. Dooley's wit and sarcasm became so popular that Dunne was forced to continue the column despite his decided preference for editorial duties and regular editorial writing. Between 1893 and 1915, he produced over 500 "Mr. Dooley" pieces, averaging 1,500 to 2,000 words each. "I wish it cud be fixed up," Mr. Dooley commented during the Spanish–American War in 1898, "so's th' men that starts th' wars cud do the fightin'. Th' throuble is that all th' preliminaries is arranged be matchmakers an' all they'se left f'r th' fighters is to do the murderin'." Although satirizing a number of other conflicts, Dunne found the horrors of **World War I** too great to continue writing in this mode and abandoned the column in favor of nonhumorous journalism.

During the 1920s, the fascination with Hollywood celebrities led to the creation of the gossip column. Initially, its function was simply to promote Hollywood movies through celebrity identification. But columnists like Louella Parsons (1881–1972) soon became a power unto themselves, making or breaking careers through the gossip they dispensed not only publicly but later as informants to the federal authorities in pursuit of Communists in the **United States**. Parsons began writing the first movie gossip column for the *Chicago Record-Herald* in 1914. She lost her job when **William Randolph Hearst** bought the paper in 1918, but moved to New York City to write a movie column for the *Morning Telegraph*. In 1922, she was hired by Hearst to write for the *New York American*, but left for California three years later after contracting what seemed to be incurable tuberculosis. When the disease went into remission, she became the syndicated Hollywood columnist for the Hearst chain, producing her popular column until 1965. She had the field of Hollywood gossip mostly to herself until 1937 when Hedda Hopper began a rival column and the two became bitter enemies. Similar power over the lives of creative artists was exercised by drama critics such as Brooks Atkinson (1894–1984). After a brief stint as a foreign correspondent, Atkinson began reviewing Broadway plays for the *New York Times* in 1925. For the next 35 years, his column did much to determine the success or failure of hundreds of productions.

During the same period, the practical **advice column** became a mainstay in most newspapers. Marie Manning (1872–1945), who used the pseudonym "Beatrice Fairfax," wrote about etiquette and romance for the *New York Evening Journal* from 1898 until her marriage in 1905 and then again during the Depression, when her column was syndicated through King Features. Her main rival in the general advice field was Elizabeth M. Gilmer ("Dorothy Dix"), who began her career in journalism as a crime reporter for the *New York Journal* (1901–1916). Her lovelorn column in the *New Orleans Picayune* was eventually syndicated and still later distilled in such books as *How to Win and Hold a Husband* (1939). Since then, "general advice" has become increasingly specialized, with columns devoted specifically to health, nutrition, sex, exercise, and a host of other modern concerns. *See also* BROUN, HEYWOOD; COLEMAN, KIT; *FEUILLETON*; McCORMICK, ANNE ELIZABETH.

COMMITTEE ON PUBLIC INFORMATION (CPI). Agency created by President Woodrow Wilson on 13 April 1917, a week after the U.S. declaration of war, to coordinate the government's information campaign and serve as a liaison with the press. It was chaired by former newspaper editor George Creel (1876–1953), who had been active in Wilson's 1916 reelection campaign. In *Mobilizing America*, written before the war, Arthur Bullard, a journalist and novelist in the tradition of the **muckrakers**, had argued that the **United States**

should make the world safe for democracy. His ideas were scrutinized by Colonel Edward Mandell House and probably reached Wilson through him. The Creel committee drew up a voluntary **censorship** code and on 10 May 1917 began publishing an *Official Bulletin of the United States*. Closely affiliated with the executive branch, the *Official Bulletin* reprinted news releases in newspaper form. The CPI's staff grew to 150,000 and, in addition to many journalists, included historians Carl Becker and Frederic L. Paxon. A 1941 study of the committee's thousands of news releases praised it for its record of honesty, but subsequent assessments have been less charitable. Though successful in the short run, its blatant propaganda contributed to disillusionment after **World War I**. The operations of the CPI were later described by Creel in *How We Advertised America* (1920) as well as in his autobiography *Rebel at Large* (1947).

CORANTOS. During the late 16th and early 17th centuries, news broadsides and **pamphlets** were published with steadily increasing frequency. It was not until the outbreak of the Thirty Years' War in 1618, however, that an enterprising printer in Amsterdam named George Veseler began the first continental news publication to appear at regular and reasonably frequent intervals. Between 2 December 1620 and 18 September 1621, Veseler issued 15 numbers of a single folio sheet, printed on both sides, of continental news in English. It was written by Pieter van der Keere or Petrus Keerius, a Dutch mapmaker. From its title *Corrant out of Italy, Germany &c*, the term "coronto" (meaning current of news) was extracted and applied to a number of similar Dutch publications, which were then adapted by London printers to the needs of English readers. On 24 September 1621, Thomas Archer, Nathaniel Bourne, and Nathaniel Butter began publishing a weekly folio-sized *Corante, or, News from Italy, Germany, Hungarie, Spaine and France* using materials from Dutch and German newssheets. The following year, at the urging of Butter, they switched from a single folio sheet to a quarto pamphlet of between eight and 24 pages. Archer left the group shortly thereafter, but Bourne and Butter continued publication until 1632. Although their newssheet had no regular name, the title on the second number, which appeared nine days after the first issue of 14 May 1622, began with the words "Weekly News." The English corantos were issued under licenses from the crown and restricted to foreign news. *See also* GREAT BRITAIN.

COSMOPOLITAN. American magazine founded in 1886 as a monthly publication for family reading. In 1887, editor John B. Walker moved it from Rochester to New York and began to compete with *McClure's* and *Munsey's*. Among its early contributors were Samuel Clemens, Henry James, Rudyard Kipling, and Arthur Conan Doyle. In 1897, its articles on popular education led to the creation of Cosmopolitan University, a correspondence school. After 1900, it was among the publications used by the **muckrakers**, but switched to popular fiction and noncontroversial articles even before its purchase by **William Randolph Hearst** in 1925.

COTTA, JOHANN (1764–1832). Founder of one of the largest publishing firms in Europe in the late 18th and early 19th century. The son of a court printer in Stuttgart and younger brother of Friedrich Cotta, a radical German constitutionalist, Johann Cotta took over the family's book shop in Tübingen in 1787. With the collaboration of Friedrich Schiller, he established its literary credentials and used the profits from literature to publish a series of periodicals devoted to a new kind of historicized political journalism emphasizing the discussion of ideas over factual reporting. In 1798, he launched the *Allgemeine Zeitung*, moved it to Augsburg in 1810, and developed it into the most widely read newspaper in the German states. Along with Cotta's other newspapers, the *Augsburger Allgemeine Zeitung* sought to achieve freedom from press controls through responsible, nonpartisan journalism. Dependent on government measures against piracy and forced to operate under various Napoleonic and restoration authorities, Cotta claimed that there was no discrepancy between serving the public and being useful to government. *See also* GERMANY.

CRANE, STEPHEN (1871–1900). Realist novelist and journalist whose writing helped to create a closer relationship between journalism and literature. Crane did intermittent reporting for the *New York Herald* and *New York Tribune* while writing his first book, *Maggie: A Girl of the Streets* (1893). For his sketch "An Experiment in Misery" (1894), he dressed as a tramp to experience how the downtrodden live. Although his masterpiece, *The Red Badge of Courage* (1895), was written without any prior personal experience of war, its immediate success forced him into the field of war reporting. His observations on the Greco–Turkish War were published as *Active Service* (1899) and his stories about the Spanish–American War (1898) were collected in *Wounds in the Rain* (1900). The hardships he endured in gathering this material broke his health, however, and he died before his 30th birthday. His success inspired other aspiring writers to use the newsroom as a springboard to fiction.

CRIME AND TRIALS, COVERAGE OF. Crime and trials have long provided the press with exciting news which can be easily obtained at relatively low cost. Most of the coverage has followed the leads and accepted the judgments of law enforcement agencies, including generally uncritical reporting of alleged waves of crime. At the same time, variations of emphasis have existed between countries and different types of newspapers within the same country. In 19th-century **Great Britain**, for example, crime reporting was generally characterized by decorum and thoroughness in contrast to the sensationalistic, moralizing style of American crime reporters. Within the British press, however, conservative middle-class newspapers often treated crime as evidence of the disorderliness of the lower classes, while radical working-class newspapers saw it as a product of social and economic inequality. In the **United States**, reporters used middle-class frames such as the evils of the city and the restrictions on women's lives to make sense of stories such as the Helen Jewett murder trial, the Beecher-Tilton scandal, and the Lizzie Borden axe murders.

The Helen Jewett murder trial has been of particular interest to journalism historians. In June 1836, Richard P. Robinson, a 19-year old office clerk, was tried for allegedly bludgeoning to death Helen Jewett, a beautiful 25-year old prostitute, in one of New York City's pricier brothels. While exploiting the opportunity to increase circulation through sensationalistic coverage of the five-day trial, most New York papers also probed into the social meaning of the murder. For those supporting his conviction, Robinson represented the supposedly corrupt and unruly lower-class clerks and artisans whose aspirations for upward mobility, as evidenced by their use of high-priced prostitutes like Jewett, threatened the fabric of established society.

For the *New York Herald*'s **James Gordon Bennett**, on the other hand, Robinson was a victim of the city's aristocracy, which had allegedly conspired with brothel owners and the police to frame Robinson so as to cover up their own licentious lifestyle.

CRISIS OF ELOQUENCE. The rapid proliferation of newsbooks during the English civil war (1642–51) created a "crisis of eloquence" among contemporary historians. This term was first used by the republican writer John Hall, himself a writer of newsbooks, to refer to the shift from personal oration to disembodied text as the prevailing medium of political persuasion. As applied by Joad Raymond, the term refers to the difficulties for reliable history which historians such as John Rushworth attributed to this transformation. Before the appearance of newsbooks, historians relying on oration knew who was saying what to whom in what context. But as newsbooks became the dominant source of information, the authenticity and authority of the spoken voice was severed and replaced by the unreliability of printed texts. This concern did not prevent historians from using the "fallen speech" of the newsbook as a source of information. In his *Historical Collections* (First Part, 1659), Rushworth, who had earlier served as a licenser of the press, made deliberate and extensive use of newsbooks. And for his exposition of the civil war in *Behemoth* (1680), Thomas Hobbes relied on a chronicle which, unknown to him, had been compiled from **pamphlets** and newsbooks. *See also* GREAT BRITAIN.

CROLY, JANE CUNNINGHAM (1829–1901). English-born journalist and early feminist who came with her father to New York City in 1841 and began her remarkable career by writing feature articles on topics of interest to women for the *New York Tribune* under the pseudonym "Jennie June." In addition to being the first woman journalist to syndicate her column, she edited the fashion pages for the *New York World* (where her husband David was editor) in the 1860s, edited *Demorest's Quarterly Mirror of Fashion* and its successor *Demorest's Illustrated Monthly* from 1860–87, served as the New York correspondent for various newspapers, was part owner and editor of *Godey's Lady's Book*, and created the first designated women's pages for the *New York Herald*, basing their content on *Godey's*. She also established the first major women's club (1868), the Women's Press Club (1889), and the magazine *Women's Cycle* (1889), the latter serving as the organ of the General Federation of Women's Clubs. Croly was the first woman to teach college journalism (at Rutgers), paving the way for other women professors of journalism such as Sara Lockwood Williams.

CROUCH, JOHN (1614?–1680). Arguably the most brazen member of a network of subversive royalist journalists during the early stages of the Commonwealth in England. Though dismissed by historians looking for serious political commentary, his scurrilous style not only served to attract a large readership but constituted an underlying commentary on what he took to be the morals of his opponents. He produced several newsbooks, the best known being *The Man in the Moon* (1649–50), an eight-page weekly. Crouch produced over a million words of crude commentaries, including ballads, elegies, and **pamphlets** as well as newsbooks. *See also* GREAT BRITAIN.

CUBA. The first newspaper in Cuba was likely the weekly *Gaceta de la Habana*, founded by the governor on 8 November 1782 but published for less than a year. It was followed in 1790 by the weekly four-page *Papel periódico* (later *Aviso*), which became biweekly in 1791 and Cuba's first daily newspaper in 1793. Over the course of the 19th century, the press gradually expanded but remained until tight control by **Spain**. Patriots, like the poet and journalist José Martí (1853–1895), were forced to use the **underground press**. Born in Havana, Martí was first convicted of subversion at the age of 16 and sentenced to a year of hard labor in Spain. In the mid-1870s, he wrote for the *Revista universal* in **Mexico** and taught at the University of Guatemala before trying to return to Cuba in 1879. Deported once again, he went to New York City, where he worked as an editor and correspondent for numerous Latin American magazines and newspapers. Through his own periodical, *La Patria*, he became a symbol of Cuba's struggle for independence from Spain.

Over the next half century, the government continued to stifle criticism primarily through **censorship**. In the mid-1930s, however, the government instituted a system of press subsidies and began placing sympathetic journalists directly on the government payroll. These policies artificially expanded the number of newspapers. By 1956, there were 33 daily newspapers in Havana alone, more than in London, with only *Prensa libre* and the *Times of Ha*

only political but highly demeaning. Despite having previously rejected drawings by the Danish illustrator Christoffer Zieler poking fun at Jesus Christ, *Jyllands-Posten* proceeded to publish the images on 30 September. They were not used, as would normally be the case for caricatures, in connection with a specific issue or story being treated more generally. When Danish Muslims protested to the prime minister, they were told to seek redress in the courts. And when this approach failed to achieve anything, they sought support in several Arab countries. Groups such as the Organization of the Islamic Conference responded by condemning **Denmark** and organizing a highly damaging boycott of Danish goods. Though insisting that the cartoons were not meant to be offensive and did not violate the law, Juste admitted that they were considered insulting by many Muslims and issued an apology, which the Danish Muslim leaders generally accepted. In February 2006, however, other Scandinavian newspapers decided to show their solidarity with *Jyllands-Posten* by republishing the cartoons. They were soon joined by newspapers in a large number of other countries. It was only after this bandwagon effect began to operate that Muslim populations in over 30 countries engaged in widespread demonstrations and protests, including attacks on the Danish and Norwegian embassies in Damascus and the Danish embassy in Beirut. By the time the violence subsided, over 300 people had died and many others had been injured. This violence was then interpreted by many newspapers and magazines as the real threat to freedom of expression.

DAVIS, RICHARD HARDING (1864–1916). The epitome of the adventurous, swashbuckling war correspondent who made journalism seem the most exciting of careers. His mother was the prominent novelist Rebecca Harding Davis and his father was editor of the *Philadelphia Public Ledger*. After attending Johns Hopkins University, he became a reporter for the *New York Sun* and later managing editor of *Harper's Weekly*. He covered the Greco–Turkish War, the Spanish–American War of 1898 (where he joined in the fighting), the Boer War (where he witnessed the rescue of Ladysmith), the Russo–Japanese War, and **World War I**. His romantic portrait of the life of a reporter in *Gallegher and Other Stories* (1891) led a reviewer in the *Pall Mall Gazette* to declare that "the Americans . . . have discovered a Rudyard Kipling of their own." His front-page articles about the Spanish–American War glorified its opportunities for chivalry and heroic death. But despite calling for the entry of the **United States** into World War I, his experiences in **Belgium** and **France** made him increasingly ambivalent about war and its "civilizing mission." His articles were syndicated for publication throughout the United States.

DAY, BENJAMIN H. (1810–1889). Founder of the *New York Sun*, the first of the **penny papers** in the **United States**. Born in Springfield, Massachusetts, he was descended from William Brewster, who sailed on the *Mayflower*. After apprenticing for six years on the *Springfield Republican*, he left for New York City where he worked as a newspaper compositor and then set up his own business as a job printer. Lacking much work because of a financial depression, he decided to try selling a small newspaper for the price of a penny. On 3 September 1833, he began publishing the four-page *Sun* under the moniker "It Shines for ALL." It was immediately a huge success; by 1835, according to Day, it had a circulation of over 19,000, which, if correct, would have made it the largest paper in the world. In 1837, he sold the *Sun* to his brother-in-law, Moses Yale Beach, for $40,000, a decision he later regretted. Day also founded the monthly *Brother Jonathan* (1842), which later became the first illustrated weekly in the United States.

DAY, DOROTHY (1897–1980). Charismatic communitarian leader whose religious fervor infused her radical social philosophy and journalism. In 1916, she moved with her family to New York City, where her father worked as a sportswriter, and began writing for radical journals such as *The Call*, *The Masses*, and the *Liberator*. After being ostracized by the radical movement for her conversion to Catholicism in 1927, she proceeded to develop an alternative Catholic social criticism. In 1933, she and Peter Maurin, a French philosopher, founded *The Catholic Worker*, a penny **tabloid** which achieved a circulation of almost 200,000 and helped to establish the communitarian Catholic Worker movement. She recounted her experiences in the movement in *The Long Loneliness* (1952).

DEFOE, DANIEL (1660?–1731). Prolific writer who arguably invented both the modern novel and modern journalism. The son of a

Protestant Nonconformist, he was barred from attending Oxford or Cambridge, but received an excellent education at the Dissenting Academy of Charles Morton. A brilliant teacher and future vice-president of Harvard College, Morton helped Defoe develop the plain and energetic style that became the earmark of his journalism. Fearing confiscation of their Bibles, the Dissenters copied them out using shorthand, a skill that also served Defoe's journalism. In 1702, he was fined and sent to Newgate Prison for writing a **pamphlet** judged to be critical of the Anglican Church. But in 1703 he was hired as a government **spy** by Robert Harley, the Tory secretary of state and later chancellor of the exchequer and lord high treasurer. With Harley's support, he started the *Review* in 1704 and disregarded the usual practice of **anonymity** by openly acknowledging himself as its author. For the next seven years, he singlehandedly produced three issues of the *Review* a week, a feat made possible in part by his development of a new journalistic style. Forsaking both the bland prose of the *London Gazette* and the rhetorical excesses of journalists like **Roger L'Estrange**, Defoe tried to reach as many readers as possible through writing that was not only clear and straightforward but also graphic, factual, and marked by at least an occasional felicitous turn of phrase. *See also* GREAT BRITAIN.

DENMARK. During the 1480s, printing made its way from **Germany** to Denmark (which included **Norway** and its dependencies until their independence in 1814). For the next century and a half, the main vehicle for disseminating printed news was the news **pamphlet** or newsbook. Each pamphlet was restricted to a particular category of news, was published in either Danish or German, and was subject to religious and later political **censorship**. The first royal privilege to issue a newspaper, understood as containing reports on diverse subjects, was granted in 1634, the same year that weekly mail service was established between Hamburg and Copenhagen. This first newspaper cribbed news from two German papers, did not have a regular title, and did not distinguish its issues by number. Three years after the death of its printer in 1654 (it may have been discontinued before then), both the Royal and the University printer in Copenhagen were given privileges and began publishing "Weekly News from Hamburg" in German.

Sometime after Denmark changed from an aristocratically elected to an absolute monarchy in 1660, the censorship of political news was transferred from university to government officials. The sanctioned printers were required to submit their copy (consisting mainly of news extracted from foreign papers) to the censor before publication and compelled to accept all revisions or deletions. In 1672, a further privilege was awarded to Daniel Paulli, who began publishing a biweeky paper in German together with a monthly in Danish; the former included a much more extensive selection of news than its predecessors, while the latter published royal ordinances along with a summary of the biweekly paper. In 1720, a weekly newspaper in French emphasizing literary, scientific, and cultural news was added to this mix. It was followed by a number of newspapers influenced by Addisonian journalism, but these eventually gave way to more broadly based dailies such as the *Berlingske Tidende* (1749) in Copenhagen and the *Fyens Stiftstidende* (1774) in Odense.

Although prepublication censorship was temporarily abolished in 1770, it was not until 1849, when Denmark became a constitutional monarchy, that it was made illegal once and for all. Following the establishment of a bicameral legislature, four main political parties emerged in Denmark, each with its own substantial national network of supporting newspapers. The most cosmopolitan of these was *Politiken*, founded by Viggo Hørup (1841–1902) in 1885. Regarded by some as Denmark's greatest journalist, Horup had turned to journalism after being defeated for office and later became a minister in the first Liberal government. He adopted several features of the New Journalism in **Great Britain**, such as smaller pages, bold headlines, and extensive illustrations, while also pursuing constitutional change.

After further reforms in 1901, papers such as *Politiken* began to deemphasize politics in favor of news. While the main political parties continued to look to newspaper ownership for a competitive edge, they found the results increasingly disappointing. In 1918, for example, a group of businessmen tried to revive the flagging Conservative People's Party by purchasing *Kobenhavn* (established as an independent daily in 1889) on its behalf. Four years later, however, they sold it to the Left Party, which discontinued it in 1931 after becoming similarly disenchanted with its capacity to deliver political dividends.

During the Nazi occupation from 1940–45, an **underground press** emerged in conjunction with the Danish Resistance. In 1943–45, K. B. Anderson (1914–1984), who had organized a national anti-Nazi youth group in the 1930s and later became foreign minister, edited two illegal papers. The creation of a unicameral parliament in 1953 led to the dissolution of the four-party system and a "quiet revolution" in the structure of the Danish press. Newspaper content also underwent substantial changes in response to competition from radio and television. Instead of resorting to sensationalism, however, the leading dailies have been able to stabilize their readerships by providing in-depth news coverage for the country's better educated citizens.

DIBAO. An official news publication in **China** dating back to the Han Dynasty (206 B.C.E.–C.E. 200). It was printed using carved wooden blocks until the invention of moveable type in 1038. Separate editions were eventually produced for different clienteles. In modern times, it was known as the *Peking Gazette*.

DOUGLASS, FREDERICK (c. 1818–1895). Editor and publisher of the *North Star* (later *Frederick Douglass' Paper*), an abolitionist weekly, from 1847 to 1859. Born as a slave in Maryland, he took his name from Sir Walter Scott's *The Lady of the Lake* and escaped from slavery in 1838. He hoped to achieve emancipation through political methods and published several autobiographical works as well as *Douglass' Monthly* (1860–63).

DUANE, WILLIAM (1760–1835). Editor of the *Aurora* and one of the most effective journalists in his day. Born to Irish parents in the colony of New York, Duane apprenticed as a printer in **Ireland** and then went to Calcutta, where he founded and edited the liberal *India World*. After being deported for his attacks on the East India Company, he worked as parliamentary reporter for the *General Advertiser* in London before leaving for America where he linked up with **Benjamin Franklin Bache**, editor of the *Aurora* in Philadelphia. When Bache died in 1798, Duane became editor and threw the paper's support behind the radical Jeffersonian republicans, who wanted to increase popular representation at the expense of the propertied classes. When armed assault failed to silence him, he was charged under the

Alien and Sedition Acts, but avoided conviction when **Thomas Jefferson** became president. Jefferson later acknowledged him as one of republicanism's "fellow-laborers in the gloomy hours of federal ascendancy." After Washington became the federal capital in 1800, the *Aurora* continued as the leading national Republican paper, but gradually shifted its focus to state politics, supporting the more egalitarian "Old School" Democrats. After Duane was forced to sell the *Aurora* in 1822 for financial reasons, the Old School movement disappeared.

DU BOIS, W. E. B. (1868–1963). African American educator, author, and journalist who fought for full equality of citizenship in the **United States**. After graduating from Harvard with a doctorate in history in 1895, he became a professor of economics and African American history, wrote several books on racial oppression, and founded the Niagara Movement against segregation. In 1910, he was appointed as director of publications and research by the National Association for the Advancement of Colored People (NAACP) as well as editor of its monthly publication, *The Crisis*, which he oversaw until 1934 when he became chairman of the Sociology Department at Atlanta University. From the late 1920s to the early 1940s, he wrote political columns for various newspapers and a further series of books. In 1961, he was invited by Kwame Nkrumuh, the president of Ghana, to begin work on an *Encyclopedia Africana*.

DUCOMMUN, ÉLIE (1833–1906). Swiss journalist, political figure, and business executive. An eloquent advocate of peace, Ducommun began his journalistic career in 1855 as editor of the political journal *Revue de Genève*. In 1865, he founded the radical journal *Der Fortschritt* [Progress] and later edited newssheets such as *Les États-Unis d'Europe*, published by the International League for Peace and Freedom. He remained involved with journalism after being appointed director of the International Bureau of Peace in Bern in 1891. In 1902, he shared the Nobel Peace Prize with Charles Albert Gobat.

DURANTY, WALTER (1884–1957). Foreign correspondent who reported on the **Soviet Union** for the *New York Times*. His legacy is currently a matter of some controversy. Born in Liverpool, Duranty studied classics at Cambridge, joined the *Times'* Paris bureau in 1914, and covered the Western Front and Versailles Peace Conference. In 1922, he was assigned to Moscow, learned the Russian language, and continued to report on the new Soviet regime despite losing a leg in a train wreck in 1924. As the Moscow correspondent for the *Times*, he obtained an exclusive interview with Joseph Stalin and won a **Pulitzer Prize** in 1932 for his series on Stalin's Five Year Plan for industrialization. He was criticized for being unduly sympathetic to Soviet aims and for his denial of the Ukrainian famine in 1933. He responded in *I Write as I Please* (1935) by saying that he was "a reporter, not a humanitarian." But his reporting on collectivization, labor camps, and show trials was colored by his belief that the Russian character was incompatible with Western freedoms and required some form of autocratic rule. In 1941, he returned to the **United States** and tried to interpret the Soviet Union to the American public in *The Kremlin and the People* (1941) and *USSR: The Story of Soviet Russia* (1944). Together with his earlier reporting, these works have been criticized for facilitating Soviet propaganda.

– E –

EBBUT, NORMAN (1894–1968). Chief Berlin correspondent for *The Times* of London from 1927 to 1937. In *Berlin Diary* (1941), American journalist William Shirer praised Ebbut as the most knowledgeable correspondent in **Germany** in the 1930s. Although he tried to report life in Nazi Germany as accurately and dispassionately as possible, his dispatches were systematically cut, rewritten, and distorted by *The Times'* sub-editors in London, compromising the ability of readers to understand the dangerous implications of the Nazis' rise to power. When *The Times'* coverage still met with Nazi criticism, editor Geoffrey Dawson wrote on 23 May 1937 that "it really would interest me to know precisely what it is in *The Times* that has produced this new antagonism in Germany. I do my best night after night to keep out of the paper anything that might hurt their susceptibilities." Despite this in-house **censorship**, Ebbut's articles still managed to present the Nazis unfavorably. In line with Joseph Goebbels's crackdown on press criticism, therefore, Ebbut was subjected to a vicious character assassination and expelled from Germany in August 1937. Fifty foreign correspondents risked the wrath of the Nazis to bid him farewell. A month after his return to England, he suffered a severe stroke, ending his career as a journalist. His years in Berlin were the focus of a television series, *The Nightmare Years* (1992).

EDITORIAL FEUD. A questionable device used by some late 19th-century American newspapers to improve circulation. In 1884, for example, two Buffalo newspapers, Edward Butler's *Evening News* and the *Evening Telegraph* owned by the fledgling chain of E. W. Scripps, began feuding over presidential candidate Grover Cleveland's adulterous affair with a shop girl. When the *Telegraph* closed in 1885, contemporaries blamed its "satanic journalism."

EDUCATION AND TRAINING. Attitudes and approaches to the preparation of journalists have long been subject to considerable cultural variations and institutional tensions. In continental Europe, the tendency has been to emphasize training on the job. The first school of journalism, the École supérieure de journalisme de Lille, was not established until 1924 and handled only a few students a year. After **World War II**, **Agence France-presse** acted as a kind of national journalism school, but further educational opportunities for prospective journalists in **France** remained quite limited until the 1960s. Only in recent decades has formal journalism education at universities and related institutions become the norm in Europe.

There has been a longstanding preference in **Great Britain** for training journalists on the job. In 1889, the National Association of Journalists began offering training to journalists, but it was not until 1919 that its successor, the Institute of Journalists, persuaded London University to offer a diploma in journalism. And it was only after World War II that the American model of journalism education began to seriously penetrate British journalism.

In the **United States**, pressures to deflect criticism of the press in the late 19th and early 20th century led to earlier and more concerted efforts to link the traditional process of training to higher education. This development added a new form of tension to the preparation process. In addition to the debate over whether journalists are best prepared in newsrooms or classrooms was added the question of the proper place of journalism educators in academia. The result was a double-squeeze for journalism educators. On the one hand, those who sought to demonstrate to employers that they develop good news-workers were considered less than fully fledged academics; on the other hand, those who emphasized the academic credentials they were giving graduates were regarded less favorably by the industry.

These points are best illustrated in the case of the United States as the birthplace of journalism education. In the 18th and early 19th centuries, Americans regarded journalism largely as a trade involving the art of printing as well as editing and writing. Young boys learned the craft by apprenticing with master printers. In this context, efforts to formalize the training of journalists were closely tied to print shop activities. The first attempt to provide a more academic form of training was undertaken by the land-grant colleges, which had been given a mandate to provide more practical education. But even they encountered opposition to incorporating journalism into their curriculae; when Norman J. Colman proposed a journalism program at the University of Missouri in 1869, it was rejected as unsuitable for academic status. In 1878, the University did agree to the creation of a course on journalism, but it was not until three decades later that the Missouri School of Journalism began operations under Walter Williams. The idea that journalism should be learned on the job remained solidly entrenched, especially among editors like **Horace Greeley**, **Edward Godkin**, and **Charles A. Dana**.

Aided by a new ethos of professionalism, the first American schools of journalism were established during the Progressive era, beginning with the Missouri School of Journalism in 1908. Four years later, the **Columbia School of Journalism** opened its door to graduate students with the help of a substantial endowment from **Joseph Pulitzer**. As the number of programs expanded, teachers and departments began to create their own societies and associations, beginning with the American Association of Teachers of Journalism in 1912. It was reorganized as the Association for Education in Journalism in 1949 and subsequently renamed the Association for Education in Journalism and Mass Communication (AEJMC). While the teachers' association was open to all journalism educators, the American Association of Schools and Departments of Journalism (AASDJ), formed in 1917, began setting instructional requirements for participation; to belong to the AASDJ, programs offering a journalism major had to devote most of their attention to the technical aspects of reporting and editing, an emphasis reflecting the fact that most instructors were former journalists. Following Walter Williams's lead at Missouri, most programs linked instruction to the production of a campus or community newspaper and turned to textbooks authored for the first time by journalism professors themselves.

The growth of journalism programs was viewed with suspicion by both universities and the press. In 1938, Robert M. Hutchins, president of the University of Chicago, told the Inland Daily Press Association that "the shadiest educational ventures under respectable auspices are the schools of journalism. They exist in defiance of the obvious fact that the best preparation for journalism is a good education. Journalism itself can be learned, if at all, only by being a journalist." Quoting this statement approvingly in an editorial on February 18, the *Washington Times* added that "we know a lot of newspaper boys with B.A., B.S., etc., degrees; and we believe their prospects are better than those of a journalism school graduate."

The technical-vocational emphasis of the emerging journalism programs was criticized on two fronts. On the one hand, it was thought to deprive students of the benefits of a broad education. But at the same time, it was taken to task for failing to achieve its own narrow purpose of preparing students for the "real" world of journalism. For example, a study by Albert Sutton found that many teachers had no credentials in journalism and that even former journalists were not always in touch with current newsroom practices. In response to these criticisms, a number of journalism educators advocated increasing the academic content of journalism programs. They rejected the argument that journalism is best learned on the job after receiving a broad liberal education. But under the influence of **Willard G. Bleyer**'s pioneering program at Wisconsin, they pushed for more public affairs and social science content in journalism education, especially courses in the new field of mass communication. For students of Bleyer like Chilton Bush, who headed the journalism program at Stanford, the goal was to transform journalists into media professionals.

While the American Newspaper Guild considered the attempt to establish professional status for journalists a ploy to help gain collective bargaining, Hutchins changed his tune and criticized schools of journalism for not doing enough to prepare their students to function as judges of public affairs. "The kind of training a journalist needs most today," the **Hutchins Commission** wrote in *A Free and Responsible Press* (p. 77), "is not training in the tricks and machinery of the trade."

The problem for journalism schools wishing to increase their emphasis on public affairs was that the vocational emphasis of the AASDJ made it difficult to pursue this approach and still receive accreditation. In 1944, therefore, a number of schools denied membership in the AASDJ formed a rival organization, the American Society of Journalism School Administrators. They also began hiring more teachers with a Ph.D. and developing courses on a range of media issues. Led by Stanford and Illinois, many programs established connections with Departments of Communication, but with mixed results. As communication evolved as a discipline, its interests became less relevant to journalism students and its own needs were not always well served by the traditional relationship.

Between 1938 and 1948, the number of students in American journalism programs grew from 6,000 to 16,000, but then slowly declined for more than a decade. Beginning in the mid-1960s, however, interest in journalism studies suddenly skyrocketed. Enrollment jumped to 33,000 in 1970 and reached 71,000 by 1979. Apart from "baby boom" demographics and the inspiration of the investigative and New Journalism of the 1970s, students were drawn back to journalism by a desire for relevant job skills and a career through which they could make a difference. Increasingly, however, they were also using their journalism background to pursue careers in public relations, advertising, and communications generally. Of the 150,000 students in some 450 journalism-related programs in the United States in 2000, only about one-quarter were primarily interested in careers as journalists.

EMPIRE PRESS UNION. Organization founded in **Great Britain** in 1909 ostensibly to overcome "mutual ignorance between Britain and her distant colonies." While Britain saw it as a way of influencing the development of colonial media, countries such as **Australia** and **New Zealand** used their periodic conferences to alter imperial communications policies regarding cable rates, news cartels, and other factors affecting the freedom and performance of the press. The relative openness of the journalistic profession in Britain and the dominions contributed to this success by encouraging a high degree of reciprocity among journalists within the Empire/Commonwealth. Freedom of the press was a major topic of debate at the postwar conferences in London (1946) and Ottawa (1950), with **Canada**, Australia, and New Zealand among its staunchest defenders.

ESTONIA. Between 1689 and 1710, a German-language newspaper called the *Revalsche Post-Zeitung* was published in Estonia. But it was not until 1806 that the first Estonian-language newspaper, the *Tartomaa Näddala-Leht*, made its appearance. In 1821, Otto Wilhelm Maasing began the *Marahwa Näddala-Leht* as an instrument of national awakening. During the first half of the 19th century, however, newspapers were generally too short-lived to accomplish much in this regard. The *Perno Postimees* (later the *Tartu Postimees*), edited by Johann Vilhelm Jannsen from 1857 to 1905, was the first newspaper to gain a secure foothold in Estonia.

In the late 19th and early 20th century, the press expanded rapidly and became increasingly politicized; by the time of independence in 1914, all of the major newspapers were associated with particular political parties. Following the coup of 1934, many of these papers were closed. During the Soviet occupation in 1940–41 and again after the war, the press began to expand again, as collectives undertook to publish their own newspapers. At the same time, the number of Russian-language publications began to rise steadily. In the period immediately before and after regaining independence, a large number of new Estonian-language newspapers and journals were created, but many were forced to undergo economic consolidation after 1995.

ETHICS, CODES OF. In 1876, the Missouri Press Association, which had been founded nine years earlier to promote excellence in journalism, drafted a list of rules of conduct for its members. But the creation of professional codes of ethics by U.S. journalists did not begin in earnest until the 1920s, when lingering dissatisfaction with the press because of its wartime propaganda was accentuated by increased sensationalism, the emergence of press agents, and declining editorial independence. In an attempt to restore public trust in the press, a number of state and national associations of reporters and editors in the **United States** drew up codes of ethics, emphasizing truthfulness, public service, and the watchdog role of the press. In 1923, for example, the American Society of News Editors (ASNE) issued its *Canons of Ethics*. It was also influenced by complaints about the impact of **advertising** on news content dating back to the 1890s. However, these codes were entirely voluntary; they had no mechanism of enforcement and exerted little practical influence over journalistic practices. Later, following criticism of the media during the course of the Warner, Kerner, and Eisenhower Commissions between 1963 and 1970, a number of individual news organizations drafted their own codes of ethics with the intention of actual implementation. However, they later became worried that these codes would facilitate suits for libel and stopped publicizing their existence.

ETYMOLOGY. The word *journalism* has long been characterized by ambiguity. According to the *Oxford English Dictionary* (2nd ed., 1989), it was first used in **France** (*journalisme*) in 1781, but did not begin to gain currency in **Great Britain** until half a century later. Reviewing a French work entitled *Du Journalisme* in 1833, the *Westminster Review* allowed that "*journalism* is a good name for the thing meant," as "a word was sadly needed." An isolated instance of *journalisme* occurred as early as 1705 in the *Journal littéraire*. But H. Mattauch found that it was actually the French term *journaliste* that first became widespread. Though it appeared in Pierre Bayle's *Nouvelles de la république des lettres* (1684) "as a sort of slip of the pen," its common usage was mainly owing to a new group of editors at the *Journal des sçavans* after 1701 who used it to refer to those involved in the production of such learned periodicals.

In Britain, the gradual substitution of *journalist* for words like *mercurist* was complicated, as in France, by its application to diarists whose journal-keeping seems to have been undertaken in some cases with an eye to circulation. The *OED* quotes **Joseph Addison**'s comment in *Spectator* no. 323 in 1712 that "my following correspondent . . . is such a Journalist as I require. . . . Her Journal . . . is only the picture of a Life filled with a fashionable kind of Gaiety and Laziness." In *An American Dictionary of the English Language* (1828), Noah Webster gave only this now archaic meaning of journalist— "the writer of a journal or diary"—which was also still one of the meanings of *journaliste*. Long before then, however, the journalist had come to be identified primarily with the activity of earning a living by editing or writing for a regularly published journal. The *OED* cites Toland's observation in 1710 that the Tories had "one Lesley for their Journalist in London, who for Seven or Eight Years past did, three Times a Week, Publish Rebellion." As this reference implies, the activities of writing and publishing were not yet regarded as distinct occupations, a situation which would continue through the 18th century.

In France, the term *journalisme* was originally used to refer to a group of public journals, or those who produced them, in a particular time or place. By the 1830s, however, the term was rapidly coming to designate the *occupation* of writing for a public journal. A similar evolution occurred in England, as evidenced in the *Westminster Review*'s comment above. In both countries, the occupation of journalism was not limited at first to a particular range of journals because the activity of writing for periodical publications was not yet associated linguistically with a new *form* of writing. It was not until the latter 19th century that *journalism* acquired the additional meaning of a particular kind of discourse. Moreover, journalistic discourse was not initially "journalism," but rather *journalese*, which the *Pall Mall Gazette* distinguished from "plain English." (In French, the pejorative term was *journaleux*.) "It is sad," said the *Athenaeum* of one writer in 1893, "to find [him] guilty of such journalese as 'transpired.'" It was because of this connotation that Charles D. Johnson proposed in an article in *Social Forces* in 1928 that the new schools of journalism be renamed schools of "journalology," so as to capture the idea of there being a science of journalism. Not surprisingly, this awkward word never caught on, but efforts to make journalism a social science would increase in subsequent years.

In the contemporary world, the word *journalism* has come to encompass both the occupation (or profession) made up of journalists and the distinctive discourse that journalists learn to produce. As a result of this lexicographical evolution, the history of "journalism" has been pushed farther into the past—although it is the more recent meaning that points to the older history. Whereas the history of journalism as an *occupation* begins with its gradual differentiation from activities such as printing starting in the late 18th century, its history as a form of *discourse* distinct from ballads, chronicles, history, and the novel commenced at least two centuries earlier. Without the prior emergence of journalism as a new form of discourse, the occupation which the word *journalism* first designated would never have arisen.

EVERYBODY'S. U.S. magazine originally founded in 1899 as a house organ of John Wanamaker's department store. In 1903, it was sold to Erman Jesse Ridgway and became a leading journal of the **muckrakers**, publishing T. W. Lawson's series "Frenzied Finance" in 1904-05 and articles by Upton Sinclair, Ben Lindsey, **Lincoln Steffens**, and others. After 1910, it turned to popular fiction and general articles and was later absorbed by *Romance*. It died in 1928.

– F –

FARRER, EDWARD (1846/50?–1916). Polemical Canadian journalist. He emigrated from **Great Britain** to the **United States** and then in 1870 to **Canada** where he worked for John Ross Robertson's *Daily Telegraph* and later for the *Toronto Daily Mail*, a Conservative paper founded by Sir John A. Macdonald. In the mid-1880s, under Farrer's editorship, the paper broke from Macdonald's control and promoted a number of controversial causes, including anti-Catholicism and commercial union with the United States. In 1890, Farrer was hired by the Toronto *Globe* to promote the Liberal policy of unrestricted reciprocity. During the election of 1891, he was accused by Macdonald of having written a **pamphlet** instructing the Americans on how to pressure Canada into accepting political union. There is evidence that he may have accepted responsibility in order to deflect attention away from the "disloyalty" of others. Under pressure from Ontario premier Sir Oliver Mowat, he left the *Globe* but continued to work on behalf of annexation, including writing signed columns for the *New York Sun*.

FEDERAL BUREAU OF INVESTIGATION. Under J. Edgar Hoover, the Federal Bureau of Investigation (FBI) periodically used its powers to undermine freedom of the press in the **United States**. During **World War II**, it monitored journalists critical of government policy and, with the approval of the administration of Franklin Roosevelt, conducted a lengthy investigation of *Washington Times-Herald* gossip columnist, Inga Arvad. In the late 1940s and 1950s, it constructed a distorted portrait of **Edgar Snow** to discredit the prominent journalist in the *New York Times* and effectively end his journalistic career. Snow's *Red Star over China* (1937) was actually banned from U.S.-sponsored libraries abroad. In 1958, the bureau began an investigation of journalist Fred J. Cook after he had criticized Don Whitehead's sycophantic *The FBI Story* (1956) in an article in *The Nation*. It later used its counterintelligence program COINTELPRO to harass left-wing journalists. *See also* CENTRAL INTELLIGENCE AGENCY (CIA).

THE FEDERALIST. Two-volume work published in March–May 1788 supporting ratification of the proposed Constitution of the **United States**. Of the 83 essays comprising the text, 77 were also published in New York newspapers between 27 October 1787 and 2 April 1788. Signed by "Publius," the essays were written by Alexander Hamilton (59), James Madison (28), and John Jay (5).

FEUILLETON. A predecessor of the modern column. It is thought to have originated in Paris on 28 January 1800 when the editor of the *Journal des débats* happened to insert a *feuilleton* (extra sheet) into the edition as it went to press. As a freewheeling journalistic genre, the *feuilleton* consisted initially of diverse tidbits of news written in an entertaining manner, primarily for the upper echelons of society, and usually containing a theatrical review. In the mid-1820s, the genre was formally introduced to Russian readers by Faddej Bulgarin in the *Northern Bee*. The term for it initially retained its original French spelling, but was later Russianized as *fel'eton*. Early in his career, Fyodor Dostoevsky wrote a number of *feuilletons* entitled "Petersburg Chronicle." Alongside the French form, a number of Russian writers developed a more polemical variant through which to engage in social criticism. There was also an attempt to elevate the *feuilleton* to greater dignity as a literary form. The result was an ongoing tension between the *feuilleton* as a "publicistic" genre in which facts took precedence and the *feuilleton* as a "belletristic" genre featuring the use of literary devices. The belletristic approach was characteristic of the *feuilleton* in the German states, but this emphasis did not prevent it from being denounced by the authorities as subversive.

FICTIONAL RADIO-TV REPORTERS. The journalist has been depicted not only in fiction and films but also on radio and television. On early American radio in particular, there were numerous shows about reporters fighting against racketeers and criminals. In October 1937, for example, CBS began broadcasting *Big Town*, featuring the fictional crusading editor Steve Wilson of *The Illustrated Press*. Written and directed initially by the former journalist Jerry McGill, the program used Hollywood film stars like Edward G. Robinson and Gale Gordon to turn it into one of radio's top ten programs. In 1948, it switched to NBC where it continued for another four years. During **World War II**, Frank H. Phares created *Foreign Assignment* for Mutual; fictitious correspondent Brian Barry (played by Jay Jostyn) fought the Gestapo in occupied **France** with the help of his beautiful assistant Carol Manning (Vicki Vola).

Reporters were also the protagonists of justice on producer Bernard J. Proctor's radio series *The Big Story*, which NBC broadcast for eight years beginning in April 1947. Though originally intended to honor reporters ignored by **Pulitzer** committees, it focused on murders and other violent crimes no longer being investigated. At the end of the show, the real reporters were called on stage and given a $500 "Big Story Award" by the sponsor, Pall Mall cigarettes. The program was so popular that Bing Crosby had to move his *Philco Radio Time* show a half an hour earlier to avoid direct competition. Both *Big Town* and *The Big Story* were also seen on early television. But the most famous fictionalized reporter on TV was Clark Kent, a.k.a. Superman. Actors such as Mary Tyler Moore and Candice Bergen have also played reporters on television.

FINANCIAL JOURNALISM. *See* BUSINESS JOURNALISM.

FINLAND. Journalists were an integral part of Finland's long struggle for national revival and eventual independence. Initially, they were composed largely of patriotic young academics and literary figures whose major concern was revival of the Finnish language. In 1775, the first Finnish-language newssheet, *Suomenkieliset Tietosanomat* [News in the Finnish Language], appeared in Turku. But even after Finland was transferred from **Sweden** to **Russia** in 1809, most of its newspapers were still published in Swedish. It was not until 1847 that the first Finnish-language newspaper, *Suometar*, began publication in Helsinki. According to George Kurian, only six of Finland's 13 newspapers were Finnish in 1860. Most of these were quite small and none was published on a daily basis. Thereafter, however, the situation began to change rapidly, aided in part by the more tolerant rule of Tsar Alexander II. By 1890, 32 of Finland's 55 newspapers were published in Finnish, including a number of dailies. Most of these papers were tied to political parties and were increasingly staffed by permanent newsworkers rather than moonlighting academics.

In 1899, Nicholas II issued a manifesto threatening Finnish autonomy and appointed Nicholas Bobrikov as governor general. As part of his plan for the Russification of Finland, Bobrikov closed down or suspended the more nationalist newspapers, deported a large number of Finnish journalists, organized an official Russian-language newspaper, and instituted vigorous **censorship**. After his assassination in 1905, however, the Finnish press quickly revived. In 1916, a year before Finland took advantage of the turmoil in Russia to declare its independence, there were several hundred newspapers in operation, and 60 of their publishers joined the newly formed Newspaper Publishers Association. However, their commitment to freedom of the press became increasingly difficult to navigate in subsequent decades as Finland was drawn back into the **Soviet Union**'s sphere of influence. During **World War II**, newspapers were issued a steady stream of warnings by government officials about how to portray events. After the war, Finland was only able maintain a degree of independence by avoiding criticism of Soviet policies. As a result, self-censorship became an element of Finnish journalism. It was not until the breakup of the Soviet Union in 1989 that Finnish journalists were able to acquire the same degree of autonomy as their Scandinavian counterparts.

Finnish journalists currently work in an environment characterized by widespread literacy, technological modernity, relative economic security, and a high degree of press freedom. Beginning in 1966, the government developed a system of direct as well as indirect press subsidies, ostensibly to preserve press diversity. One indirect subsidy went to the postal service to maintain low rates for newspapers; another was given to news agencies to help cover telecommunication costs. Despite failure to get the approval of Parliament, the government also introduced two direct subsidies: one to assist newspapers with their transportation and delivery costs; the other to political parties for their publications in accordance with their percentage of seats in Parliament. Although the indirect subsidies were discontinued in the mid-1990s, the direct ones still remain, albeit at somewhat reduced levels. They do not, however, constitute a substantial threat to freedom of the press. Although the direct subsidies initially politicized news by enabling the major parties to run their own news agencies, the recent trend is toward the rise and use of independent news agencies.

FIRST, RUTH (1925–1982). White activist, scholar, and journalist who campaigned against the apartheid regime in **South Africa**. Her parents, who came to Johannesburg from Latvia, helped to found the South African Communist Party, which she joined. After being interned for 117 days during a government crackdown in 1962, she went into exile in London and worked as a freelance writer. She later taught at various universities, including the Universidade Eduardo Mondlane in Mozambique. She continued to write against both capitalism and apartheid until she was assassinated by a parcel bomb sent to her in Mozambique. Her story was told in the 1988 film *A World Apart*, based on a screenplay by her daughter Shawn Slovo.

FLOWER, BENJAMIN ORANGE (1858–1918). American editor of various reform-minded magazines such as the *Arena* from 1886 to 1911. Historian Arthur M. Schlesinger credited him with preparing the way for the **muckrakers**. Attributing many of the country's social ills to its laissez-faire economy, he called for better education, child labor reform, women's rights, improved housing, and public works programs. Believing that "no evil can withstand the enlightened and aroused conscience of a nation" (*Arena* from March 1894), he praised the realism of Upton Sinclair, **David Graham Phillips**, and other muckraking novelists.

FRANCE. Until the French Revolution, the only sanctioned news sources in France were the *Gazette de France* (1631) and, much later, the daily *Journal de Paris* (1777). However, 17th- and 18th-century Parisians could also obtain news through *nouvellistes de bouche*, who sang their reports to illiterate passers-by; *nouvellistes à la main*, who distributed handwritten newssheets to those who could read; and foreign-produced newspapers such as *Gazette de Leyde*. During the *ancien régime*, a Republic of Letters also emerged with the publication of journals such as Denis de Sallo's ***Journal des sçavans*** (1664), which contained scientific news, and Donneau de Visé's *Mercure galante* (1672), which related literary news. Even on the eve of the Revolution, however, there were only about 20 journals produced by about 100 journalists in all of France.

Following the assembly of the Estates General in 1789, dozens of new political journals such as *Le Père Duchesne* sprang up. But as the Revolution proceeded, the press was subjected to even stricter controls than during the *ancien régime*. Article 11 of the Declaration of the Rights of Man and Citizen offered a guarantee of freedom of expression, but was not realized in practice. In January 1800, Napoleon closed down 60 of Paris's 73 newspapers; established the *Moniteur universel* as his official newspaper; and wrote anonymous articles himself for publication. It was not until 1819 that **censorship** was sufficiently relaxed for liberal journals such as the *Constitution* and *Minerve* to emerge.

Even during the Restoration (1814–30), however, the government sought to control the press through **stamp taxes** and a system of "caution" money which required owners to deposit surety for fines that might later be incurred. It also launched numerous vexatious prosecutions for minor infringements of regulations, resulting in heavy fines and even imprisonment. These measures were generally more effective in the provinces than in Paris, where most of the national newspapers survived. In some cases, however, they did so only by resorting to **venality**, or the acceptance of financial payments in return for favorable coverage of issues such as slavery in France's colonies.

During the July Monarchy (1830–48), controls over the press became even harsher. But at the same time, increased literacy also fueled a growing demand for news and led to the creation of new services and products. In 1835, the Parisian translator and **advertising** agent Charles-Louis Havas (1783–1858) created the **Havas** news agency, the world's first such organization. Havas began by offering the French press translations of news from European papers. With the aid of railway development, it gradually monopolized the sale of news and advertising to the provinces. Part of its success lay in its willingness to allow subscribers to pay in advertising space as well as cash. Over a century later, it was transformed into **Agence France-presse**, the leading news agency in France today.

Havas initially restricted itself to government-sanctioned information of little interest to most Parisians. To exploit the expanding Parisian market for other forms of news, novelist Émile de Girardin (1802–1881) founded and began editing *La Presse* in 1836. The first low-priced newspaper in France, *La Presse* provided popular news items and serialized novels for its readers, but also reflected Girardin's passion for social reform. Its operation remained exceptional, however; there were still too few readers and too little advertising for a popular press to emerge. In 1846, the total circulation of all Parisian dailies was still less than 200,000 and most newspapers depended on their connections to political parties or factions to survive.

It was not until the last third of the 19th century that the newspaper gradually became a mass medium in France. The process began with Polydore Milhaud's creation of *Le Petit journal* (1863–1944). By confining itself to sensationalized news, it was able to avoid the tax on political papers and sell for a third of the price of its competitors. By the late 1860s, it had several hundred thousand readers and began spawning a few competitors such as *Le Petit parisien* (1876–1944), which aimed at the "little man," but also attracted lower middle- and middle-class readers through its serialized novels and fashion and financial news. The initial success of these more popular papers was furthered by a new press law in 1881, which reduced the heavy bureaucratic requirements for establishing and maintaining a newspaper and drastically cut the system of press violations.

But the full transformation of *Le Petit Journal* and *Le Petit Parisien* into mass-circulation papers only occurred after the invasion of the American New Journalism of **Joseph Pulitzer** in the form of *Le Matin* (1884–1944). Launched by a team of American journalists, *Le Matin* greatly extended the popular devices used to build a mass audience and inspired *Le Petit journal*, *Le Petit parisien*, and later *Le Journal* (1892–1944) to do the same. On 18 October 1903, for example, *Le Petit parisien* introduced its first contest, offering 250,000 francs in prizes for guessing the number of grains of wheat in an illustrated and measured bottle. By then it had over a million readers, climbing to 1.4 million by 1914.

On the eve of **World War I**, the four main mass-circulation newspapers—*Le Petit journal*, *Le Petit parisien*, *Le Matin*, and *Le Journal*—were selling 4.5 million copies a day or 75 percent of daily newspaper sales in Paris and 40 percent of daily sales in France. Even then, however, their advertising revenues were still quite low. *Le Petit parisien*, the most commercial of the four, derived less than 15 percent of its income from advertising. Lacking even this modest revenue stream, the political papers remained thoroughly dependent on subsidies from their own parties or factions as well as additional government bribes. This continuing system of venality extended to payments from a host of foreign governments, including Russia which used them to silence coverage about its inability to ever provide a return on French investments.

Whatever its faults, the pre-World War I French press attracted readers in high numbers. On a per capita basis, the circulation of daily newspapers among adults was at or near the top in continental Europe. Since then, however, daily newspaper readership levels have declined fairly steadily and France now lags behind many other European countries. It also has fallen behind English-speaking countries such as the **United States** and **Canada** where a similar trend has been occurring. A complex set of factors has contributed to this situation. Collaboration with the enemy in wartime led to a loss of credibility for some publications; financial pressures during the interwar years forced many papers to cut costs and reduce quality; distribution costs have remained particularly high compared to other European countries; the concentration of newspaper ownership, which went largely unregulated until the mid-1980s, has contributed to reduced diversity; the frequent use of the press by politicians to advance their own careers has at times alienated readers; and strikes such as the one at the *Parisien libéré* in 1975–77, one of the longest in French labor history, have taken their toll. After **World War II**, the government began creating a complex system of press subsidies to stabilize the press. But the price of quality newspapers such as *Le Monde* has remained very high in comparison with their counterparts in other European countries.

The state of French journalism training and recent employment practices have also been factors. Although the first journalism school in Europe was created at the Catholic University of Lille in 1924, further programs were not established until after World War II and journalism education did not become a priority until the 1960s. Even then, most journalists did not partake of it. Less than one-third of French journalists currently have formal journalism **education**. Many of those who do not have a professional degree work as *pigistes*, a remuneration category between regular wage-earning on a monthly basis and various freelance arrangements. Traditionally, there has been a high rate of turnover among French journalists. The *pigistes*, who are essentially "piece-rate" workers paid by the article, have aggravated this trend. Between 1995 and 2005, their number doubled to almost 20 percent of card-carrying journalists. About two-thirds of them work for the press, generally for lower pay, and their positions are more vulnerable than those of titular wage earners. They are also less likely to regard themselves as professional journalists, especially in a culture where journalists still see themselves more as moralists and intellectuals than as objective reporters. *See also* FRONDEUR JOURNALISM.

FRANK LESLIE'S POPULAR MONTHLY. Magazine founded in the **United States** by Frank Leslie in 1876. It was part of a stable of Leslie magazines in which artwork was a central part of the content. By the time of his death in 1880, Leslie's magazine empire was close to ruin, but was subsequently revived by his widow, Miriam Folline Squier Leslie. In 1904, the magazine passed out of the family's hands, but continued as *Leslie's Monthly Magazine* until 1906 when it was sold and became *The American Magazine*.

FRANKLIN, BENJAMIN (1706–1790). American statesman, diplomat, and scientist who is generally considered to be the "father of American journalism," though his tombstone epitaph, in line with the terminology of the time, began "The body of Benjamin Franklin, Printer . . ." He was one of the first journalists to espouse not only freedom of the press but the principle of balanced news and editorial coverage, arguing in his "Apology for Printers" (1731) that editors should cover both sides of a controversy.

Born in Boston, the tenth and youngest son in a family with 17 children, Franklin began an apprenticeship at the age of 12 in the printshop of his half-brother James, where he was able to indulge his love of reading. After discovering a volume of the *Spectator*, he used it, like the young Voltaire, as a model for his own writing style. His talent for satire was first displayed in his series of "Silence Dogood" letters in the influential *New-England Courant*, which his brother established in 1721 and he took over during the inoculation crisis the following year. After a quarrel with his brother in 1723, he ran away to Philadelphia, worked briefly for printer Samuel Keimer, and then left for England in 1724 in the hope of buying his own **printing press.** Unsuccessful in this endeavor, he returned to Keimer's printshop in 1726 and began saving for his own publication. In the meantime, he formed a discussion group called the Junto, which led to the creation of America's first subscription library in 1727. In 1728, Franklin left Keimer to go into a magazine venture with printer Hugh Meredith. Following his departure, Keimer established the weekly *Universal Instructor in All Arts and Sciences, and Pennsylvania Gazette*, but in 1729 agreed to sell it to Franklin, who promptly shortened its title to the *Pennsylvania Gazette*.

Under Franklin's editorship until 1747, the *Gazette* became the liveliest and most prosperous newspaper in the colonies, publishing his early Busy Body papers and introducing such features as weather reports into American journalism. A good editor, he wrote, "ought to be qualified with an extensive Acquaintance with Languages, a great Easiness and Command of Writing and Relating Things clearly and intelligibly, and in a few Words; he should be able to speak of War both by Land and Sea; be well acquainted with Geography, with the History of the Time, with several interests of Princes and States, the

Secrets of Courts, and the Manners and Customs of all Nations." Not surprisingly, he found that "men thus accomplish'd are very rare in this remote Part of the World."

In 1732, Franklin founded both the *Phildelphia Zeitung*, the first foreign-language newspaper in the colonies, and *Poor Richard's Almanack*; while the former failed after a few issues, the latter continued until 1758, selling as many as 10,000 copies annually. He also began the *General Magazine* (1741), one of the first magazines in the colonies. In 1758, he and William Hunter were appointed deputy postmasters general for the colonies. They discontinued the practice of free newspaper delivery to subscribers, but allowed publishers to exchange newspapers by post free of charge. Franklin's career up to this point became the subject of his *Autobiography*, written between 1771 and 1789 but not published in the **United States** until 1794. Tracing his rapid rise from obscurity to eminence, it contributed to the American myth of the self-made man. Franklin helped to draft the Declaration of Independence and was an influential member of the Constitutional Convention.

FRONDEUR JOURNALISM. Term used by Nina Gelbart to designate the political criticism that emerged in state-sanctioned journals in **France** after the accession of Louis XVI in 1774. During the last years of Louis XV's reign, Chancellor Maupeou had not only exiled the *parlements* (law courts) for their bold use of the right of remonstrance against the crown but had cracked down on writers and journalists. Recently created newspapers were eliminated and the royalist **censor** Marin was placed in charge of the *Gazette de France*, reducing the opposition press to **newsletters** and **pamphlets** once again. With Maupeou's dismissal, hopes were raised for greater journalistic freedom and a number of new journals were launched. In 1775, a group of frustrated dramatists-cum-editors, whose works had been rejected by the Comédie-Française, banded together to attack its privileged, exclusive position through a network of about 10 mutually supportive journals, including the *Journal du théâtre*, *Journal des dames*, and *Lettres sur les spectacles*. In addition to supporting the *parlements*, they soon expanded their critique to include other absolutist institutions such as the Académie française and the state-protected *Gazette de France* and *Mercure de France*. They believed the stage, the press, and the law should inform the public irrespective of social rank.

FULLER, MARGARET (1810–1850). Feminist writer and literary editor of the *New York Tribune*. Born in Cambridgeport, Massachusetts, Fuller was a child prodigy in languages and literature and a friend of Ralph Waldo Emerson. Through him, she became involved in Transcendentalism and edited its quarterly magazine, *The Dial*, from July 1840 until July 1842, when Emerson took over. She joined the *Tribune* in 1844 and wrote critical articles on equality for women, the treatment of African Americans, the prison system, Irish immigrants, and poverty. Following the publication of *Woman in the Nineteenth Century* (1845), she left for Europe as *Tribune* correspondent, had a son in **Italy** by revolutionist Giovanni Angelo, whom she later married, and supported Giuseppe Mazzini during the Revolution of 1848. On the voyage home, she and her new family drowned in a wreck off Fire Island near New York City. The body of her child was the only one recovered and her manuscript on the Roman revolution was lost.

– **G** –

GARRISON, WILLIAM LLOYD (1805–1879). Militant anti-slavery editor. Garrison first began attacking slavery in his early twenties as manager and editor of a series of journals, landing in a Baltimore jail for seven weeks after being convicted of libel. On 1 January 1831, he launched his *Liberator*, initially a small, weekly publication printed on a hand-press with borrowed type. Rejecting the gradualist approach of earlier abolitionist editors, Garrison so angered Southerners that the State of Georgia offered a $5,000 reward for his arrest and conviction. In 1833, he helped to organize the American Anti-Slavery Society, which then founded the *Emancipator* as its official organ. When Garrison's opponents left the Society in 1840, they took the abolitionist paper with them. In addition to the *Liberator*, which he continued until the Thirteenth Amendment ended slavery in 1865, Garrison also founded the *National Anti-Slavery Standard*, edited first by novelist Lydia Maria Child and later by Maria Weston Chapman of the Boston Female Antislavery Society. In later life, Garrison turned his attention to other reform causes, including women's suffrage and the treatment of native peoples.

GARVEY, MARCUS (1887–1940). Political activist and publisher who promoted black nationalism among the peoples of the African diaspora and influenced African leaders such as Kwame Nkrumah. After being expelled from his native Jamaica for his role in the printers' strike of 1907, he published newspapers in Costa Rica and Panama and worked for *The African Times and Orient Review* in London. In 1916, he settled in New York City where he advocated black self-reliance through the Universal Negro Improvement Association (UNIA) and publications such as *Negro World*. Pursued by J. Edgar Hoover and the **Federal Bureau of Investigation (FBI)**, he was convicted of mail fraud in 1922 and eventually deported to Jamaica. In addition to furthering Jamaican independence, he continued his campaign to uplift blacks worldwide through *The Black Man*, an international newspaper published in London.

GENTLEMAN'S MAGAZINE. The first national magazine in **Great Britain**. It was founded as a monthly by printer-journalist Edward Cave in 1731 and was run by him until his death in 1754. It began as a digest of material from other periodicals and, according to Samuel Johnson's famous *Dictionary*, was the first publication to be called a *magazine*, meaning storehouse. However, it later focused on publishing original content supplied by its readers, including, for a time, Johnson himself. During the 18th century, it was the most successful publication of its kind, reaching a circulation of 15,000 copies a month by the mid-1740s. Cave signed himself "Sylvanus Urban" to attract middle-class readers in both London and the countryside. Through ingenious packaging, he managed to circumvent the 1712 tax on advertisements and also likely used his position in the post office to drain **advertising** revenues away from his competitors. The magazine continued publication until 1914.

GERMANY. During the late 18th century, the German-speaking territories of Europe underwent the first of a series of "reading revolutions" that included rapid growth in newspapers and journals. This expansion created new opportunities for journalists, who increasingly saw themselves as contributing to the good of society. For Karl Philipp Moritz, editor of the *Vossische Zeitung* in the 1780s, the ideal newspaper provided both enlightenment and leadership for society. At that time, however, few journalists would have agreed with Ludwig Schlözer, editor of *Stats-Anzeigen*, that journalism is society's best protector against despotism. As James Retalleck has argued, journalists like **Johann Cotta** did not see any need to limit the state's power or facilitate public participation in politics. For conservatives, indeed, the danger of newspapers was that they gave people the false impression that they were sufficiently informed to hold a valid opinion about current affairs.

Throughout the 19th century, this negative assessment of journalism was encouraged by the political elite. Retalleck relates how King Friedrich Wilhelm IV of Prussia expressed concern lest journalism "be placed in a position of equal dignity" with science and literature, while Chancellor Otto von Bismarck dismissed journalism as a dumping ground for those unable to find a calling in life. Both regarded journalism as a potentially subversive political force. This kind of attitude delayed the development of German journalism as a profession and hindered attempts by German journalists to improve their low socioeconomic status. Despite their high level of education, most 19th-century German journalists were too poorly paid to survive on their writing alone, but had to work as librarians, postmasters, or printers as well. Their lower middle-class status was reflected in the working arrangements at larger newspapers such as Cotta's *Augsburger Allgemeine Zeitung*, where they labored in close physical proximity to the technical staff and even lived with them in the building where production took place.

Fearing the potential power of the press over public opinion, 19th-century German governments continued to limit its freedom. The Press Law of 1874, for example, restricted it to the printing of "established facts." As a result, most newspapers still concentrated on literature, art, music, theater, religion, science, and fashion rather than hard political news or public affairs. While Article 118 of the constitution of the Weimar Republic gave every German "the right to express his opinion freely," it did so only "within the bounds of the general laws," and laws reducing free expression soon became extensive. These laws hindered newspapers supporting Germany's experiment with democracy without preventing the attacks of its enemies. Alfred Hugenberg, who owned the powerful press agency Telegraph Union (TU) along with several other wire services, a massive group of newspapers, and a major advertising agency, used his control over much of the news received by Germans to lead the way in undermining public support for the Republic. Although a few journalists such as **Carl von Ossietzky** sought to engage in critical investigative reporting, the traditional emphasis on culture and education also undermined the capacity of German journalism to prevent the rise of Hitler or resist the brutality of the Nazis after they came to power on 30 January 1933.

Almost overnight, the Nazis turned the press into a near monopoly of the party. Except for the *Berliner Tageblatt* and *Frankfurter Zeitung*, virtually all opposition and Jewish-owned newspapers were immediately suppressed and expropriated. Other publications, such as the *Vossische Zeitung* which dated back to 1703, were forced to sell out to Eher Verlag, the Munich publishing house owned by Max Amann which had issued *Mein Kampf.* Eher Verlag became in effect a lucrative Nazi newspaper trust, eventually cornering four-fifths of German circulation. At the same time, all newspapers were placed under a Press Division within Joseph Goebbels's Ministry for Public Enlightenment and Propaganda and subjected to tight **censorship** along with radio, film, and most other cultural institutions. In addition, the party acquired the *Völkischer Beobachter*, a morning newspaper in Munich, and turned it into an official paper. It was edited by the National Socialist philosopher Alfred Rosenberg and distributed throughout the country in various editions; at its peak, it had a circulation of about 1.2 million.

Under the Reich Press Law of 4 October 1933, all reporters and editors were required to pass tests of German citizenship and prove they were not Jewish or married to Jews. At a news conference each morning, Goebbels gave precise directives to the editors of Berlin's dailies and correspondents from other cities on what to feature in the day's news; similar instructions were sent to Germany's smaller newspapers. All journalists were expected to praise Hitler and follow the National Socialist line. Even sports journalists had to submit to the directives of the Ministry of Propaganda. Not content to leave direct propaganda to the *Völkischer Beobachter*, the official party organ, Goebbels also founded his own newspaper, *Der Angriff*, in which he reserved the right-hand column of the front page for a personal diatribe signed "Dr. G." An afternoon paper in Berlin, its title (meaning "the assault") and subtitle—*For the Oppressed against the Oppressors*—were themselves regarded by Goebbels as effective propaganda.

For a brief period, an attempt was made to court foreign correspondents by assigning them luxurious quarters and entertaining them lavishly. When this approach did not work to the degree desired, it was replaced by various forms of intimidation, including the expulsion of journalists like **Norman Ebbut**. Controls soon reached the point where correspondents could not verify unofficial information without risking the lives of their sources.

After the war, censorship was abolished and the **United States** and **Great Britain** sent reporters to Germany to prepare a new generation of objective, democratically inspired journalists. This assistance helped the West German media to recover more quickly than their East German counterpart and contributed to their later dominance in Germany. As newspapers revived, they maintained much looser ties with re-emerging political parties and established a system in which the most influential papers—currently *Frankfurter Allgemeine Zeitung*, *Die Zeit*, and *Süddeutsche Zeitung*—are no longer owned by, or even official mouthpieces for, political parties. Through its connections with the Munich Journalism School and the Hamburg Journalism School, *Süddeutsche Zeitung* has also been instrumental in improving the quality of journalism **education** in Germany. While Germany's traditional emphasis on erudite journalism has continued, more sensational news genres have also appeared. The most popular newspaper in Germany is currently the **tabloid** *Bild Zeitung*, which is also the fifth largest newspaper in the world. *See also* BENJAMIN, WALTER.

GIWA, OLADELE (1947–1986). Nigerian journalist. Despite their extreme poverty, his parents managed to send him to Oduduwa College in Ife in 1964, where he first acquired his love of journalism and became one of the editors of the school paper. After graduation, he was able to land a job as a news assistant at the Nigerian Broadcasting Corporation, Ibadan. In 1971, he began studying English at Brooklyn

College, and after graduation worked briefly at the *New York Times*. After returning to Nigeria, he worked first for the *Daily Times*, writing two popular columns ("Parallax View" and "Press Snaps"), then as a founding editor for the *Sunday Concord*, and finally at *Newswatch*, a magazine dedicated to **investigative journalism** which he helped to establish in 1985. He first came into conflict with the security authorities in 1982 for publishing a government White Paper before its official release. After the Lagos High Court ruled that he had been illegally detained, he received damages and a public apology from the chief of police. On 19 October 1986, he was killed in his home in Lagos by a letter bomb in the midst of his investigation of the country's security agencies.

GLAVLIT. Semi-official abbreviation for the **Soviet Union**'s main instrument for **censorship** and the protection of "state secrets." Created in 1922, its real function was to prevent the publication of any information that might undermine the goal of creating a totalitarian society. It eventually encompassed not only all printed materials, including newspapers, but also radio and television. Its early directives prohibited the publication of statistics about unemployment, homelessness, suicide, and crime; information about crop failures, natural disasters, industrial accidents, and any form of civil unrest; and reports on things like sanitary conditions in prisons and internment camps, the availability of medications, the exportation of grain, and the movements of government officials. Much like George Orwell's fictional Ministry of Truth, Glavlit also engaged in the canonization of Joseph Stalin and the concomitant degradation and eventual erasure from memory of his political opponents. At the same time that it prohibited any criticism of its own operations, it placed local censors in the difficult position of having to reconcile its numerous proscriptions with the desire of Communist Party executives to demonstrate economic progress in their respective areas. Its apparatus grew steadily over ensuing decades, reaching 70,000 censors in the late 1980s.

GODKIN, EDWARD L. (1831–1902). Founding editor of *The Nation* (1865) and spokesman for the Mugwumps in Gilded Age America. Born in **Ireland**, Godkin studied law briefly but then turned to journalism and covered the Crimean War (1854–56) for the *London Daily News*. In 1856, he emigrated to New York and continued his work as a correspondent during the Civil War. After the war, he helped create *The Nation*, became its first editor, and established its reputation for lively and independent political opinion. In 1881, he sold the financially troubled magazine to the *New York Evening Post*, but continued as editor until 1889. In 1883, he also became editor-in-chief of the *Evening Post*, succeeding Carl Shurz. An admirer of English aristocratic ideals, Godkin believed that America lacked a genteel tradition and stability. In the Mugwump tradition, he favored moral persuasion as an instrument of reform. Editorially, he supported free trade, honest government, and a number of liberal reforms. But he also opposed many American reform movements and held low opinions of native Americans, African Americans, Irish Catholics, and immigrants who were not Anglo-Saxons. He favored Chinese exclusion, radical Reconstruction, and civil service reform through which to place a minority of well-educated men in government jobs.

GOLDSMITH, OLIVER (1730?–1774). Irish-born author and journalist. After studies in Dublin, Edinburgh, and Leiden, he tried his hand at various professions before finding his métier as a miscellaneous writer for his landlord's *Monthly Review* in London. In 1759, he began his own publication, a weekly essay paper called *The Bee*, and completed his critical *Enquiry into the Present State of Polite Learning in Europe*. He also contributed to other periodicals, including a series of "Chinese Letters" on London customs for the *Public Ledger* in 1760–61, before switching from journalism to biography, history, poetry, and the writing of popular novels such as *The Vicar of Wakefield* (1766).

GRADY, HENRY W. (1850–1889). A leading Southern editor during the reconstruction era in the **United States**. After studies at the Universities of Georgia and Virginia, he worked as a reporter in Rome, Georgia. In 1872, he became editor and one-third owner of the newly founded *Atlanta Herald*, but it eventually fell victim to the financial depression of 1873. From 1877 to 1880, he worked as a freelance correspondent for the *Atlanta Constitution* and various other papers in both the North and the South, acquiring a national reputation for his political coverage and use of interviews. In 1880, he bought a quarter interest in, and became managing editor of, the *Constitution*. He aggressively expanded its readership by broadening its news coverage, while continuing to report major stories and write editorials himself. His famous speech on "The New South," delivered in December 1886, helped to improve relations between the North and South.

GREAT AWAKENING. An example of how new media, in this case weekly newspapers, can give rise to textual events—events which exist in people's minds more by virtue of their being reported on than because of their actual impact. The term Great Awakening was not used until the mid-19th century, but the phenomenon in question is not simply a historian's construction. In the late 1730s and early 1740s, a substantial Anglo-American community believed they were participating in, or at least witnessing, a "remarkable Revival of Religion." The process by which this belief arose began in 1733 when a substantial number of sinners apparently found salvation in the small town of Northampton, Massachusetts, about 100 miles from Boston. Religious revivals of this sort had occurred previously in Northampton and other colonial towns. But instead of remaining a small and isolated event, the alleged awakening stimulated other local revivals, which were then taken as evidence of an intercolonial and later a transatlantic awakening.

The critical first step occurred when Jonathan Edwards, the pastor of Northampton, produced *A Faithful Narrative* in which he interpreted the spiritual redemption of hundreds of Northampton inhabitants (over a two-year period) as "an extraordinary Work of God." Published in 1737 by John Guyse and Isaac Watts in London, Edwards's narrative became a model for other accounts that quickly followed. Accelerating this process was the preaching tour of the young English evangelist George Whitefield, beginning in October 1739. Whitefield attracted crowds estimated at 20,000 to his sermons in Boston and Philadelphia and received extensive press coverage. By the early 1740s, revivalists were reporting awakenings in scores of communities. But it was the minister and publisher Thomas Prince of Boston who first linked these local accounts into a single intercolonial revival. In 1743, Prince began publishing the various narratives modeled on Edwards's narrative in a new journal called *Christian History*. It led to other revival magazines and later began reprinting narratives published in **Great Britain**, thereby helping to create the idea of a transatlantic revival. Almost as quickly, however, the "event" came to an end. By the mid-1750s, the Great Awakening was over, in part because anti-revivalists such as Charles Chauncy in Boston began to argue that a few scattered and highly publicized revivals did not add up to a single grand movement.

GREAT BRITAIN. The origins of British journalism can be traced back to the 16th century when, in response to growing demand for news, publishers produced increasing numbers of small printed **pamphlets** dealing with local as well as foreign affairs. At the same time, however, the Crown steadily augmented its controls over the press. Under Elizabeth I, state **censorship** removed all criticism of the queen from pamphlets and diluted their content generally. In 1621, James I took steps to ban the importation of Dutch **corantos** as well as the production of English imitations, but relented at the last minute by giving a monopoly to Nicholas Bourne and Nathaniel Butter on the condition that they restrict themselves to foreign news. Under Charles I, even this form of news production was suppressed with the help of the Star Chamber and Court of the High Commission.

During the initial phase of the English civil war (1642–51), both the royalist and parliamentary camps made use of weekly newsbooks to appeal to public opinion, financing them in part through the use of **advertising**. These newsbooks included verses written by sympathetic poets in support of each side's perspective. After the execution of Charles I, however, the Commonwealth created a monopoly over news once again. The first English newspaper, the *London Gazette* (1665), also began with a news monopoly. Though an organ of the state, it accompanied official news and announcements with a degree of public commentary on government edicts.

Until the final expiry of the Licensing Act in 1695, independent newspapers turned to advertising not only for additional revenue but as a means of camouflaging news and opinions. This practice of including commentary within the body of paid advertisements helped to establish advertising as an integral part of the English newspaper. Despite government attempts to limit its growth through duties and taxes, advertising increased steadily during the 18th century and contributed to the expansion of the British press. In populations with low literacy and economic stagnation, advertising does not necessarily operate as a spur to newspaper growth. But by the late 18th century, advertising had entered into a symbiotic relationship with circulation by providing the resources through which newspapers could attract the readers desired by advertisers through the diversification of content. In addition to better information about trade and commerce, newspapers gradually included more news about the daily life of 18th-century society, with its cockfights, public executions, sideshows, professional theater, and balloon flights. At the same time, however, coverage continued to favor elite power structures. The treatment of **crime**, for example, contributed to **moral panics** and harsher prosecution and sentencing practices.

The end of economic controls over the press in the mid-19th century was followed initially by increased manipulation of the press by politicians. Lord Palmerston was particularly effective in seducing favorable coverage from newspaper editors on his way to becoming prime minister in 1855. At the same time, however, the mainstream press began to undergo a steady process of popularization. Even before **William T. Stead** launched the New Journalism in the 1880s, provincial papers tried to attract more readers through syndicated serial fiction.

During the early 20th century, the British press underwent the "Northcliffe Revolution" as London-based papers such as the *Daily Mail* and the *Daily Express* used larger headlines, more photographs, and various features to attract lower middle-class and working-class readers throughout the country. The press became divided between nationally circulated "quality" or "prestige" broadsheets and mass-market **tabloids**. Before **World War II**, the tabloids not only contained political coverage, albeit of a sensationalist nature, but were used by owners such as **Lord Northcliffe** and **Lord Beaverbrook** to pursue and exercise political influence. Many of their editors and journalists also used their newspaper careers as a springboard into politics or received honors in return for political support. After the war, however, the gap increased between the "newspapers of opinion" and the tabloids, which relied more and more on accidents, crime, and bizarre occurrences to attract readers. Tabloidization became increasingly a matter of de-politicization. At the same time, the "quality" press, which provided a fairly balanced representation of British political opinion, began to come under the increasing control of large conglomerate corporations. The main force counterbalancing these trends has been a growing professional consciousness among British journalists through education, **codes of ethics**, and various occupational organizations. *See also* ADDISON, JOSEPH; DEFOE, DANIEL; EMPIRE PRESS UNION; *GENTLEMAN'S MAGAZINE*; HALL, JOSEPH; *REVIEW*; *SPECTATOR*; STEELE, RICHARD; *TATLER*; *THE TIMES*.

GREELEY, HORACE (1811–1872). Newspaper editor and founder of the *New York Tribune*. Born in Amherst, New Hampshire, Greeley worked briefly as a compositor and job printer in New York City before he and another partner founded the *New Yorker* (1834), a weekly journal devoted to the arts and literature. To supplement its meager profits, Greeley also wrote on politics for the *Daily Whig* and edited Whig campaign sheets. These endeavors brought him into contact with New York Whig leaders, who encouraged him to found the *New York Tribune* on 10 April 1841. Less sensational than other **penny papers** of its day, the *Tribune* exerted a profound influence on American politics over the next 30 years. Greeley's vigorous editorials supported not only Whig causes such as protective tariffs but Fourierism, the organization of labor, a homestead law, women's rights, and, above all, antislavery. In 1856, he helped to organize the new Republican Party, but had mixed success in navigating intraparty politics and the difficult issues involved in mending the Union. In 1872, his unsuccessful attempt to run for the presidency as a Liberal Republican, together with the death of his wife shortly after his defeat, led to a mental breakdown and his own death not long thereafter.

GRUB STREET. Originally a real street, located in the Moorfields area of London, where criminals, prostitutes, and other forms of lowlife congregated. By the mid-18th century, according to Samuel Johnson's dictionary, it was also inhabited by struggling writers such as himself. By then it had become a derisory term for hack writers, especially journalists, and a metaphor for bad writing generally.

– H –

HALL, JOSEPH (1574–1656). English bishop and early news critic. In *Mundus Alter et Idem* (1605), he poked fun at the news publication *Mercurius Gallobelgicus* (1594–1635), a digest of military and diplomatic news which was published twice a year by Michael ap Isselt in Cologne and circulated widely in England. Although the term *Mercurius* (the common term for journalist or reporter at the time) was meant to let its author off the hook for its contents (he was a mere "messenger"), the digest was chided for its unreliability by both John Donne and Bishop Hall. "Mercurius Britannicus," whom Hall has relate a fantastic journey through various lands of vice, begins his voyage in the company of "Gallus" and "Belgicus." After they give up and return home, Britannicus is left to make up his own lies like an efficient "Mercurius." Hall's work is thus an early satire on both travel and the lies that journalists tell. *See also* GREAT BRITAIN; JONSON, BEN.

HARPER'S MAGAZINE. American magazine founded in 1850 as *Harper's Monthly Magazine*. Under editor Henry Mills Alden, it added political and social journalism to its initial literary emphasis. In 1901, it was purchased and edited by George Harvey, a former journalist who had made a fortune in railway building. It became *Harper's Magazine* in 1925.

HARRIS, BENJAMIN (1673–1716). English bookseller and editor. During the brief lapse of licensing in 1679, Harris published the biweekly *Domestick Intelligence* in London, but was imprisoned regardless for his vehement anti-Catholicism. With the act's revival, he left for Boston and on 25 September 1690 published one issue of a three-page newssheet on the Nine Years War (1689–97) entitled *Publick Occurrences, Both Foreign and Domestick*. Modeled on the **London Gazette**, it was immediately suppressed by the governor and his council for criticizing the government's conduct of the war with **France**. Harris wanted to give his readers a "Faithful Relation" of events so as to bring about the "Curing, or at least the Charming of that Spirit of Lying, which prevails amongst us." To this end he proposed relying on reports from credible citizens and printing the names of those who circulated false rumors. After the final lapse of the Printing Act in 1695, Harris returned to London to publish the short-lived *Intelligence, Domestic and Foreign*. In 1699, following another stint in jail for publishing false news, he successfully established the *London Post*.

HAVAS. See AGENCE FRANCE-PRESSE; FRANCE.

HEARST, WILLIAM RANDOLPH (1863–1951). Controversial American press baron. His father, George Hearst, was a mining magnate, U.S. senator, and owner of the *Examiner* in San Francisco, where the younger Hearst was born. After returning from Harvard in 1887, he persuaded his father to hand him the reins of the *Examiner* and experimented with various pictorial and typographical devices to increase its appeal. In 1895, he purchased the *New York Morning Journal* and began an uncompromising and ultimately successful circulation battle with **Joseph Pulitzer**'s *New York World*. He increased the size of the *Journal*, cut its price to a penny, and lured reporters from other papers with higher salaries. His use of what became known as **yellow journalism** included whipping up popular support for a war with Spain over Cuba in 1898, but he also championed unpopular causes when he believed in them. He eventually created an immense media empire that included motion picture and radio companies as well as 18 newspapers and 9 magazines. Though he managed to get elected to the House of Representatives in 1903, he ran unsuccessfully for mayor of New York City and for governor of New York and was also denied the Democratic Party's presidential nomination. Although his papers initially supported progressive legislation, he later became politically conservative and strongly opposed the New Deal.

HEMINGWAY, ERNEST (1899–1961). One of America's greatest novelists and short-story writers, Hemingway was also sporadically a journalist. After graduating from high school in Oak Park, Illinois, in 1917, he worked for six months as a cub reporter for the Kansas City *Star*, a paper known for its excellent news coverage and crusades for better government; its style guide became a touchstone for his writing generally. During the final months of **World War I**, he served as an ambulance driver on the Italian Front, where he won the Silver Medal of Military Valor from the Italian government and was himself badly wounded. After convalescing and returning to Oak Park, he took a job as a feature writer at the *Toronto Star* in 1920 and later covered the Greco–Turkish War for the paper before being fired for inadequate reporting. Although he found it increasingly exasperating, his journalism helped to pay the bills while he developed as a writer among the "lost generation" in Paris. In 1937, he went to **Spain** to cover the Spanish Civil War for the North American Newspaper Alliance. He initially supported the fascist Nationalists, but was persuaded by the propaganda films of Joris Ivens to switch his allegiance to the Republican insurgents, even breaking with John Dos Passos over his friend's more neutral stance. Late in **World War II**, Hemingway reported from **France** for *Collier's* magazine. In various letters, he later asserted that he had killed anywhere from 26 to 122 German soldiers, presumably while serving as an unarmed, noncombatant correspondent. A recent study has concluded, however, that these claims were exaggerated, if not entirely fictitious.

HOAXES. Hoaxes have long been used by newspapers to increase circulation. The most famous was the so-called "moon hoax," a fraudulent 18,000-word story serialized in the *New York Sun* between 25 and 31 August 1835. It was purportedly based on an article in the *Supplement to the Edinburgh Journal of Science*, which had actually ceased publication two years earlier. Written by reporter Richard Adams Locke (1800–1871), the story alleged that renowned astronomer Sir John Herschel had discovered not only planets in other solar systems but life on the moon in the form of a tiny moon bison, a blue unicorn, and a *Verspetilio homo*, or man-bat, whose behavior was said to be quite lacking in decorum. These life forms had been observed through a massive telescope, which had supposedly since been damaged beyond repair. The moon story sent the *Sun*'s circulation soaring, from about 4,000 copies a day to over 19,000, and was plagiarized by other newspapers hoping to get in on the boom. Only arch-rival **James Gordon Bennett**'s *New York Herald* called the story a hoax. A content analysis by Brian Thornton found that, while most editors and letter-writers emphasized the importance of truth in journalism, they did not seem to resent the hoax, which, as the *Sun* itself said, likely provided temporary relief from debates over slavery. To Bennett's great annoyance, the *Sun* never admitted that the story was a fraud.

On 13 April 1844, the *New York Sun* published another hoax, this time a fictitious story by Edgar Allan Poe in the guise of a regular news article. The story claimed that a week or so earlier eight men had, with the assistance of a two-day gale, managed to cross the Atlantic in only 75 hours in "Mr. Monck Mason's Flying Machine" (a hot-air balloon inflated with coal gas).

Hoaxes continued into the early years of the 20th century. In December 1909, for example, six years after the first flight by the Wright brothers, businessman Wallace Tillinghast fooled the Boston *Herald* into thinking that he had flown an airplane from Worcester to New York City and back one night in September of that year. Other New England newspapers picked up and amplified the false story, increasing their circulations in the process.

HONDURAS. Printing was not introduced into Honduras until 1830 when Francisco Morazán began publishing the official *Gaceta del gobrierno* in Tegucigalpa. It later moved to Comayagua and underwent several name changes before returning to its original location in 1877 and settling for its present title, *La Gazeta*, in 1890. In 1834, Honduras passed a law proclaiming freedom of the press, but for the next half century Hondurans had to depend on Panamanian, Guatemalan, and **Cuban** newspapers for non-official news. President Luis Bográn was essentially correct in claiming that his administration from 1883–91 was the first to allow an opposition press. The creation of the independent weeklies *El Tren* and *El Bien público* in the 1880s was followed by the establishment of a few indigenous dailies in the 1890s, beginning with the *Diario de Honduras* in 1893. Although Bográn's successor continued his policy of press freedom, President Terencio Sierra sentenced Juan Ramón Molina to hard labor for a hostile editorial in the *Diario*. When the paper's subsequent editor criticized Sierra's successor in turn, it was forcibly shut down in December 1903.

Closing papers and exiling their editors continued to occur as a matter of presidential whim over the next 20 years. But the most repressive measures were enacted during the 16-year dictatorship of

President Tiburcio Carías Andino beginning in 1933. During the Caríato, the press was reduced to a single government paper, *La Epoca*, edited by Fernando Zepeda Durón and funded by a supposedly voluntary 5 percent contribution from the salaries of civil servants. After 1948, a measure of press freedom allowed the reestablishment of independent papers, but most engaged in self-censorship and their reach remained minimal. In the mid-1950s, the circulation of Honduras's six newspapers was only 44,000; 30 years later, there were still only four major dailies for a population of about 4.5 million.

HORSERACE JOURNALISM. Election coverage that emphasizes the conduct of the campaign, including the strategies of the candidates, rather than their positions on policy issues. Instead of describing campaign events and speeches, horserace journalism focuses on who's ahead and why. Although aspects of American horserace journalism can be traced back to colonial days, its domination of campaign coverage is largely the result of television. In the **United States**, according to one study, the amount of policy-oriented coverage declined from one-half to one-ninth between 1972 and 1992. Researchers have found at least three reasons for the trend toward strategy-oriented election coverage: the length of campaigns; the resistance of journalists to media management by campaign operatives; and the pressures of the marketplace in which news organizations must compete for audience share.

HOT NEWS DOCTRINE. A doctrine originating in the Supreme Court decision *International News Service v. Associated Press* 248 U.S. 215 (1918). During **World War I**, the International News Service had taken breaking news stories from uncopyrighted **Associated Press** reports. The Court decided that news organizations have a limited property right on the facts of news for a short period after publication. The doctrine was later expanded in scope before being narrowed by Congress and the courts.

HOWE, JOSEPH (1804–1873). Political reformer and editor of the *Novascotian* in British North America. In 1835, he published a letter signed "The People" accusing the magistrates and police of Halifax of fleecing the poor of at least $30,000 a year for the previous 30 years. He was charged with criminal libel for "seditiously contriving, devising and intending to stir up and incite discontent among His Majesty's subjects." Since the trial of **John Peter Zenger** in New York a century earlier, juries had acquired the right to decide not only whether the accused had published the statements in question but also whether they were libelous. As a result of subsequent changes in procedural rules, however, prosecutions for seditious libel were often still successful in **Britain** and its remaining colonies. In conducting his own defense, Howe focused on the idea that malice is a necessary aspect of a libel. Previously malice had been ascertained by examining the statements themselves to see whether they were likely to disturb the peace. But Howe argued that intention should be taken into account in determining malice and that he should be given an opportunity to show "the state of my own mind at the time I published the letter." This ploy enabled him to argue that he had not acted maliciously, that his claims of corruption were true, and that there was a "great and overwhelming public necessity" to monitor the government's actions. His acquittal did not immediately change the law of libel. After Howe entered politics, his successor as editor was imprisoned for libel.

HUMAN INTEREST STORIES. In *News and the Human Interest Story* (1940), Helen MacGill Hughes suggested that it was the **penny papers** that invented the human interest story. But 18th-century newspapers like **Benjamin Franklin**'s *Pennsylvania Gazette* had earlier carried a degree of human interest material. In a political and economic study of the human interest story in 20th-century British **tabloids**, James Curran argued that it serves the interests of the elite by disempowering its readers. Instead of understanding events in terms of deep-seated causes, the human interest story explains things in terms of chance and luck. In a more recent study of the media coverage of the entrapment of a Kentucky man in a cave for 17 days in the winter of 1925, Gary Fine and Ryan White acknowledge that such stories seldom contribute to political action. But they also maintain that human interest stories of this kind, which are "closely linked to the current tabloidization of the press and television," create the "shared identification" necessary for "social cohesion and the maintenance of a **public sphere**." In a similar vein, folklorist Russell

Frank argues that the personal experience narratives of journalism, which remain "staples of newspaper writing," help "to make sense of experience and to bind readers into a symbolic community."

HUTCHINS COMMISSION. Commission on Freedom of the Press (1944–47). It was chaired by Robert M. Hutchins (1899–1977), president of the University of Chicago (1930–45) and author of *Education for Freedom* (1943). In 1942, **Henry Luce** invited Hutchins, his personal friend and fellow Yale alumnus, to organize a commission to formulate a statement on freedom of the press. Luce was concerned about increasing **news management** or the self-conscious control of news by government press agents. On 28 February 1944, Hutchins announced the creation of a 13-member commission. Funded to the tune of $200,000, its members—which included no one currently working for a newspaper—promptly forgot about Luce's main concern and focused instead on the impact of concentrated media ownership on the performance of the press. The commission set forth the results of its deliberations on 26 March 1947 in a slim report entitled *A Free and Responsible Press*. The report emphasized that freedom of the press carries with it the obligation to act responsibly, which became known as the social responsibility theory of the press. The commission redefined a free press to mean one which reflects the views of all citizens and conveys the full spectrum of ideas in society. It concluded that freedom of the press in this sense was in danger because of the growth of communications empires. It suggested that if the press did not take steps to clean up its own house, government action might be necessary. Its preference, however, was for nongovernmental mechanisms such as press councils and mandatory retraction and right of reply provisions. *See also* UNITED STATES.

– I –

INDIA. In 1780, James Hicky, an expatriate Irishman, founded India's first newspaper, the weekly *Bengal Gazette*. Its criticism of the East India Company, for whom Hicky worked, led to the imposition of a licensing system, which delayed the growth of an indigenous press;

in 1830, there were only 16 Indian-owned and operated newspapers, about half the number of Anglo-Indian publications. During this period, the indigenous press retained elements of the Mughal news-gathering system, using *Akhbār* in their titles, publishing in Persian, and emphasizing news about rulers and their courts.

After the elimination of licensing in 1835, Indian newspapers began to multiply and to model themselves on the Anglo-Indian press. But as a result of the Sepoy Mutiny or First War of Independence in 1857–58, India was brought under the direct rule of the crown and the Indian press was closely monitored through the Press and Registration of Books Act of 1867. By the 1870s, there were about a hundred Indian newspapers, but many had only a few hundred subscribers and only a few had a circulation of more than 3,000. Most of their owners led a hand-to-mouth existence and labored to put them out without the assistance of any regular staff. The papers were usually double-sheets and, unlike the Anglo-Indian press, carried almost no **advertising**, relying instead on wealthy patrons, local rajas or zaminders, and subscriptions, which were sometimes adjusted to the subscriber's income; in a few cases, local governments subsidized them by purchasing a fixed number of copies. They could not afford to subscribe to news agencies like Reuters, but had to rely on the Anglo-Indian press for news of the outside world and reached at most about 100,000 of India's 200 million inhabitants.

In response to criticism of the Second Afghan War, the Viceroy's Council passed the Vernacular Press Act in 1878 for "the better control of publications in Oriental languages." Framed on the model of the Irish Coercion Act of 1870, the act empowered the district magistrates to discipline any Indian-language publication for "seditious writing." In **Great Britain**, William Gladstone pointed out the hypocrisy of not giving the editors of Indian-language newspapers the same liberties as English-language critics of the government. As a result of criticism, the act was repealed two years later.

Despite periodic **censorship**, harassment, and even deportation, indigenous papers and magazines continued to multiply and through these publications Indian nationalism began to grow. While a few English newspapermen like **Robert Knight**, founder of *The Times of India* (1861) and the *Statesman* (1875), were supportive of Indian nationalism, Anglo-Indian papers such as the *Pioneer* and the *Civil and*

Military Gazette tried to stifle its development. They were particularly opposed to efforts by the educated Indian intelligentsia to gain admission to the ranks of the military and civil service, a cause promoted by Anglo-Indian papers such as *Hindu, New Indian,* and *Indian Social Reformer.* This uncompromising attitude led many educated Indians to abandon the idea of some form of constitutional accommodation in favor of outright independence. Many of the early nationalist leaders had close ties to the press as owners as well as journalists; among those at the first meeting of the Indian National Congress in Bombay in 1885 were the editors of the *Dyan Prakash, The Maratha, The Kesari, The Nababibhakar, The Indian Mirror, The Nassim, The Hindustani, The Tribune,* and *The Indu Prakash.*

During the late 19th century, Indian Muslims, especially those in Bengal, also turned to journalism to promote their own sense of nationalism. The British partition of Bengal in 1905 was followed by reduced freedom for both communities. The protests and violence provoked by the partition led the British to conclude that freedom of the press was inapplicable in India. Expressions of enmity were construed as disaffection, which was taken as equivalent to sedition. Various repressive measures were instituted to intimidate the nationalist press: bookshops were raided, suspicious mail was intercepted, meetings and schools were infiltrated by secret agents, and numerous authors, publishers, and printers were arrested and prosecuted. The Newspapers Act of 1908 and Indian Press Act of 1910 gave district magistrates the power to seize newspapers even for veiled hostility to British rule; prison terms ranged from one to six years and were sometimes accompanied by heavy fines.

Despite these measures, the Indian press became increasingly linked to the struggle for independence. During the interwar years, prominent leaders of the nationalist movement, including Mahatma Gandhi, continued to own or edit newspapers to advance their ideas. The *Swarajya,* founded by T. Prakasam in Madras in 1922, served as a training ground for journalists such as Khasa Subba Rao. The Indian Muslim leader, Mohammad Ali Jinnah, likewise founded several daily and weekly newspapers to promote his policies. During the turbulent pre-independence decade, the Indian press became increasingly assertive. With the outbreak of **World War II**, papers such the *National Herald,* founded by Jawaharlal Nehru in 1938, were closely watched by the imperial government; content was censored and fines and jail sentences were imposed on journalists.

On 8 August 1942, the Indian National Congress, prodded by Mahatma Gandhi, demanded that the British immediately cede control of India. In response, the government arrested Gandhi and the main Congress leaders and banned the press from covering the so-called "Quit India" movement. Several newspapers, including the *National Herald*, ceased operations in protest, while others went underground in order to adopt a directly confrontational approach. However, the clandestine writers were openly criticized by Gandhi upon his release from prison in May 1944 and journalists once again conformed to the practice of working within the constraints of British censorship.

Following independence in 1947, the Indian media enjoyed substantial freedom from government controls. During the Emergency Rule of Indira Gandhi in 1975–76, restrictions were briefly imposed on speech and the press. But thereafter the number of newspapers increased dramatically (from fewer than 900 to almost 4,500 two decades later) and the press adopted a more adversarial and investigative role. Both developments stimulated the development of facilities for the training of journalists. The first program in journalism was started at Aligarh Muslim University in 1938 by Sir Shah Muhammad Sulaiman. After independence, other universities began to add journalism to their offerings. Today most Indian universities have programs in journalism, including half a dozen or so doctoral programs, and additional training is available through the Asian Media Institute based in Chenai. Newspapers such as *The Times of India* and *Malyala Manorama* have also established institutes for the advancement of journalism. Such training has tended to homogenize and further Westernize Indian journalism. *See also* AKBĀR NAWĪS; BESANT, ANNIE.

INDONESIA. The earliest newspapers in Indonesia were established by the Dutch in the late 18th century and were mainly devoted to European news. The first paper to cover local events was the *Bataviasche Courant*, founded in 1816; later renamed the *Javasche Courant*, it continued publication until the **Japanese** occupation in 1942. By the mid-19th century, there were several dozen newspapers and magazines in Jakarta and elsewhere, but most had small circulations and led precarious existences. The first fully indigenous newspaper was the *Medan Prijaji* [Officialdom], founded in 1907. It was soon joined by more nationalist papers such as *Budi Utomo* [High Endeavor] in 1908. The Chinese-Indonesian community also began to establish newspapers, mostly using Batavian Malay.

Following their occupation in 1942, the Japanese banned all Dutch and most Indonesian newspapers and established several papers of their own. In response, an **underground press** developed which was closely tied to nationalist ambitions. After the war, however, successive Indonesian governments maintained close control of the press. Mochtar Lubis, editor of *Indonesia Raya* (1949–74), was jailed by both the Sukarno and Suharto governments. Only since the resignation of Suharto in 1998 has the press begun to acquire a measure of freedom, leading to a rapid growth in news media. In 1996, for example, there were 77 daily newspapers; by 1999, this number had increased to 172.

INFORMATION SUBSIDIES. Term used by Oscar H. Gandy Jr. to designate the practice whereby well-resourced organizations are able to secure preferential treatment from journalists by supplying them with information on a regular basis. The concept challenged the traditional concept of gatekeeping.

INSTANT ANALYSIS. The practice, initially, whereby the American television networks followed a president's speech with an immediate commentary. After Vice-President Spiro T. Agnew denounced the practice during his assault on the news media in 1969–70, it was temporarily banned on CBS by chairman William S. Paley. As the practice spread to include all major political pronouncements, politicians sought to regain control through the use of their own "**spin doctors**."

INTERNATIONAL HERALD TRIBUNE. The first newspaper to be available simultaneously throughout the world. Its origins go back to 1887 when James Gordon Bennett Jr. founded the *Paris Herald* as a European edition of the *New York Herald*. Known in Paris as "Le New York," it underwent frequent editorial changes under the tempestuous Bennett. It was part of the merger between the *Herald* and the *New York Tribune* in 1924 and became the *International Herald*

Tribune when the ***New York Herald Tribune*** closed in 1966. It began electronic transmission in 1980 and came under joint ownership of the ***New York Times*** and ***Washington Post*** in 1991.

INVESTIGATIVE JOURNALISM. Investigative reporting generally seeks to uncover some event, practice, or phenomenon that certain persons or part of society would prefer to keep hidden from view. To this end, it often makes use of methods of inquiry that go beyond traditional reporting techniques. Where conventional methods such as interviews are still relied upon, there is an expectation of additional insight and depth.

In the **United States**, the beginnings of investigative journalism are often associated with the **muckrakers** of 1900–1914. But a tradition of investigative reporting was already growing in both Europe and America before the muckraking movement made its appearance. In **Great Britain**, for example, journalist Henry Mayhew's series on the London poor clearly meets the criteria of investigative journalism. It was carried by the *Morning Chronicle* between October 1849 and October 1850, partially reprinted between December 1850 and March 1852, and later published as *London Labour and the London Poor* (4 vols., 1861–62). The series grew out of an assignment to look into sanitary conditions in one of London's slums where cholera was raging; shocked at the horrors he found, Mayhew spent two years documenting the larger picture of London poverty. Though praised by William Thackeray and others for its "tale of wonder and horror," Mayhew's account (as "Metropolitan Commissioner") has since been criticized for its lack of methodological sophistication. But such criticism misses the point: it was not meant to be a work of social analysis, but a piece of higher journalism that resulted, as F. S. Schwarzback has pointed out, from Mayhew's ability to follow "his reporter's nose wherever it led him." Mayhew did not discover London poverty, but he did temporarily pierce the protective cover around it; it was 40 years before the middle classes became conscious of it again.

Another worthy precursor of investigative journalism is Henry Demarest Lloyd (1847–1903). After graduating from Columbia, Lloyd married the daughter of William Boss, co-owner of the *Chicago Tribune*, and rose to the position of chief editorial writer. In "The Story of a Great Monopoly," published in the *Atlantic Monthly* in 1881, he used what he called the photography of facts to counter social Darwinist arguments supporting the rapacious practices of John D. Rockefeller and the Standard Oil Company. It was later expanded and published as *Wealth Against Commonwealth* (1894). After falling out with publisher **Joseph Medill**, Lloyd resigned from the *Tribune* in 1885 to devote himself exclusively to the literature of protest. In *A Strike of Millionaires Against Miners* (1890), he championed the cause of Illinois coal miners.

Although the muckrakers were part of the larger Progressive movement in prewar America, there is no necessary connection between investigative journalism and the pursuit of reform. During the 1920s, investigative reporting shifted its focus from widespread social abuses to narrower cases of individual and administrative corruption and wrongdoing. After being hired by the *St. Louis* (Missouri) *Post-Dispatch* in 1914, for example, Paul Y. Anderson (1893–1938) immediately set about exposing official corruption in East St. Louis. He helped to convict those responsible for a race riot in 1917, facilitated the release of 52 Americans still in prison in the early 1920s for their opposition to **World War I**, and contributed to impeachment charges against a federal judge. His career as an investigative reporter reached its peak in 1929 when he almost single-handedly reopened the Teapot Dome scandal, a feat for which he won a **Pulitzer Prize**. Though a contemporary called him "the last of the muckrakers," his concern was with particular cases of political corruption rather than anything endemic to the political system as a whole.

In "golden age" accounts of investigative reporting, **Watergate** remains the archetype of the genre and the pinnacle of its achievement. It is thought to have made investigative reporting respectable and to have launched a new era in its practice. But unlike the investigative journalism of magazines like *The Nation* in the 1950s and newspapers like the *New York Times*, the *Los Angeles Times*, and the *Washington Post* in the 1960s, it was singularly concerned with political and administrative corruption and these remained the main targets of post-Watergate investigative reporters like **Jack Anderson**. The formation of Investigative Reporters and Editors (IRE) in 1975 helped to legitimize investigative reporting as a distinct set of journalistic practices, but did little to broaden its agenda. At the same time, revelations about the domestic surveillance activities of the **Central Intelligence Agency (CIA)** by reporters like Seymour Hersh were subject to increasing self-censorship by the mainstream press. *See also* ASAHI PAPERS; McWILLIAMS, CAREY; *PENTAGON PAPERS.*

IRELAND. The first newspaper in Ireland to publish for more than a few months was the *Flying Post*, founded by Cornelius Carter in 1699. During the 18th century, other newspapers were established, but the imposition of **stamp taxes** and other repressive measures kept their numbers and circulations low. Three years after Ireland became part of **Great Britain** through the Act of Union of 1800, there were still only seven newspapers in the country, compared to 236 in 1905. Examining the 19th century as a whole, Jacques Delacroix and Glenn R. Carroll concluded that the creation of new papers was closely related to levels of political turbulence. For example, the largest number of new foundings occurred in 1848 in the midst of the Great Famine of 1845–51. As political turmoil increased thereafter in response to recurring outbreaks of famine, the average number of newspapers in business in any given year more than doubled from 91 in 1841 to 194 in 1891, despite the fact that the population was stagnant or in decline. This expansion included the first nationalist newspapers, beginning with *The Nation* which Charles Gavan Duffy, John Blake Dillon, and poet Thomas Davis founded on 15 October 1842 as the mouthpiece of the romantic Young Ireland movement. Within a year, it had a readership of 250,000, making it the largest newspaper in Ireland. Despite continuing tight controls over the press, it was soon joined by more radical nationalist papers, the most influential being the *Freeman's Journal.*

The increasing politicization of the Irish press on behalf of nationalism was accompanied by the participation of journalists in radical nationalist politics. Journalists were prominent members of the Irish Republican Brotherhood (IRB) or Fenians during the 1860s and tried to use their craft to delegitimize British rule; one-tenth of those IRB members under surveillance in the 1880s were journalists, editors, or newspaper proprietors. Despite their role in nationalist politics, however, late 19th-century Irish journalists made considerable progress toward professionalism. Michael Foley has shown how they developed the same skills and norms as journalists in Britain and the

United States, including shorthand and interviewing and a commitment to accuracy and impartiality. They also avidly supported the Association of Journalists (1889), renamed the Institute of Journalists in 1892, with its goal of promoting professional status, supplying *Cork Examiner* editor and proprietor Thomas Crosbie as president in 1894. Through professionalism, they were able to develop middle-class careers not only in London, North America, and elsewhere but more importantly in Ireland itself, where it enabled them to work for any given paper regardless of its politics.

This professionalism continued to serve Irish journalists after the establishment of the Irish Free State in 1922 and helps to explain their antipathy to projects such as the Irish News Agency (INA). Following **World War II**, there was a growing feeling that Ireland's case against partition had never been properly heard because news to the outside world was filtered through a British news agency. In 1949, therefore, Sean MacBride, leader of the new political party Clann na Poblachta, convinced the government to establish the INA. As John Horgan has related, however, its operations immediately alienated Irish journalists, who resented not only its orientation to foreign media but the degree of government control exercised over their own work as journalists. Although the INA was closed in 1957, government attempts to manage the media, especially in broadcasting, have continued to challenge Irish journalists' professional norms. As in many other Western countries, moreover, this threat has been exacerbated by the emergence of media giants such as Independent Newspapers, which have sought, among other things, the right to syndicate journalists' material without paying royalties. For protection against such incursions, Irish journalists have turned increasingly to trade union and **professional organizations** such as the National Union of Journalists (NUJ), the world's largest union of journalists. *See also* MITCHELL, JOHN.

IRWIN, WILL (1873–1948). American journalist and press critic. After graduating from Stanford University in 1899, he worked as a reporter for the *San Francisco Chronicle* and then joined the *New York Sun* in 1904. Following the San Francisco earthquake in 1906, he wrote "The City That Was," a nostalgic portrait of the city as he had known it. In 1911, after a year and a half of research, he wrote a 15-part mildly **muckraking** series entitled "The Power of the Press" for *Collier's* magazine, mainly criticizing the daily press for lagging behind the times but also pointing to abuses by advertising interests. Subtitled "A Study of Journalism in Its Relation to the Public," the series sought to educate the public so that it might better control the press. Several decades before the **Hutchins Commission**, Irwin developed the ideal of a free but responsible press as a basis for assessing the performance of journalism. The series was eventually reprinted as *The American Newspaper* (1969). During **World War I**, Irwin went abroad as a correspondent, scored a beat on the first use of poison gas by the Germans, and related his experiences in *A Reporter in Armageddon* (1918). He later campaigned to get the United States to join the League of Nations and criticized the growth of public relations in *Propaganda and the News* (1936). Following his retirement, he wrote *The Making of a Reporter* (1942).

ISKRA **[THE SPARK].** Journal set up by **Vladimir I. Lenin** in 1900 after returning from exile in Siberia. Despite being subjected to surveillance, the Russian Social Democratic Workers' (SDW) Party decided to produce two newspapers, *Iskra* and *Zaria*, and arranged for Lenin to go to **Germany** to set them up. On his way to Germany, he visited St. Petersburg illegally and was arrested and interrogated. *Iskra* was published in Munich and then smuggled into **Russia** through Prague as well as by émigrés and sailors plying the Alexandria-to-Odessa sea route. In 1901, Sergei V. Zubatov, head of Moscow's Secret Political Police Department, enacted a series of measures to counteract its appeal to the masses and create divisiveness within the SDW. *Iskra* ceased publication in 1903 following a conflict at the party's Second Congress between the Bolsheviks Lenin and Georgi Plekhanov and the Menshevik members of the paper's editorial board such as Paul B. Axelrod.

ITALY. The first newspaper in Italy was printed in Genoa in 1639 and was soon followed by a number of other papers. During the late 17th century, the first scientific journals made their appearance and helped to usher in an age of international science by including foreign articles.

In comparison with several other European countries, however, newspapers developed more slowly in Italy. When the French revolutionaries arrived in the 1790s, they required cities like Mantua to begin publishing a revolutionary newspaper. During the 19th century, low literacy rates continued to stifle the growth of newspapers, while the prevalence of local dialects favored regional over national newspapers.

At the beginning of the 20th century, the most influential paper in Italy was the *Corriere della Sera* in Milan. It was directed and edited by Luigi Albertini, a self-styled "conservative liberal" who opposed Enrico Corradini and other nationalists concerned about Italy's military preparedness. After his takeover in 1922, Benito Mussolini continued to rely on the Milanese newspaper *Il Popolo d'Italia*, which he had established in 1914 with funds from industrial and political interests, as his official news organ, while using *Il Tevere*, which he founded in 1924 and placed under Telesio Interlandi, as an unofficial mouthpiece. Mussolini also benefitted from the generally supportive attitude of the Vatican press; when the socialist member of parliament Giacomo Matteotti was murdered in the summer of 1924 after denouncing Fascist disruptions of the elections that year, the Vatican newspaper *Osservatore Romano* ignored Mussolini's responsibility for the violence and merely called upon the courts to secure justice. During the 1930s, the Catholic Church produced numerous popular religious magazines which continued to uphold Fascism, glorifying patriarchy and rebuking challenges to civil authority.

After the war, journalists like Giovanna Zangrandi denounced Fascism, rationalizing their earlier support as a temporary aberration. The postwar period saw the emergence of numerous weekly newspapers, but many were little more than scandal sheets. In 1970, Italy had 70 daily newspapers, compared to 88 today. During the same period, the readership of dailies rose from about 5 million to roughly 6 million. At the same time, however, Italy continues to have one of the lowest aggregate daily newspaper circulations in Europe. Apart from its tradition of strict controls over the press, the main reason for this situation is the lack of a popular press or newspapers with mass appeal.

– J –

JAPAN. During the Edo period, news was distributed in Japan by means of *kawaraban*, or woodblocks containing printed text and illustrations, which were marketed with the help of *yomiuri* or singing vendors. Their popularity rapidly declined following the introduction of newspapers in the Meiji period (1868–1912). In 1861, two years after Japan was opened to foreign residence, Englishman Albert William Hansard began the *Nagasaki Shipping List and Advertiser*. It was soon followed by a number of Japanese newspapers, which supported Shogunate officials when they took steps to curtail the operations of Scotsman J. R. Black's *Nisshin Shinjishi* (1872) and *Bankoku Shimbun* (1876) as part of its campaign against extraterritoriality. A new press law required newspaper owners and editors to be Japanese citizens but also limited the capacity of indigenous papers to engage in political commentary. In addition, regulations were passed prohibiting Japanese citizens from helping Black with the production or distribution of the *Bankoku Shimbun*. This "affair" constituted an important step in the Japanese government's campaign to end extraterritoriality and reinforced the tendency to limit political news to small-circulation newspapers such as the *Yokohama Mainichi Shimbun* (1871) and the *Tokyo Nichi-ninchi Shimbun* (1872) which were aimed at intellectuals.

The most popular papers, which assumed the format of a tabloid or *Ko-shimbun* (small paper), stuck mainly to entertainment. The popularization of the Japanese press was stimulated in part by the introduction of a phonetic-based system of shorthand known as *sokki* in the mid-1880s. Before the adaptation of Western stenography by Takusari Kōki Takusari and his students, the use of cumbersome Chinese figures created a gulf between the spoken and written word. The pale reflection of colloquial Japanese in written language was reinforced in printed texts by the economic constraints of publishing. The sudden and widespread use of *sokki* contributed to popularization of the press by enabling reporters to provide more immediate, realistic, and seemingly objective coverage of political debates. It also brought into existence the new, albeit short-lived, genre of *sokkibon*, or colloquial transcriptions of oral stories accompanied by reading glasses, which even the highbrow papers began to incorporate.

These developments played a major role in the three-fold increase in Japanese newspaper circulation in the decade after 1877. In 1896, Takahashi Jiji, publisher of the small magazine *26th Century*, formed an alliance with Kuga Katsunan, publisher of the *Nihon Shimbun*, to pressure the government to adopt the principles of ministerial responsibility and freedom of the press. The government responded by suspending the two publications, but after its fall in 1897 a bill was passed providing for a degree of press freedom. This freedom was limited, however, by the press club system (*kisha kuraku*) under which club members restricted their criticism in return for exclusive access to news sources in government, industry, and the civil service.

During the period of democracy from 1918 to 1932, democratic, party-led governments devised controls over the press that were stricter than those of their oligarchic predecessors. Under the military regime from 1932 to 1945, the press clubs operated as part of the state's propaganda machine, actively promoting Japan's mobilization for war. While this role was curtailed during the American occupation, the clubs' exclusive news-gathering privileges remained relatively intact. The press club system continues to dominate Japanese journalism despite objections from foreign news services. Each news "beat" is monopolized by a specific "club" of journalists; to gain access to the prime minister, a government ministry, the stock exchange, and so forth, a journalist must be a member of the club with responsibility for reporting the area in question. Each club controls its own membership, which has historically been closed to foreign journalists, and is usually provided with generous facilities by the agency being covered. The journalists in each club can only report information that is available to all other members of their club and cannot seek information outside their specific news jurisdiction.

Tom Brislin has argued that this highly structured system eliminates competition between journalists, prevents any kind of **investigative journalism**, and results in self-**censorship** by the Japanese press. As he also points out, however, there are a couple of ways that newspapers can get at least partially around these controls. Because each major newspaper also owns a **news magazine** whose reporters are excluded from the press clubs, it can publish non-official information, including rumors and innuendos, through its magazine subsidiary and then report the existence of these stories itself without violating press club practices. In addition, frustrated press club members can leak information to a major foreign newspaper and then later provide second-hand coverage of the story. *See also* ATOMIC BOMB; WORLD WAR II.

JAURES, JEAN (1859–1914). French journalist and socialist leader. When the French socialists temporarily split into two camps in 1899, he led the French Socialist Party, which favored peaceful revolution and accommodation with the state. In 1904, he cofounded the newspaper *L'Humanité*, in which he denounced nationalism as hostile to socialism. His opposition to armed conflict with **Germany** in 1914 led to his assassination by a fanatical nationalist. *See also* FRANCE.

JEFFERSON, THOMAS (1743–1826). Third president of the **United States** and a staunch supporter of the principle, if not always the practice, of freedom of the press. "[W]ere it left to me to decide whether we should have a government without newspapers, or newspapers without a government," he wrote in 1787, "I should not hesitate a moment to prefer the latter." He won election in 1801 despite the opposition of about 80 percent of America's 235 newspapers. In 1809, after years of tirades against him in the press, he commented that "nothing can now be believed which is seen in a newspaper." Overall, however, he retained a faith in the Miltonian self-righting principle. "[T]he only security of all," he wrote in 1826, "is in a free press."

JENKINS JOURNALISM. "Jenkins" was originally a fictional character introduced by the British humor magazine *Punch* in 1843 as a **caricature** of the obsequious purple prose on the society pages of the *Morning Post*. The term probably made its way to the **United States** through the Civil War-era humor magazine *Vanity Fair*, which used it to attack the excessively prying and windy prose of the *New York Herald*. Andie Tucher quotes William A. Wheeler's definition of Jenkins in his *Explanatory and Pronouncing Dictionary of the Noted Names of Fiction* (1865): "cant name for any snobbish penny-a-liner . . . whose descriptions of persons and events in fashionable and aristocratic society betrayed the ingrained servility, priggishness, and vulgarity of his character." In 1867, Samuel Clemens changed the name of his 1865 spoof on such bombastic reporting from "The Pioneers' Ball" to "'After' Jenkins." During the 1870s and 1880s, the focus of the term gradually shifted from fawning banality to what struck many critics as the increasingly intrusive character of Gilded Age journalism. Its use reflected the initial unease over the new practice of interviewing.

JONES, GARETH (1905–1935). Welsh **investigative journalist** for *The Times* of London who first exposed the famine in the Ukraine of 1932–33. After graduating from Cambridge in languages in 1929, he began work as a foreign policy advisor for British Prime Minister David Lloyd George. He made his first trip to the **Soviet Union** two years later with American financial assistance and published his observations as *Experiences in Russia: A Diary* (1931). After covering the coming of the Nazis to power, he ignored travel restrictions and secretly returned to the Soviet Union. On 29 March 1933, he reported under his own name in the *Manchester Guardian* that "from every part of Russia . . . [came] the cry, 'There is no bread. We are dying.'" Though confirmed by earlier unsigned stories by Malcolm Muggeridge, who was also in the Soviet Union for *The Guardian*, Jones's reports were denounced by **Walter Duranty** of the *New York Times* as the product of a "diplomatic duel between **Great Britain** and the Soviet Union." Unsupported by other journalists and banned from the Soviet Union, Jones traveled to the Far East and was killed by bandits in Inner Mongolia under suspicious circumstances.

JONSON, BEN (1572–1637). English playwright and early media critic. In *Volpone*, or *The Fox* (1606), he drew attention to the political purposes behind the dissemination of news through royal proclamations and private **newsletters**. In later writings such as *News from the New World* (1620), he shifted his attention from the power of news to the falsity of information being conveyed in increasingly public forms of news. His most thorough analysis, *The Staple of News* (1626), criticized news for its inferiority to poetry and lamented the monopolistic control exercised by the printers' syndicate over its publication. The title pointed to the growth of news as an article of mass consumption.

JORDAN, ELIZABETH GARVER (1867–1947). Journalist, author, and suffragist. Jordan worked for the *New York World* for 10 years before becoming assistant editor of the *Sunday World* and later editor of *Harper's Bazaar*. Her journalism ranged from hard news to **human interest stories** and a daily fiction column based on actual events. During her coverage of the sensational Lizzie Borden murder trial in 1893, at which she was the only woman reporter, she became convinced of the defendant's innocence. In addition to writing 28 novels and a number of plays, she edited *The Sturdy Oak* (1917), a suffrage novel by 14 authors, and corresponded with women's suffrage advocates and prominent literary figures such as Frances Hodgson Burnett, Julia Ward Howe, Henry James, and Samuel Clemens.

JOURNAL DES SÇAVANS. The first learned periodical in Europe. Influenced by a proposal of François Eudes de Mézeray, it began publication as a quarto pamphlet of 12 pages on 5 January 1665. In its first issue, it announced that its purpose was "to give information concerning new happenings in the Republic of Letters." Published weekly until 1792, it provided news of scientific research and inventions, reviews of important new books, obituaries of famous men, the decisions of tribunals and universities, and current events in academia. It spawned a number of imitations, including the *Acta eruditorum* (1682–1731) in Leipzig and Pierre Bayle's *Nouvelles de la république des lettres* (1684–1718) in Rotterdam. Norman Fiering notes that their goal was to provide the infrastructure for a new republic of letters that had become too large and dispersed to maintain contacts through interpersonal communication.

JUDGE. Satirical American weekly magazine founded in 1881 by a group of writers and artists who had resigned from the popular comic weekly *Puck* after H. C. Bunner took over as editor. Despite its artistic merits, *Judge* struggled to survive until the Republican Party saw the merits of having a rival to the Democratic *Puck* and provided it with aid. By the end of the 1880s, it had surpassed *Puck* in circulation and had the field of bold satire to itself after its competitor expired in 1918. During the Depression, it tried to survive by becoming a monthly but folded in 1939.

– K –

KALTENBORN, H. V. (1878–1965). One of the first radio news commentators. He worked as a reporter for the *Milwaukee Journal* and *Brooklyn Eagle* for two decades before branching into radio, beginning with the first editorial over the air on 4 April 1922. During the 1920s, he broadcast news and analysis for station WEAF in New York City. Released by the *Eagle* in 1930 for financial reasons, he landed a job at CBS doing weekly talks on current affairs. In 1936, he paid his own way to cover the Spanish Civil War for $100 a week. His coverage of the Munich crisis in 1938 solidified his reputation as the "suave voice of Doom." In 1940, at the peak of his popularity, he switched to NBC to report the action from overseas. President Harry S. Truman delighted in mimicking his 1948 election-night prediction that Thomas Dewey would be victorious. Kaltenborn's insistence on expressing his own views contradicted the Federal Communication Commission's early policy against editorializing on the airwaves and later led to a number of confrontations with NBC. He recounted his career in *Fifty Fabulous Years* (1950) and *It Seems Like Yesterday* (1956).

KENNAN, GEORGE (1845–1924). American journalist who traveled widely in search of stories, including a 5,000-mile trek across **Russia** by dogsled and a trip to Mt. Pelée after its eruption. He also covered the Spanish–American and Russo–Japanese Wars. In each case, he followed up his newspaper articles with a book: *Siberia and the Exile System* (1891), *Campaigning in Cuba* (1899), and *The Tragedy of Pelée* (1902).

KLEIST, HEINRICH VON (1777–1811). A tragic German figure, better known for his poetry and plays in the *Sturm und Drang* tradition than for his journalism. Obsessed with countering the Napoleonic domination of Prussia, he made a brief foray into newspapering by founding the pocket-sized *Berliner Abendblatter*, Berlin's first evening daily, in October 1810. It used various devices to criticize French hegemony, including short reports on Paris fashions which contrasted the display of riches in the French capital with the plight of the Prussian economy under war reparations and the

Continental System. Subjected to increasing **censorship**, the *Berliner Abendblatter* ceased publication in March 1811. Eight months later, Kleist committed suicide with his lover.

KNIGHT, ROBERT (1825–1890). Economist, government official, and the first Anglo-Indian press owner to advocate self-rule for **India**. After acquiring controlling interests in the *Bombay Times* in 1859 and the *Bombay Telegraph* in 1864, he amalgamated the two papers into *The Times of India*. He was one of the few British journalists to recommend clemency after the "mutiny" of 1857. Having incurred the censure of most of the British community in Bombay, he moved to Calcutta in the early 1870s and founded the *Statesman*. It continued his brand of adversarial journalism into the 20th century.

KOREA. In the mid-1880s, the Chosun dynasty replaced its centuries-old court gazette with a number of more modern news publications using classic Sino-Korean characters. Then, during a brief period of relative freedom under Russian suzerainity in the 1890s, the first privately owned newspapers were established. The first of these independent papers was *Tongnip Sinmun*, founded in April 1896 and published three times a week. It used only the Korean alphabet and focused on human rights, national sovereignty, and other issues of interest to the educated elite. It was followed by a number of other nonofficial newspapers, including the first Korean daily, *Maeil Shinmun*, in January 1898.

Following the **Japanese** annexation in 1910, however, all newspapers were closed, except for a few organs of the new regime like *Maeil Shinbo*. In 1920, the Japanese attempted to defuse an emerging movement for independence by adopting the unusual strategy of relaxing controls over the press. As a result, private newspapers such as *Chosun Ilbo* and *Dong-A Ilbo* were able to begin operations. During the interwar years, the Japanese also established a form of public radio broadcasting. But with the outbreak of **World War II**, control over radio content was even more rigidly controlled and the independent newspapers were suppressed once again.

After the Japanese were defeated in August 1945, the **United States** abandoned the idea of a multilateral trusteeship over Korea and unilaterally declared the 38th parallel as the dividing line between a

Soviet-occupied zone in the north and an American zone in the south. Under the American military occupation from 1945 to 1948, the South Korean press was regulated with increasing severity by the Department of Public Information. Despite adopting even stricter controls, the South Korean government of Syngman Rhee was unable to stifle the press entirely and criticism of his dictatorial regime in the major national dailies contributed to its downfall during the April 1960 (Students') Revolution.

Following a formal guarantee of press freedom by the newly elected parliament of the Second Republic, there was an explosive growth of the media in South Korea. But the military coup by General Park Chung Hee in May 1961 used various decrees to establish even more repressive controls than under Rhee. The licenses of various regional newspapers were cancelled, several newspaper companies were forced to consolidate, and it was made a criminal offense to criticize the government, even indirectly through foreign media. Although Park's assassination was followed by another brief period of press liberalization, the military regime of Chun Doo Hwan reenacted most of the usual repressive measures through the Basic Press Act of 1980.

Only since 1987, when two new sets of regulations governing the press and broadcasting were instituted, have the South Korean media experienced a sufficiently long period of reasonable freedom to develop their own internally generated journalistic practices. There has been an explosion of new papers, many with large circulations and an adversarial attitude toward the government.

In North Korea, on the other hand, the regimes of Kim Il Sung (1948–94) and his son, Kim Jong Il, maintained a virtually unchallenged hold over the press. In his struggle against the Japanese, Kim Il Sung had recognized the capacity of popular journalism to promote revolution, but the use of popular modes of expression, including the practice of publishing in both Korean and Chinese, was only tolerated in conjunction with Communist objectives. Under Kim Jong Il, moreover, the concept of *Jucheism*, which originally stressed the importance of national development, was transformed into a cult of the leader. So tight are the controls over the press that even an **underground press** has not been able to gain a foothold. In 1999, Freedom House assigned North Korea the worst possible combined score (100 out of 100) on its criteria of press freedom and the situation has deteriorated since then.

KOSSUTH, LAJOS [LOUIS] (1802–1894). The son of a poor Hungarian noble, Kossuth trained as a lawyer and then entered politics in the mid-1820s. Despite using published letters as a means of criticizing the **Austrian** Hapsburg monarchy, he was eventually imprisoned for high treason, but released in 1840 in response to public demand. In 1841, he became editor of the semiweekly Liberal party newspaper, *Pesti Hirlap*, in which he advocated various feudal reforms and an independent legislature for Hungary. Though dismissed from the paper in 1844 after an argument over his salary, he continued to fight for political and economic independence. In 1849, after Hungary received its own constitution, Kossuth became minister of finance and later regent-president, but overplayed his hand and was unable to prevent the Austrians from using **Russian** forces to end the revolution in Hungary. He continued to practice journalism while in exile in England, writing columns for the liberal *Sunday Times* and the radical *Atlas* and criticizing British domestic and foreign policies.

– **L** –

LATIN AMERICA. For most of the colonial period, the Spanish and Portuguese authorities in America restricted political discussion by curtailing the development of printed news. In the Viceroyalty of **Peru**, the official *Gaceta de Lima* was published intermittently between 1715 and 1767, but in New Spain, New Granada, and Río de la Plata, there was an almost complete absence of printed news. Following the French Revolution, however, an incipient **public sphere** emerged as various cultural elites organized academic and literary societies and launched a series of news publications. While *El Mercurio Peruano*, begun by the Sociedad de Amantes del País in 1791, was mainly devoted to science and literature, later newspapers delved into political subjects as well. By 1809, there were six different newspapers in Mexico as well as a public news agency of sorts called the "Mexico Seat of News Important to the Public," begun by Juan Nazario Peimbert y Hernández in 1803.

A common practice, which the viceroy of Mexico later prohibited, was to place boxes at locations such as tobacco shops so people could submit news, advertisements, and letters to the editor. The Peruvian government responded by reviving the *Gaceta* and later began two other newspapers of its own, the *Telégrafo Peruano* (1793) and the *Minerva Peruano* (1805); similar publications were organized in Mexico and elsewhere. However, despite their small readerships and government attempts to restrict discussion to politically conservative ideas, the independent newspapers helped to foster a rudimentary civil society in Latin America which contributed to the independence movements of the 1810s and 1820s. In addition to countering government propaganda, independent journalists provided much of the philosophical and legal justification for independence.

Beginning in the 1830s, literary intellectuals such as Andrés Bello in Venezuela turned to journalism to help shape the identity of newly independent Latin America. Eschewing the growing emphasis on factual reporting in American journalism, they put the stamp of their own rhetorical style and ideological beliefs on what they wrote and established a tradition of belletristic journalism which continues to play an important role in Latin America's literary culture. During the middle decades of the 19th century, the press enjoyed considerable freedom in most Latin American countries. But as the century progressed, dictatorships developed in Mexico, Argentina, and elsewhere and the press once again adopted an oppositional role to government. In the case of Mexico, the Díaz dictatorship subsidized various papers in an attempt to neutralize their impact on public opinion.

For much of the 20th century, the Latin American press has struggled to retain a reasonable degree of freedom. In 1926, the Inter American Press Association (IAPA) was organized to promote freedom of the press, but did not meet again until 1942 and had to fight back attempts by Communists and various governments to gain control. In 1951, however, its pressure helped to overthrow the suppression of Gainza Paz's *La Prensa* by Juan Perón. In addition to struggling against dictatorial regimes, the Latin American press has also had to contend with American cultural penetration.

Despite these substantial obstacles, it has served as an important vehicle for the various processes of modernization. Contrary to media imperialism hypotheses, moreover, coverage of American and

European affairs by the elite Latin American press declined steadily during the postwar period, from almost 50 percent in 1949 to just over one-third by 1982. The greatest threat to Latin American journalism remains the precarious state of liberal democracy. An examination of the 273 journalists around the world who died on the job between 1982 and 1989 found that Latin American countries like Columbia and Peru were among the most dangerous, with numerous reporters having been murdered while covering stories related to corruption, drugs, and **crime**. *See also* ARGENTINA; BEALS, CARLETON; BRAZIL; CHILE; CUBA; HONDURAS; MEXICO; PARAGUAY.

LE MONDE. Newspaper founded in **France** in 1944 by Hubert Beuve-Méry, who developed it into one of the most prestigious institutions in the Fourth and Fifth Republics. It represented a break from the interwar period when French newspapers were dependent on powerful political and financial interests.

LENIN, V. I. (1870–1924). From the outset, newspapers played a pivotal role in Vladimir Lenin's revolutionary strategy. In 1895, he and G. V. Plekhanov organized *Rabotnik* as the main organ of the Social Democratic Workers' (SDW) party. It was published in Geneva and then distributed in **Russia**. It was later replaced by *Iskra* [The Spark], published from 1900 to 1903 with Lenin as head of the editorial board. In 1910, it was succeeded by *Zvezda* [Star] and *Pravda* [Truth]. Forbidden by the czar in 1914, *Pravda* was revived by Lenin in March 1917. Following the October Revolution, Lenin appealed for the creation of a loyal proletarian press. In Petrograd, the Bolsheviks' district committees established literary colleges to transform industrial workers into professional reporters. At the same time, however, Lenin sanctioned increasingly strict **censorship** on the grounds of protecting the socialist revolution against counterrevolutionary forces.

L'ESTRANGE, ROGER (1616–1704). Political journalist in late 17th-century England. Following the restoration of Charles II, which he supported in various **pamphlets**, he produced a stringent set of *Considerations and Proposals in Order to the Regulation of the Press*

(1663). He was rewarded by being appointed as Surveyor of the Press and in this capacity briefly held a monopoly over the publication of news. His later dogmatic and scurrilous political newspaper, *The Observator: In Question and Answer* (1681–86?), was organized in the form of a dialogue. *See also* GREAT BRITAIN.

LEVELLERS. A short-lived opposition group in Parliament during the English civil war. Led by John Lilburne, they explicitly related freedom of the press to good government and argued that Milton's self-righting principle in *Areopagitica* provides a safeguard for greater democracy. As they pointed out in a **petition** to Parliament on 18 January 1649, "if Government be just in its Constitution, and equal in its distribution, it will be good, if not absolutely necessary for them, to hear all voices and judgments, which they can never do, but by giving freedom to the Press, and in case any abuse their authority by scandalous **pamphlets**, they will never want advocates to vindicate their innocency." Despite the moderate tone of this argument, they did not receive a sympathetic response to their petition. Parliament immediately enlarged the crime of treason to include seditious publications and attempted, albeit unsuccessfully, to convict Lilburne for such supposedly treasonous ideas. *See also* GREAT BRITAIN.

LIANG QICHAO (1873–1929). Prominent journalist and press theorist in the late Qing period who has been credited with modernizing the Chinese press by creating a new style of journalism. However, recent commentators have tended to downplay his originality and impact. Influenced by the missionary periodical *Wanguo Gongbao*, whose publishers he met and briefly worked for, Liang founded seven reform papers after **China**'s defeat at the hands of **Japan** in 1895. The most prominent of these was *Shiwubao* through which Liang sought to create a national community. In 1902, Liang wrote the first comprehensive history of newspapers in China. Although previously critical of Western newspapers for their scandalmongering, inaccurate and biased coverage, and excessive verbiage, he now transferred these negative characteristics of the Western press to the foreign-owned papers still operating in China and treated Western papers outside of China as a model to be emulated. According to Zhang Volz, Liang's ultimate ideal of journalism as a vocation governed by moral virtue and dedicated to social improvement combined the Confucian emphasis on conscience with modern liberalism. For Liang, the journalist should not only educate the public about social issues but serve as its conscience and the ultimate arbiter of truth and justice.

LIBELLISTES. Downtrodden Parisian pamphleteers of the 1770s and 1780s. According to Robert Darnton, they comprised a counterculture with revolutionary aspirations. Lacking literary style and standing, they were treated with contempt by the very *philosophes* whom they sought to emulate and were accorded none of the benefits of the salons, academies, privileged journals, and honorific posts. While **Grub Street** had a few institutions of its own, such as the *musées* that sprang up in the 1780s and journals such as the *Les Nouvelles de la republique des lettres et des arts*, these did not curtail the frustration of would-be *philosophes* such as Marat, Brissot, and Carra, who produced a barrage of scurrilous *libelles* against a regime that had no place for them. In the final years before the Revolution, by Darnton's account, it was not the bourgeois *philosophes*, but the marginal writers of Grub Street, who were the main ideological opponents of the *ancien régime*.

For Jeremy Popkin, on the other hand, the obscure Grub Street scribblers were not primarily embittered, penniless, aspiring men-of-letters. On the contrary, they were the pawns of second-rank members of France's traditional political elite working on behalf of, and with the collusion of, some of its first-rank members in opposition to others. Prominent political figures like d'Eprésmesnil, Lafayette, and the Duc d'Orléans used their wealth to draw into their fold printers such as Pierre-Jacques Le Maître, who in turn hired lowly writers such as Brissot, Carra, and Gorsas to produce the requisite text. Though occasionally caught and arrested for their pamphlet campaigns, printers like Le Maître were generally let off lightly because of the reluctance of the political elite as a whole to maintain the traditional limitations on political journalism.

LIPPINCOTT, SARA JANE CLARKE (1823–1904). The first female correspondent for the *New York Times*. In 1844, using the pseudonym "Grace Greenwood," she began writing informal letters for newspapers, a format she retained for the rest of her career. Her letters dealt with issues such as slavery, capital punishment, and women's rights. In 1849, she became an editorial assistant for *Godey's Lady's Book*, but was fired after offending Southern readers with her anti-slavery views. During the Civil War, she gave lectures to raise funds for injured soldiers and was called "Grace Greenwood, the patriot" by President Abraham Lincoln. In her travel correspondence from Europe in the 1870s, she promoted the value of greater freedom for women while simultaneously titillating her readers with references to women's bodies and their sexual vulnerability.

LIPPMANN, WALTER (1889–1974). American philosopher-journalist and press critic whose journalism won him numerous awards, including **Pulitzer Prizes** in 1958 and 1968. In 1906, he entered Harvard where he was influenced by the pragmatism of William James and idealism of George Santayana and met fellow students **John Reed** and T. S. Eliot. After his graduation in 1909, he worked as a political advisor in upstate New York, relating his disappointing attempt to apply theory to practice in *A Preface to Politics* (1913). The following year, he helped to found the liberal *New Republic* and reflected further on the role of the intellectual in politics in *Drift and Mastery*. Following the entry of the **United States** into **World War I**, he was an assistant to the secretary of war and helped President Woodrow Wilson draft his Fourteen Points. Wilson's failure to "make the world safe for democracy" led him to question his earlier support for America's entry into the war.

In 1921, Lippmann joined the *New York World*, became editorial page editor, and proceeded to make its editorial page one of the best in the country. Ironically, however, he also developed a highly pessimistic assessment of the role of journalism in a democracy. The press, he argued in *Public Opinion* (1922), could never inform the public adequately for it to participate effectively in policy-making. It is "too frail to carry the whole burden of popular sovereignty, to supply spontaneously the truth which democracies hoped was inborn." Instead of being influenced by a faulty public opinion created by journalists, politicians should be guided by "organized intelligence" produced by an intellectual elite. "The press," Lippmann wrote, "is no substitute for institutions. It is like the beam of a searchlight that moves restlessly about, bringing one episode and then another out of darkness into vision. Men cannot do the work of the world by this light alone. They cannot govern societies by episodes, incidents, and eruptions."

Lippmann expanded on this theme in *The Phantom Public* (1926), at the same time that he was exerting a positive influence on public opinion through his own journalism. During the 1928 trial of the United States Radium Corporation for exposing its women workers to lethal levels of radiation, for example, he supported the Radium Girls editorially. The case, he said, called "not for fine-spun litigation but for simple, quick, direct justice."

After the Depression killed the *World* in 1931, Lippmann began writing the syndicated column "Today and Tomorrow" for the *New York Herald Tribune*. He initially supported President Franklin D. Roosevelt and the New Deal, but in *The Good Society* (1937) worried that national planning was paving the road to dictatorship. During the postwar period, he continued his negative treatment of public opinion in works such as *Essays in the Public Philosophy* (1955). In a final abandonment of pragmatic liberalism, he returned to the idea of "natural law" as the ultimate basis for determining the national interest. As a result of his own reading of that basis, he became one of the first journalists to question American involvement in the Vietnam War, earning the wrath of the Lyndon Johnson administration.

LITERARY JOURNALISM. An ambiguous category whose membership varies depending on whether it is defined as journalism that achieves certain "literary" attributes (e.g., **Daniel Defoe, Joseph Addison**) or as journalism practiced by writers whose greatest accomplishments are thought to be in the field of literature (e.g., Charles Dickens, George Orwell). Many of those included in the canon fulfilled both definitions (e.g., **Stephen Crane**). Literary journalism has generally been associated with attempts to develop a new kind of journalism (e.g., **Benjamin Franklin, Tom Wolfe**).

During the final years of the Restoration (1815–30), the French novelist Stendhal (1783–1842) turned to journalism to comment on the world of letters. He wrote hundreds of pages of unsigned and pseudonymous articles and reviews for the British press criticizing the contemporary literary and publishing scene in **France**. Written first in French and then translated for journals such as the *Paris*

Monthly Review and the *London Magazine*, these writings were a witty journalistic riposte to critical press reactions to Stendhal's own contribution to French literature. More frequently, however, writers have dabbled in journalism before settling into their literary career. Samuel Clemens (1835–1910) was a reporter for the Virginia City *Territorial Enterprise* in 1862 and an assistant editor of the monthly literary magazine *The Galaxy* (1866–78), contributing a department of "Memoranda" devoted to humorous sketches. Before becoming a novelist, Edward Bellamy (1850–98) worked for the *New York Evening Post* and then edited the *Springfield* (Massachusetts) *Union* from 1872–77. After the publication of *Looking Backward: 2000–1887* (1888), he founded two journals, the *Nationalist* (1889–91) and the *New Nation* (1891–94). In some cases, their journalism was of high quality and continued to play an important role alongside their other work. Albert Camus (1913–1960) was a courtroom reporter for the *Alger republicain* and upset the local authorities by campaigning for political and economic reforms on behalf of the Algerian Muslims. After joining the French Resistance in 1942, he wrote leading articles for underground newspapers such as *Combat*, which he also edited from 1944 to 1947. *See also* HEMINGWAY, ERNEST; STEINBECK, JOHN; ZOLA, EMILE.

LLOYD, THOMAS (1756–1827). "Editor" of the *Congressional Register*, the most complete reports of the earliest debates of the U.S. House of Representatives. The *Register* was issued with some difficulty more or less weekly from 6 May 1789 until 8 March 1790, when its publication on a subscription basis suddenly ended—inexplicably breaking off in mid-sentence. With a reputation as the best shorthand writer in the new republic, Lloyd persuaded Congress to let him record, edit, and print accounts of its proceedings. Although other reporters were also allowed in the House, Lloyd was permitted to sit near the speaker where speeches could be heard most clearly. This convenience, he told his subscribers, enabled him "to assure the public of the greatest degree of accuracy in detailing the words, sentiments, and opinions delivered by its members." While some members complained of inaccurate reporting and contemplated removing the reporters altogether, James Madison thought the inaccuracies were unintentional and defended the publication of the debates. After returning to his birthplace in London, Lloyd fell on hard times and spent the rest of his life drifting from one job to another.

LONDON GAZETTE. The official newspaper of **Great Britain** with editions in London, Edinburgh, and Belfast. It was first published as the *Oxford Gazette* by Leonard Litchfeld, the University Printer, on 14 November 1665 to provide news to Charles II and his courtiers, who had fled to Oxford to escape the Great Plague and were afraid of being contaminated by London papers. Even before the king returned to London, it became the responsibility of **Henry Muddiman**, who continued it subsequently as the *London Gazette* (beginning with No. 24 on 5 February 1666).

LOS ANGELES TIMES. One of the most respected newspapers in the world. It originated in 1882 when the Mirror Company took over the bankrupt *Los Angeles Daily Times* (1873) as its printer and placed it under the editorship of Harrison Gray Otis, a former lieutenant colonel in the Union army. A militant, anti-union conservative, Gray became sole owner of the *Times* in 1886 and used it to promote the development southern California. About the same time, Harry Chandler joined the paper on the business side and consolidated its circulation and regional influence. He was later succeeded by his son Norman, who retained the paper's conservative politics. For more than half a century, however, it remained little more than a parochial California paper. It was not until the 1960s that the Harry Chandler's son, Otis, shifted its emphasis to quality national and international news.

LUCE, HENRY R. (1898–1967). American media mogul. The son of Presbyterian missionaries in **China**, Luce worked briefly as a reporter for the *Chicago Daily News* and the *Baltimore News* after his graduation from Yale in 1920. In 1923, he and Briton Hadden, a college classmate, founded *Time* as a weekly newsmagazine. Following Hadden's death in 1929, Luce began the business monthly *Fortune* (1930), the weekly radio news program *March of Time* (1931), and the popular weekly photojournalism magazine *Life* (1936). He assembled a group of brilliant young writers like Archibald MacLeish, Dwight Macdonald, and **James Agee**, but kept them on a short leash.

A fervent Republican, he continued to build up his media empire and used it to promote big business at the expense of labor and entry of the **United States** into **World War II**. He and his talented wife, Claire Boothe Luce, traveled to China in 1941 to report on conditions there; she also reported from Europe, **Africa**, and **India** under contract to *Life*. After the war, Luce promoted an aggressive American stance against the **Soviet Union** and Communist China. *See also* TIMESE.

LUNA. An anti-fascist literary and cultural journal produced weekly at the end of the Spanish Civil War by a group of 17 republican intellectuals who had taken refuge in the **Chilean** embassy in Madrid after General Francisco Franco's victory. They also produced a newspaper, *El Cometa*, but only had sufficient resources to produce one copy of each issue. In 1940, the group escaped to Chile where they continued their work in exile.

LUXEMBURG, ROSA (1871–1919). Polish-born activist who used both journalism and academic writing to help create the Polish Social Democratic Party and the **German** Communist Party. Harassed by Poland's **Russian** authorities for embracing Marxist socialism while still in high school, she emigrated to Zurich where she received her doctorate in law and political science in 1889. After graduation she began editing *The Workers' Cause*, but a year later became a German citizen and moved to Berlin where the German Social Democratic Party was in ascendancy. In *Reform or Revolution* (1899), she gained prominence within the socialist movement by attacking revisionist Eduard Bernstein's case for "evolutionary socialism" or gradual reformism as a betrayal of Marxist principles. After witnessing the revolution in Poland and Russia in 1905, she concluded that the general or mass strike was the most effective weapon for overthrowing capitalism. Despite being imprisoned during **World War I** for her antiwar activities, she continued to promote her radical views through **pamphlets** such as "Crisis in the German Social Democracy" (1916), signed with the pseudonym "Junius." In January 1919, her belief in mass participation led her to support the ill-prepared insurrection by the Spartacus League in Germany. In the course of its crushing, she was captured and brutally put to death without trial.

– M –

MACGAHAN, JANUARIUS ALOYSIUS (1844–1878). American war correspondent. In 1869, he travelled from his hometown Pigeon Roost Ridge, Ohio, to Paris to further his education. Two years later, he was hired by the *New York Herald* to cover the Franco–Prussian War (1870–71) and Paris Commune. In 1873, defying **Russian** orders and pursued by Cossack and Turkoman forces, the bearded, bearlike MacGahan rode a thousand miles across Central Asia, including the Kyzil Kum desert, to overtake a Russian army and cover its conquest of the Khanate in the walled city of Khiva. His account of his exploits, *Campaigning on the Oxus* (1874), made him famous. After returning from **Asia**, he covered the Carlist War in **Spain** and then accompanied the 1875 Arctic expedition of the ship *Pandora*. In 1876, he was hired by the *London Daily News* to go to **Bulgaria**, where Turkish soldiers had killed some 15,000 Christians. MacGahan reported having seen "the remains of babes and little children slaughtered by the hundreds, of immense heaps of bodies of maidens—first violated and then murdered." Together with similar testimony from an American diplomat, his reports turned public opinion against the Ottoman Empire and encouraged the Russians to attack. During the Russo–Turkish War of 1877–78, through which Bulgaria gained its independence, MacGahan contracted typhus and died in Constantinople.

MACKENZIE, WILLIAM LYON (1795–1861). Scottish-born journalist and political reformer. Raised by his poor but proud mother and a voracious reader from an early age, Mackenzie emigrated to Upper **Canada** in 1820 and tried his hand at various business endeavors before founding the *Colonial Advocate* in Queenston on 18 May 1824. Later that year, he relocated the paper to York (present-day Toronto) where, despite partial demolition of his **printing press** in 1826, he escalated his attacks upon the Tory authorities or so-called Family Compact. In 1828, he was expelled for the first of five times from the Legislative Assembly for libel, each time being re-elected by his constituency. In 1834, he gave up publication of the *Colonial Advocate* to become the first mayor of Toronto, but two years later founded the *Constitution* as a vehicle for the Reform party. Following the party's defeat, he made a futile attempt at rebellion and was forced to flee to the **United States**, where his attempt to set up a provisional government on Navy Island in the Niagara River led to his imprisonment for 18 months for violation of the neutrality laws. During the 1840s, he worked as a journalist until a general amnesty allowed him to return to Canada. He rounded out his tempestuous career as a member once again of the Legislative Assembly. His grandson, William Lyon Mackenzie King, was a Liberal prime minister of Canada.

MACNEIL-LEHRER REPORT. Unorthodox nightly news program on the PBS network in the **United States** beginning in 1976. It tried to break free from the traditional format of commercial network newscasts with their numerous short items. Anchored by Robert MacNeil in New York and Jim Lehrer in Washington, the program examined a single major news story each night, using experts and other journalists. It was scheduled at 7:30 P.M. to reduce competition as well as serve as a follow-up to regular network newscasts.

MACROSTORIES. Concept developed by Marvin Olasky in *Central Ideas in the Development of American Journalism* (1991). For Olasky, a macrostory consists of a worldview that is integrated and condensed into an interpretive, narrative framework for making sense of the news. Derived from the main theologies and ideologies of an age, macrostories are applied to "discretionary" news items rather than "obligatory" ones such as accidents or disasters. According to Olasky, three successive, though overlapping, macrostories have had a commanding influence over European and American journalism: the "official" macrostory, or the world as seen in terms of the needs of the state; the Reformation-inspired "corruption" macrostory, or the unsurprising abuse of authority by naturally sinful individuals; and the "oppression" macrostory, which shifts the blame for corruption from human frailty to flawed social systems. Compared to the sociological concept of media frames, which has dominated recent analyses of news coverage, the concept of macrostories provides a better basis for relating journalism to history, but is arguably too narrow and reductionist as applied by Olasky.

MALAYSIA. The first newspaper in Malaysia was the *Straits Times*, an English daily founded in 1845 in Kuala Lumpur. For most of the 19th century, Malaysian journalism was confined to English publications such as the *Malay Mail* in Kuala Lumpur and the *Free Press*, owned by William Makepeace in Singapore. In the 1890s, however, a few indigenous weeklies, such as *Seri Perak* and *Jajahan Melayu*, were founded to give a voice to the Malay intelligentsia. In 1907, moreover, one of Makepeace's editors, Mohd Eunos Abdullah, founded the vernacular *Utusan Melaya*, published three times a week and modeled on the *Free Press*. Related to royalty and the son of a prominent merchant in Singapore, Eunos had graduated from the Raffles Institute in 1894 and then gone to work for Makepeace a few years later. Called the father of Malay journalism by W. R. Roff, he also founded and edited the only vernacular daily in Malaysia, the *Lembaga Melaya*, in 1914. In the same period, a number of other vernacular newspapers and magazines were begun, including the Islamic reform journals *Al-Iman* and *Neracha*.

During the interwar period, the vernacular press continued to grow, despite restrictions in the 1930s aimed at deterring the spread of Communism. Some, like the *Warta Malaya* founded by Onn b. Ja'afar in 1931, began to criticize the British occupation of Malaysia. Following the **Japanese** takeover in 1942, many of Malaysia's newspapers were suspended. After **World War II**, the British enacted emergency controls over the media in response to ethnic unrest and increased Communist agitation. During the 1960s, a temporary state of equilibrium was achieved through the political alliance of different ethnic parties. But the withdrawal of the Malaysian Chinese party from the government in 1969 threw the country into turmoil. A new state of emergency was declared and press freedom was curbed once again. Since then, the Malaysian media have been subject to various forms of control, such as stringent permit requirements. In recent years, the government has combined corporate ownership with legislative regulation.

THE MARCH OF TIME. Quasi-**newsreel** which made its appearance in movie theaters beginning in 1935. Cofounded by Louis De Rochemont and Roy E. Larsen for the publishers of *Time* and *Fortune* magazines, it revolutionized the style of the newsreel by adding staged scenes to authentic newsreel footage and adopting an editorial point of view. Although giving the newsreel greater impact and realism, the docudrama technique involved questionable journalistic ethics as audiences were not informed of its use. In 1943, Louis de Rochemont was succeeded as producer by his younger brother Richard. Among the most successful episodes was "Inside Nazi **Germany**," produced in 1938. Some of the productions were censored in the **United States** as well as Europe.

THE MASSES. Artistic, witty, and irreverent left-wing magazine founded by Max Eastman (1883–1969) in New York City in 1913. In addition to essays by journalists like **John Reed**, the publication drew upon the talents of numerous women contributors, who used it to promote feminism and pacifism. In 1917, it was suppressed by the federal government. Eastman was tried twice for sedition, but both trials ended in a hung jury.

"MAY FOURTH" JOURNALS. On 4 May 1919, the citizens of Peking led by the local university students protested in the streets against the Versailles treaty confirming previous secret agreements which gave **Japan** all of **Germany**'s Shangdong rights in return for its naval assistance. The date gave its name to a new movement of nationalism and cultural introspection in **China** which was carried on in part through a large number of new newspapers and periodicals. With names like *The Dawn*, *New Society*, and *Plain People*, the "May Fourth" journals tended to use a simple vernacular style to reach as many people as possible with their campaign for national and cultural renewal.

McCLURE'S. Popular monthly magazine founded by S. S. McClure, the self-styled "inventor" of muckrake journalism, together with John S. Phillips on the eve of the Panic of 1893. Modeled in part on **George Newnes**'s *Strand Magazine*, it initially focused on adventure stories, romances, and noncritical articles, but during the Spanish–American War of 1898 began to adopt a more outspoken attitude on matters of public interest. This critical stance continued after 1900 when McClure hired a group of talented journalists whom President Theodore Roosevelt was later to denigrate as **muckrakers**. When McClure returned from Europe in 1906 with a grand scheme for expanding the company and also proposed discontinuing muckraking because of Roosevelt's attack and lost **advertising** revenues, Phillips left the magazine and took **Lincoln Steffens, Ida M. Tarbell**, and **Ray Stannard Baker** with him. Following this "palace revolution" (McClure's words), the magazine began losing money and in 1912 McClure was forced to sell his beloved publication and become a salaried employee of its new owners. To help pay off its outstanding debts, the company proposed serializing McClure's autobiography without compensation in exchange for any profits from its sale in book form. Written largely by Willa Cather from interviews with McClure, *My Autobiography* tells the story of McClure's triumphs over adversity in the typical Horatio Alger motif.

McCORMICK, ANNE ELIZABETH (1882–1954). Born in England as Anne O'Hare, McCormick was raised in the **United States**, where she attended college and began her journalistic career in Cleveland as associate editor of the weekly *Catholic Universe Bulletin*, to which her single-parent mother also contributed. After **World War I**, her husband's business travels provided her with an opportunity to write about postwar conditions in Europe for the *New York Times*. During the early 1930s, she won recognition for her stories on the rise of Benito Mussolini and, in 1936, began writing a thrice-weekly column entitled "In Europe." The same year, she became the first woman member of the *Times'* editorial board, writing two unsigned editorials a week. She was the first woman to win a **Pulitzer Prize** for foreign correspondence (1937) and the recipient of several other prestigious awards. In addition to Mussolini, her interviewees included Winston Churchill, Adolf Hitler, Joseph Stalin, Franklin Roosevelt, and Harry S. Truman.

McWILLIAMS, CAREY (1905–1980). Prolific writer and editor of *The Nation* from 1955 to 1975. He first joined *The Nation* in 1945 as a contributing editor after a career in law. A champion of racial minorities and the oppressed, he continued its devotion to investigative reporting, developing special series on the **Federal Bureau of Investigation (FBI)** in 1958 and the **Central Intelligence Agency (CIA)** in 1962. He led the attack on American policy in Vietnam and was in the forefront during **Watergate**.

MEDILL, JOSEPH (1823–1899). American newspaper owner who was instrumental in forming (and credited with naming) the Republican Party. In 1855, a few years after founding the *Leader* in Cleveland, Medill purchased an interest in the *Chicago Tribune* and gradually gained absolute control over its operations. A strong supporter of Abraham Lincoln, he held several important public service appointments and, in 1871, was elected mayor of Chicago.

MEET THE PRESS. Long-running American radio and TV program featuring live interviews of major newsmakers by a panel of prominent journalists. Created for the MBS radio network in 1945 by Martha Rountree and Lawrence Spivak in association with the *American Mercury* magazine, it went on television on 6 November 1947 and marked the beginning of public affairs journalism on American TV. In addition to Rountree and Spivak, its moderators have included Ned Brooks, Bill Monroe, Marvin Kalb, and Chris Wallace.

MENCKEN, H. L. (1880–1956). Known as the "Sage of Baltimore," Mencken was the leading member of a new breed of American ("The right of *Americans* to be so called," he wrote in 1947, "is frequently challenged, especially in **Latin America**, but so far no plausible substitute has been devised") social critic during the interwar period. Born into an upper-class German family in Baltimore, he was raised on the writings of Nietzsche and Schopenhauer. He worked for the *Baltimore Morning Herald* from 1899 until its demise in 1906 and then joined the *Sun* papers of Baltimore. He and G. J. Nathan co-edited the *Smart Set* from 1914–23 and then cofounded *The American Mercury* as its successor, which Mencken edited from 1924–33. In *The American Language* (1919), which grew in subsequent editions to almost 800 pages, he tried to show how the American language is different from English. Some of his best criticism was published in *Prejudices* (6 vols., 1919–27). Among his main targets was pretentiousness, as evidenced in his "Bulletin on 'Hon.'" in *American Speech* (no. 2, 1946). Noting that members of Congress continued to insist that they be described as *Hon.* in the *Congressional Record*, he added wryly: "The Hon. Mary T. Norton of New Jersey . . . not contented with the frequent *Honing* she gets from the *Record*'s reporters, once actually spoke of herself as 'I, *Hon.* Mary T. Norton' in a solemn House document."

MERCURIUS POLITICUS. English newsbook founded in June 1650 under the editorship of Marchamont Nedham (or Marchmont Needham). It served as a vehicle of propaganda for the Commonwealth-Protectorate until the return of Charles II in 1660 whereupon it was closed. From 1655 to 1659, it had an outright monopoly of news. Until January 1652, John Milton was officially responsible for its registration, but not for its content, giving rise to debate as to whether he actually contributed to the publication. In addition to news, its early numbers contained a series of articles by Nedham in support of the party in power. Nedham was probably influenced by Milton, with whom he had become close friends. After the execution of the king in January 1649, Nedham had been imprisoned and Milton had been assigned to examine his writings; it was only through Milton's positive evaluation that he was chosen to edit *Mercurius Politicus.* In switching from a jocular to a more serious tone and in drawing selectively from his own writings, Nedham seems to have done so with an eye to Milton's expressed convictions. *See also* GREAT BRITAIN.

MERKEL, GARLIEB (1769–1850). Livonian journalist and activist who was instrumental in developing a modern press system in the Baltic provinces of **Russia**. In his famous pamphlet *The Latvians* (1794), he attacked the harsh treatment of the peasantry by the German aristocracy and called for the abolition of serfdom in Livonia and **Estonia**. His writings contributed to the agrarian reform law of 1804. After visiting Weimar in 1797, where he was influenced by Johann Gottfried von Herder, he moved to Berlin and published various newspapers and magazines in the fight against Napoleon. After Prussian defeats at Jena and Auerstedt, he fled to Riga and continued his opposition in *Der Freimutige* and other papers. In addition to establishing the basis for a political press in **Germany**, his journalism publicized the ideas of the Enlightenment.

MERZ, CHARLES (1893–1969). Editorial page director for the *New York Times*. In 1920, he and **Walter Lippmann** conducted a study of the *Times*' coverage of events in **Russia** since the October Revolution of 1917. Published as a 42-page supplement to the *New Republic* on August 4, "A Test of the News" concluded that "from the point of view of professional journalism the reporting of the Russian revolution is nothing short of a disaster." During the 1955 hearings by the Senate Internal Security subcommittee, chaired by Sen. James O. Eastland (D-Miss.), on possible Communist infiltration of the New York press, Merz wrote a key *Times'* editorial criticizing both the subcommittee and his own paper's actions in dismissing several of its reporters for taking the Fifth Amendment. In "The Voice of a Free Press," published on 5 January 1956, Merz acknowledged that some *Times'* employees had been associated with Communist organizations in the past, but insisted that the *Times* alone should decide whom it would employ. "We do not believe in the doctrine of irredeemable sin," he wrote. "We think it is possible to atone through good performance for past error." *See also* CENSORSHIP.

MEXICO. As in **Latin America** generally, the newspaper continues to struggle in Mexico in terms of both readership, with very limited circulation, and as a basis for a **public sphere**. Although the Spanish introduced printing to Mexico in the early 16th century, strict controls were maintained over the press. Around 1660, small-circulation newspapers such as the *Gacetade* in Mexico City made their appearance and used cartoons to engage in a degree of criticism. However, it was not until the 1720s and 1730s that substantial journals such as the *Gaceta de Mexico* and *Mercurio de Mexico* were established. Their stated purpose was to provide moral uplift and a record of events in New Spain. They focused on **crime** and natural disasters rather than political events. Even literary compositions were looked upon with suspicion by the colonial authorities.

After Mexico achieved independence from **Spain** in 1819, there was hope for an American-style political public sphere among editors such as José Joaquin Fernández de Lizardi (1776–1827), who had championed independence in his weekly *Pensador Mexicano*. But except for the brief period of the restored republic (1867–76), successive presidents turned a deaf ear to pleas for press freedom and used newspaper closures, the imprisonment of journalists, and outright bribery to intimidate and manipulate the press.

During the Revolution of 1910, the charismatic Pancho Villa used archetypal American images of himself to achieve favorable coverage in the American press. After the Revolution, hopes for greater freedom led to the creation of a number of new papers. In 1916, for example, Felix Fulgencio Palavicini established *El Universal* for the specific purpose of promoting the ideals of the Revolution. After gaining power in 1929, however, the Partido Revolucionario Institutional (PRI) established a monopoly over political power that was not seriously challenged until the late 1980s. When the Mexico City paper *Excélsior* began showing signs of greater independence in 1976, the government simply ousted its editor. In some cases, violence has been used against journalists to keep them in line. But newspaper owners themselves have generally made sure that their employees do not challenge the official line. Mexican journalists base most of their coverage on official news releases which are accepted uncritically; a content analysis of daily newspapers in Mexico City in the mid-1980s found that over 90 percent of stories were favorable to the government ministry providing the information.

During the 1990s, an independent press was finally able to gain a foothold in Mexico with the founding of papers such as *Público* in Guadalajara and *Reforma* in Mexico City. They began to modify the practices of the traditional officialist press and to gain new readers in the process. However, most newspapers are still owned by wealthy individuals with close political connections to the state.

MITCHELL, JOHN (1815–1875). Irish journalist and leader of the Irish American nationalists. In 1848, he founded the *United Irishman* and contributed to the abortive Young Ireland revolt, for which he was convicted of sedition and transported to **Australia**. In 1853, he escaped to the **United States**, where he edited the proslavery journal *Citizen* and wrote the Irish revolutionary classic *Jail Journal* (1854). Following imprisonment in 1865 for his support of the Confederacy during the Civil War, he edited the *Irish Citizen*. Shortly before his death, he returned to **Ireland** and was elected to Parliament.

MOBILIZING INFORMATION. Concept developed by James B. Lemert in *Does Mass Communication Change Public Opinion After All?* (1981). A number of previous studies had concluded that public opinion is an inherently lethargic force. But Lemert presented evidence that it can lead to politically effective action in cases where journalists provide the public with adequate "mobilizing information"—in particular, the names and addresses of persons or organizations who might take action if contacted by members of the public. According to Lemert, journalists usually only provide information designed to change public opinion without including the means for the public to act upon its new opinion.

MORAL PANIC. Term originating in British sociology and cultural studies in the 1970s and applied by the national press of **Great Britain** beginning in the mid-1980s in connection with issues such as drug addiction, child abuse, and single motherhood. As first used by Stanley Cohen in *Folk Devils and Moral Panics* (1972), a moral panic occurs whenever certain interest groups respond to the strains and uncertainties accompanying social change by using the mass media to project their fears on to a convenient scapegoat or "folk devil" (e.g., the Mods and Rockers in 1960s Britain). In *Policing the Crisis: Mugging, the State, and Law and Order* (1978), on the other hand, Stuart Hall and his neo-Marxian colleagues saw moral panics as deliberate attempts by the ruling elite to maintain its authority in the current period of declining hegemonic consensus by diverting the attention of the masses from the actual causes of eroding social conditions to more superficial issues.

For still other academics, however, moral panics are in fact genuine, spontaneous public responses to real troubling conditions as revealed more or less accurately by the media. The press used the term pejoratively for the most part until the killing of toddler James Bulger in 1993, when some media commentators began to criticize "left-wing" criminologists for dismissing a real crime epidemic and crisis of values as a mere "moral panic." Recently academics such as Arnold Hunt have begun a needed critique of the concept, which arguably has become too ambiguous in meaning and rhetorical in purpose to have much remaining analytical utility.

MOREL, EDMUND DENE (1873–1924). British journalist who played an influential role in the campaign against slavery in the Belgian Congo. He was born in Paris, but raised mainly in England. He first became aware of a vast slave system in the Congo Free State through his work with a Liverpool shipping company and in 1900 began writing against it in various magazines, including the *West African Mail*, which he founded in 1903. A year later, he organized the Congo Reform Association and used it to enlist the support of writers such as Joseph Conrad, Arthur Conan Doyle, Anatole France, and Mark Twain. Doyle based one of his characters in the *The Lost World* (1912) on Morel. A pacifist, Morel was imprisoned during **World War I**, but in 1922 defeated Winston Churchill to win a seat as a Labour M.P.

MORRISON, GEORGE ERNEST (1862–1920). Australian physician who gave up medicine to become a journalist in **China**. Known as "Chinese Morrison," he served as the Beijing correspondent for *The Times* of London from 1897 to 1912, sending particularly memorable dispatches during the Boxer Rebellion. Author of *An Australian in China* (1895), he also worked as an advisor for the government of Yuan Shikai.

MOTT, FRANK LUTHER (1886–1964). Professor of journalism and early authority on American journalism and the press. From 1925–30, he co-edited the *Midland* with John T. Frederick. While director of the school of journalism at the State University of Iowa (1927–42), he wrote a **Pulitzer Prize**–winning *History of American Magazines* (3 vols., 1930, 1938; vol. 4, 1957) and published *American Journalism: A History* (1941; rev. ed. 1950). He also served as editor of *Journalism Quarterly* (1930–35). During his tenure as dean of the school of journalism at the University of Missouri (1942–51), he edited *Journalism in Wartime* (1943) and wrote *Jefferson and the Press* (1943), *Golden Multitudes: The Story of Best-Sellers in the U.S.* (1947), and *The News in America* (1952).

MUCKRAKERS, AMERICAN. Group of well-educated journalists and novelists who engaged in exposure and protest during the Progressive era in the **United States**. Anticipated by Henry Demarest Lloyd and **Benjamin Orange Flower** in the 1880s and 1890s, the muckraking movement gained momentum during the period of agrarian revolt and began to influence public opinion after 1900 when popular magazines such as *McClure's*, *Everybody's*, *Collier's*, *Cosmopolitan*, and the *Independent* began to embrace investigative reporting.

The term *muckraker* was first used by President Theodore Roosevelt on 14 April 1906 in a speech rejecting charges of corruption in politics. Roosevelt compared certain journalists to the Man with the Muckrake in John Bunyan's *Pilgrim's Progress* (1678), who was so intent on raking muck that he could not see a celestial crown overhead. In the same speech, however, Roosevelt also hailed "as a benefactor every writer or speaker who . . . with merciless severity attacks evil, provided always that he remembers that the attack is of use only if it is absolutely truthful."

According to Mark Neuzil, Roosevelt's muckrake speech was aimed as much at **William Randolph Hearst**, whom he regarded as his chief political rival for the presidency, as at the muckraking journalists themselves. Although journalists such as **Lincoln Steffens**, **Ida M. Tarbell**, **Ray Stannard Baker**, **David Graham Phillips**, T. W. Lawson, William Hard, Mark Sullivan, and **Samuel Hopkins Adams** took his epithet as a badge of distinction, Roosevelt helped to delegitimize their quest to save American democracy. By 1911 or so, the muckraking movement was not only running out of steam but was being deliberately undermined as *Everybody's*, *Collier's*, *Hampton's*, and the *Arena* were destroyed, bought out, or transformed by the interests they threatened. Muckraking contributed to reforms such as the Pure Food and Drug Act, workmen's compensation laws, conservation measures, and direct primaries. But it was also largely restricted to issues affecting white Americans and generally remained captive to the prevailing stereotypes of African Americans.

MUCKRAKERS, JAPANESE. The muckraking movement was not confined to the **United States**. In early 20th-century **Japan**, a group of popular journalists and other writers also sought to expose the social costs of industrialization. Their numbers included Arahata Kanson, Kōtoku Shūsui, Sakai Toshihiko, and Uchimura Kanzō and they provided valuable assistance to the farmers of the Watarase Valley in their fight against pollution by the Ashio copper mine. Unlike their American counterparts, however, they were generally more interested in showing that "the social problem" had arrived in Japan than in finding concrete ways of alleviating urban poverty, labor exploitation, and industrial pollution. Intent on proving that capitalist industry was destroying the moral basis of Japanese society, they failed to offer an alternative to the Meiji dream of progress, leaving the door open for a replacement in the form of an emperor-state ideology.

MUDDIMAN, HENRY (1629–1692). First editor of the *London Gazette*. He began his journalistic career by publishing two newsbooks, *Parliamentary Intelligence* and *Mercurius Publicus*, when Parliament reconvened in 1659. His monopoly over news production was given to **Roger L'Estrange** in 1663, but reacquired in 1665 at which time he began the *Gazette*.

MURDOCH, RUPERT (1931–). Australian-born global media baron. After studies at Oxford, Murdoch worked briefly at **Lord Beaverbrook**'s *Daily Express* and then began buying newspapers in **Great Britain** and **Australia**, beginning with his father's small *Adelaide News*. Eventually, his Sydney-based News Corporation owned papers on every continent except **Africa**. In 1986, Murdoch challenged the three American networks by creating the Fox Network. In the late 1990s, he also developed Fox National News, an all-news cable network. A key to his economic success has been control over the production as well as the delivery of content. But the extent of his holdings raises serious questions for the practice of journalism within his vast empire.

MURROW, EDWARD R. (1908–1965). Distinguished American broadcast journalist. Murrow joined CBS in 1935, became its European director in 1937, and gained fame for his dramatic broadcasts beginning "This—is London" during the Blitz. After **World War II**, he produced *See It Now* and *Person to Person* for CBS on television. His finest hour came on 9 March 1954 when *See It Now* broadcast "A Report on Senator Joseph R. McCarthy," directly exposing the distortions and false claims on which McCarthy had based his witchhunt against alleged Communists. In 1961, President John F. Kennedy appointed him as director of the United States Information Agency (USIA). The year before his death, he was awarded the Presidential Medal of Freedom, the nation's highest civilian honor.

– N –

THE NATION. Magazine founded by abolitionists in New York City on 6 July 1865. Its first editor was Wendell Phillips Garrison, the son of **William Lloyd Garrison**. In 1881, it was purchased by Henry Villard and converted into a weekly literary supplement for his *New York Evening Post*. In 1918, his son, **Oswald Garrison Villard**, transformed it into a liberal current affairs magazine. During the 1920s, it published **Carleton Beals**'s articles on U.S. policy in Latin America and Paul Y. Anderson's exposure of the Teapot Dome scandals. In 1937, it was purchased from New York banker Maurice Wertheim by managing editor Freda Kirchway, who served as editor and publisher until 1955. As a result of its support for labor, economic reform, and civil liberties, it was monitored for many years by the **Federal Bureau of Investigation (FBI)**. It is currently the oldest weekly magazine in America.

NATIONAL ENQUIRER. Originally the *New York Enquirer*, a weekly broadsheet founded by **William Randolph Hearst** in 1926. In 1952, it was purchased for a small sum by Generoso Pope Jr. and turned into a **tabloid** focusing on blood and gore. John R. Vitek III suggests that it may have been financed initially by Mafia money. Its circulation soon reached one million, but then stalled. In 1957, Pope renamed it the *National Enquirer*, switched its focus to celebrity news and self-help features, and began marketing it in supermarkets, where it was selling 6 million copies a week at one point. In 1971, Pope moved it to Lantana, Florida, and hired numerous British journalists to produce its materials. It later spawned several clones, which have reduced its circulation by about two-thirds.

NATIONAL POLICE GAZETTE. Sensationalist paper published in New York City and distributed nationally from 1845 until it went bankrupt in 1932. During the editorship of founder George Wilkes, it focused on criminal biographies and police scandals; after being purchased in 1866 by George Matsel, New York's chief of police, lurid sex was added to the mix; and under Richard K. Fox, who acquired it in 1877, coverage of boxing became an additional staple. *See also* CRIME AND TRIALS, COVERAGE OF.

NETHERLANDS. In 1579, the northern provinces of the Low Countries acquired independence from **Spain** through the Union of Utrecht. Aided by a policy of press freedom, the Republic of the

United Netherlands became an intellectual and publication center for Protestantism. Following the Catholic suppression of a Protestant revolt in Bohemia in 1618, printers in Amsterdam began issuing **corantos** (Spanish for *current*) to provide the European Protestant community with news about such events. Similar newssheets were created in other Dutch cities, all of them published in French as the most widespread language in Europe. The first full-fledged newspaper in the Dutch Republic was Adriaen Vlacq's *Post-Tydingen Uyt's Graven-Haghe*, which began publication in The Hague in 1656. The subsequent expansion of newspapers included a number of international gazettes written in French and profitably marketed to readers in **France** and other European countries where **censorship** still prevailed. These influential papers made use of correspondents in the major cities of Europe. One of the most respected and reliable was the *Gazette de Leyde*, founded in 1680.

During the 18th century, freedom of the press continued to be extended not only to Dutch newspapers but to journals published by refugees fleeing religious intolerance in other European countries. Under the influence of the French Revolution, however, a repressive constitution was adopted in 1798 and an authoritarian government, the Staatsbewind, established three years later. When the new reactionary regime was ridiculed by J. C. Hespe in 1802, he was tried for various crimes and banned from the provinces of Holland, Zeeland, and Utrecht. The Staatsbewind also revoked freedom of the press, making it a crime to criticize government, and suppressed the venerable *Gazette de Leyde* after it aroused Napoleon's wrath.

Partial freedom of the press was restored in the constitution of 1815, enabling statesmen like Jon Rudolph (1798–1872) to use the press to advocate further reforms. But although the first daily newspaper was created in 1830, the development of a daily press did not begin in earnest until the enactment of the constitution of 1848. Even then, press freedom was not granted in the Dutch colonies. In 1856, the colonial government in the Netherlands East Indies (now **Indonesia**) enacted specific restrictions on freedom of the press. When these regulations were attacked by liberal papers such as *Bataviaansch Handelsblad* edited by H. J. Lion, the minister of colonial affairs, J. J. Rochussen, took legal action, and in 1860 Lion was sentenced to 18 months in prison.

Until **World War II**, most Dutch newspapers closely reflected the political and religious beliefs of their editors. During the war, underground newspapers such as *Trouw* and *Het Parool* took great risks to counter the information in papers that were either taken over by the Nazis or, like the previously liberal *New Rotterdam Daily*, voluntarily became pro-German. After the war, most Dutch newspapers maintained close relations with a particular political party. During the 1960s and 1970s, however, many papers began to reduce their party ties.

NEW-ENGLAND COURANT. Literary newspaper founded by James Franklin (1697–1735) in 1721. Shortly after its creation, it became embroiled in a war of words with the *Boston News-Letter* over the controversial practice of inoculation during the smallpox epidemic that was then raging in Boston. Whereas the *News-Letter* supported local Puritan minister Cotton Mather's advocacy of inoculation, the *Courant* lined up with the Boston physicians who, seeking to establish their own jurisdiction over medicine, opposed its experimental use. After James Franklin was jailed for criticizing the theocracy, his younger half-brother Benjamin took over as editor. As the first colonial American paper to be published without government approval, the *Courant* helped to establish the principle of editorial independence. It ceased publication around 1726. *See also* FRANKLIN, BENJAMIN; UNITED STATES.

NEWNES, GEORGE (1851–1910). Late Victorian and Edwardian editor, publisher, and proprietor who founded a series of British magazines in the spirit of the New Journalism. Among the more successful of these were *Tit-Bits* (1881), the *Review of Reviews* (1890), *Strand Magazine* (1891), and *Country Life* (1897). Each publication was carefully crafted to serve the desires of a particular audience. Newnes also founded the *Westminster Gazette* in 1893 as a Liberal evening paper. In 1898, he became involved in an unsuccessful venture to develop a device called the Home Mutoscope through which people could watch filmed news events.

NEW REPUBLIC. The leading magazine of American liberalism. It was founded in 1914 by Herbert Croly, **Walter Lippmann**, and Walter Weyl and promoted Croly's vision of a new nationalism in which the state would use its regulatory power to control corporate capitalism, improve social welfare, and reinvigorate democracy. With the help of contributors like John Dewey, Thorstein Veblen, and **W. E. B. Du Bois**, it attracted 40,000 subscribers by 1918. Over the next half century, its influence and balance sheet ebbed and flowed in conjunction with the fortunes of political liberalism, declining in the 1920s, reviving in the 1930s, experiencing difficulties during the early postwar period, and regaining strength as an opponent of the war in Vietnam in the late 1960s. Since then, it has moderated its traditional knee-jerk liberalism and placed increasing emphasis on broader social and cultural issues.

NEWS, CONCEPTS OF. *1. The Communicative Concept of News.* In an essay entitled "News as a Form of Knowledge," first published in 1940, the American sociologist **Robert E. Park** suggested that different forms of knowledge might be placed along a continuum on the basis of their degree of precision. He then argued that news is located at some point between a superficial and fragmentary personal "acquaintance with" certain events and a formal, exact, and verified "knowledge of" those events. This approach provides a defense against criticisms of news that judge it by criteria of accuracy and depth that are more applicable to history or sociology. But it still leaves news, and the journalists who produce it, vulnerable to charges of distorting reality.

It could be argued, however, that news is not primarily about constructing reality but rather is mainly concerned with facilitating communication about reality. Once they have answered the basic "who, what, when, and where" questions, most news stories shift their focus from what happened to what different people think has happened—and especially why it happened. They also begin to consider its significance, but again through the opinions and judgments of others. The reader, listener, or viewer learns more about the events in question, but indirectly, through the assessments collected by the journalist. To the extent that this account is correct, it follows that journalism should be judged less from the standpoint of a knowledge paradigm and more in terms of the range and kinds of "voices" that it allows to speak about "the news." From this standpoint, objectivity in the form of perfect balance may *not* be the most appropriate value in terms of achieving a better understanding of events. If, for example, 95 percent of the relevant scientific community believe that serious climate change is a reality, should journalists "balance" their views with those of the skeptics? Nor, when it comes to appreciating significance, are experts necessarily more worthy of being heard. As John Dewey once said, when it comes to knowing the effects of a new policy in our daily lives, only the person wearing the shoe can say whether it fits.

2. *News as Counter-Information.* Viewing news as a form of knowledge presumes that it should provide us with a comprehensive and balanced picture of social reality. It treats the journalist as a kind of historian on the run. But while both the journalist and the historian must be selective in what they include in their accounts, the basis upon which journalists make their choices is fundamentally different from that of the historian. For the historian, a major consideration in deciding whether to include a particular event is whether it contributes to the overall interpretation being developed. In this context, the audience plays little, if any, role in the process of selection. As Stuart Hall pointed out in "A World at One with Itself" (1973), however, the selection of news "rests on inferred knowledge about the audience" in that "news items which . . . break the pattern of expectations and contrast with our sense of the everyday . . . have greater salience for journalists than others."

In other words, the journalist begins with a certain notion, which may or may not be accurate, of how the public, or some segment of it, views the world. The journalist then proceeds to scan the flow of events for occurrences that, if known, would require the public to modify its view of reality in some respect. Such occurrences could include the expression of viewpoints. According to this argument, it is its status as counter-information (information that runs counter to public perceptions) that makes an event or opinion newsworthy— that gives it relevance or human interest.

3. *News as Countervailing Information.* The communicative and counter-informational concepts of news can be combined to produce a conception of news as not merely distinct from, but a force working against, propaganda. In *Propaganda: The Formation of Men's Attitudes*, first published in French in 1962, the French social philosopher Jacques Ellul suggested that propaganda is any deliberate and organized attempt to distort reality, as it is perceived to exist, in order

to influence or modify the behavior of some other group. Apart from legal penalties that are sometimes imposed against those who consciously distort the truth (e.g., Holocaust denier Ernst Zundel), the only constraint on propaganda is what might be called the imperative of credibility. This is the principle that people will not generally distort the truth beyond the point at which they anticipate a loss in their own credibility.

Several institutions contribute to the operation of this imperative. One of the most important of these in modern democratic societies is the educational system. But even more important for society as a whole is the institution of journalism. To the extent that it presents the views of various sides on contentious issues, it encourages people to be at least somewhat more open and honest in their public pronouncements than they might otherwise tend to be. This balance does not in itself eliminate attempts to lead the public astray, but the press also discourages deception by including countervailing information that makes it easier to recognize deliberate distortion.

4. News as Frontline Humanism. To regard news merely as countervailing information is to throw the baby out with the bath water. Journalists have always sought to provide insight about human events for its own sake, but their perspective is essentially that of the humanist rather than the social scientist. For the social scientist, the problem with human perception is that we often see too much in the sense of indiscriminately absorbing information about all aspects of social reality. The task of the social sciences is to discover, verify, and account for the more important and recurring relationships between different types of events. For the humanist, on the other hand, the problem is that we see too little. We do not, without further reflection, grasp the historical, the moral, or the religious dimension of reality. The task of the humanities is to help us see life more fully and deeply through history, philosophy, literature, poetry, and religion. From this standpoint, the journalist is primarily a humanist, concerned with concrete events rather than relations between event-types. Given the constraints of time and resources which govern journalistic production, however, the journalist might best be described as a *front-line* humanist; a foot soldier who carries out vital functions in the battle for human understanding, but is at a comparative disadvantage in comprehending the overall campaign.

5. News as Ideology. For students of political economy, the above concepts of news are too idealistic and naive. They ignore the extent to which journalism is ideological in the sense of being knowledge tied to a particular power interest. For political economists, the selection, gathering, and presentation of news are ultimately governed by power relations and the larger structures of society. There are many versions of this argument, but it is usually acknowledged, as Stuart Hall once put it, that news serves elites less through "the wilful, intentional bias of editors and newscasters" than through "the institutional ethos of the news media as a whole." In a typical sociological study of how news gets "manufactured," S. Cohen and J. Young pointed out that this ethos includes certain underlying assumptions about the legitimacy of existing political and economic arrangements. Confronted with groups or movements that deny this legitimacy, the journalist "characterizes them as 'meaningless,' 'immature' or senseless,' as involving a misunderstanding or reality rather than an alternative interpretation of its nature." In this manner, journalism serves to reinforce the status quo.

5. The Normative Concept of News. In considering the nature of news, Stuart Hall also noted that items can be considered newsworthy if they "infringe social norms." This idea has been further developed by the American sociologist Jeffrey Alexander, who suggests that the selection of news is closely tied to the moral issues facing a society. According to Alexander, every society shares a relatively small number of basic values, which generally remain quite stable over long periods of time. These values, he argues, are operationalized in the everyday lives of citizens through the development of a much more numerous set of norms, or practical rules as to how to realize one or more of society's underlying values in a particular situation. Because these situations or circumstances are always changing, a society is continually confronted with the need to reconsider its normative choices. What makes most stories newsworthy, Alexander claimed, is that they involve one or more normative dilemmas. The role of the journalist is not so much to resolve such dilemmas as to highlight their existence and initiate public discussion aimed at working out new norms. "The entire professional concentration on what is 'newsworthy,' 'fresh' as opposed to 'stale,'" he wrote, "can be viewed as flowing from this normative function."

NEWS DOCTORS. Research companies hired at great expense by local television stations to improve the image and ratings of their newscasts. News consultants first emerged in the **United States** in the 1960s, but American consultants are now also working abroad. Apart from the fact that they have tended to have a homogenizing impact on TV news, they also reduce the role of journalistic values in determining what is news.

NEWSLETTERS. One of the earliest forms of news dissemination. Their development was facilitated by the growth of private and state postal networks in the 16th century. They continued to play an important role even after the introduction of **corantos** and in fact constituted one of their main sources of information. After 1625 or so, however, their significance fluctuated in accordance with the ups and downs of state **censorship**. In the second half of the 17th century, **Henry Muddiman** in the office of the Secretaries of State sent newsletters to subscribers twice a week containing manuscript records of English Parliamentary and court news. Other newsletters were produced by professionals like the Whig Giles Hancock and the Tory John Dyer as well as by London scriveners and solicitors. They provided fuller coverage of domestic events, especially of Parliamentary proceedings, than did newspapers. Though too expensive for ordinary people to buy, some were available through coffeehouses.

NEWS MAGAZINES. In 1923, **Henry Luce** launched *Time*, the first major weekly newsmagazine in the **United States**. Luce hired a large staff of reporters, writers, researchers, and **columnists** for the publication. It was later challenged by *Business Week* (1929), *Newsweek* (1933), and *U.S. News and World Report* (1948). While *Newsweek* tried to match *Time*'s coverage of most categories of news, *Business Week* and *U.S. News and World Report* narrowed their focus to business/industry and national/international news respectively. Various imitations of *Time* were also created in Europe, including *Der Spiegel* in **Germany** in 1946 and *L'Express* in **France** in 1953. In *The Newsmagazines* (1958), Ben Bagdikian criticized them for being unreliable, oversimplified, and conservatively slanted. *See also POLITISCHE JOURNAL*; TIMESE.

NEWS MANAGEMENT. Governmental control over the flow of information to the public through leaks, press releases, and public relations rather than through **censorship** or the withholding of information. In *Dependency Road* (1981), Dallas Smythe defined it as "deliberate actions by organizations and individuals outside the mass media which shape the agenda and content . . . of media information, issues, or points of view which are helpful (or harmful) to the interests of those who take such actions" (71). The term *news management* was first used by the American journalist **James B. Reston** in testimony before a House Government Operations subcommittee in 1955. "Most of my colleagues here have been talking primarily about the suppression of news," Reston said. "I would like to direct the committee, if I may, to an equally important aspect of this problem which I think is the growing tendency to manage the news."

During the American Civil War (1861–65), John Hay (1838–1905), the personal secretary of President Abraham Lincoln, engaged in an early form of news management by placing some 132 **anonymous** letters and editorials in both Democratic and Republican newspapers. The letters in the (St. Louis) *Missouri Republican* in particular are thought to have helped secure the loyalty of the border states. However, historian Michael Schudson has argued that Woodrow Wilson was the first U.S. president to engage in systematic news management during peacetime in connection with the Treaty of Versailles. During the Depression, the administration of Franklin D. Roosevelt created a press bureau in every department to channel news to the public. Though not using the term, publisher **Henry Luce** was primarily concerned about management of the news in funding the **Hutchins Commission** during **World War II**. Since then, the extent and sophistication of news management has grown steadily, aided by the common practice of hiring journalists and graduating journalism students to serve as the interface between government and the press. The ethical and professional implications of this practice are seldom discussed by journalism educators, whose market is substantially enlarged by the dual career paths that their training provides.

NEWSREELS. Short motion pictures which accompanied the main features in movie theaters from the 1910s to the early 1960s when television made them seem redundant. Nine to ten minutes in length, each issue usually covered eight or nine topics headed by a title and shown in order of significance. While Anglo-American newsreels deliberately combined journalism with show business and were often superficially upbeat, they provided audiences with vivid images of many important world events. In **Italy**, Benito Mussolini established the Istituto Nazionale L'Unione Cinematographica Educativa or LUCE Institute in 1925 to coordinate the use of newsreels as an instrument of Fascist propaganda in Europe and South America. During the German occupation of **France** in **World War II**, newsreels such as the Vichy government's *La France en marche* were used to shape public opinion on behalf of collaboration.

NEW YORK HERALD. Influential **penny paper** founded by **James Gordon Bennett Sr.** in 1835. It was known for its full, but often sensational, news coverage and use of feature writers like Samuel Clemens and **Richard Harding Davis**. In 1870–71, it financed Henry Morton Stanley's trip to Africa in search of David Livingston. In 1924, it was sold to, and then merged with, the *New York Tribune* to form the *New York Herald Tribune*.

NEW YORK HERALD TRIBUNE. The chief rival of the *New York Times* in terms of quality journalism during the interwar and early postwar period. It was created in 1924 through the merger of the *New York Herald* and the *New York Tribune*. During the late 1920s, **Walter Lippmann** and Joseph Alsop helped to establish its reputation for literate commentary. It later pioneered the Sunday news-in-review section. After **World War II**, however, its circulation steadily declined, despite drawing on the talents of writers such as **Tom Wolfe**, Gloria Steinem, and Jimmy Breslin. It ceased publication on 24 April 1966.

NEW YORK SUN. The first of the American **penny papers**. Founded by **Benjamin H. Day** on 3 September 1833, it consisted of four pages, measuring about 7.5 x 10 inches, with three columns on each page. It was the first paper to be hawked in the streets by newsboys, who paid 67 cents per 100 papers. It reached a circulation of 5,000 by January 1834 and doubled this figure by the end of the year. In 1838,

Day sold the *Sun* to his brother-in-law and production assistant, Moses Beach (1800–1868). In 1848, Beach created the first European edition of an American paper, the weekly *American Sun*. The same year, he turned the *New York Sun* over to his sons, Moses Sperry Beach and Alfred E. Beach. Initially known for its police stories and scientific **hoaxes**, the *Sun*'s reputation improved under editor **Charles A. Dana**, though consistency was never its strong point; it attacked government corruption, but also opposed civil service reform. In 1950, it merged with the *New York World-Telegram*.

NEW YORK TIMES. Daily morning broadsheet founded by Henry J. Raymond, George Jones, and Edward B. Wesley on 18 September 1851 as the *New-York Daily Times*. Long regarded as the most authoritative source of news in the **United States**, it became the *New York Times* on 14 September 1857. It helped to create the Republican Party in 1854 and supported the party editorially until Raymond's death in 1869. Jones, who had become business manager in 1856, then assumed full control of the paper and directed its successful campaign (together with *Harper's*) to break the power of Tammany Hall boss William H. Tweed. After a period of decline, the paper was purchased in 1896 by **Adolph Ochs**, who sought to distinguish it from its **yellow journalism** competitors through the slogan "All the News That's Fit to Print." Under Ochs, it developed a reputation for accuracy and foreign correspondence, winning its first **Pulitzer Prize** for its coverage of the Western Front in 1918.

After **World War I**, Edwin L. "Jimmy" James, who had been the paper's chief correspondent with the American Expeditionary Force, expanded its foreign coverage as chief European correspondent. Although the *Times* has continued as the gold standard for American journalism, it has tended to lag behind on matters of style, layout, and general accessibility. A study of its stories (and those of the *Los Angeles Times*) over the period from 1885 to 1989 found—in contrast to novels during the same period—a gradual drop in readability, largely as a result of the use of longer words. Its reporting has also never been beyond criticism. It has been criticized, for example, for its failure to make Americans aware of the Holocaust. In May 2003, reporter Jayson Blair was forced to resign following allegations of plagiarism and news fabrication. The paper was able to repair its image in the Blair case, however, by maintaining the need for high journalistic standards and accepting responsibility for their violation.

NEW YORK TIMES V. SULLIVAN (1964). U.S. Supreme Court decision which held that the First Amendment applied to libel law. The decision originated from a libel suit brought by L. B. Sullivan, a public official in Alabama, against the **New York Times** and four ministers for an advertisement about a civil rights demonstration. After the jury awarded the plaintiff $500,000 and the Alabama Supreme Court upheld the judgment, the *New York Times* made an appeal to the U.S. Supreme Court. At the time, the common law of libel still did not regard either truth or good intentions as an absolute defense. The *Times* argued that this situation seriously undermined the capacity of the media to criticize government policies or officials. The U.S. Supreme Court agreed and set a minimum requirement for plaintiffs of demonstrating media negligence, or failure to exercise reasonable care. In the case of public figures or officials, the bar was raised still higher to a demonstration of actual malice, or reckless and knowing disregard of the truth so as to injure reputation. Although celebrated by the press at the time and later expanded in scope, the decision failed to insulate the media against numerous costly libel actions.

NEW YORK TRIBUNE. Daily newspaper founded in 1841 by **Horace Greeley**, who edited it until his death in 1872. Under managing editor **Charles A. Dana** from 1849–62, it managed to marry radical politics with trustworthy, nonsensationalized news. During the Civil War, it became the most powerful Republican paper in the country. After Greeley's death, it was taken over and edited by **Whitelaw Reid**, owner of the *New York Herald*, and gradually became a voice of conservatism. In 1924, Reid's son, Ogden Reid, merged the *Tribune* and *Herald* to form the **New York Herald Tribune** and ran the new paper until his death in 1947.

NEW YORK WORLD. Daily newspaper founded by **Joseph Pulitzer** in 1883. To increase its circulation, Pulitzer made use of illustrations, colored comics, feature articles, and stunt journalism. His competition with **William Randolph Hearst** for circulation during the Spanish–American War in 1898 gave rise to the term **yellow journalism**.

The *World* later abandoned sensationalism and gained respect for its independent views and bold attacks on political corruption.

NEW ZEALAND. For most of their history, New Zealand journalists looked to **Great Britain** for their standard of excellence and tried to be "more English than the English themselves." A content analysis of metropolitan newspapers in the early 1930s found that they contained more political news dealing with the internal affairs of England (37 percent) than *The Times* itself (30 percent). Recently, however, historians of journalism in New Zealand have looked to the **United States**, and especially its frontier West, for a better comparison with the country's journalistic development. While allowing for significant differences between the two trajectories, they have found a number of parallels between American and New Zealand journalism history. An even more appropriate comparison might be with another British Dominion like **Canada**, which underwent the same transition from colony to nation.

As in the British North American colonies, the first newspaper in New Zealand, the *New Zealand Gazette* begun by Samuel Revens in 1840, was an official newspaper and papers challenging Crown Colony policies were initially subject to closure. As opposition papers grew in strength, however, they led the campaign for self-government. In both New Zealand and British North America, they tended to be associated more closely with politicians than with parties, especially compared to the United States where they were a major instrument of party organization. In both New Zealand and Canada, reporting (as opposed to the use of exchanges) was slower to develop than in the United States, in large measure because of correspondingly greater interest in overseas than in local news. At the same time, however, there developed a higher and more uniform degree of political control over news in New Zealand than in Canada or the United States, where commercialization involved a strong populist element.

One factor behind this pattern of control may be the relative absence of major non-indigenous challenges (such as the division between French and English in Canada) to New Zealand's quest to develop a sense of national identity. But the immediate cause lay in the degree to which New Zealand newspapermen were not only involved in politics as members of the House of Representatives but used their positions in government to assert control over the news system. The process began in 1866 when a group of newspaper owners in the House, including future prime minister Julius Vogel of the *Otago Daily Times*, persuaded the government to take over the internal **telegraph** system being developed to link the country's constituent parts. It was the main instrument by which news arriving by ship in New Zealand ports was then distributed further and the plan was to create a subscription service under their own control. Although this arrangement soon broke down, a series of competitive approaches also failed and a government-based monopoly was restored in 1879 in the form of the United Press Association. This approach was later repeated in the case of broadcasting and lasted until the Broadcasting Authority Act (1968) achieved some dispersal of political control.

In the early 1980s, New Zealand received a mediocre rating on press freedom, despite the absence of **censorship** or any of the customary measures of repression. One reason was probably the heavy-handed approach some politicians still adopted toward journalists. In 1980, for example, the Prime Minister banned members of *The Dominion* from his press conferences unless their papers agreed to publish material that had been cut from one of his previous statements. He also tried to prevent the accreditation of a *Listener* columnist for a Commonwealth conference. Since then, however, such episodes have been few and far between. New Zealand's largest and most influential newspapers, the *New Zealand Gazette*, *The Press*, and *The Dominion*, are among the most free in the world, cooperate along with other papers with the New Zealand Press Council, and are no longer prone to being browbeaten by politicians.

NORTHCLIFFE, LORD (1865–1922). British newspaper proprietor who broadened the constituency for mass journalism, the so-called "Northcliffe Revolution." Born Alfred Harmsworth near Dublin, he established several popular weeklies and used the profits from these ventures to purchase the *Evening News* in 1894 and found the *Daily Mail* in 1896. An inexpensive and attractive morning newspaper, the *Daily Mail* used imperialism, contests, and banner headlines to attract lower middle-class and working-class readers. After the turn of the century, Northcliffe entered the world of quality journalism by purchasing the Sunday *Observer* in 1905 and, to the dismay of some, *The Times* of London in 1908. As owner of *The Times*, he helped to turn around its declining financial fortunes. In 1917, he led the British mission to secure America's support in the war and the following year served as Director of Propaganda in Enemy Countries. After disagreeing with the prime minister over the composition of the postwar government, he was excluded from the British delegation to the Paris Peace Conference.

NORWAY. Under Danish rule since the 15th century, Norway could only obtain newspapers through the post office in Copenhagen until well into the 18th century. Although a newspaper was begun in Bergen in 1721, its printer was forced to discontinue it after a publisher in Copenhagen complained that it was a reprint of his own paper. It was not until 1763 that a regular newspaper, *Norske Intelligenz Seddeler*, was established and it was subject to **censorship**. When the Danish monarchy temporarily relaxed controls over the press in 1770, a host of **pamphlets** emerged complaining about Norway's inferior position. Written by a group of younger, university-educated men who had come to Copenhagen, the pamphlets promoted an early form of national identity, but were not generally reprinted in Norway's newspapers at the time. It was not until the end of the 18th century that newspapers began to call for independence. With the defeat of Napoleon in 1814, **Denmark** turned Norway over to **Sweden**, but the Norwegians managed to limit Swedish control through a new democratic constitution with specific provision for freedom of the press.

During the course of the 19th century, most newspapers became aligned with one of Norway's numerous political parties, but often exercised a substantial degree of editorial independence. When owner Olaf Madsen tried to reduce the news-hole in favor of **advertising** in *Verdens Gang* in 1910, editor Olaf V. Thommessen portrayed it as an attack on editorial freedom, resigned along with many of his staff, and founded his own newspaper. During the Nazi occupation, an **underground press** arose after the more outspoken papers were shut down and their editors imprisoned or murdered. After the war, the various political groupings provided start-up funding to reestablish the party press, but only those newspapers with substantial advertising were able to survive.

In 1969, in an attempt to maintain a diversity of political views, the government began a system of state subsidies to newspapers with small circulations or stiff competition from other papers. Though deemed a failure by many commentators, this policy continued into the 21st century, though with a substantially reduced budget.

– O –

OBSERVER. Sunday newspaper in **Great Britain** with a reputation for informed commentary. Founded in 1791 by W. S. Bourne, it exerted little influence during the 19th century. After being purchased by **Lord Northcliffe** for £4,000 in 1905, however, it rose to prominence under the editorship of J. L. Garvin. In 1911, Northcliffe sold the paper to William Waldorf Astor for £45,000. More recently, it has been owned by an American oil company (1976), the Lonrho corporation (1981), and the *Guardian* newspaper (1993).

OCHS, ADOLPII S. (1858–1935). Publisher who built the *New York Times* into one of the world's great newspapers between 1896 to 1935. Born to German-Jewish immigrants in Cincinnati, he moved with them to Tennessee after the Civil War and began working as a printer's devil for the *Knoxville Chronicle* in 1869. In 1878, having worked his way up to journeyman printer, he borrowed $250 and bought a controlling interest in the near-moribund *Chattanooga Times*, which he skillfully revived by making it one of the South's most dignified and trustworthy papers. Two decades later, he used much the same formula to rescue the *Times*. At the time of its purchase for a mere $75,000 in 1896, the *Times*' circulation was down to 9,000 daily and its debts were accumulating rapidly.

"OFF THE RECORD." During the 20th century, journalists in the **United States** and elsewhere developed a distinction between regular interviewing and "off-the-record" discourse. In the case of the former, it is considered ethically acceptable to publicly disclose anything said by the interviewee; in the case of the latter, there must be either indirect attribution ("sources at the scene said . . .") or, in the case of what is called "deep background," no attribution at all. In cases of attribution, the journalist regards him/herself as responsible only for accurately reproducing what was said, not for the truthfulness of those statements.

OSSIETZKY, CARL VON (1889–1938). German journalist and pacifist. After **World War I**, he served briefly as secretary of the German Peace Society in Berlin and then joined the antiwar *Berliner Volkszeitung* as foreign editor. After the paper's editorial staff attempted unsuccessfully to found a new political party, Ossietzky switched first to the political weekly *Tagebuch* and then to Siegfried Jacobsohn's *Die Weltbühne*. When Jacobsohn died suddenly in December 1926, Ossietzky took over as editor-in-chief and continued his predecessor's unpopular efforts to expose the secret rearmament of Germany in violation of the Treaty of Versailles. Despite imprisonment in 1927 and 1931, Ossietzky refused to abandon the campaign and from 1933–36 was incarcerated in concentration camps at Sonnenburg and Esterwegen-Papenburg where his health rapidly deteriorated. After he was awarded the Nobel Peace Prize in 1936, he was refused a passport to travel to **Norway**, press coverage of the award was muzzled by the government, and Germans were prohibited from accepting any future Nobel prizes.

– P –

PACIFICA. Alternative noncommercial radio network founded by visionary Lewis Hill in Berkeley, California, in 1949. It later added affiliate stations in New York, Los Angeles, Houston, and Washington, D.C. It was originally an experiment in pacifist broadcasting. Following Hill's suicide in 1957, it became less radical, but contributed to the counterculture of the 1960s and the opposition to the Vietnam War. In 1969, Seymour Hirsch broke the Mai Lai story on the Pacifica network. During the 1970s, the network switched its focus from national to community issues.

PAINE, THOMAS (1737–1809). Political pamphleteer who helped to shift American popular opinion in favor of independence. After emigrating from **Great Britain** in 1774, he worked in Philadelphia as editor of *The Pennsylvania Magazine*. His **pamphlet** *Common Sense* (1776) was the first call for American independence; it was reprinted in numerous patriot newspapers and sold an estimated 500,000 copies at a time when the American colonies had only three million inhabitants. During the Revolutionary War, he was instrumental in maintaining morale through 16 essays known as the "Crisis" papers. "These are the times that try men's souls," he began in the first of these in December 1776.

PAMPHLETS. As a cheap and easily transportable form of print, the pamphlet was restricted, at least in **Great Britain** according to Joad Raymond, to a maximum of 12 sheets or 96 modern pages (though most pamphlets were smaller). It was meant to accommodate a variety of contents, including news of episodic events. In **Italy**, news pamphlets as well as **newsletters** were called *avvisi* and were handwritten even after the development of typography. By the 1530s, however, some Italian news pamphlets were being printed, leading later scholars to refer to them as *avvisi a stampa* (in Rome they came to be known as *relazioni*). As postal services expanded and became more regular, the production of news pamphlets was gradually synchronized with the weekly schedule of couriers. In Venice, whose commercial empire made it the center of 16th-century newswriting, the first weekly news pamphlets were printed in 1566. Costing a *gazzetta*, the smallest denomination of the Venetian coinage, they came to be known as gazettes. In **Spain**, news pamphlets were called *relacíons*, while in **France** they were referred to as *occasionnels* if they were official and *canards* if they were not.

PARAGUAY. The first printed news vehicles in Paraguay were official publications, beginning with the *Repertorio nacional* (1841–51), which contained only administrative acts and decrees. It was followed by *El Paraguayo independiente* (1845–52) and its successor *El Semanario* (1853–68), a newspaper edited by the president himself. Beginning in the mid-1850s, a few independent newspapers were founded, but none lasted more than a couple of years. The first daily newspaper, *Nación Paraguaya* (1872–74), was also an official government paper. During the last quarter of the 19th century, however, independent papers such as *La Democracia* (1881–1904) were able to gain a more secure foothold. Until a **telegraph** line was installed in 1895, it had to wait six or seven days for world news to make its way upriver from Buenos Aires in **Argentina**. Following **World War I**, Paraguayan journalism experienced unprecedented freedom. In this atmosphere of tolerance, however, pro-fascist factions such as the Frente de Guerra were also able to establish newspapers propagating their extreme right-wing ideology. In the 1940s, the military government of President Higinio Morínigo created an official government newspaper, confiscated a number of opposition papers, and established the Departamento Nacional de Propaganda to control the rest. Since then, even nonpartisan newspapers have continued to suffer from periodic harassment, **censorship**, and closure. In 1984, for example, Paraguay's largest circulation daily, the **tabloid** *ABC Color*, was shut down.

PARK, ROBERT E. (1864–1944). American sociologist who pioneered social science research on the press. Born in Red Wing, Minnesota, Park studied philosophy with John Dewey at the University of Michigan and then worked as a journalist at various newspapers for the next 11 years. Dissatisfied with newspapering, he returned to academia for an M.A. at Harvard and Ph.D. in Germany and then taught philosophy at Harvard until 1913 when he became a professor of sociology at the University of Chicago. A leader in the "Chicago School" of sociology, his most notable publications on journalism were *The Immigrant Press and Its Control* (1922) and "The Natural History of the Newspaper," *American Journal of Sociology* (1923). Though overly deterministic, the latter was one of the first attempts to place the history of journalism within a larger conceptual framework.

PARLIAMENTARY REPORTING, ORIGINS OF. In the late 17th century, the authors of **newsletters** in **Great Britain** sometimes ignored the ban on parliamentary reporting by including brief reports on House of Commons debates. But there was no attempt at regular coverage until 1711 when Abel Boyer took advantage of a loophole to publish accounts of the parliamentary recess in his monthly magazine, *The Political State of Great Britain*. In the early 1730s, the *Gentleman's Magazine* and *London Magazine* began copying from the *Political State* and later produced versions of their own. After the Commons tightened the regulations in 1738, the magazines pretended to report on mythical assemblies until various reprimands and lack of public interest forced them to stop. In 1757, an oversight in the new Stamp Act favoring periodicals of over five pages prompted the creation of several new papers, but their attempts to report on Parliament were beaten back again.

In the late 1760s, however, excitement over political events created renewed interest in Parliament. Printer John Almon began writing accounts for the triweekly *London Evening Post* and then founded the monthly *London Museum* in January 1770 to provide "an accurate Journal of the Proceedings and Debates of the Present Parliament." His lead was followed by other monthly magazines and a number of newspapers, including William "Memory" Woodfall's *Morning Chronicle*. Though only a few debates were reported at length and even these were still disguised as the proceedings of the "Robinhood Society" or "A Great Assembly," the Commons again became alarmed and in 1771 prosecuted eight of the offending papers. At this point, however, **John Wilkes** used his authority as alderman of London to give refuge to several of the printers. Although the Commons won a token victory, Wilkes's action effectively ended the ban on Parliamentary reporting by making long-term enforcement an unenviable prospect.

For a time, many newspapers continued the pretense of concealing debates and speakers and were slow to expand their coverage or even abandon the practice of pirating accounts. By 1774, however, readers had come to expect prompt and substantial reports and at least seven papers were responding to this demand with their own versions. That year reporters also gained access to the House of Lords, which may have helped to preserve its own relevance in the process. Even then, the results were uneven. Not without foundation did William Pitt and others complain that the coverage was still filled with inaccuracies. It was not only difficult to hear speeches clearly from the gallery but, as James Stephen of the *Morning Post* recalled, "no man was allowed to take a note for the purpose. We were obliged therefore to depend on memory alone and had no assistance in the work, one Reporter for each House being all that any Paper employed." A comparison of the newspaper reports of the period with the verbatim accounts that

Henry Cavendish later compiled using shorthand found that the former "are best regarded as the creation of imaginative artists, who often worked with scanty materials." Even the legendary coverage of Woodfall did not convey the actual phrases used by speakers. Although Parliament finally allowed note-taking in 1783, reporting continued to be unreliable owing to the inadequacies of shorthand and difficulty of hearing speakers clearly.

PARSONS, ALBERT RICHARD (1848–1887). Anarchist editor who was hanged for his alleged part in the Haymarket riot. As editor of *The Alarm*, a weekly newspaper published by the International Working People's Association, he was a key leader in the movement for an eight-hour day. At a peaceful protest meeting on 4 May 1886, the evening after police had fired upon strikers at the McCormick harvester factory in Chicago, someone threw a bomb that killed 11 people, including seven policemen. Parsons came forward voluntarily to stand trial after eight radical leaders were indicted. Four of the seven leaders convicted were hanged, including two other journalists, August Spies and Adolph Fischer. A review of the trial later condemned its methods.

PEARSON, DREW (1897–1969). Controversial newspaper columnist and NBC radio commentator. As a correspondent for the *Baltimore Sun* in the late 1920s, he began the practice of using inside sources, especially diplomats from other countries. After he became head of the *Sun*'s Washington bureau, he met Robert S. (Bob) Allen, his counterpart at the *Christian Science Monitor*. In *Washington Merry-Go-Round*, a best-seller published anonymously in 1931, they exposed the embarrassing shortcomings of various public figures. After their identities were discovered, they were both fired, but were soon hired by the United Features syndicate to collaborate on a syndicated daily column with the same name and intent as their book. The column eventually reached an estimated 20 million readers through several hundred papers. **Jack Anderson** later replaced Allen as Pearson's coauthor.

PENNY PAPERS. Although the American Revolution democratized many segments of U.S. society, the daily press still remained out of reach of many of the republic's citizens. Intended primarily for the political elite, the six-penny papers or "blanket sheets" (so named because of their 24 x 35 inch dimensions) cost $8–10 (about 10 days' pay for the average worker) for a year's subscription, payable in advance, or 6 cents for a single copy, though many could not be purchased in that manner. Moreover, the elite papers contained little of relevance to the clerks and artisans in America's rapidly growing cities. In the late 1820s, a number of less expensive labor newspapers were founded: the *Mechanic's Free Press* (1828) in Philadelphia and the more influential *Workingmen's Advocate* (1829) in New York City. But they too failed to address the interests of most potential readers.

Between 1830 and 1833, several newspapers in Boston dropped the subscription price to $4 a year. But the major change in marketing the news came in 1833 when **Benjamin H. Day** founded the first of the penny papers, the *New York Sun*. Following the practice of London papers such as the *Morning Herald*, it emphasized **crime** news and was soon followed by a host of imitators in New York and other east coast cities: the *New York Transcript* (1833); the *New York Herald* (1835) under proprietor **James Gordon Bennett Sr.**; the *Boston Daily Times* (1836) founded by George Roberts and William H. Garfield; the *Philadelphia Public Ledger* (1836), established by printers William M. Swain, Arunah S. Abell, and Azariah H. Simmons; the *Baltimore Sun* (1837), also owned by Swain and his partners; the *New York Tribune* (1841) under editor **Horace Greeley**; the *Savannah* [Georgia] *Morning News* (1850) founded by William Tappan Thomas; and the venerable *New York Times* (1851) established by Henry J. Raymond. Within a few years of their creation, the *Sun* had a circulation of 30,000 and the *Herald* one of 20,000.

Eight of the first ten penny papers were founded by enterprising artisans like Day who had few resources but were able to exploit the final days of the inexpensive hand-cranked flatbed press to generate a new urban market for news. Within a few years, most had installed Napier presses capable of producing 2,000 copies an hour. The early penny papers made the news more appealing through sensationalism and humor, but they also pursued it more comprehensively and aggressively. The *Herald* included Washington and foreign news, used every available device to obtain news more quickly, and created "beats" such as finance, theater, society, and sports. While some of the penny papers did not support a particular political party, none ignored political topics, especially the debate over slavery. Greeley's *Tribune* championed various humanitarian reforms, including anti-slavery, while Thompson's *Morning News* condemned abolitionists and their political supporters.

PENTAGON PAPERS. Articles and documents published in the *New York Times* in 1971 leading to a historic court case over the question of prior restraint. In 1967, Robert S. McNamara commissioned a history of the involvement of the **United States** in Vietnam; the end product was a 40-volume study classified as top secret. In 1971, Daniel Ellsberg, an analyst at a research institute with close ties to the administration of Richard M. Nixon, gave the *Times* a copy of sections dealing with the Tonkin Gulf incident and the subsequent commitment of American air and ground forces to the Vietnam War. On 13 June 1971, the *Times* began publishing a series of articles based on the leaked materials, revealing, among other things, that President Lyndon Johnson had drawn up plans for military action before the Tonkin Gulf incident in 1964. When the Department of Justice obtained a temporary restraining order on the grounds of national security, the *Times* and a number of other newspapers appealed the order. In a 6-3 decision (*New York Times v. United States*) on June 30, the Supreme Court upheld the right of the papers to continue publishing the materials. However, it failed to draw a clear line between government secrecy and the public's right to know. While three members of the majority held that the courts could not suppress publication under any circumstances, the other three maintained that prior restraint was constitutional in situations where there was an immediate and grave threat to the nation. The case thus set a weak precedent for interpreting the First Amendment as prohibiting prior restraint. *See also* CENSORSHIP.

PERU. During the 17th and 18th centuries, a number of temporary newssheets were published in the viceroyalty of Peru. But the first regular news publications were primarily literary productions, beginning with *El Mercurio Peruano* in 1791 and followed by *Diaro erudito* and *El Semanario crítico*. After Napoleon invaded **Spain** in

1803, these periodicals were joined first by political **pamphlets** and later by newspapers such as *El Peruano* and *El Satélte del Peruano*, all of which began to question the colonial system. In 1814, however, the viceregal government took steps to suppress this literature, later turning *El Peruano* into an official state gazette. In 1822, Guillermo del Río and three associates created the *Diario de Lima* to provide the citizens of Lima with political and military news as well as commentary on society, religion, and the theater. But it lasted only 25 issues and other news publications suffered a similar fate.

The first successful commercial newspaper was *El Comercio*, established in Lima in 1839 to represent the interests of wealthy landowners, bankers, and exporters. In 1903, the moderate conservative paper *La Prensa* was created by Pedro Beltran to serve the newly emerging industrial interests; it was Peru's leading daily in terms of serious national and world coverage until the 1980s when the costs of technological modernization forced it to fold. The first evening daily was *La Cronica*, begun in 1912; by 1980, it had parlayed sensational **tabloid**-style content into the largest circulation of any paper in Peru, but later lost pride of place to *El Comercio*.

Most newspapers in Peru have been closely associated with prominent families and particular socioeconomic interests. The largest papers have been those based in Lima, but none of these has been able to acquire national status; regional papers have remained dominant in the provinces and even these have been directed primarily at the non-Indian population. Historically, Peruvian journalists have suffered from high unemployment and low pay. Apart from senior editors, many journalists still work on a part-time basis, relying on single assignments on an unpredictable basis. At the same time, they regard journalism as a privileged calling and see themselves as constituting the sole channel of information to the Peruvian people.

For much of its history, the Peruvian press has been subject to strict **censorship**. After **World War II**, President Manuel Prado reduced state controls over the media and a number of new dailies were founded, including *La Hora* in 1950 and *Correo, Expreso, Ojo,* and *Extra* in the 1960s. But between 1969 and 1974, President Velasco Alvarado instituted a series of harsh measures against the press, culminating in the complete nationalization of the Peruvian media. His approach was moderated only slightly by President Moralez

Bermudez (1976–80). Following the election of President Fernando Belaunde in 1980, the nationalized papers were returned to their former owners, but freedom of the press was only partially restored. During the 1990s, President Alberto Fujimori again resorted to censorship, but was unable to stifle harsh criticism of his fraudulent election in 2000.

A few months after Fujimori's resignation in November 2000, the International Press Association removed Peru from its "watch list" of countries in danger of losing freedom of the press. Although Peruvian journalists have continued to face various forms of intimidation from the government and its enemies, the daily press has undergone a notable resurgence in recent years. In 2007, there were 57 daily newspapers with an aggregate circulation of 5,700,000, compared to 34 dailies with a circulation of 828,000 during the Bermudez regime in 1977. Over the same period, the circulation of dailies rose from 51 per 1,000 to 342 per 1,000.

PETITIONS. During the medieval and early modern periods, popular discussion of political matters was expressly prohibited. In **Great Britain**, for example, the sale of domestic news was actively discouraged and the disclosure of parliamentary debates was made a crime. The only exception to this rule of secrecy was the privilege to petition the central authority for the redress of local grievances. But this privilege was limited to corporate entities and their petitions were not understood as an expression of the "will of the people." They did not, therefore, seriously stem the flow of political messages from the top of society to the bottom. With the invention of printing, however, the petition acquired the capacity to send messages in the opposite direction and thereby undermine the traditional norms of secrecy and privilege. During the English civil war in particular, associations of private persons began to issue printed petitions and to invoke the authority of public opinion as a means of lobbying Parliament. Though ignored by the authorities in accordance with what David Zaret calls the "the paradox of innovation," these new practices contributed to the emergence of a **public sphere**. *See also* LEVELLERS.

PHILIPPINES. The first newspaper in the Philippines, a short-lived government publication called *Del Superior gobierno*, was not published until 1811, almost three centuries after the Spanish took control. It was followed by a number of other Spanish papers, including the first daily, *La Esperanza* (1846), and a bi-monthly publication called *El Pasig* (1862) in Spanish and Tagalog. But it was not until 1889 that the first vernacular newspaper, *El Ilocano* founded by Isabelo de Los Reyes (1864–1938), was able to gain a reasonably secure foothold, lasting until 1896. After being exiled to **Spain** in 1897, Reyes began translating the New Testament into Ilocano, the language of northwestern Luzon.

On 12 June 1898, the Philippines gained independence from Spain with the help of an American fleet under Admiral George Dewey. However, the **United States** then decided to colonize the country and proceeded to establish its own newspapers, beginning with Franklyn Brooks's *The American* (1898) and Carson Taylor's *Manila Bulletin*, while at the same time suppressing nationalistic ones.

In 1920, future president Manuel L. Quezon finally managed to establish the first Filipino newspaper, the *Philippines Herald*, but its influence was undermined by the advent of radio, which quickly became an entertainment medium under American control. Ironically, it was under the otherwise repressive **Japanese** occupation from 1941–45 that the use of Tagalog was encouraged as part of a policy of "Asia for Asians." After the war, journalists like Amado Vera Hernandez were part of the general preoccupation with the question of cultural identity—whether, after four and a half centuries of colonialism, Filipino culture had been lost forever. For the next quarter century, the Philippine press experienced something of a golden age. But there were disturbing trends as well: a few large Manila dailies were exerting increasing influence over the country's media; and many journalists saw nothing wrong in accepting payments from the government in addition to their regular salaries.

On 21 September 1972, President Ferdinand Marcos imposed martial law and instituted strict **censorship**. The assassination of opposition leader Benigno Aquino in 1983 led to the creation of underground newspapers and radio stations that helped to mobilize the people for the People Power or EDSA Revolution of 1986. Following the ouster of Marcos and ratification of the 1987 Constitution, the repressive measures taken against the opposition journalism were lifted and a number of new papers soon appeared.

PHILLIPS, DAVID GRAHAM (1867–1911). Indiana-born member of the **muckrakers**. After graduating from college in 1887, Phillips worked as a reporter in Cincinnati before moving to New York City where he was a reporter, columnist, and editor at the *New York World* from 1893 until 1902. Through the royalties from his novel *The Great God Success* (1901), he was able to work as a freelance journalist while dedicating himself to fiction. His series on "The Treason of the Senate" for *Cosmopolitan* magazine in April 1906 exposed the practice of rewarding campaign contributors and was eventually influential in the passage of the Seventeenth Amendment in 1913 for the direct election of senators. He wrote some 20 novels with muckraking elements related to contemporary social problems. In *Susan Lenox: Her Fall and Rise*, written in 1908 but not published until 1917, he exposed slum life and political corruption.

POLIGRAPHI. A group of satirical **pamphlet** writers influenced by Pietro Arentino in mid-16th century **Italy**. Their numbers included Nicolò Franco, Lodovico Domenichi, Ortensio Lando, and Guido Landi. Their writings reflected the general malaise arising from the acquiescence of the Italian ruling classes to Spanish hegemony. While some of the *poligraphi* called for a rejection of civic life in favor or rural solitude, they themselves lived off their writings and discussed their ideas in the literary academies and vernacular printshops of Venice and other urban centers.

"POLITICS AS A VOCATION" (1918). Famous essay by the **German** political and social theorist Max Weber which also deals with the status and role of journalists. While acknowledging that journalists do not have the autonomy of academics, Weber argued that journalism is not only an important avenue for developing political leaders but provides leadership on public issues in its own right. Contrary to most contemporary assessments, Weber thought that the discretion exercised by journalists overall is "above the average of other people." In terms of preparing honorable politicians, journalism is even preferable to scholarship, because journalists must be able to produce "at once and 'on order,'" are subject to "incomparably greater temptations," and carry a greater responsibility for the consequences of their writing. "If the life of a young scholar is a gamble," Weber observed, "still he is walled in by firm status conventions, which prevent him from slipping. But the journalist's life is an absolute gamble in every respect and under conditions that test one's inner security in a way that scarcely occurs in any other situation."

POLITISCHE JOURNAL. Founded in 1781 by Gottlob Benedikt von Schirach (1743–1804), who dominated its production, it quickly became the most successful magazine in the **German**-speaking world. Despite carrying no **advertising**, it made political news into a profitable commodity by providing rationally organized background context for what it took to be the most significant current political events of the day. To obtain reliable news, Schirach cultivated favorable relations with German princes and their officials. The Hamburg publisher Bohn promoted the journal at the Leipzig book fair and elsewhere. The magazine contributed to the development of a pan-German public opinion and sense of identity. After Schirach's death, the publication was continued by his son Wilhelm.

POLITKOVSKAYA, ANNA (1958–2006). Russian journalist born in New York City where her Soviet Ukrainian parents worked as diplomats at the United Nations. After graduating from Moscow State University in 1980, she worked for *Izvestia* (1982–93), as a reporter and editor for *Obshchaya Gazeta* (1994–99), and as a columnist for *Novaya Gazeta*. Her critical coverage of the war in Chechnya and various Russian authorities led to numerous death threats. In 2001, she received the Amnesty International Global Award for Human Rights Journalism, one of many such awards. On 7 October 2006, she was shot and killed in the elevator of her apartment building.

PORTUGAL. During the repressive Salazar regime (1926–1974), the state not only exercised strict control over the press but actively discouraged efforts by groups such as the National Union of Journalists to provide better education for journalists. Since then academic programs in journalism have been established at various universities, but many Portuguese journalists still lack formal training. The most prestigious newspaper for print journalists is the *Diario de noticias*, Portugal's "newspaper of record," followed by the more popular *Jornal de noticias* and the staunchly independent *Publico*. Portugal's national news agency LUSA, founded in 1987, is also among the preferred employers for reporters. Although the current constitution formally guarantees freedom of the press, Portuguese history dictates against taking press freedom for granted; the code of ethics adopted by the Syndicate of Journalists in 1993 makes it a duty for journalists to oppose any attempts to restrict access to information or curtail freedom of publication.

PRAVDA **[TRUTH].** The official organ of the Central Committee of the Communist Party in the former **Soviet Union**. Named after the Bolshevik faction of the Russian Social Democrats, it was established by **V. I. Lenin** in 1910. By 1912, its influence was generating considerable fear within official circles. On 8 July 1914, its publication was forbidden, but it was revived by Lenin on 5 March 1917. Its editors included Joseph Stalin and Nikolai Bukharin. It continued to serve as the official party organ until 1991.

PRINTING PRESS, ORIGINS OF. Modern journalism is inconceivable without the printing press or printing from moveable type, but the origins of this "invention" have long been a matter of controversy and mystery. Credit usually goes to Johann Gutenberg (c. 1400–1468) for developing typography around 1439. In 2001, however, Blaise Agüeras y Arcas and Paul Needham at Princeton University used a computer to analyze the famous Gutenberg Bible and other early works printed by Gutenberg and found that no two letters were exactly the same, so that the texts could not have been produced using hard-cast moveable type. They speculated that the modern punch matrix system was introduced by another craftsman a few years after Gutenberg's death, but provided no clue as to whom that might have been. In *1434* (2008), subtitled "The Year a Magnificent Chinese Fleet Sailed to **Italy** and Ignited the Renaissance," Gavin Menzies claims that it was an expedition from Ming **China** led by Admiral Zheng He that brought moveable type to Europe. However, Menzies provides only two pieces of indirect evidence for this claim: a Venetian senate decree of 11 October 1441 against the "evil" practice of "printed playing cards and coloured figures," presumably for undermining their preferred artistic production; and the fact that Venice soon became the printing capital of Europe. Cards, however, would most likely have been produced by block printing. No explanation is given as to how typography, like the massive Chinese expedition itself, could suddenly appear like a gift from Santa Claus—where the fact of its being given registers no physical, visual, or documentary impression. Part of the mystery of the printing press is dissolved when it is recalled that it was the coalescence of several technologies over a span of time and that the economic incentive for the final component (moveable type) was in place for more than a century.

PROFESSIONAL ORGANIZATIONS. Beginning in the late 19th century, journalists in various countries began to organize societies and associations for the purposes of protecting their rights and status and promoting professionalism generally. One of the earliest of such organizations was Concordia, which was founded in Vienna in 1859, but it was largely social in nature. In 1885, however, French journalists organized the Association of Parisian Journalists not only to promote social esprit but to pursue greater financial security through medical and retirement programs. In 1889, British journalists created a similar professional organization called the Institute of Journalists.

The stated purpose of the Institute of Journalists was to "secure the advancement of all branches of Journalism; to obtain for Journalists, as Journalists, formal and definite professional standing; and to promote and serve in every possible way the interests of the profession of the Press." By 1894 it had 3,556 paid members. During the next two decades, it created provident and orphan funds; secured the right of journalists to remuneration for testifying in court; and advanced the right of journalists to be present at inquests. Its repeated attempts to develop an examination scheme to control entry into journalism faltered over differences about the desired level of openness to the field and the role of education in producing journalists. According to Mark Hampton, however, its more senior members were generally opposed to limiting entry on the basis of expert knowledge. Their concern was primarily to improve the social image and status of journalists. For the leaders of the Institute, professionalism rather than trade unionism was seen as the most appropriate means to these goals. At the same time, however, they were divided as to what made journalism a profession. For some, indeed, journalism was less a profession in its own right than an apprenticeship for other professions or careers.

In the **United States**, journalists followed the lead of their British counterparts by organizing the Society of Professional Journalists (SPJ) in 1909 to protect their First Amendment rights and promote ethical behavior. The SPJ now has almost 10,000 members, maintains a legal defense fund, publishes the magazine *Quill*, and makes its own annual awards for journalistic excellence. In 1922, editors at the larger dailies decided to establish their own organization, the American Society of Newspaper Editors (ASNE). The idea was first conceived by Caspar Yost, editor of the *St. Louis Globe-Democrat*, during a trip with some fellow editors to Glacier National Park in 1912 at the expense of railway magnate James H. Hill. But it was not until 1922 that Yost was spurred by mounting criticism of the press to organize a meeting of midwestern editors in Chicago at which ASNE was established. One of the first projects of the association was to draft a code of ethics emphasizing truthfulness, sincerity, and devotion to the public interest. In addition to sponsoring several awards, ASNE runs a variety of projects aimed at promoting editorial diversity, balance, and excellence. Though initially limited to editors at daily newspapers in cities with a population over 100,000, ASNE is now more inclusive in its membership.

During the same period, the first international organizations made their appearance, beginning with the International Federation of Journalists (IFJ) in 1926. It now has approximately 140 member-unions in 103 countries, making it the largest international organization in the world. Its purposes are to defend press freedom and promote professional and industrial rights. In 1946, journalists from primarily socialist countries organized the International Organization of Journalists (IOJ), but it ended in 1991 following the collapse of Communism. Elsewhere, however, international organizations promoting the interests of journalists have multiplied and flourished.

PUBLIC JOURNALISM. A controversial American-based movement against several traditional news values. Also known as civic journalism, the movement was launched in the mid-1990s by journalists Jay Rosen and Davis "Buzz" Merritt. It arose from their belief that citizens are becoming increasingly alienated and disengaged from politics and public life and that current journalistic practices are partly to blame. They considered the main failings of traditional news coverage to be threefold: its excessive use of conflict as a means of framing stories; its "watchdog" preoccupation with the wrongdoings and failures of governments; and its contentment with identifying problems without being concerned about solutions. Taken together, these biases were thought to produce a sense of helplessness among ordinary citizens in the face of vast social problems.

As an alternative, advocates of public journalism propose that journalists not only encourage citizens to become involved in the democratic process but actively facilitate problem-solving by bringing together citizen groups, public officials, and other relevant constituencies. While this approach has been criticized for abandoning journalistic objectivity, it could be argued that it is a logical extension of the role played by journalism generally in facilitating productive discussion within the **public sphere**.

PUBLIC SPHERE. Concept applied to Western political and media development by Jürgen Habermas in *The Structural Transformation of the Public Sphere*, first published in German in 1962, but not available in English until 1989. Habermas has been mainly interested in what he calls the political public sphere as opposed to related cultural spaces. The political public sphere is essentially any communicative space in which individuals can freely, rationally, and critically discuss matters of public interest or policy in their capacity as private citizens; by his account, this space first emerged in British coffeehouses in the late 17th and early 18th centuries. More recently, Joad Raymond and David Zaret have argued that its origins can be traced back to the 1650s in conjunction with newsbooks and **petitions**, while Leth Goran relates its rise to the **corantos** published in support of Protestantism in the Dutch Republic beginning in 1618 and in England a couple of years later. It is questionable, however, whether the discussion that occurred through these earlier media had the degree of protection from state repercussions that Habermas takes as the earmark of a genuine public sphere. Habermas does, however, overlook the extent to which the political public sphere became dependent for its operation on journalism. Not only did the press become the main locus of its existence but a public sphere within the press clearly only existed to the extent that journalists facilitated it. By excluding government officials and institutional representatives from participation in the ideal public sphere, moreover, Habermas also ignores the extent to which the public sphere has always been a normative democratic practice with evolving views as to who should and should not participate in its discussions. As feminist critiques of his use of the concept have made clear, there has always been a gendered dimension to its articulation as a contested democratic ideal.

PULITZER, JOSEPH (1847–1911). American pioneer of the so-called New Journalism. Pulitzer emigrated to the **United States** in 1864 after his upwardly mobile Hungarian Jewish family was bankrupted by his father's death. He fought for the Union in the final year of the Civil War and then became a reporter for the St. Louis *Westliche Post* under the guidance of **Carl Schurz**, later becoming its managing editor and part owner. In 1878, he launched the St. Louis *Post-Dispatch* and used its profits to purchase the *New York World* in 1883. During the 1880s, he introduced various techniques of "new journalism" to his various newspapers and began to attack what he perceived to be the growing corruption of big business. A firm believer in the development of journalism as a profession, he provided an endowment in 1903 for the creation of the **Columbia School of Journalism**.

PULITZER PRIZES. In addition to endowing the **Columbia School of Journalism**, **Joseph Pulitzer** established a fund for annual prizes for distinction in letters, drama, music, and newspaper work, now known as the Pulitzer Prizes. The newspaper prizes were made on the recommendation of an advisory board of the Columbia school and stimulated other organizations to create similar awards for good reporting. In 1917, when the first prizes were awarded, there was only one Pulitzer for reporting, but by 1958 there were four. The awards provided an incentive for many newspapers to engage in civic campaigns; in *The Pulitzer Prize Story* (1959), John Hohenberg found that almost one quarter of the prizes given between 1917 and 1958 were for "exposing graft and corruption in government on local, state, and national levels." War reporting was the next most awarded category during that period, though it was actually exceeded by prizes for reporting and editorializing about U.S. racial conflict and civil liberties if the two are combined. In recent decades, a better balance has been achieved overall through increased emphasis on areas such as labor, economics, education, and medicine.

PYLE, ERNEST TAYLOR (1900–1945). America's most popular war correspondent during **World War II**. Born in Dana, Indiana, "Ernie" worked as a roving correspondent in the early 1930s; it was during this period that he honed his special skills as an observer and storyteller. After becoming the managing editor of the *Washington Daily News*, he began writing a syndicated column for the Scripps-Howard chain in which he focused on the lives and dreams of ordinary Americans. He retained this approach as a war correspondent by writing about the personal experiences of enlisted men and overcame his own feelings of fear and depression to create a sympathetic image of the American infantryman which still resonates today. In 1944, he won a **Pulitzer Prize** for distinguished correspondence. The following year, he was killed by Japanese machine gun fire on Ie Shima. Many of his columns were reprinted in *Ernie Pyle in England* (1941), *Here Is Your War* (1943), *Brave Men* (1944), *Last Chapter* (1946), and *Home Country* (1947).

– R –

RALPH, JULIAN (1853–1903). Highly regarded reporter for the *New York Sun* from 1875 to 1895. While at the *Sun*, he wrote thousands of stories on a wide range of topics, including many of the major trials of the period and both the Greco–Turkish and the Boer War. In 1895, he left the *Sun* for **William Randolph Hearst**'s *New York Journal* and later worked for the *London Daily Mail*. Called "the prince of reporters" by one of his colleagues, he also wrote close to 150 magazine articles, 14 books, and an autobiography.

REED, JOHN (1887–1920). American journalist, poet, and adventurer who became the hero of a generation of radical intellectuals. Born into a wealthy family in Portland, Oregon, Reed went to Harvard University where he served on the editorial board of the *Harvard*

Monthly and *Lampoon* and was class orator and poet. Upon graduating in 1910, he traveled in **Great Britain** and **Spain** before returning to work for the *American Magazine*. He later became a reporter for the radical magazine *The Masses*, where he met his future wife, writer and feminist Louise Bryant. He spent four months with Pancho Villa and his soldiers, covering the Mexican revolution for *Metropolitan Magazine* and the *New York World* and writing *Insurgent Mexico* (1914). With the outbreak of **World War I**, he left for Europe and later turned his reports from the eastern front into the book *The War in Eastern Europe* (1916).

With the help of Max Eastman and some other friends, he and his new wife were able to travel to **Russia** in time to witness firsthand the October Revolution of 1917. He became a close friend of **V. I. Lenin** and recorded his experiences in *Ten Days That Shook the World* (1919). His pro-Bolshevik articles for *The Masses* contributed to its indictment on the grounds of sedition. Upon returning to the **United States**, he worked for the left-wing journal the *Liberator*, threw himself into the embryonic Communist movement, and was instrumental in the foundation of the illegal Communist Labor Party. He returned to Russia in 1920 as a delegate of this party to the Comintern but caught typhus and died. He was given a state funeral and became the only American to be accorded the honor of being buried in Red Square.

REID, WHITELAW (1837–1912). Ohio-born reporter, author, and diplomat whose distinguished Civil War correspondence led **Horace Greeley** to appoint him as managing editor of the influential *New York Tribune* in 1869. After Greeley's death during the presidential campaign of 1872, Reid took over the paper and ran it until 1905 when he became ambassador to England. He used the *Tribune* to advance the argument for American overseas expansion and helped to embody imperialist goals in the treaty concluding the Spanish–American War (1898). He also served as minister to France (1889–92) and was the Republican candidate for vice president in 1892.

RESTON, JAMES BARRETT (1909–1995). Influential American journalist and author of works such as *The Artillery of the Press* (1967). After his family emigrated from **Scotland** in 1920, he began a lengthy journalistic career at the *Springfield* (Ohio) *Daily News,* joined the **Associated Press (AP)** in 1934, and first worked for the *New York Times* in its London bureau in 1939. Following the American entry into **World War II**, he took a leave from the *Times* to establish the U.S. Office of War Information in London. After the war, he rejoined the *Times* as a correspondent and rose through the ranks to become associate editor in the mid-1960s and vice president in the early 1970s. From 1974 to 1987, he wrote a nationally syndicated column that dealt cogently with national and world affairs. Known as "Scotty," he won a **Pulitzer Prize** for national reporting in 1945 and again in 1957.

THE REVERBERATOR **(1888).** Short comedic novel by Henry James which takes newspaper journalism as its main subject. It first appeared as a serial in *Macmillan's Magazine* between February and July 1888. Based on an actual case, its plot revolves around the indignant reaction of a French aristocratic family after a visiting American girl indiscreetly reveals its inner life to George Flack, correspondent for the fictional American society paper *The Reverberator*. The novel reveals James's dismay not only over the contemporary rise of the personal interview as an invasive journalistic practice but over the public's willingness to participate in this invasion of privacy.

REVIEW. News publication produced in its entirety by **Daniel Defoe**. It began on 17 February 1704 with the cumbersome title *A Review of the Affairs of France: And of All Europe, as Influenced by That Nation . . . with an Entertaining Part in Every Sheet, Being Advice from the Scandal Club to the Curious Enquirers; In Answers to Letters Sent Them for That Purpose.* This was later shortened to *The Review of the State of the British Nation.* Published twice and later three times a week with an initial print run of 400, it continued with only a few intermissions until 11 June 1713 when government intervention brought it to a close. Sales reached a peak of about 1,000 copies in 1705–06 and then declined to about half of that by 1712. Defoe recovered some of his costs through commercial advertising and promoted the new culture of credit through allegorical figures like Lady Credit, though still expressing anxieties over some of its moral implications. He deliberately projected his own persona into the text and introduced elements of interviewing into news stories. The general idea for his "Scandalous Club" department was probably borrowed from Henry Care's paper *Pacquet of Advice from Rome* (1678–79).

RIIS, JACOB (1849–1914). Journalist-photographer who crusaded for the reform of slum conditions and contributed to both social realism and the **muckraking** movement. Born in Ribe, **Denmark**, he came to New York City as a penniless immigrant in 1870 and worked at various trades until 1877, when he got a job as a police reporter for the *New York Tribune*. While covering accidents and **crime**, he experienced first-hand the poverty, squalor, and disease in the city's slums. After joining the *New York Evening Sun* in 1888, he began working on a photographic essay on the underside of urban life, which *Scribner's Magazine* published in 1889. It was later expanded into *How the Other Half Lives* (1890), a groundbreaking examination of the social toll of unregulated industrial capitalism. When Theodore Roosevelt became police commissioner (1893–95), he became friends with Riis and accompanied him on all-night investigations of the crowded tenement district. In addition to contributing to improved housing, Riis's campaigns led to the creation of schools and playgrounds in slum areas and improvements in the municipal water supply. Riis wrote several books and lectured widely about the evils of slum life, but the most enduring account of his crusades is his autobiography *The Making of an American* (1901). Roosevelt described him at one point as New York's "most useful citizen."

ROMULO, CARLOS PENA (1899–1985). Philippine journalist and diplomat. After working as a reporter while still in his teens, Romulo did his M.A. at Columbia University and then taught English at the University of the Philippines. In 1933, he returned to journalism as publisher and editor of the *Philippines Herald*. He became the first Asian to win a **Pulitzer Prize** in journalism (1942) for his series on the political and military situation in East Asia. When the **Japanese** invaded the Philippines, he became a press aide to General Douglas MacArthur. In 1949, he was elected president of the United Nations General Assembly. Despite his earlier liberalism, he supported **censorship** while serving as secretary of education and foreign secretary under President Ferdinand Marcos, a contradiction which has marred his reputation as a Filipino patriot.

ROOSEVELT, ELEANOR (1884–1962). Influential first lady who carved out a career in journalism for herself. Following the election of her husband, Franklin D. Roosevelt, as president in 1932, she developed a close relationship with Lorena A. Hickok, who taught her how to use the media and suggested that she hold her own press conferences, making her the first president's wife to do so. Hickok also helped her to develop a nationally syndicated newspaper column called "My Day," which she also broadcast on radio. In addition to promoting the presidency, she used her journalism to develop her own identity as a champion of minorities, women's rights, youth, and the poor. In the process, she provided women journalists with an opportunity to cover national politics.

ROSS, HAROLD (1892–1951). Founder and first editor of the *New Yorker*. Born in Colorado, he began his journalistic career as a reporter for various California newspapers and served as editor of *Stars and Stripes* during **World War I**. After the war, he edited magazines such as *Judge* before founding the *New Yorker* in 1925 as the voice of the American liberal community. In addition to assembling a brilliant staff of editors and writers, he developed its unique mixture of articles, short stories, poetry, and cartoons and created its "Profile" and "Talk of the Town" features.

ROYALL, ANNE (1769–1854). Self-styled protector of democracy whose lifelong concern to expose bureaucratic and religious corruption, fraud, and waste culminated in *Paul Pry* (1831–36) and *The Huntress* (1836–54), two small news publications produced in Washington, D.C. Born Anne Newport, Royall turned to writing after being left with few means by her husband's death in 1812. She traveled widely and wrote several books before turning to journalism at the age of 62. Her "newspapers" consisted mainly of editorials and letters-to-the-editor.

RUSSIA/SOVIET UNION. Although printing began in Russia in 1553 under Ivan IV, the first newspaper was not established until 1702, when Peter the Great created the semi-official *Vedomosti* or *Gazette*. The first private newspaper was the *Moskovskie Vedomosti*, founded by M. V. Lomonosov in 1756, shortly before Catherine II began her reign. But for the next century, poverty, illiteracy, and poor transportation limited the further development of newspapers. During the reign of Paul, the importation of foreign books was banned and private presses were suppressed in the capitals. After becoming tsar in 1825, Nicholas I appointed a special committee to **censor** the press even more closely, forcing writers such as I. G. Golovin and Alexander Herzen to publish their journals and books in Paris and London, respectively.

When Alexander II became emperor in 1855, there were still only a few daily newspapers and these were either owned or subsidized by the government. As part of his efforts to improve education and increase literacy, Alexander encouraged the creation of privately owned newspapers by easing censorship restrictions and allowing street sales and commercial advertising. The first independent commercial newspaper was *Golos* [The Voice], a reformist daily founded by Andrei A. Kraevsky in Moscow in 1863. Among those who took advantage of this freedom to engage in highly polemical journalism was Fedor Dostoevsky (1821–1881). Some of the liberal journals were actually sponsored by conservative Moscow merchants, who agreed with the view of Slavophile journalists that Russia needed to industrialize to avoid becoming subservient to Europe. Despite their hatred of absolutism, leading liberal newspapers such as *Russkoe Slovo* and *Sovremmik* also supported the tsar's military expansion into Siberia and the Caucasus. By 1870, there were 79 Russian-language newspapers in operation, almost five times as many as a decade earlier. The new popular papers borrowed the French newspaper feature known as the ***feuilleton***, which consisted of random slices of popular culture. In addition to building circulation, the *feuilleton* helped to create public opinion by reflecting back to readers their own tastes and opinions.

At the turn of the century, the Russian press was still subject to censorship. In his 1905 poem "What You Can Write About," Vladimir Vasil'evich Trofimov (1874–1916) satirized the situation as follows:

> Never write about bureaucrats,
> Officers or soldiers,

About strikes, political movements,
Clergy, intellectual ferment,
About peasants or ministries,
Executions or Cossack atrocities,
About police, arrests,
Robberies or manifestos,
But everything else—
Must be exposed without fail!

As a result of the 1905 revolution, the press was temporarily freed from prepublication controls, facilitating further increases in newspaper circulation and enabling a few individuals like Aleksei S. Suvorin (1834–1912), millionaire publisher of the large daily *Novoe vremia*, to use journalism as a means of social mobility. At the same time, however, the government retained a number of irritating postpublication controls and used the St. Petersburg Telegraph Agency, established by Finance Minister Sergei Witte in 1904, to propagandize its own programs, especially industrialization, among the middle class. And after Bolshevik publications such as *Iskra* and *Pravda*, established by **V. I. Lenin** in 1900 and 1910 respectively, accelerated their attacks on the imperial regime, the authorities cracked down on independent newspapers once again.

On his way to power, Lenin wrote that all citizens should have the right to express their opinions in the press. But after acquiring it in November 1917, he abandoned any pretense of freedom of the press, immediately closed over 300 opposition papers, and established a system of tight controls. He also banned the conservative American press from the country, resulting in general acceptance of his interpretation of events within the **United States**. In the new Soviet Union, the Bolsheviks set about to harness the press to the revolutionary task of remaking society. During the Leninist period (1917–1925), an official newspaper for the Soviet state (*Izvestia*) was founded to go along with the Communist Party paper *Pravda*; a formal censorship office known as *Glavlit* was set up in 1922; and a state information system run by the Telegraph Agency of the Soviet Union (TASS) was created in 1925.

In staffing the newspapers of the new regime, Soviet officials were initially concerned to secure professional competence as much as ideological steadfastness among journalists. They believed that unless journalists were proficient, they would not be able to educate the peasantry and curb corruption and nepotism in the Party and state. At the same time, however, most Bolsheviks with newspaper experience had already been drawn into the bureaucracy, leaving the press in the hands of relative novices, many of whom were not even Party members. Despite the belief that only proletarians (and later peasants) could be good Communists, therefore, leaders of the press corps were forced to staff their newspapers with a number of non-Communist (or recently converted) intelligentsia and white-collar workers. To overcome this situation, the Bolsheviks established the **State Institute of Journalism** or GIZh in 1921 to train a new group of journalists with approved political and class identities. It was the first school of journalism in the country, as attempts in tsarist Russia to provide professional training for journalists had never progressed beyond the planning stage. But the Institute also found it difficult to recruit a sufficient number of adequately prepared students who were Communists with the required class background and for a time quietly allowed nonsanctioned students to attend. It was not until 1930, when the Institute's faculty was purged and a new curriculum was established, that applicants with nonsanctioned identities were no longer admitted.

A shift in emphasis from educating professionals to training propagandists was symbolized the same year by renaming GIZh the Communist Institute of Journalism. During the New Economic Policy (1921–28), however, the information infrastructure was generally too primitive for propaganda to work effectively. Although **Glavlit** exercised tight control over official information, Jeffrey Brooks notes that newspaper publishers, unchecked by market forces, ignored popular taste so that the materials they produced were of no interest to most readers. Though intended for lower-class readers, the Soviet newspaper *Bednota* failed to gain a large audience, especially after payment was introduced in 1921. In late 1923, therefore, the Bolsheviks created *Krest'ianskaia gazeta*, a weekly **tabloid** for those considered not ready for serious material. It was joined by two other state-run tabloids, *Rabochaia gazeta* and *Rabochaia Moskva*. While these papers still failed to attract a mass audience of common readers, they did acquire a following among activists and government employees hoping to become involved in the new institutions of public life.

After Joseph Stalin came to power in 1928, attempts to cultivate readers in stages came to an end. The press became a sterile, obedient servant of the Communist party, providing little more than official speeches and stories about the achievements of Soviet socialism. During the 1930s, radio also became Stalin's mouthpiece, although an Aesopian language was developed to express a degree of coded criticism and music and children's literature flourished. For the next 25 years, the Soviet press became a virtual propaganda agency on behalf of Stalinism, revealing none of its abuses and corruption.

Following the death of Stalin, Nikita Khrushchev facilitated a revival of journalism by elevating the press to the role of trusted servant. Led by his son-in-law, Aleksei Adzhubei, editor of *Izvestia* from 1959 to 1964, an attempt was made to reconstitute journalism and Soviet society more generally on the basis of what Thomas Wolfe describes as the idea of an ideal socialist "person" or *chelovek*, specifically understood as having an independent political voice. Newspapers also adopted a number of Western features, such as larger headlines, shorter news items, and greater use of photographs. The revelation of Stalinist horrors also drove circulation to unprecedented heights. After Khrushchev's removal from power in 1964, the Communist Party once again sought to establish its control over the press. But while the rhetorical figure of the *chelovek* was undermined, it was not eliminated from Soviet journalism, eventually being taken up again during *perestroika* and *glasnost*.

With the collapse of the Soviet Union and Communist Party in December 1991, there was an explosion of journalism intent on reforming the Russian nation that remained. The new Russian Constitution of 1993 specifically provided that "The freedom of the mass media shall be guaranteed. Censorship shall be prohibited." However, various legal measures have since been used to reestablish much of the traditional self-censorship of the Russian press.

– S –

SAUDI ARABIA. The first newspaper in Saudi Arabia was *al Hijaz*, which the Ottoman authorities began publishing in Mecca in 1908. It was devoted mainly to literary materials for the country's small literate minority, a characteristic subsequently of both the official government journal *Umm al Qura* and private papers such as *Sawt al Hijaz* and *Madinah al Manawarah*. The latter publications ceased operations during **World War II**, but were resumed with more focus on news after the war. They were soon joined by a number of other private newspapers serving the personal interests of the new oil-based elite. In 1962, the government responded to this growth by creating the Ministry of Information to monitor the press. The new Ministry enacted a press code (1964), licensing all publishing operations, restricting the right to establish a new periodical, and regulating content. The code gave the Ministry control over the selection and tenure of newspaper editors and the right to close newspapers. In 1971, the Ministry also set up the Saudi Press Agency to supply the media with pro-government information. Lest even these measures leave too much to chance, a royal decree in 1982 set forth explicit guidelines for self-**censorship**.

Within the confines of this system, the Saudi Arabian press and its readership has still managed to grow. In 1980, the country had 10 dailies and 8 non-dailies, with roughly estimated circulations per 1,000 of 28 and 3 respectively. Today, there are 13 dailies and some 200 non-dailies with a combined circulation per 1,000 of about 60. The leading dailies are currently *Ar-Riyadh* and *Al-Jazirah* in Arabic, *Riyadh Daily* in English, and the regional Arabic daily *Sharq Al Awsat*, which the Saudi Research and Publishing Company (SRPC) began in London in 1978. All remain subject to close government scrutiny, however. In 2007, the Paris-based organization Reporters Without Borders ranked Saudi Arabia last in terms of press freedom, below Libya, Syria, and Iraq.

SCHURZ, CARL (1829–1906). German-born American senator, minister to **Spain**, and secretary of the interior, who was also active for much of his life as a journalist. He began his journalistic career as editor of the *Neue Bonner Zeitung* in **Germany** before emigrating to the **United States** where he founded the *Watertown* (Wisconsin) *Deutsche Volks-Zeitung*. After the Civil War, he worked as the Washington correspondent for the *New York Tribune*, edited the *Detroit Daily Post*, and then became co-owner of the *St. Louis Westliche Post*, where he gave **Joseph Pulitzer** his first job as a reporter. He was later chief editor of *The Nation* and from 1892 to 1897 wrote the weekly lead editorials for *Harper's*.

SCOPES TRIAL. Famous "monkey trial" in Dayton, Tennessee, in July 1925 over the right to teach evolution in the public schools. John Thomas Scopes, the physics teacher who volunteered to be the defendant in the case, was represented by Clarence Darrow, while the volunteer prosecutor was the former Progressive leader William Jennings Bryan. The **Associated Press (AP)** and United Press both sent correspondents, the most well-known being UP's Raymond Clapper. Owing in part to the sensational coverage of **H. L. Mencken**, the trial was front-page news for three weeks and was framed by the press as an epic struggle between science and religion. Papers such as the *Chicago Tribune* portrayed Bryan as a reflection of rural ignorance. Edward Caudill has argued that the press was biased in favor of evolutionism because of the affinities between science and journalism. But the press itself had originally been skeptical of Charles Darwin's theory and had only gradually come to accept it as scientific fact. Moreover, the textbooks used to teach Darwin in Tennessee schools actually misrepresented how contemporary scientists understood evolution and were thus quite capable of being criticized on scientific grounds. Bryan's death a week after the trial was prematurely taken as symbolic of the death of religious fundamentalism.

SCOTLAND. The development of an indigenous national press occurred at a somewhat later date in Scotland than in England. Early Scottish newsbooks such as *The heads of severall proceedings in the present Parliament* (1641) and *Mercurius Scoticus* (1651) only contained news obtained in London and soon gave way to English publications like a *Diurnal of some Passages and Affairs* (1652) and *Mercurius Politicus* (1654) which were first published in London and then reprinted in Edinburgh or Leith. On the last day of 1660, Thomas Sydserf began publication of the first newspaper manufactured in Scotland, a weekly quarto of eight pages called *Mercurius Caledonius* (subtitled "Comprising the Affairs in Agitation, in Scotland, with a Survey of Foreign Intelligence"), but it only lasted until the end of March 1661. A similar fate awaited most other late 17th-century Scottish newspapers, with the exception of the official *Edinburgh Gazette* (1680).

By the early 18th century, however, papers such as the *Edinburgh Flying Post* (1708), the *Edinburgh* (later *Scots*) *Courant* (1710), the Edinburgh *Evening Courant* (1718), and the *Caledonian Mercury* (1720) were operating on a profitable basis; the highly respected *Mercury* continued until 1867, while the *Courant* lasted until 1871. The *Courant*'s first proprietor, James Watson, also printed a Scottish version of *The Tatler* edited by Robert Hepburn. Apart from using the publication to address anxieties resulting from the Union of 1707, Hepburn has his character, Donald MacStaff, implore his supposed cousin, Steele's Isaac Bisckerstaff, to take account of Edinburgh in his discussions of social manners. While less popular than cheap street literature such as chapbooks and broadsides, 18th-century Scottish newspapers disseminated an increasingly wide variety of information and opinion and consciously promoted national identity, even giving preference to advertisements that included some kind of national appeal.

By the 1820s, the Scottish political press had come to be marked by extreme partisanship, with one particularly immoderate attack resulting in a duel and the death of its author. At the same time, newspapers were finally developing outside of the main cities. In the 1830s, several of the unstamped newspapers in Glasgow, including one owned by workers themselves, helped labor leaders such as Alexander Campbell to organize trade unions and promote universal suffrage, better factory conditions, and improved education. But as in the rest of **Great Britain**, the abolition of the **stamp tax** in 1855 undermined the radical press by enabling inexpensive dailies to siphon off many working-class readers.

During the 1920s and 1930s, Scottish newspapers not only began to concentrate on stories with specific Scottish content but deliberately excluded English stories. For most of the postwar period, the Scottish press was clearly biased toward the Labour Party. After the British *Daily Mail* launched a Scottish edition in 1995, however, several of Scotland's main papers moved away from Labour in an effort to secure new readers. A content analysis of Scottish newspaper election coverage after devolution in 1997 found greater emphasis on providing voters with information and evaluative material than in British papers generally.

SEE IT NOW. Television public affairs program produced by **Edward R. Murrow** and Fred W. Friendly for CBS. An adaptation of their radio program *Hear It Now*, it went on the air on 18 November 1951 and lasted until 9 July 1958 when CBS board chairman William S. Paley decided to discontinue it. Broadcast live, it set the standard for honest, accurate reporting. On 9 March 1954, it exposed the witch-hunting tactics of Senator Joseph R. McCarthy.

SELDES, GEORGE (1890–1995). American investigative reporter and news media critic. He began his long career in journalism in Pittsburgh at the age of 19. At the end of **World War I**, he was court-martialed for allegedly breaking the Armistice by trying to publish an exclusive interview with Paul von Hindenburg in which the head of the German army emphasized the role that the **United States** had played in winning the war. During the 1920s, Seldes worked as an international reporter for the *Chicago Tribune* and was expelled from both the **Soviet Union** and **Italy** for his critical reports. After leaving the *Tribune*, he wrote two books in which he included stories that the paper had refused to publish. He also produced two major critiques of the press: *Freedom of the Press* (1935) and *Lords of the Press* (1938). In 1940, he began *In Fact*, a **newsletter** devoted to **investigative journalism**. Despite being blacklisted after Joseph McCarthy accused him of being a Communist, he published over 20 books on topics and events generally ignored by the mainstream media.

SHENBAO. Highly profitable commercial newspaper founded by the British merchant Ernest Major in the treaty port of Shanghai in 1872. Though managed by a British company, it was written by Chinese literati and soon had a circulation of between 8,000 and 10,000. It made use of strange and fantastic stories, a strong personal editorial voice, and a letters-to-the-editor column to attract a wide audience. After the failure of the 1898 reform movement, it purchased the central government's official gazette. In 1909, it was taken over by a Chinese comprador. The decline in the cost of paper during **World War I** enabled it to invest in new equipment and expand its staff, measures which helped to increase its circulation from about 20,000 before the war to about 150,000 by the early 1920s.

SHIELD LAWS. Laws that provide varying degrees of protection for journalists' confidential sources, and in some cases the information itself obtained through them, by promising not to reveal their identity. In the **United States**, the first state-level shield law was passed by Maryland in 1886 and remained the only such law until New Jersey followed suit in 1933. By 1950, 10 states had shield laws, increasing to some two dozen states by the early 1990s. Efforts to pass a federal shield law have yet to meet with success, however, and one study found that journalists were less likely to go to jail for refusing to identify a source in states *without* shield laws than in states with them.

SINGER, BERNARD (1893–1966). Polish journalist. Born in Warsaw, Singer helped to establish the Polish Folkist Party before turning to journalism. After a stint as a reporter for the Jewish daily *Haynt*, he joined the staff of *Nasz Przeglad* in 1925 and traveled widely as an international correspondent until 1941. After the war, he worked at *The Economist* in London. In his memoirs, published in 1959, he recounted his travails as a Polish Jew.

SMALLEY, GEORGE W. (1833–1916). The dean of 19th-century foreign correspondents, "G. W. S." (as he signed his articles) first established his reputation by his accurate account of the battle of Antietam for the *New York Tribune*. In 1866, he was transferred to London to cover the Franco–Prussian War (1870–71) and sent one of the earliest news cables across the Atlantic. The following year, he organized a London bureau to coordinate news from the *Tribune*'s reporters scattered across Europe. He also arranged for a news exchange between the *Tribune* and the *London Daily News*, the first such agreement by an American newspaper. In 1895, he ended his work as an international columnist for the *Tribune* to serve as the London correspondent for *The Times* in the **United States**. He played a key role during the British Guiana-Venezuelan boundary dispute.

SNOW, EDGAR (1905–1972). American journalist who provided the most influential reporting on the Communists' rise to power in **China** through unparalleled access to its leadership. Born to a middle-class

Kansas City family, Snow attended the University of Missouri and **Columbia School of Journalism** and worked for the *Kansas City Star* in 1927 before leaving for New York to work briefly in advertising. "I was twenty-two," he recalled in *Journey to the Beginning* (1958), "and I had picked up a few dollars in Wall Street speculation which gave me just enough of a stake, I thought, to finance a year of parsimonious traveling and adventuring . . . I had, on my itinerary, allotted six weeks to China." Landing a job with J. B. Powell's *China Weekly Review* in Shanghai in 1928, he remained in China for the next 13 years and became a prolific contributor to newspapers and magazines in China, the **United States**, and **Great Britain**. In 1936, he slipped through the Kuomintang blockade and made his way to the Communist base at Yen-an in north-central China. He spent several months with Mao Zedong (Mao Tse-tung) and wrote *Red Star over China* (1937), a highly sympathetic account of the Communists' struggle for power. "The description of the 'Long March' almost makes Xenophon's heroes shrivel into chocolate soldiers," wrote one reviewer. "That alone makes this book the great adventure book of the year; but it is of even greater importance as a handbook for the historian and the political scientist." Despite its one-sided treatment, the book has remained a primary source on the early history of the Communist movement. Upon returning to the United States in 1941, Snow worked for the *Saturday Evening Post*. He revisited China in 1960 and wrote *The Other Side of the River: Red China Today* (1962). It was through Snow that the Chinese leadership signaled their willingness to receive U.S. President Richard Nixon in Beijing.

SOB SISTERS. Derogatory term originally referring to women reporters covering the sensational 1907 trial of wealthy playboy Harry Thaw for the murder of prominent architect Stanford White in New York City. According to the early press historian Ishbel Ross (1936), it was coined by journalist Irvin S. Cobb to describe the sentimentalized accounts of Winifred Black, Dorothy Dix, Nixola Greeley Smith, and Ada Patterson, who produced most of the female-authored coverage of the trial. However, although most subsequent journalism historians have accepted this attribution, a recent study of the extensive trial coverage by Jean Marie Lutes found references to women reporters as the "pity platoon" and "sympathy squad" but no specific mention of "sob sisters." Nonetheless, the term came into use in the 1910s to characterize women reporters generally so as to restrict their opportunities and diminish their accomplishments as journalists. Lutes's study argues that the coverage by male reporters was actually no less sentimental than that of their female counterparts, but did not give rise to similar stereotypes.

SOCIAL CONTROL IN THE NEWSROOM. Concept articulated by Warren Breed in an article first published in the journal *Social Forces* in 1955. Breed argued that, whereas newspaper owners in the past had sometimes exercised direct control over content, news operations had become too large and complex for owners to manipulate coverage on a regular basis. Breed maintained, however, that they still exercised control indirectly by establishing implicit news policies to which newsworkers adhered because of feelings of obligation or esteem and aspirations for promotion and achievement. The news worker "learns to anticipate what is expected of him so as to win rewards and avoid punishments." Subsequent sociologists of news have refined this concept to include unconscious processes governing the selection of news.

SOUTH AFRICA. The first newspaper in South Africa, the *Cape Town Gazette and African Advertiser*, was begun by British settlers in 1800, not long after their arrival in the Cape area. It was later followed by English-language papers like the *Eastern Province Herald* (1845), the *Natal Witness* (1846), the *Natal Mercury* (1852), the *Daily News*, (1854), the *Cape Argus* (1857), the *Daily Dispatch* (1872), the *Cape Times*, (1876), the *Diamond Fields Advertiser* (1878), and *The Star* (1887). The Dutch-speaking population, whose forbears had begun settlements along with the Portuguese in the mid-17th century, did not create a newspaper until 1828 when they founded *Die Zuid Afrikaan*. As the British came to dominate the Cape Town area, those of Dutch descent moved north and established newspapers such as *De Staats Courant* (1857), *De Volksten* (1873), and *Di Patriot* (1876), the latter being the first newspaper in Afrikaans. But the number of papers in Afrikaans lagged well behind those in English, a situation which continues across South African media today. In this period, the native African population also established a few newspapers, principally *Imvo Zabantsundu* (1884) and *Ilanga Losa* (1904).

As a result of the British victory in the Anglo–Boer War (1889–1902), the Dutch republics of Transvaal and Orange Free State were amalgamated with Natal and Cape Town in 1910 to form the Union of South Africa. There ensued a long struggle between the English-speaking whites and nationalist Afrikaners, with black South Africans trying to gain a measure of influence through organizations such as the South African Native National Congress, organized in 1912 and transformed into the African National Congress (ANC) in 1923. During the interwar period, the moderate English-speaking United Party maintained the upper hand with the help of influential papers such as the *Rand Daily Mail* (1902) and newspaper chains like the *South African Associated Press* (now *Times Media*). The Afrikaners tried to counter their influence through new papers such as *Die Burger* (1915) and newspaper chains of their own such as *National Pers* and *Perskor*. But many of their number continued to prefer English-language newspapers. As a result, they began a campaign to infiltrate institutions such as the South African Broadcasting Corporation (SABC), which became a governmental agency in 1936.

Following the victory of Daniel François Malan's National Party in 1948, the Afrikaners consolidated their control over the SABC and used it to help establish the oppressive policy of apartheid. In conjunction with apartheid, the state attempted to exercise total control over the dissemination of news and information. By the late 1960s, however, there was some criticism of apartheid within the National Party itself by members such as Schalk Pienaar, editor of the Sunday newspaper *Die Beeld* and later *Beeld*. Pienaar tried to achieve "reform from within" of the Afrikaner establishment by criticizing the moral hypocrisy of apartheid and calling for justice for all South Africans. In 1977, however, the National Party continued the kind of deceit about which Pienaar had complained by secretly founding *The Citizen* as a state propaganda organ. Though this ploy was later exposed, even the liberal English-language press remained highly supportive of the status quo and opposed the organized mass resistance to apartheid that emerged in the mid-1980s. As a result, anti-apartheid whites, aided by foreign funding, began to establish alternative publications, such as the English-language *Weekly Mail* and

Sunday Nation and the Afrikaans-language *Vrye Weekblad* and *South* (1987). These independent papers not only helped activists to mobilize but provided South Africans generally with news about the struggle against apartheid (and the government's brutal countermeasures) that was absent in the mainstream media. Together with international pressure and growing economic problems, the alternative media contributed to National Party leader F. W. de Klerk's decision in 1989 to dismantle the infrastructure of apartheid and negotiate with Mandela and the ANC to create a democratic and multiracial South Africa. *See also* FIRST, RUTH.

SOVIET UNION. *See* RUSSIA.

SPAIN. Per capita readership of newspapers has always been quite low in Spain and television has now overtaken print as the primary source of news. For much of their history, Spanish journalists have contended with state **censorship**. During the 18th century, restrictions on freedom of the press were generally avoided by concentrating on news about the arts, literature, and science rather than politics and religion. But resistance to the Napoleonic occupation gave rise to political journalism which led in turn to press controls. After numerous oscillations, these controls reached their peak under the fascist regime of Francisco Franco, who created a National Press and Propaganda Agency to monitor the press. Following the death of Franco in 1975 and the enactment of a new constitution in 1978, the Spanish press was finally released from the shackles of prepublication censorship. For the first time, Spanish newspapers could safely engage in critical and even **investigative journalism**. At the same time, however, the government continued to register journalists and to influence the flow of news through its own massive news agency, *Agencia* (EFA), first created by Franco in 1938.

During the second half of the 19th century, a number of figures used the Spanish press to pursue their political and social ambitions. From 1866 to 1874, for example, Ruggiero Bonghi advanced his career as a member of Parliament by writing a column on foreign affairs entitled "Rassegne Politiche" for *Nuova Antologia*. Similarly, Rafael Gasset y Chinchilla used his ownership of Madrid's *El Imparcial* to join the political and social elite, culminating in his appointment as minister of agriculture in 1900. After the turn of the century, however, the politician-as-journalist was displaced in stature and influence by the intellectual-as-journalist. In contrast to the Anglo-American press, the most important figures in modern Spanish journalism have not been reporters, but university professors like José Ortega y Gasset who published much of their writing in newspapers and helped to found and operate influential periodicals. This tradition of the *periodista* had less to do with political censorship than with practice of treating the public dissemination of ideas as newsworthy events.

Most journalists in Spain are now graduates of university journalism programs, a practice encouraged by the fact that a journalism degree is required for membership in any of the various **professional organizations** belonging to the National Federation of Associations of the Press. Currently, the main programs in journalism are offered at the University of Madrid and the University of Navarre. Typically, these programs have accommodated large numbers of students; for example, even after limiting enrollment in 1980, the Madrid program admitted over 600 new journalism students. For graduates seeking employment at a prestigious national newspaper, the preferred choice is clearly *El País*, followed by *ABC* and *El Mundo*. A socialist newspaper founded by the communications group PRISA in Madrid in 1976 after the death of Francisco Franco, *El País* played an important role in Spain's transition to democracy and is currently the largest paper in Spain. A general news **tabloid** founded in Madrid in 1989, *El Mundo* originally supported the right-wing Popular Party, but later became more politically independent. It currently ranks second in national circulation.

SPECTATOR. Literary newspaper begun by **Richard Steele** and **Joseph Addison** on 1 March 1711 and continuing until 6 December 1712. Building on the enormous popularity of *The Tatler*, it was aimed at a broad readership and was published on a daily basis (except Sundays) by Sam Buckley. At its height, it was selling 3,000 copies a day. Apart from Steele and Addison, who together wrote 510 of the publication's 555 issues, contributors included Alexander Pope and Addison's cousin, Eustace Budgell. Addison's witty, satirical essays utilized a fictitious club presided over by "Mr. Spectator," a man of travel and learning who frequents London as an observer but keeps clear of political strife. A victim of the **stamp tax**, the *Spectator* was succeeded initially by a more political weekly publication called the *Guardian* on 12 March 1713 and then revived by Addison under its old title for 80 numbers on 18 June 1714. In 1828, Robert Stephen Wintoul started a radical weekly by the same name to support Lord John Russell's reform bill. Among the imitators of the *Spectator* was the satirical magazine *Drone*, begun by Russian journalist Nikolai Ivanovich Novikov (1744–1818) in 1769. Even its approach to social injustice was too much for Catherine II, however, who suspended it in 1774.

SPEED, JOHN GILMER (1853–1909). Author of the first content analysis of a newspaper. A grand-nephew of the poet John Keats, he worked as a civil engineer in Louisville before leaving for New York where he became managing editor and later publisher of the *World*. He used his position to compare the content of four New York dailies in 1881 and 1893, finding increased levels of gossip and scandal in the news. He criticized the New Journalism for displacing the kind of news that he believed readers needed to function as citizens in a democracy and for providing examples of poor behavior that readers might imitate. His study provided a foundation for later academic critiques of the newspaper as a social institution.

SPIES, JOURNALISTS AS. The world of journalism has periodically intersected with that of espionage. For 20 years, Pietro Bizzarri, a minor Protestant writer in 15th-century **Italy**, provided the English government with weekly political intelligence in the form of a **newsletter** in exchange for a pension. **Daniel Defoe** spied first on behalf of Tory leader Robert Harley and then for the Whigs. During the American Revolution, James Rivington, the king's printer and a detested arch-Tory, whose office was mobbed and who was hanged in effigy for supporting the Royalists in his *New-York Gazette and Universal Advertiser*, was actually employed in George Washington's secret service. In 1852, the well-known Danish journalist Edgar Bauer (1820–1886), who had earlier been jailed by Prussian authorities for his involvement in radical political activities, was recruited by the chief of the Copenhagen police to spy on various revolutionary groups in London; the police then passed along his intelligence to their counterparts in Dresden, Hanover, and Vienna.

In *The Invasion of 1910*, which the *Daily Mail* serialized in March 1906, and *Spies for the Kaiser* (1910), William Le Queux warned that a German invasion of **Great Britain** would be preceded by an army of spies disguised as waiters, barbers, and tourists. Influenced by such works, a new Official Secrets Act was passed which only required the prosecution to show that the accused "appeared" to be a spy. This criterion was more than sufficient to convict a German journalist Max Schultz of spying in November 1911. During the war, **Germany** did in fact send dozens of agents to Britain as spies; a majority of these agents used business ventures as covers, but many posed as journalists. One security service analysis summarized these covers in percentages as follows: businessmen (55), journalists (25), workmen (10), and people with no occupation or traveling for their "health" (10).

Before joining *Time* magazine in 1939, Whittaker Chambers wrote for the American Communist party newspaper and engaged in espionage on behalf of the **Soviet Union**. During **World War II**, the well educated and respected **Japanese** journalist Osaki Hotsumi ran a successful spy ring in Japan on behalf of what he thought was the Communist International. Osaki used his government connections to channel information to Richard Sorge, a Tokyo-based German journalist with supposed Nazi sympathies who actually reported to Red Army intelligence but led Osaki to believe that he represented the Comintern. Both Ozaki and Sorge went to the gallows on the same day, but Osaki later acquired cult status as what John J. Stephen calls "a redemptive symbol of Japan's conscience." *See also* BURCHETT, WILFRED; CENTRAL INTELLIGENCE AGENCY (CIA).

SPIN DOCTORS. Term first used in the mid-1980s to refer to the various consultants, media handlers, and party officials whose job is to interpret events in a manner favorable to particular politicians or political campaigns. As part of the larger process of **news management**, spin doctoring creates a further barrier between the journalist and public figures.

SPORTS JOURNALISM. Following the lead of the *Spectator* (1711–12), 18th-century newspapers in **Great Britain** gradually increased their coverage of sporting events as part of their local fare. The early Sunday papers placed even greater emphasis on sports, paving the way for the first journals devoted exclusively to sports. Like the *Weekly Dispatch* in Britain, the *American Turf Register* (1831) was dedicated to horse racing. But in 1831, William Trotter Porter founded the *Spirit of the Times* and broadened its content to include cricket, foot racing, nautical sports, and prize fighting. The same year, Henry William Herbert was banished from England by his nobleman father after piling up debts at Cambridge. Arriving in New York City, he began writing novels and other literary works, but soon turned to sports reporting to supplement his income. To avoid compromising his literary reputation, he adopted the pen name "Frank Forester" and became America's first regular sports reporter.

During the late 1830s, **penny papers** such as the *New York Sun* and the *New York Herald* began covering sports, but were slow to compensate their reporters. Henry Chadwick, who developed the baseball box score while writing for the *Herald*, was not paid for his efforts until 1862. After the Civil War, the *Spirit of the Times* and the *New York Clipper* led the way in promoting baseball as the "national game," a task later taken over by magazines like *Sporting Life* (1883) and *Sporting News* (1886). After helping to establish the American League in 1900, *Sporting News* took over the *Clipper*'s title as the "Bible" of baseball. Almost all baseball reporters engaged in boosterism, promoting their own city's team and mythologizing its best players. The first major exception to this rule occurred during the 1890s when reporters criticized owners who controlled more than one team. The players themselves remained demigods until 1919 when the press got wind of the fact that some of the Chicago White Sox players had taken steps to fix the World Series. Before long, however, baseball reporters became promoters once again, a practice reinforced by the fact that the ball clubs paid their expenses.

Prize fighting, which had long been excoriated in much of the press as an affront to public decency, was a greater promotional challenge. But in the 1880s, Kyle Fox, publisher of the *National Police Gazette*, exploited the deeds of boxer John L. Sullivan to help professionalize boxing and make himself wealthy in the process. During the 1890s, football became even more popular, aided by the development of pages devoted specifically to sports. Both sports provided gratuities to sports writers in return for covering their matches, an arrangement which continued unimpeded until 1975 when the American Society of Newspaper Editors (ASNE) tried to eliminate such freebies.

In contrast to the current treatment of sporting performances as an accumulation of statistics, baseball writers such as Peter Finlay Dunne at the *New York Times* developed a picturesque, humorous, and exaggerated style of coverage that regarded actions on the field like a performance at the ballet. The promotion of particular sports or sports figures by media owners and journalists continued during the 20th century. In the 1920s, for example, Grantland Rice devoted many of his syndicated articles to bolstering the reputation of golfer Bobby Jones.

By then, however, the traditional paternalistic view that the sports page should cultivate the participation of youth by covering amateur as well as professional sport was giving way to sports reporting as a circulation- and career-builder. Jazz-age sports journalists like Rice placed increasing emphasis on professional athletes as cultural heroes. Rice was among those whose coverage helped to transform football from a college social event into a supreme test of manhood and preparation for life in a highly competitive society. Though some sportswriters have questioned the practices of owners in running their teams and leagues, especially in times of labor strife, most have continued to function as apologists for "the game," be it baseball, football, basketball, hockey, or their lesser rivals. Most continue to focus almost exclusively on men's sports. A recent survey of sports editors in the southeastern **United States** found that many simply assumed that women's sports are less worthy of coverage without making any effort to discern their readers' interests.

STAMP TAX. Economic measure designed to control the outpouring of political propaganda in **Great Britain** after the expiry of the Licensing Act in 1695. Introduced in 1712 by the Tory government of Robert Harley with the support of most Whigs, the Stamp Act required newspaper and periodical publishers to pay a duty of a halfpenny for each copy of a halfsheet of paper plus an additional shilling for each **advertisement**. At the time, most papers were printed on a halfsheet (folded in two) and sold for a penny. While also raising revenue and providing information about circulation rates, the act was mainly intended to discourage the growth of the press, which was still regarded as a threat to political stability by Whigs and Tories alike. A loophole in the original act temporarily enabled publishers to escape most of the tax by increasing the size of their newspapers to one and a half sheets. In 1725, however, Parliament plugged this loophole and improved enforcement of the act. As a result of successive increases in the duty, the cost of a single newspaper represented a day's pay for an ordinary worker by the century's end. The act failed, however, to achieve the results intended; instead of preventing the growth of the press, it further entrenched the system of political patronage.

STARS AND STRIPES. Military newspaper first published by U.S. troops in Paris between 8 February 1918 and 13 June 1919. Edited by Lieutenant Guy T. Vishniskki, who had worked for the Wheeler Syndicate in New York, the original 71 issues set a pattern for soldier journalism by being sentimental, irreverent, funny, and honest. Its original staff included Private **Harold W. Ross**, later of the *New Yorker*, Captain **Franklin P. Adams,** and Lieutenant Grantland Rice. It was joined by a number of other armed forces newspapers during **World War II**. Although generally supportive of its publication, Generals Douglas MacArthur and George Patton preferred that it take its material straight from the War Department's Army News Service rather than seek out the views of enlisted men.

STATE INSTITUTE OF JOURNALISM. Founded in Moscow in the fall of 1921 as part of the Commissariat of Education, the State Institute of Journalism or GIZh was the early **Soviet Union**'s flagship school of journalism. Its purpose was to prepare trustworthy Communists to run the mass press, but during the 1920s it also accepted students who were not from the proletarian or peasant class. It began as a one-year program but was later expanded to three years. Its first rector was Konstantin Novitskii. In 1924 it was transformed into a specialized Communist Institution of Higher Education and in 1930 was renamed the Communist Institute of Journalism. During the course of their studies, students did apprenticeships at national and local newspapers.

STEAD, WILLIAM T. (1849–1912). Key figure in the development of the New Journalism in **Great Britain**. The son of a Congregational minister in Northumberland, Stead combined a puritanical temperament with a passionate liberal and imperialist ideology. He began his career as a journalistic crusader at the *Northern Echo* in Darlington, quickly turning the fledgling provincial newspaper into a vehicle of social and moral reform. In 1876, he attacked Prime Minister Benjamin Disraeli's refusal to come to the aid of Bulgarian Christians during their rebellion against **Turkey**. In 1880, after a decade at the *Echo*, he became John Morley's assistant at the *Pall Mall Gazette*, the most notable afternoon paper in London. When Morley was elected to Parliament in 1883, Stead took over as editor of the sedate publication and used illustrations, interviews, and sensationalism to make it the most influential paper in Britain. An apostle of Britain's supreme naval power, he wrote a series of articles on "The Truth about the Navy" that led to important naval reforms.

After being attacked for his crusade against "white slavery," Stead left the *Gazette* in 1890 to found the *Review of Reviews* as a monthly periodical through which to propagate his own views. His writing inspired both the imperialist project of Cecil Rhodes and the arbitration and armament reduction plan of Andrew Carnegie. In 1911, he wrote a letter to the editor of the *London Daily Express* refuting the claim that English women were being lured to Mormon communities in Utah and forced into polygamous marriages. Nominated five times for the Nobel Peace Prize, he was among those who died on the *Titanic*'s maiden voyage.

STEELE, RICHARD (1672–1729). Born and educated in Dublin, Steele was educated at Charterhouse in London where he met **Joseph Addison**, whom he later joined at Oxford. After leaving Oxford without a degree for a career in the army, he became a successful comedic playwright and in 1707 was appointed editor of the government sponsored *London Gazette*. In 1709, while still a Gazetteer, he began *The Tatler* with the collaboration of Addison. After *The Tatler* was ended for political reasons, Steele and Addison began the *Spectator* in early 1711. Steele wrote 229 of *The Tatler*'s 271 issues and 236 of the *Spectator*'s 555 issues.

STEFFENS, LINCOLN (1866–1936). A University of California-educated leader of the American **muckrakers** during his association with *McClure's* from 1902–11. In books such as *The Shame of the Cities* (1904) and *The Struggle for Self-Government* (1906), he focused on political corruption and the alliance between business and politics. **William Randolph Hearst** called him the "best interviewer he ever encountered." His experiences as a muckraker were later chronicled in his *Autobiography* (1931) and influenced journalists such as **George Seldes**.

STEINBECK, JOHN (1902–1968). **Pulitzer Prize**-winning novelist who worked as a journalist during the Depression and **World War II**. By the mid-1930s, Steinbeck had published several famous novels but was still struggling financially. In 1936, therefore, he went to work for the *San Francisco News* to report on the labor problems in central California, an experience that provided the basis for *The Grapes of Wrath* (1939). He then worked in Europe as an accredited correspondent for the *New York Herald Tribune*. In 1942, he was commissioned by the U.S. government to write *Bombs Away*, an account of American fliers in training. The following year he left for London and later filed stories for the *Tribune* from North Africa and **Italy**. Frustrated by military **censorship** (on one occasion, he filed Herodotus's account of an ancient battle and even it was censored), he tried to compensate by giving readers an idea of the compromising conditions under which war correspondents generally worked. Because of his previous criticism of the American socioeconomic order, Steinbeck's wartime writing was monitored, to his annoyance, by the **Federal Bureau of Investigation (FBI)**. His collected wartime correspondence for the *Tribune* was published as *Once There Was a War* (1958).

STONE, I. F. (1907–1989). Radical American journalist. Born Isidor Feinstein in Philadelphia, he worked as a reporter, editorial writer, and columnist for the *Philadelphia Daily Record*, *P.M.*, the *New York Post*, and other papers during the interwar period. In 1940, he became the Washington editor of *The Nation*. In *The Hidden History of the Korean War* (1952), which was boycotted by the mainstream press, Stone claimed that the attack by the North was not premeditated but provoked by South **Korea** and Taiwan, an interpretation inconsistent with documents subsequently released from Soviet archives. In 1953, he began the **newsletter** *I. F. Stone's Weekly*, inspired by **George Seldes**'s political weekly *In Fact*. Produced almost single-handedly by Stone and his wife, it became *I. F. Stone's Bi-Weekly* in 1967 and achieved an international reputation for its **investigative journalism** and tough-minded criticism until ill health forced Stone to discontinue it in 1971. Stone also wrote ten books, including *The Trial of Socrates* (1989).

SUBSCRIPTION READING-ROOMS. During the early 19th century, when newspaper circulation was still hindered by print technology, illiteracy, poor communication, post office restrictions, and heavy taxation, the middle and working classes in **Great Britain** made use of subscription reading-rooms to overcome these obstacles. Most reading-rooms provided a selection of government and opposition papers, as determined by their subscribers, as well as books and **pamphlets**. By 1830, most towns, large or small, had their own reading-rooms, and through their operation each copy of a paper reached, on average, perhaps 25 additional people.

SWEDEN. The first newspaper in Sweden, the *Ordinari Post Tijender*, was begun in 1645 by the postmaster in Stockholm to dispel rumors about current hostilities with **Denmark**. Published in accordance with a royal ordinance, it was issued weekly under varying titles and relied on reports from non-German newspapers for news about the final stage of the Thirty Years War (1618–48). Its production was later shifted to the chancellery, but was subject to numerous disruptions until 1720, when it was finally established on a permanent basis. For several decades after 1730, a number of Danish journals consciously borrowed stylistic devices from **Joseph Addison** and **Richard Steele**'s *Spectator* as a way around the prevailing **censorship**. Even after the turn of the 19th century, Swedish newspapers remained expensive and reached only a small segment of the population. The first paper to offer a wide range of news, editorial content, and entertainment was *Aftonbladet* [Evening News], which began publication in 1830.

Increasing calls for freedom of the press in liberal newspapers such as *Courier*, *Argus*, and *Anmarken* eventually succeeded in eliminating prepublication censorship in 1849. Spurred by greater press freedom as well as urbanization and Industrialization, the Swedish press grew rapidly in the latter part of the century; between 1884 and 1904, for example, the number of daily newspapers more than doubled. As in other Scandinavian countries, most newspapers became the mouthpieces of particular political parties, but without any permanent security of ownership. In 1851, conservative groups outbid the prominent liberal politician Lars Johan Hierta (1801–1872) for ownership of the leading Stockholm newspaper *Aftonbladet*. In 1906, a consortium of Conservative Party leaders acquired a majority ownership of the Liberal *Svenska Dagladet* in Stockholm, after which its editorial policy soon followed suit. Prominent party figures served as editors as well as owners: for example, Arthur Engberg (1888–1944) of the Social Democratic Party, edited *Arbetat* from 1918–24 and *Social-Demokraten* from 1924–32.

During the 20th century, Swedish newspapers gradually placed increasing emphasis on news and developed news forms of reportage. Before **World War I**, for instance, a number of Stockholm papers used female "flaneur" reporters to provide a stark look at the social life of the city after dark. It was not until the end of the 1960s, however, that an independent political journalism emerged in Sweden.

– T –

TABLOIDS. Newspaper type associated with pandering to the lowest common denominator through sensationalism, emotionalism, and scandalmongering. The word *tabloid* (combining *tablet* and *alkaloid*) was originally trademarked by a British pill manufacturer. But **Lord Northcliffe** stole the term to describe the *Daily Mail*, which he established in 1896. He wanted the paper to be like a small, concentrated, effective pill, containing all the news needed within one handy package, half the size of a conventional broadsheet. In the **United States**, the first tabloid was the *New York Daily News*, launched by Joseph M. Patterson in 1919. Within two years, it had built up the largest circulation of any newspaper in the country. By the 1960s, there were more than 50 tabloids in the United States. Most continue to provide sensationalized coverage and make extensive use of pictures, features, and sports. A recent study by Matthew Baum has found that entertainment-oriented news media such as tabloids actually provide a significant amount of information about high-profile domestic and foreign policy crises; in so doing, they manage to reach politically inattentive individuals who would otherwise remain uninformed about such issues.

TARBELL, IDA MINERVA (1857–1944). Member of the American **muckrakers**. After graduating from Allegheny College in 1880, she began investigating industrial relations. Influenced by the experience of her father, an independent oil producer in the Pennsylvania oil region, she attacked the ruthless business tactics of the Standard Oil Company in a series of articles published in *McClure's* in 1902 and 1903. These became the basis for her two-volume *History of the Standard Oil Company* (1904), a classic example of the literature of exposure of the muckrakers. As a journalist, Tarbell considered herself "one of the boys" and opposed women's suffrage.

THE TATLER. A sort of literary newspaper first published by **Richard Steele** in **Great Britain** on 12 April 1709. It was issued three times a week until 2 January 1711. Steele and **Joseph Addison** combined the highly personal and reflective tradition of Montaigne's *Essais* (1580) with the educational moralizing of Francis Bacon's *Essayes* (1597) to create a vital new journalistic form. Jonathan Swift, who contributed a number of essays, allowed Steele to disguise his authorship by using his popular character, Mr. Bickerstaff, as the fictitious writer of the paper. A host of other fictitious characters also populated the text, including Sir Roger de Coverley, Will Wimble, and Sir Andrew Freeport. Printed like contemporary newspapers on both sides of a folio halfsheet, *The Tatler* generally satirized upper-class moral conventions in matters of everyday like education, fashion, and marriage from the standpoint of middle-class Christian morality. Initially, each issue included a number of topics; later, as the advertising content increased, each number was devoted to a single subject.

After the fall of the Whig government in 1710 and the identification of *The Tatler*'s real authorship, Tory journalists, including Swift, began attacking the politics of the publication; Steele and Addison initially responded in kind, but then decided to bring *The Tatler* to a close and launch a new publication which would stay clear of politics. Two months after *The Tatler* ended, a new set of fictitious characters made their appearance in the ***Spectator***.

TAXES ON KNOWLEDGE. During the 18th century, successive governments in **Great Britain** tried to curtail the expansion of the press by placing duties on newspapers, advertisements, and paper. It was not until the second third of the 19th century that these "taxes on knowledge" were gradually removed. In 1833, the government lowered the duty on advertisements from 3s.6d to 1s.6d. Three years later, it reduced the duty on newspapers from 4d to 1d and the duty on paper to 1 1/2d per lb. All three duties were eventually abolished: the advertisement tax in 1853; the newspaper tax in 1855; and the paper tax in 1861. Each of these developments was followed by an increase in newspaper circulation.

TELEGRAPH. From the beginning of telegraphy in the 1840s, the press and the telegraph exerted a mutual influence on each other. The desire of the press to obtain news as quickly as possible was a factor in the decision to prioritize one-way transmission over two-way interaction. At the same time, reporting distant news as it was breaking required newspapers to develop networks of reporters and, given the "15-minute rule" governing individual use of the telegraph, to cooperate with other papers to a greater extent than under the exchange system. The result was the creation of news agencies such as the New York Associated Press. The telegraph also changed the nature of news by emphasizing events related to markets, the weather, and sports, which could be easily condensed for transmission. News became crisper and greater emphasis was placed on events likely to have a strong emotional impact on readers. Because of the costs involved in obtaining foreign news by telegraph, however, editors often had to be highly selective, resulting in erratic treatment of certain events.

THAILAND. The first newspaper in Thailand was founded by Christian missionaries in 1844. The subsequent growth and freedom of the press fluctuated in accordance with the country's political leadership; at times, ironically, experiencing greater autonomy under absolute rulers than during constitutional regimes. In some periods, the press seems to have been its own worst enemy. In 1955, for example, the military temporarily relaxed controls over the press; but within a few years, these were reinstituted, in part because of the immoderate manner in which the press had used its freedom to attack the government.

During the late 1960s and early 1970s, press restrictions (including **censorship** and a ban on new publications) were again reduced and a large number of new papers appeared, many representing new political parties and struggling to obtain an adequate share of circulation. Once again, the volume of criticism and degree of sensationalism rose to what, for the government at least, was a disturbing and unproductive level. Some of the new papers engaged in extortion and blackmail to obtain financing. An attempt by Prime Minister M. R. Kukrit Pramoj, founder of the uncharacteristically balanced paper *Siam Rath*, to encourage more responsible journalism through an ethics monitoring committee proved a failure. Instead of consolidating constitutional democracy, the press contributed to its downfall in yet another violent coup in 1976. Since then, Thailand has continued to swing from military dictatorships to limited democracy and back again, while journalism remains a poorly regarded and lowly paid occupation.

THAT WAS THE WEEK THAT WAS. Innovative British television program which featured satirical skits about current events and public figures. Conceived and produced by stage dramatist and broadcast personality Ned Sherrin, *TW3* (as it came to be known) went on the air in 1963. Though well received, it fell short of attracting a mass audience. Its regular company included the TV personality and humorist David Frost. While NBC's attempt to transfer it to American television met with failure, it was a major influence on the producers of the highly popular but controversial Canadian public affairs program *This Hour Has Seven Days*.

THOUGHT-NEWS PROJECT. A scheme devised by Franklin Ford (1849–1918), a shadowy American visionary who believed that existing newspapers did not adequately inform the public. In 1887, Ford quit as editor of Bradstreet's *Journal of Trade, Finance and Economy*, the leading business journal of its day, and headed west in the hope of interesting academics in his plans for a new kind of newspaper. At the University of Michigan, John Dewey, George Herbert Mead, and **Robert E. Park** saw merit in his plan for a "Journal of Enquiry and Record of Fact," but parted ways after the press ridiculed the plan. Ford seems to have envisaged a situation in which journalists and intellectuals would work together to produce accurate, insightful accounts of social trends relevant to the "general interest." This information would then be sold to newspapers across the country as well as published in their own paper. By this means, as Ford's *Draft of Action* (1892) proposed, "truth and commerce" would be "at one."

THE TIMES (LONDON). One of the world's great newspapers, long known for its accurate news and editorial independence. Founded in London by John Walter in 1785 as *The Daily Universal Register* to advertise a system of syllabic printing, it became *The Times* on 1 January 1788. Despite obtaining a printing contract from the board of customs and a direct treasury subsidy of £300 a year, it was in serious financial difficulties in 1803 when Walter passed the ownership and editorship over to his son. A shrewd businessman, the second John Walter revived the paper by hiring better writers, establishing a faster and more reliable newsgathering system, and expanding its **advertising**. During the Napoleonic Wars, he entered into a fierce competition with the Whig *Morning Chronicle* and Tory *Morning Post* to be the first to print the latest news from the continent. *The Times* was the first newspaper to print by steam, assigned its reporters to specific "beats," and took pride in having the fewest printing errors of any of its competitors. More significantly, by placing the paper on a sound economic foundation, Walter II enabled it to become independent of government and party patronage, a strategy which further increased its prosperity. *The Times*, wrote Samuel Taylor Coleridge in 1811, is the only newspaper which "without impudence can dare call itself independent or impartial."

Under Thomas Barnes, who replaced John Stoddart as general editor in 1819, the paper became not only politically independent but politically influential. Barnes made its long leading articles the main feature of the paper for politically engaged members of society. Though successfully resisting the efforts of party managers to influence its editorial voice, it was not, however, as representative of public opinion as it claimed. The public opinion that it best represented was that of the upper middle class, whose ascendancy in mid-Victorian society was what gave *The Times* much of its power.

Under John Thadeus Delane, who succeeded Barnes in 1841, *The Times* reached the pinnacle of its influence. "We all know," wrote an English critic in 1855, "that this country is ruled by *The Times*." Throughout the tenure of John Walter III, who had taken over as owner in 1847, *The Times* (by then nicknamed "The Thunderer") retained its primacy in the field of political opinion, though Delane's support of the South during the Civil War suggested a weakening perception of where **Great Britain**'s long-term interests lay. But during the last third of the 19th century, it began to experience economic difficulties as competition from the popular press increased and its production methods became increasingly outdated. This situation was exacerbated in 1887 when it lost both prestige and over £200,000 when it was revealed that it had purchased 10 forged letters during its campaign against Charles Parnell.

Between 1878 and its acquisition by **Lord Northcliffe** in 1908, *The Times'* circulation dropped from 60,000 to 38,000. Although North-cliffe instituted numerous changes in an attempt to restore its fortunes, it retained its cumbersome broadsheet format, continued to reserve the front page for small commercial advertisements, and maintained a formal style for personal references. In 1922, the Northcliffe estate sold the paper to John Jacob Astor V. He retained ownership until 1967, when Canadian media magnate Roy Thomson purchased the paper. After a lengthy strike in 1981, Thomson was forced to sell the paper to **Rupert Murdoch** of **Australia**. Under Murdoch, *The Times* eventually began to modernize by adopting a more compact format with news on the front page and providing its news online.

TIMESE. The kind of term *Time* magazine might have devised to label its own obsessively playful and idiosyncratic use of language, especially its propensity to label current events and phenomena with clever new compounds on the assumption that ordinary English is insufficiently descriptive for its purposes. In *American Speech* (1940), Joseph J. Firebaugh suggested the *Time's* stylistic mannerisms reflected a Menckian social philosophy of "irreverence towards authority," but other commentators have been less charitable toward its efforts to, as described by Henry Luce III, son of *Time* founder **Henry Luce**, "enrich the idiom." In an update to Firebaugh's assessment, Yates argued that *Time*'s use of language revealed "an inconsistency in values amounting almost at times to ethical schizophrenia." Of the 150 words that Yates considered to be "possibly coinages by *Time*" for the years 1968–77, only a handful have become part of common parlance (e.g., chillout, Disneyfication, superbug, televangelist). The others were either too closely tied to passing events (e.g., Carterphobia, Koreagate, Nixspeak) or overzealous attempts to be clever with words (e.g., crediholics, outcumbent, superbaul) to have any lasting impact or utility. *See also* LUCE, HENRY R.; NEWS MAGAZINES.

TOP NEWS STORIES. In 2006, *USA Weekend* and Newseum, the interactive museum of news, conducted a year-long survey of Americans about the top news stories of the 20th century. The top ten stories for the public (with the ranking by journalists in square brackets) were:

1. U.S. drops atomic bomb (1945) [1]
2. Japan bombs Pearl Harbor (1941) [3]
3. Men first walk on the moon (1969) [2]
4. Wrights fly first airplane (1903) [4]
5. JFK assassinated in Dallas (1963) [6]
6. Antibiotic penicillin discovered (1928) [11]
7. U.S. women win right to vote (1920) [5]
8. U.S. stock market crashes (1929) [10]
9. New polio vaccine works (1953) [21]
10. DNA's structure discovered (1953) [12]

The survey found considerable differences between male and female participants. Men tended to vote for stories about war and technology, while women (whose top story was the discovery of penicillin) gave preference to medicine and social issues. While the survey found surprising agreement overall between journalists and the public, journalists tended, like men, to downplay pure science and medicine. For example, "Einstein conceives relativity" (1905) was 12th for the public, but only 19th for journalists. The Newseum Web site (www.newseum.org/century) listed the top 100 stories by voting group.

TURKEY. The first Turkish newspapers appeared during the final century of the Ottoman Empire as the Sultan Mahmud II (1808–39) and his sons, Abdülmecid I (1839–61) and Abdülaziz (1861–76), tried to stave off collapse through a series of reforms. An official gazette was founded in 1831, followed by two nonofficial publications: the *Ceride-I Havadis* in 1840 and *El-Cevaib* in 1861. Edited by Ahmed Faris and his son Selim, the latter was influential throughout the Turkish and Arabic world. In 1867, it was joined by *Muhbir*, a political newspaper founded by Ali Suavi to further propagate reform. After opposition papers were banned in March of that year, it moved to London but died a year and a half later. *El-Cevaib* survived until 1884, when it too was suppressed. In 1895, *Yeni Azir* [New Century], currently Turkey's oldest daily newspaper, was allowed to begin operations in Ismir, and Turkish nationalists such as Ahmed Ferid (1878–1971) soon began to use the press to promote the Young Turk movement.

Late Ottoman newspapers continued to use Arabic characters as the basis of the Turkish language, resisting the efforts of modernizers to replace these with Latin characters. In doing so, they were supported by the Young Turks and their Committee of Union and Progress, which opposed this form of Europeanization. In 1911, however, Zekeria Sami Efendi began printing the content of his newspaper *Esas* in Monastir (now Bitola) in both an Arabic and Latin-based version of Turkish. Following his creation of the modern Republic of Turkey in 1923, Kemal Atatürk sided with the modernizers and made Latin the script for printed Turkish. This policy initially deprived newspapers of many of their readers, but eventually facilitated substantial growth.

During Atatürk's presidency, a number of new dailies were founded in Turkey, including *Cumhuriyet* (1924), which is still published in Istanbul. The Anadolu Ajansi [Anatolian Agency], which Atatürk had established in 1920, continued as the main Turkish news agency. It placed correspondents throughout the country, but relied on external news agencies for foreign news. It was not until the creation of the cooperative news agency Turk Haberler Ajansi in 1950 that Turkish correspondents began gathering news in other countries.

After Atatürk's death in 1938, the Turkish press remained subject to tight controls. Following a coup d'état in 1960, however, Turkey acquired a new constitution guaranteeing freedom of the press.

Newspapers acquired greater influence and diversity and schools of journalism began to flourish. In general, the Turkish press became one of the most independent in the Middle East, though various forms of repression continued to operate. In recent years, media ownership of Turkey's 45 daily newspapers has become increasingly concentrated in the hands of a few corporations. While this process initially provided the press with more power to resist government **censorship**, it has reached the point of threatening journalistic autonomy in its own right, with one conglomerate (Doğan Group) now owning 70 percent of the Turkish media. Of the three largest dailies currently being published, *Milliyet*, *Sabah*, and *Hürriyet*, two are Doğan properties.

TYPEWRITER. A key technology in the emergence of modern journalism beginning in the mid-1880s. Although a number of patents were taken out for mechanical writing devices in the 18th and early 19th century, the typewriter did not become a staple of journalism until near the end of the 19th century. In 1867, a group of amateur inventors in a small Milwaukee machine shop developed a clumsy writing contraption. Foremost among these was Christopher Latham Sholes, former editor of the *Milwaukee Sentinel*. Through the constant prodding of journalist-promoter James Densmore, Sholes gradually improved his writing machine to the point where it was commercially feasible. By then, however, the two were heavily in debt. In 1873, they sold the rights to manufacture and market their typewriter to the Remington Arms Company in Ilion, New York, which began marketing its Model 1 typewriter in 1867. By 1885, the demand for typewriters from business, government, and newspapers exceeded the supply and rival machines began to enter the marketplace. In addition to providing numerous job opportunities for women, the typewriter transformed journalism by speeding up the writing and editorial processes. It enabled newspapers to feed wire services much more quickly. The first electric typewriter appeared around 1935.

– U –

UNDERGROUND PRESS. Following in the footsteps of the *Guardian*, a radical paper founded in New York City in 1948, and *I.*

F. Stone's Weekly, hundreds of underground newspapers arose in the United States during the 1960s to oppose the Vietnam War, promote the sexual revolution, and challenge the "establishment" generally. Inspired by figures like Allan Ginsberg, Bob Dylan, Jack Kerouac, Lenny Bruce, and Norman Mailer and aided by their own press associations, papers such as the *Village Voice* (1955) in Greenwich Village, the *Los Angeles Free Press* (1964) founded by Art Kunkin, and the campus-based *Berkeley Barb* (1965) provided an uninhibited perspective on the American political and social scene before the movement petered out in the 1970s.

UNITED STATES. The first newspapers to be published on a regular basis in colonial America were initiated by postmasters, who had franking privileges and access to both European papers and official government information. On 24 April 1704, the Boston postmaster John Campbell hired Bartholomew Green to begin printing a **newsletter** he had previously distributed to New England governors in handwritten form. Indicative of its origins was the fact that it still left the last page blank so readers could add their own news before distributing it further. With a clientele of about 250 subscribers, the *Boston News-Letter* remained the only newspaper in the American colonies until 21 December 1719, when William Brooker, Campbell's successor as postmaster, started the *Boston Gazette*. Although licensing had expired, Brooker secured government approval of each issue before publication.

The practice of combining printing and editorial functions began with the *New-England Courant*, which James Franklin (1697–1735) founded as a literary newspaper in 1721. It helped to raise colonial American printers above the status of their counterparts in London and later enabled them to take an active role in the struggle for independence from **Great Britain**. After separation, this partisanship remained an entrenched characteristic of American journalism. President John Adams complained, not unjustifiably, that he was a constant object of scurrilous misrepresentations and lies. Even **Thomas Jefferson** eventually became disenchanted with the excesses of the press, despite his strong belief in the necessity of its freedom. A highly personal and vitriolic style of journalism continued throughout the antebellum period.

As American politics evolved into a contest between two main political parties, newspapers were caught between two contradictory roles: to provide citizens with the information and ideas necessary to understand and participate in political discussions; and to serve as the main organizing device for the competing parties. In the absence of a strong party infrastructure, editors came to play a key role in maintaining party unity. At the federal level, both the Federalists led by Alexander Hamilton and the anti-Federalists led by Thomas Jefferson and James Madison subsidized the press for practical as well as ideological reasons.

The main organ for the Federalists was initially the *Gazette of the United States*, a semi-weekly newspaper founded by John Fenno in New York in 1789. It followed the government to Philadelphia, the new nation's temporary capital, in 1790, became a daily in 1793, and changed its name to *United States Gazette* in 1804 before terminating publication in 1818. To counter its influence, Jefferson and Madison helped Philip Freneau (1752–1832) found the semi-weekly *National Gazette* in October 1791. Known as the "poet of the American Revolution," Freneau was a graduate of Princeton, had edited the *Freeman's Journal* in Philadelphia during the Revolutionary War, and became one of the leading journalists of his day. Madison contributed at least 19 unsigned articles to the *National Gazette*, including one on "Public Opinion" in December 1791.

During the 1830s, editors such as Duff Green (1791–1875) and Francis Preston Blair (1791–1876) continued to play a key role as political party organizers. After editing the *St. Louis Enquirer* for a year, Green moved to Washington in 1825, purchased the *United States Telegraph*, and began backing Andrew Jackson for president. After Jackson was elected, Green's paper became the main Democratic organ and Green became a member of Jackson's so-called kitchen cabinet. Blair was also a member of the same informal group as editor of the *Washington Globe*, which he had begun editing in 1830; before its demise in 1845, the *Globe* received some $500,000 in government printing contracts. Blair later supported Martin Van Buren as president, but was forced to sell his interest in the *Globe* when Polk won the Democratic leadership in 1844. In 1856, he presided over the first national convention of the Republican Party, which his anti-slavery views had led him to help found. Though an influential advisor to

President Lincoln, he opposed radical Republicanism and later returned to the Democratic fold.

The first major challenge to this close relationship between politics and the press came from the **penny papers**, which rapidly accelerated the positive feedback relationship that occurs between **advertising** and circulation when readers are given popular content at an affordable price. Because of their concern to convey as much information as possible in the few pages available, 18th-century papers had organized most of their news into a series of short items. When longer pieces had been included, they had usually been organized chronologically. This practice was continued by the early 19th-century party press, but the penny press not only used longer pieces more frequently but applied a chronological framework less rigidly. It also moved even further away from the terse, dry language of 18th-century papers, using similes, metaphors, and other stylistic devices in its coverage of accidents and **crime**.

In colonial America, a few women such as Elizabeth Timothy in South Carolina and Mary Katharine Goddard in Maryland had assisted their fathers or husbands with the printing of newspapers and in a few cases inherited and ran the papers on their own. But it was not until the second third of the 19th century that American women became reporters or editors in their own right. Sarah Josepha Hale began editing *Godey's Lady's Book*, while **Anne Royall** wrote about federal fraud in her two Washington papers, *Paul Pry* and *The Huntress*. **Margaret Fuller** was both editor of *The Dial* and a correspondent for **Horace Greeley**'s *New York Tribune*. Mary Clemmer Ames, Amelia Bloomer, Paulina Wright Davis, Elizabeth Cady Stanton, Lucy Stone, and Jane Swisshelm also helped to establish a place for women in American journalism.

During the half-century between the end of the Civil War and the outbreak of **World War I**, American newspapers underwent a remarkable transformation. At the beginning of the period, newspapers were still relatively small publications, with modest circulations, a relatively narrow range of content, limited advertising, and unimpressive graphics. By 1914, the modern American newspaper was clearly in evidence, with its banner headlines, big stories, news photographs, comic strips, sports pages, and extensive display advertising. Throughout this period, there was a remarkable growth in the number of daily newspapers, increasing from fewer than 400 in 1860 to 850 by 1880 and then more than doubling again to some 2,200 by 1914. Between 1860 and 1900, the number of daily newspapers in the United States increased from 387 to 1,967.

During the immediate post-Civil War period, influential papers such as the *San Francisco Chronicle* (1865), the *Boston Globe* (1872), the *Chicago Daily News* (1876), and the *Kansas City Star* (1880) were founded. At the same time, a number of older papers were refashioned so as to gain greater respectability: during the 1870s, **Charles A. Dana** turned the *New York Sun* into a "newspaperman's newspaper," while **Adolph Ochs** made the *New York Times* the nation's paper of record. As competition for stories became more intense, editors pushed their reporters to find new and provocative news angles. Reporters such as **Julian Ralph** worked harder to cultivate relationships with public figures as sources of information. What became known as the New Journalism began symbolically with **Joseph Pulitzer's** purchase of the *New York World* from Jay Gould in 1883. Pulitzer gradually expanded the paper from 8 to 16 pages, improved its news coverage, added more illustrations, and engaged in various crusades and stunts, and held contests to attract readers. By 1887, the *World's* circulation had increased from 20,000 to 250,000, the largest in the country. During the late 1890s, its leadership was challenged by the *New York Journal*, which **William Randolph Hearst** had purchased in 1895. Using scare headlines, fake stories and pictures, and jingoistic propaganda, the *Journal's* **yellow journalism** enabled it to catch up to the *World* in circulation by 1897. Its success led to the imitation of some of its tactics by other newspapers.

Despite their continuing marginalization generally, women journalists were primarily responsible for the stunt journalism through which the New Journalism pursued new readers. Women journalists also benefitted through this competition with the creation of the first women's pages by journalists like **Jane Cunningham Croly** ("Jennie June"). At the same time, however, U.S. journalism remained a predominantly male domain. Although solitary women journalists covered a few late 19th-century trials, it was not until the 1907 trial of Harry Thaw in New York that a group of women reporters were allowed to attend and even then were placed under intense scrutiny and labeled as "**sob sisters**" for sympathizing with the accused.

During the first third of the 20th century, American newspaper owners generally remained hostile toward the unionization of their employees, opposed wages and hours legislation, and even fought against the application of child labor laws to their carriers and news hawkers. They did so on the grounds of that theirs was a privileged industry that should be exempt from regulations governing other industries. While critics such as **Will Irwin**, Upton Sinclair, and **Walter Lippmann** began to question these exploitive practices, it was not until the Depression that the press came into conflict with the New Deal legislation of President Franklin Roosevelt and was effectively challenged to change its ways. The initial confrontation occurred in 1933–34 over the National Industrial Recovery Act, which required businesses to draft cooperative agreements increasing employment, shortening working hours, raising wages, and stabilizing profits. It also required collective bargaining and gave the president the authority to license businesses. The American Newspaper Publishers Association (ANPA), which was given responsibility for the newspaper code negotiations, eventually agreed to wage and hour provisions, an open shop, and child labor regulations. But it also demanded that the president accept a clause declaring his commitment to the First Amendment and joined the National Association of Manufacturers and the U.S. Chamber of Commerce to lobby against other New Deal legislation.

For its part, the American public did not accept the argument that social welfare measures such as the Social Security Act and the Fair Labor Standards Act constituted a threat to freedom of the press. It believed that newspaper owners were trying to avoid making reasonable adjustments to new socioeconomic conditions. In the presidential election of 1936, it gave its overwhelming support to Roosevelt, despite the fact that most newspaper editorials had supported the Republican candidate, Alf Landon. The following year, the Supreme Court dealt a further blow to the newspaper publishers. In *Associated Press v. National Labor Relations Board*, the court declared that "the publisher of a newspaper has no special immunity from the application of general laws." Publishers were required to recognize the American Newspaper Guild (ANG) and were prohibited from firing an employee because of union activities. This confrontation contributed to the declining public image of the press and led to efforts such as the **Hutchins Commission** to restore that image.

While interwar journalists were gradually acquiring greater rights as employees, their places of employment were being subjected to greater shocks through newspaper concentration and consolidation. After peaking at about 2,200 before World War I, the number of daily newspapers began a long process of decline—to 1,942 in 1930 and fewer than 1,800 four decades later. For many observers, the most disturbing aspect of this decline was the steady reduction in the number of cities with two or more daily newspapers. In 1923, there were 502 cities with two or more dailies; a decade later, there were only 243. In New York City, for example, the *Herald* and *Tribune* merged in 1924 to become the *New York Herald Tribune*, while the *World* died in 1931. This process continued after the war as American families flooded into the suburbs. Between 1953 and 1973, the number of cities with two or more daily papers dropped from 91 to 37. Among the casualties in New York City were the *New York Sun* in 1950, the *Brooklyn Eagle* in 1955, and the *New York Mirror* in 1963. The deaths of the *New York Herald Tribune* in 1966 and the *Washington Star* in 1981 signaled that not even New York City and Washington, D.C., were capable of supporting two quality daily newspapers.

Faced with declining numbers, newspapers and their press associations were in no mood to extend a welcoming hand to the new medium of radio as an alternative source of news. As early as February 1922, the **Associated Press (AP)** cautioned radio stations against using its news over the air. By the late 1920s, however, an increasing number of stations were ignoring this warning, especially those owned by newspapers, and both the Columbia Broadcasting System (CBS) and National Broadcasting Company (NBC) networks began gathering news for their various affiliates. In 1933, therefore, both the wire services and the ANPA resolved to stop cooperating with the new radio industry, refusing to carry its program logs and filing news piracy suits against a number of stations. In a temporary capitulation, CBS and NBC agreed to finance a Press-Radio Bureau which would supply broadcasters with AP, United Press (UP), and International News Service (INS) bulletins under very restrictive conditions: stations could make only two five-minute newscasts a day, one in the morning after 9:30 A.M. and one in the evening after 9:30 p.m. However, this Biltmore Agreement (named after the hotel in New York City where it was negotiated) was soon scorned by many stations, which turned to new independent services such as Transradio for news. A few stations, beginning with KMPC in Beverly Hills, also began hiring their own reporters to gather the news. Rather than risk being shut out of broadcasting, UP and INS broke ranks by allowing stations to make unrestricted use of their news and AP followed suit in 1939.

Less threatening initially to newspapers were the public or current affairs programs on radio, beginning with NBC's *University of Chicago Round Table* in 1933. It was followed by *The American Forum of the Air*, carried on the Mutual Broadcasting System (MBS) network, and *People's Platform*, which CBS created in 1939. Although ***America's Town Meeting of the Air***, which began on the NBC Blue Network in 1935, was fairly influential, these programs were generally scheduled at nonpeak hours and drew small audiences compared to the entertainment-oriented programming that dominated early American radio broadcasting. After the war, several of these programs were transferred to television, but remained marginalized and tended to attract rather than deflect those who read newspapers. This was the case for both ***Meet the Press***, which NBC shifted to TV in November 1947, and *Face the Nation*, which CBS began in November 1954 (ABC later responded with *Issues and Answers*). The one prime-time television public affairs program with any pretense to popularity was ***See It Now***, which **Edward R. Murrow** adapted from *Hear It Now* in November 1951. However, it only lasted until 1958.

The threat of broadcasting to newspapers was limited by regulatory indecision over the role that radio journalism should play. During the 1930s, the Federal Communications Commission (FCC) left broadcasters largely to their own devices. But in 1941, it criticized station WAAB for its practice of "editorializing" on the air. It declared that because of the "limitations in frequencies inherent in the nature of radio, the public interest can never be served by a dedication of any broadcast facility to the support of his [*sic*] own partisan ends." Although **Walter Winchell** and a few others continued to make opinionated commentaries over the air, the argument that "a truly free radio cannot be used to advocate the causes of the licensee" discouraged most stations from jumping on the editorial bandwagon. In various decisions in 1945 and 1946, however, the FCC also instructed broadcasters to make sufficient time available for those who wished to purchase it to present their particular viewpoints. This concert hall conception of public affairs ran counter to the broadcaster-initiated discussion model of programs like *Town Meeting of the Air* and in 1949 was abandoned in favor of the original approach. Broadcasters were now instructed to devote a reasonable amount of time to discussions of important public issues and to present contrasting views on those issues. This requirement became known as the Fairness Doctrine and was intended to encourage public affairs programs. At the same time, the FCC reversed its policy against editorializing, saying that "overt licensee editorialization, within reasonable limits and subject to the general requirements of fairness . . . is not contrary to the public interest."

While this decision facilitated news commentaries, the rules governing balance had a chilling effect on public affairs programming generally and the Fairness Doctrine was eventually abandoned (in the 1980s) as counterproductive.

Despite these limitations on its development, however, broadcast journalism steadily eroded newspaper readerships—primarily through television news. In 1948, CBS began the first network newscast on American TV with *Douglas Edwards and the News*. NBC followed a year later with *Camel Newsreel Theater*, which was soon changed to *Camel News Caravan*. It was sponsored by Camel cigarettes and was anchored by John Cameron Swayze, who wrote his own script and delivered it without cue cards, but was still less popular than Edwards. Both programs were 15 minutes and consisted mainly of "talking heads" and a few still pictures and maps. In the fall of 1956, Bill McAndrews, the president of NBC News, replaced the *Camel News Caravan* with the *Huntley-Brinkley Report*, which featured two actual reporters as anchors and tried to keep the audience's attention by having one in New York City and the other in Washington. When it began to pull ahead in the ratings, CBS responded by replacing Douglas Edwards with the venerable Walter Cronkite. In 1963, when network newscasts doubled in length, Americans told a Roper poll that they were getting a majority of their news from television.

Between the mid-1950s and the mid-1970s, the audience for network news increased from about 15 million viewers to about 55 million viewers a night. By then, ABC was rapidly gaining ground, especially after teaming Harry Reasoner (hired away from CBS in 1970) with Barbara

Walters (lured from NBC in 1976). These "races" together with the advent of cable produced a steady increase in the amount of TV news. CBS, NBC, and ABC expanded their weeknight newscasts to an hour and two all-news networks were created: the Cable Satellite Public Affairs Network (C-Span) in 1979; and the Cable News Network **(CNN)** in 1980. In the late 1990s, C-Span and CNN were joined by two other 24-hour news channels: FoxNews and MSNBC.

The response of newspapers to radio and TV news has been twofold. The first reaction has been to diversify and popularize their content. Not all journalists have been pleased with the results. In 1938, O. K. Bovard resigned from the *St. Louis Post-Dispatch* after 40 years of service because of what he regarded as the paper's increasing reliance on comics, horoscopes, racehorse tips, and other such "trivial and banal" features. This trend was particularly evident in the **tabloids** which, beginning with the *New York Daily News* in 1919, made their appearance during the interwar period.

The second response was to place greater emphasis on clarity and simplicity of style. During the 1920s and 1930s, newspaper writing had become increasingly complex as reporters sought to engage in more analysis and interpretation. After the war, social scientists such as Robert P. Gunning and Rudolph Flesch began to criticize it for its poor readability. In *The Art of Plain Talk* (1946) and *The Art of Readable Writing* (1949), Gunning recommended that journalists write as they speak by using simpler words and sentences. Flesch developed a system known as the "fog index" to help the Associated Press simplify its writing. Under their influence, editors began to favor a clearer, more succinct style, using shorter words and sentences and single-sentence paragraphs.

These responses were epitomized by the creation of *USA Today* by Allen H. Neurath in 1981. In an attempt to adapt the newspaper to the age of television, *USA Today* made extensive use of color, graphics, and statistics along with shorter and lighter news items. However, while many smaller, group-owned newspapers adopted some of *USA Today*'s innovations, most of the larger U.S. dailies still regard in-depth coverage and sophisticated analysis and interpretation as their best protection against alternative sources of news. They have tried to maintain quality news coverage and have rejected *USA Today*'s tendency to reduce controversial issues to a debate between two polarized positions.

– V –

VENALITY. The practice of buying favorable press coverage. In the 1720s, the government of **Great Britain** paid Elizee Dobree £800 a year to drop "Cato's Letters" from the *London Journal*. During the 1730s, Robert Walpole paid various writers and publishers some £50,000 for articles favorable to the government. A half century later, seven of London's 10 dailies, including *The Times*, were receiving secret government subsidies. This practice was also common in **France**, where it continued throughout the 19th century. When the movement to abolish slavery began to gain strength in the late 1830s, colonial delegates drummed up contributions from the plantocracy with which to bribe Parisian newspapers into opposing emancipation. During the Russo–Japanese War of 1904, **Russia** secured substantial French loans by bribing French newspapers into presenting a favorable, and highly misleading, view of the Russian war effort.

VICE-VERSA. The first gay newspaper in the **United States**. It began publication in 1947 using a **typewriter** and carbon paper and initially had no masthead, bylines, or **advertising**. Together with a 1958 Supreme Court decision allowing gay materials to be sent through the mail, its subsequent development paved the way for a number of gay publications with national circulation.

VILLARD, OSWALD GARRISON (1872–1949). Son of the American railroad magnate Henry Villard (1835–1900), who also worked as a journalist, Oswald Villard rose through the ranks of journalism to become president of the *New York Evening Post* (1900–1918), which his father had purchased in 1881, and owner of *The Nation* (1918–35).

– W –

WALL STREET JOURNAL. Conservative U.S. financial and business newspaper published nationally from Monday through Friday. It was first issued by Dow Jones and Company, a news agency which reporters Charles H. Dow and Edward D. Jones established in New

York City in 1882 to provide information to Wall Street's financial district. In 1889, Dow and Jones changed its name from the *Customers' Afternoon Bulletin* to its current title. During the 1890s, Dow began an index of leading stocks as a daily indicator of the market's performance. In 1902, Clarence Walker Barron, who later founded *Barron's* magazine for investors, purchased both Dow Jones and Company and the *Wall Street Journal*. Some of his **columnists** scandalized the publication by selling their opinions on stock movements. Following his appointment as managing editor in 1941, Bernard Kilgore broadened the paper's coverage, while making its articles and columns livelier and better researched. The result was an extraordinary increase in circulation, rising from 65,000 in 1950 to over 1,000,000 by the time of Kilgore's death (as president) in 1967. Until the publication of *USA Today*, the *Journal*'s circulation was the highest in the **United States**.

WAR CORRESPONDENTS, EARLY. Who was the first war correspondent? In his classic study, *The First Casualty* (1975), Phillip Knightley began his account of war correspondence with William Howard Russell (c. 1820–1907), who covered the Crimean War (1854–56) for *The Times* of London. Russell described himself as "the miserable parent of a luckless tribe" and may have been the first correspondent to focus on the appalling conditions he observed. But he was not without his predecessors. The American journalist George F. Kendall accompanied the advance of General Zachary Taylor across the Rio Grande during the war with **Mexico** in 1846. He then set up a pony express system ("Kendall's Express") to relay dispatches back to the daily *Picayune* in New Orleans and was himself injured in one of the battles. In his *Historical Dictionary of War Journalism* (1997), Mitchel P. Roth takes Kendall and other Mexican war correspondents as his starting-point. But Kendall was also a co-founder of the *Picayune* and had used the paper to campaign for war. He was not, therefore, a war correspondent in the modern sense of being a specialized reporter. One of the first owner-editors to hire reporters to cover a war of sorts was **James Gordon Bennett Sr.** In December 1837, Bennett sent an unnamed correspondent to cover the rebellion of **William Lyon Mackenzie** in Upper **Canada** for the *New York Herald*. While the dispatches themselves proved disappointing, they did lead other papers to send their own correspondents to cover the armed uprising. There are, however, even earlier examples of war correspondence. In 1815, for example, James Morgan Bradford, who edited a small weekly called *The Time Piece*, wrote an account of the Battle of New Orleans for his paper. A few years before then, Henry Crabbe Robinson provided even more impressive coverage of Napoleon's campaigns in Spain and Germany for *The Times*. But the first example of printed war correspondence may well have occurred on 3 May 1775 when Isaiah Thomas, editor of *The Massachusetts Spy*, published his earlier eyewitness account of the battle of Lexington.

WASHINGTON POST. One of the leading newspapers in the world and the anchor of a media empire which includes *Newsweek* magazine. Founded as a Democratic paper by Stilson Hutchins in 1877, it was economically conservative for the next 60 years. In 1933, it was purchased at a bankruptcy sale by Agnes and Eugene Meyer for $825,000. After the war, they transferred their voting stock to Philip and Katharine Graham (their daughter), who used it to attack McCarthyism and promote civil rights. In 1963, Katharine Graham took control of the paper and hired Benjamin Bradlee to improve its national and international coverage. The *Post* remains famous for having broken the **Watergate** story, publishing the ***Pentagon Papers***, and rejecting Vice President Spiro T. Agnew's attacks on the press.

WASHINGTON PRESS CORPS. During the Civil War, the larger American newspapers created special correspondents to obtain war news from Washington. After the war, the reporters who remained in Washington gained considerable independence and stature within their news organizations by cultivating politicians as sources. Initially, the focus was mainly on Congress as presidents tried to remain distant from reporters. The first woman correspondent in Washington was Jane Swisshelm, followed by **Sara Jane Lippincott**. William McKinley was the first president to cultivate a formal relationship with correspondents, making the White House a regular "beat." During the Progressive era, newspaper correspondents like David S. Barry, whose ongoing coverage of Washington required good relations with its politicians, defended the Senate against charges of corruption by popular magazine writers like **David Graham Phillips**, whose **muckraking** operated under no such restraints. During the presidency of Theodore Roosevelt, a few executive branch agencies began using their own publicists. But Woodrow Wilson's secretary, Joe Tumulty, was the first to serve in effect as a press secretary, although the term itself was not used until 1929. Tumulty met daily with the press, relaying the words of the president through his own voice, and maintaining contact with correspondents after America entered **World War I**. While President Herbert Hoover's tendency to ignore reporters in favor of editors undermined press relations to some degree, his decision to allow direct quotations at press conferences was very well received. Franklin D. Roosevelt worked much harder at cultivating key journalists by providing lots of lively copy about his programs. During his first term as president, Dwight D. Eisenhower became disillusioned with traditional press coverage and decided to use televised press conferences as a way of reasserting control. A television studio was constructed in the White House and the Hollywood actor Robert Montgomery was hired to coach him on his presentations. Eisenhower also hired former journalist James Hagerty to serve as the White House's first "director of communications." Whereas Eisenhower's press conferences were filmed for broadcast later, President John F. Kennedy allowed the television networks to carry them live. In contrast to Kennedy's deft manipulation of the press, President Richard Nixon saw it as the enemy and assigned Vice President Spiro T. Agnew the task of reining it in. Among recent presidents, Ronald Reagan remains the icon of managing White House coverage.

WATERGATE. Scandal that led to impeachment proceedings against U.S. President Richard M. Nixon and his resignation in August 1974. It resulted from the revelation of a series of unethical and in some cases illegal activities engaged in by the Nixon administration to maintain itself in power. The first sign of such activities occurred in June 1972 when police caught five men who had broken into the national headquarters of the Democratic Party in the Watergate office-apartment complex in Washington, D.C. While most of the press ignored the burglary, *Washington Post* reporters Carl Bernstein and Bob Woodward eventually traced it to a larger operation involving key White House personnel. In 1973, Woodward and Bernstein won a **Pulitzer Prize** for their reporting and turned Watergate into the apotheosis of investigative reporting in *All the President's Men* (1974). During Senate committee hearings to investigate the affair, former presidential counsel John W. Dean III revealed the existence of a White House "enemies list" that included numerous reporters, **columnists**, and media executives.

WELLS, IDA B. (1862–1931). African American journalist and author who devoted her life to fighting against racial discrimination, exploitation, and violence. Born a slave in rural Mississippi, she began her journalistic career in 1887 with an article in *Living Way* relating her personal experience of discrimination on U.S. railroads. Following her editorial condemnation of the lynching of three African American businessmen for opening a grocery store in Memphis, Tennessee, in 1892, a white mob destroyed the office of the weekly *Memphis Free Speech and Headlight*, of which she was part owner, and threatened to burn her at the stake. Undeterred, she continued her crusade against lynching, first as a columnist for the *New York Age* and later as a lecturer in the northeast and British Isles. In addition to inspiring the formation of anti-lynching leagues, she began the African American women's club movement, established the first suffrage club among African American women, and helped to organize the NAACP. After her marriage to Chicago lawyer and newspaper publisher Ferdinand L. Barnett, she served as editor of the *Chicago Conservator* and as a foreign correspondent for the *Chicago Inter-Ocean*.

WHITE, THEODORE H. (1915–1986). American political journalist. He won the **Pulitzer Prize** for general nonfiction for *The Making of the President, 1960* (1962). At the end of **World War II**, he was appointed as chief of *Time* magazine's China Bureau, but resigned a year later after a dispute with **Henry R. Luce**. His account of John F. Kennedy's victory was the first of a series of journalistic treatments of presidential elections. He also wrote *In Search of History* (1978) and *America in Search of Itself* (1982).

WHITE, WILLIAM ALLEN (1868–1944). Long-time editor of the *Emporia* (Kansas) *Gazette*, which he bought in 1895 and through which he achieved a national reputation as a liberal-minded Republican. Although the *Gazette* only sold a few thousand copies, White's editorials were widely quoted and reprinted. White used fictional works such as *Stratagems and Spoils* (1901) and *A Certain Rich Man* (1909) to expose corruption in the manner of the **muckrakers**. Upon the death in 1925 of Frank A. Munsey, who ruined a number of America's best newspapers, White wrote famously: "Munsey contributed to the journalism of his day the talent of a meat packer, the morals of a money changer and manners of an undertaker."

WILKES, JOHN (1725–1797). English journalist, Member of Parliament (MP), and demagogue with a reputation for depravity whose fight against the supposed tyranny of George III made him a popular hero and contributed to the establishment of freedom of the press. In 1757, after studies at the University of Leiden, he was elected (with the assistance of his wife's wealth) MP for Aylesbury as a supporter of William Pitt. Following the resignation of the Grenville-Pitt ministry in 1761, he was encouraged by Earl Temple to found *The North Briton* (1762) as a vehicle for attacking the Earl of Bute, George III's favorite minister. With Bute's resignation, he switched his attack to the new Grenville ministry, ridiculing the speech from the throne in the famous issue No. 45 in April 1763. Arrested under a general warrant for seditious libel, he argued that MPs could only be imprisoned on charges of treason, a claim which Parliament also adjudged to be seditious. In the ensuing struggle, Wilkes's arrest was deemed to be unconstitutional. But in 1764, he was charged with obscenity for his contribution to an *Essay on Women*, expelled from the House of Commons, and forced to flee to Paris to escape imprisonment. Upon his return in 1768, he was elected as MP for Middlesex, but not allowed by the king's supporters to take his seat. He then surrendered himself to the authorities and was imprisoned for 22 months. During the popular protests to secure his release, violence ensued and Wilkes's reputation as a symbol of the fight of liberty against despotism was enhanced.

Following his incarceration, Wilkes became an alderman of London. In this capacity, he helped to secure greater freedom of the press by providing immunity to printers charged with violating the ban against **parliamentary reporting**. The Commons' refusal to recognize his election by Middlesex voters on three further occasions provided

Wilkes with a final libertarian cause, the right of the people to elect their own representatives. Supporters, including Edmund Burke and the unknown writer Junius, organized a nationwide **petition** on his behalf. Ironically, after finally gaining admission to the Commons in 1774, Wilkes lost popular favor for his actions in suppressing the Gordon riots in 1780.

WINCHELL, WALTER (1897–1972). Highly popular American columnist whose newspaper style and radio showmanship were derived from his early years in vaudeville with Eddie Cantor and George Jessel. After a stint at the *Vaudeville News* in the early 1920s, Winchell began to build a reputation for himself as a brash, no-holds-barred writer for the *New York Evening Graphic* before moving his long-running column "On Broadway" to the *New York Daily Mirror* in 1929. In December 1932, he began broadcasting the freewheeling *Walter Winchell's Journal*, a rapid-fire 15-minute commentary and gossip program on NBC radio. Broadcast on Sunday evenings, the program had more than 20 million listeners at its peak. In 1955, it was transferred from the Blue Network (by then ABC) to Mutual for a final season. For his attacks on all and sundry, Winchell gathered most of his information personally: during the 1930s, he berated Hitler, the Nazis, and American isolationists; after the war, he switched his guns to domestic Communists, supporting the witch-hunt of Senator Joseph McCarthy. When he called the voters "damn fools" in 1943, the show's sponsor (Jergens Lotion) and the network began **censoring** his scripts. After his eventual retirement from radio, Winchell narrated *The Untouchables* for ABC-TV.

WISNER, GEORGE (1812–1849). Generally regarded as the first police reporter. After working for several newspapers, he joined the staff at **Benjamin Day**'s *New York Sun* in January 1834 as a court reporter. He later bought a half interest in the paper, but separated from Day in June 1835. His support for the immediate abolition of slavery, which he frequently introduced into his writing, brought him into conflict with Day, who favored gradualism. Although generally using a factual approach, he often tilted his stories or added editorial comments so as to play up the mistreatment of African Americans, whom he generally referred to as "blacks." According to Gary L. Whitby, his divergence from Day over abolition may have contributed to the 1834 pro-slavery riot in New York.

WOLFE, JOHN (1548?–1601). London printer and bookseller known for his ties to the propaganda activities of Queen Elizabeth. After being denied a printing privilege in 1579, he led a rebellion against the Stationers' Company and went to prison twice for asserting, among other things, that it was "lawfull for all men to print lawfull books what commandement soever her Majestie gave to the contrary." A few years later, however, he joined the company, accepted a substantial privilege himself, and became responsible for hunting down and prosecuting violators of the licensing system. He eventually acquired more presses in England than any other commercial printer, all the while serving as one of the main instruments of surreptitious government publication. In 1589, he joined other London printers in responding to the desire for news of English troops in **France** by publishing a series of short news reports. These Elizabethan news quartos were the first continuous news publication in England.

WOLFE, TOM (1931–). American journalist and novelist who both practiced and dissected a new style of reporting which he called the New Journalism. In his genealogy, it originated in works such as Truman Capote's *In Cold Blood* (1965) and Hunter Thompson's *The Hell's Angels* (1967) as an alternative to the abandonment of social realism by writers such as Beckett, Kafka, and Tolkien. Instead of writing historical "neo-Fabulist" myths set in foggy swamps and forests, the New Journalists used "factualized fiction" to critique contemporary society from a highly personal standpoint. Wolfe's main contributions to this genre were *The Kandy-Kolored Tangerine-Flake Streamline Baby* (1965), *The Electric Kool-Aid Acid Test* (1968), and *Radical Chic and Mau-mauing the Flak Catchers* (1970).

WORLD WAR I. During the Great War of 1914–1918, journalists were faced with unprecedented pressure to join, assist, or at least avoid compromising the huge propaganda machines which were created by both the Entente and Central Powers and which targeted the home population as much as the enemy. In **Britain**, the government was particularly successful in securing the support of newspaper owners like **Lord Northcliffe**, though its own military was slower to appreciate the morale-building role that most correspondents were prepared to play. Stephen Badsey has argued that what made this cooperation possible was the general policy of placing favorable interpretations on "the facts," rather than fabricating events or focusing on enemy atrocities. Together with their control of the transatlantic **telegraph**, this approach helped the British to win the major propaganda battle of the war: the struggle over American public opinion. In **Germany**, where the press was **censored** rather than co-opted, the less sophisticated methods of its propagandists weakened their efforts to keep the **United States** on the sidelines. Among the journalists who contributed to the British propaganda victory was Philip Gibbs (1877–1962). In works such as *The Soul of the War* (1915), he adhered to the standard refrain about German atrocities and Allied bravery. After the war, however, he tried to reveal its horrors and the extensive use of propaganda in *Now It Can Be Told* (1920) and *More That Must Be Told* (1921).

Before entering the war in April 1917, the U.S. federal government, aided by state and local agencies, instituted wide-ranging **censorship** of printed materials. It also suppressed outright socialist publications such as *The Masses* and the influential *International Socialist Review* (ISR), published by Charles H. Kerr & Company in Chicago. Upon joining the Allies, President Woodrow Wilson created the **Committee on Public Information (CPI)** to control press coverage and distribute government propaganda. Headed by former journalist George Creel, the CPI engaged in a more selective use of the facts than the British Ministry of Information, portraying the war as a glorious fight for democracy and freedom against a despicable enemy. Only a few American journalists, such as **Richard Harding Davis**, succeeded in showing the destructiveness and dehumanization of the war. In **France**, the possibility of transcending sensationalistic appeals to patriotism was even more remote, although one study has found that papers outside of Paris tended to report the war more objectively. Even in the case of the British, however, wartime propaganda contributed to the widespread disillusionment with journalists in the 1920s.

WORLD WAR II. During World War II, the roles played by journalists ranged from criticism to boosterism to outright propaganda. In

Germany, Joseph Goebbels, the propaganda minister, used newspapers, magazines, radio, and film to control domestic perceptions of the war. He also tried to influence foreign opinion, especially in the case of **Italy** where there was opposition to fighting on the Axis side. Of particular importance in this regard was the periodical *Segnale* [Signal], which was published in half a dozen languages every two weeks from April 1940 until the end of the war. Goebbels was less successful as a foreign propagandist, however, in part because of rivalry with Joachim von Ribbentrop, the Nazi foreign minister.

In the **Soviet Union**, the Communist Party kept tight controls not only over the information disseminated to the Russian people but also over what the Allies could report. Ironically, while the British were able to extract substantial intelligence information from the news reports of the German-controlled French press, the Anglo-Soviet wartime alliance enabled the Russians to exercise almost total control over the British press corps in Moscow. All foreign correspondents were required to stay in the Hotel Metropole, base their reports almost entirely on Russian newspapers, and even then submit them to Soviet **censors**. Under no circumstances were they allowed to go to the Front and they were denied a visa to return to the Soviet Union if they engaged in any criticism while on leave. The result was that any questioning of Soviet political intentions was effectively eliminated.

In contrast, newspapers in **Great Britain** escaped strict censorship during the war, even though **tabloids** such as the *Daily Mirror* were quite critical of Churchill's administration. What made this possible was their strong support of the British war effort generally. Unlike the Soviet press, which kept the population in the dark about German advances until August 1941, the British media provided a fairly clear picture of the course of the war.

In the **United States**, coverage of the war brought numerous values into conflict. Early in 1942, the federal Office of Censorship drew up guidelines for editors and publishers and then used volunteer veteran journalists to disseminate and supervise them at local newspapers across the country. These provisions were later broadened to include descriptions of advance military knowledge of enemy resources as a result of an incident involving the *Chicago Tribune*. On 7 June 1942, following the battle of Midway, the *Tribune* published a front-page story implying that the United States had broken the **Japanese** naval code. At the insistence of the Navy, U.S. Attorney

General Francis Biddle convened a grand jury to investigate whether the *Tribune* should be indicted for compromising national security. According to Dina Goren, the decision not to indict the paper was based on the subsequent realization that the story had not actually tipped off the Japanese that their code had been broken. For its part, the *Tribune* never allowed that it might have undermined the national interest and attributed the investigation to President Franklin Roosevelt's prejudice against the paper.

As the war proceeded, the Office of Censorship was particularly concerned to suppress news about the development of the **atomic bomb**. But most journalists had a clear sense of what was necessary to avoid compromising the war effort and voluntarily cooperated with the censorship guidelines. In the case of editorial cartoonists, their images of the enemy were generally so hostile that no form of direct oversight was considered necessary. The main exception to the belief that journalists could be trusted to do their duty was the **Federal Bureau of Investigation (FBI)**, which closely monitored critics of the government such as Inga Arvad, a Washington *Times-Herald* columnist.

To ensure that the media promoted patriotism as fully as possible, however, the government also created the Office of War Information (OWI) in 1942 and placed CBS news commentator Elmer Davis (1890–1958) in charge. For women, being patriotic meant taking jobs in previously male-dominated fields and then, after the war, relinquishing these jobs to returning soldiers. It also meant becoming a "kitchen patriot" by changing patterns of food consumption in line with rationing needs, a campaign in which journalists and home economists worked together with the OWI and War Advertising Council. In line with the OWI's efforts to get women to give up paid employment after the war, employee magazines and War Department publications such as *Yank, the Army Weekly*, treated "Rosie the riveter" as a temporary wartime exigency. Women journalists, who had also benefitted from increased opportunities as reporters, photojournalists, and broadcasters because of the war, were similarly expected to retire or return to the women's pages.

The discrimination faced by women journalists during the war was suffered by African American journalists as well. The only African American accredited as a war correspondent by the U.S. government during the war was the Ohio journalist Ralph W. Tyler, although Em-met J. Scott, special assistant to the Secretary of War for Race Relations, was later assigned to be an observer of prejudice in the Allied Expeditionary Force. Aware of the segregation experienced by black soldiers fighting for American democracy, the African American press strongly supported the war but began to insist that "victory in war" be followed by "victory at home" (the so-called Double V campaign of **W. E. B. Du Bois**). The African American artist Charles Alston voluntarily prepared numerous editorial cartoons for the OWI, but remained a militant opponent of racial discrimination.

A further dimension of American press coverage during the war was its treatment of Japanese Americans as a threat to national security. While a number of Japanese-language newspapers had supported Japan's foreign policy in the late 1930s, they all abandoned their allegiance to Japan after Pearl Harbor. Nonetheless, a number of Japanese American editors and publishers were arrested and their papers shut down. Those that remained were afraid to speak out against plans to inter 110,000 Japanese Americans and were themselves terminated in May 1942 when the internment began. The mainstream press contributed to the public hysteria that culminated in the internment. Ironically, interred journalists such as Paul Yokota were allowed to produce camp newspapers and write editorials about the abuse of their rights without being censored.

– Y –

YOUNG, ARTHUR (1741–1820). An unsuccessful farmer who began the genre of agricultural journalism in **Great Britain** by popularizing new farming techniques in the 18th century. During the 1760s, he made extensive tours of farms in England and Wales and published his observations in numerous **pamphlets**. To supplement his income during the economic downswing in the 1770s, he reported on parliamentary debates for the *Morning Post.* In 1784, he began publishing his *Annals of Agriculture* to publicize recent experiments in farming and provide a forum for agricultural debates. George III, Edmund Burke, George Washington, and **Thomas Jefferson** were among those who requested Young's advice. During a lengthy tour of farming in **Italy** and **France**, he witnessed the outbreak of the French

Revolution and later published an account of its underlying causes in the countryside in his *Travels in France during the Years 1787, 1788, 1789*. In 1793, he was appointed secretary of the newly created Board of Agriculture. Although he carefully assembled a wealth of statistics on things like grain yields, his data did not always support his generalizations.

YELLOW JOURNALISM. Term variously used to describe a set of newspaper features (screaming headlines, garish illustrations), a sensationalistic, self-promotional style of news coverage, and a discourse about the legitimacy of those features and style. As a set of news tactics, it was an accentuation of **Joseph Pulitzer**'s New Journalism resulting from **William Randolph Hearst**'s attempts to beat him at his own game. The term "yellow press" was coined in 1896 by Erwin Wardman, editor of the *New York Press*. It was tied to Richard F. Outcault's popular comic "Hogan's Alley," whose character wore a yellow nightshirt and was dubbed the Yellow Kid. Sensationalistic coverage was usually balanced by more sober accounts of the same events. For example, James Creelman's sensationalistic treatment of the Japanese conquest of Port Arthur (Lüshun) in November 1894 for the *New York World* was offset by A. B. de Guerville's reporting for the *New York Herald*. After witnessing the fall of the city firsthand, de Guerville flatly rejected Creelman's claim that there had been a massacre of the city's Chinese inhabitants.

– Z –

ZENGER, JOHN PETER (1697–1746). Printer and journalist in colonial New York who won praise as "the morning star of liberty." After emigrating from the German states in 1710, he apprenticed as a printer and in 1733 established the *New York Weekly Journal* with the support of a political faction opposed to Governor William Cosby. The following year, he was prosecuted for seditious libel after a series of satirical attacks on Cosby. Zenger's attorney, Andrew Hamilton, made the relatively new argument that the truth cannot be libelous and the jury should decide whether Zenger's attacks were true. Zenger's acquittal did not immediately establish a legal precedent under British law. A century later, **Joseph Howe** had to fight essentially the same battle after criticizing the local magistrates in Nova Scotia. But the Zenger case did make colonial American authorities much more reluctant to challenge criticism that made use of satirical techniques. There were no further prosecutions of printers for seditious libel in the American colonies. In 1790, Pennsylvania enacted the first state law recognizing truth as a defense and the jury's right to determine its applicability.

ZINOVIEV LETTER. Letter published by the conservative *Daily Mail* on 25 October 1924 a few days before the British general election. Purportedly written by the senior Soviet official Grigori Zinoviev, it urged the British Communist Party to create dissension within the British armed forces. In the context of the Labour government's controversial trade treaty with the **Soviet Union**, its publication compromised the chances of the Labour party for reelection. Considered by some to be a fake, it was originally obtained by the government but then leaked to the press.

ZOLA, EMILE (1840–1902). French journalist-turned-novelist who is regarded as the founder of naturalism in literature. His journalism was characterized by anti-Catholicism and social reform. In 1898, he was sentenced to prison for libel as a result of his open letter to President Félix Faure on the front page of the Paris daily *L'Aurore*; entitled "J'Accuse," it attacked the army general staff on behalf of Alfred Dreyfus, an army officer who had been convicted of treason. Though escaping to England and granted an amnesty a few months later, Zola did not live to see the eventual full exoneration of Dreyfus. He died in his sleep from carbon-monoxide poisoning under suspicious circumstances—many years later, a roofer claimed on his deathbed that he had blocked the chimney for political revenge.

Appendix 1
Daily Newspaper
Circulation in Selected Countries

The reading of daily newspapers varies greatly throughout the world. According to Gale's pressreference.com (as of 2007–2008), the circulation of daily newspapers per 1,000 population for the following countries is as follows:

Country	Number of Dailies	Total Circulation	Circulation per 1,000
Norway	82	2,578,000	720
Finland	55	2,304,000	545
Sweden	93	3,700,000	541
Switzerland	104	2,666,000	454
Germany	382	23,946,000	375
Austria	16	2,503,000	374
Denmark	31	1,481,000	347
Netherlands	35	4,443,000	346
United States	1,476	55,945,000	264
Canada	104	5,167,000	206
Bulgaria	43	1,400,000	203
Australia	48	3,030,000	196
Ireland	6	567,000	191
France	86	8,799,000	190
Belgium	28	5,167,000	187
Spain	136	4,300,000	129
Portugal	83	686,000	83
Argentina	106	1,500,000	61
Brazil	465	7,883,000	61
India	398	30,772,000	50
Indonesia	172	4,782,000	36

Appendix 2
Daily Adult Newspaper Readership in United States for Selected Years

There has been growing concern in many countries about declining levels of newspaper readership. However, the statistics for adult readership vary from one source to another and even the same source can use different methods for its calculations, resulting in considerable confusion as to how serious the problem may be. In the United States, the Newspaper Association of America (NAA) provides the following figures for the selected years below:

Year	Total Daily Adult Readership	% of Adult Population
1970	98 million	77.6
1980	106 million	66.9
1990	113 million	62.4
1997	112 million	58.3

In 1997, the average weekday readership by age was 18–24 (48.1 percent), 25–34 (48.2), 35–54 (61.3), and 55+ (69.6). These figures represented drops from 70.8, 72.7, 81.0, and 75.5 for these age groups respectively from 30 years earlier (1967), indicating that only older adults were reading newspapers at more or less the same level throughout this period.

In 1998, NAA began basing its estimates of daily adult newspaper readership on the top 50 markets, rendering direct comparisons with its previous data invalid. Using the new method, daily adult newspaper readership in that year was estimated at 58.6 percent. By 2007, it had dropped to 48.4 percent. In the latter year, adult readership remained about 5 percentage points higher for men than for women. As of 2007, an estimated 53.6 percent of those who have finished college still read daily newspapers, compared to 46.0 percent for high school graduates.

Bibliography

CONTENTS

INTRODUCTION

Although the field of journalism history is still relatively young, there is now a vast literature dealing specifically with journalism as opposed to the press, the media, or communication more generally. While the quality of this literature varies greatly, there are a few works that can be considered as "classics," a somewhat larger number of works that represent scholarship at its best, and a plentiful supply of workmanlike studies on which to build our understanding even further. In terms of the evolution of journalism as a field of study, examples of these three categories can be seen as falling into five main overlapping areas: freedom of the press, objectivity and journalism, the invention of journalism, the professionalization of journalism, and journalism and the Internet. Other areas of research obviously exist, but they have generally been more peripheral to date to the field's advancement. Insofar as the works included in each section below are generally recommended as good places to begin for those interested in journalism history, the following discussion will put them into a comparative context and speak briefly about their relative strengths and weaknesses. In terms of Internet sites, Gale's pressreference.com is by far the best and was used in conjunction with pubished materials for many of the entries on individual countries.

For reasons of space, the bibliography itself has been restricted to English-language materials. It has also been limited to works published since 1980, except for a few books and articles that remain particularly valuable and were used for one or more components of this dictionary. A short section of relevant Web sites has been included, but with a few singular exceptions, the main contribution of the Internet to journalism history lies in the online databases such as JSTOR, Communication and Mass Media Complete, Project Muse, and the Wilson indexes through which much of the periodical literature referenced below can now be accessed electronically.

Freedom of the Press

Early studies of the press revolved around its long struggle for freedom. They did not necessarily focus on the role of journalists, but certainly showed that journalists were key figures in the ongoing battle against censorship and state controls. The most significant of these early works was Fred S. Siebert's *Freedom of the Press in England, 1476–1776: The Rise and Decline of Government Control* (Urbana: University of Illinois Press, 1952), which remains worth reading. Though focusing on England, Siebert showed that journalists in colonial America were equally committed to freedom of the press, a claim supported by Robert W. T. Martin's *The Free and Open Press: The Founding of American Democratic Press Liberty, 1640–1800* (New York: New York University Press, 2001).

A few years after *Freedom of the Press in England, 1476–1776* was published, Siebert collaborated with Theodore Peterson and Wilbur Schramm to produce a popular textbook entitled *Four Theories of the Press* (Urbana: University of Illinois Press, 1956) in which the authoritarian, communist, and even the libertarian "theory" of the ideal press-state relationship were treated as inferior to what they took to be a new social responsibility theory of the press. However, by excessively polarizing the libertarian and social responsibility approaches, *Four Theories* opened the door to one-sided critiques of the concept of social responsibility like that of John Merrill in *The Imperative of Freedom: A Philosophy of Journalistic Autonomy* (New York: Hastings House, 1974). "American journalists," he declared, "like most journalists in the Western world, while still chanting the tenets of libertarianism, are marching into an authoritarian sunset under the banners of 'social responsibility.'" Although the restrictive format of *Four Theories* was formally laid to rest by John Nerone's edited collection, *Last Rights: Revisiting Four Theories of the Press* (Urbana: University of Illinois Press, 1995), it had ceased to be a factor long before then.

Outside of journalism courses, the major study motivating further studies of press freedom in the United States was Leonard Levy's iconoclastic *Legacy of Suppression* (Cambridge, Mass.: Harvard University Press, 1960). Levy argued that the framers of the First Amendment did not have a strong libertarian conception of freedom of expression and that Americans have never been as committed to a free press as its apologists would have one believe. Although Levy later modified this assessment in *Emergence of a Free Press* (New York: Oxford University Press, 1985), his main line of argument continued to generate counter-studies such as Lucas A. Powe Jr.'s *The Fourth Estate and the Constitution: Freedom of the Press in America* (Berkeley: University of California Press, 1991).

Similar, though generally much smaller, literatures dealing with press freedom exist for many other countries. But for students interested in the larger picture in areas like Europe, Africa, and Asia, the choices remain much more restricted. In the case of Europe, a good place to begin is Robert Goldstein's *The Political Censorship of the Arts and the Press in Nineteenth-Century Europe* (New York: St. Martin's Press, 1989). One of the main problems in the case of Asia and Africa is that the best works in terms of scholarship, such as John Lent's *Guided Press in Southeast Asia: National Development vs. Freedom of Expression* (Buffalo: State University of New York, 1976), have been overly influenced by Anglo-American conceptions of freedom. In recent years, this defect has been reduced somewhat by works that combine an academic approach with actual journalistic experience. In *The New Africa: Dispatches from a Changing Continent* (Gainesville: The University Press of Florida, 1999), for example, Robert M. Press draws upon his years as a journalist in Africa for the *Christian Science Monitor* to produce a more nuanced account of the conditions necessary for journalists to function effectively in developing countries.

Objectivity and Journalism

From the standpoint of putting journalism itself front and center, studies on freedom of the press, despite their relevance to the journalistic enterprise, constituted a false start for journalism history. What got the field going was a sudden change of focus to the culturally based norms, values, and ideals shaping journalistic practice. This paradigm shift was accomplished almost single-handedly by Michael Schudson in *Discovering the News: A Social History of American Newspapers* (New York: Basic Books, 1978), a gracefully written work sparkling with ideas about the relations between journalism and society. Schudson's basic thesis was that the first glimmerings of objectivity as a new ideal arose in conjunction with the emergence of a democratic market society in Jacksonian America; that is, one characterized by wide participation. In the case of journalism, this commercial egalitarianism took the form of transforming the newspaper into a readily available consumer good, a task accomplished by the penny papers with their emphasis on factual, nonpartisan news.

Schudson's work inspired a series of further explorations into the origins and development of objectivity, from Dan Schiller's *Objectivity and the News: The Public and the Rise of Commercial Journalism* (Philadelphia: University of Pennsylvania Press, 1981) to David T. Z. Mindich's *Just the Facts: How "Objectivity" Came to Define American Journalism* (New York: New York University Press, 1998). These studies have added new twists to the story, but none is as broad, original, and readable as Schudson's history.

Schudson assumed that the ideals of journalism are a close reflection of the culture of the dominant class. But to what extent has objectivity been consonant with that culture outside of the United States? In "The Long Road to Objectivity and Back Again: The Kinds of Truth We Get in Journalism," an overview essay in George Boyce, James Curran, and Pauline Wingate, eds., *Newspaper History: From the Seventeenth Century to the Present Day* (London: Constable, 1978), Anthony Smith showed that the concept of objectivity has functioned at times as a protective ideal in Great Britain, but has generally declined as a goal for day-to-day practice. Similarly, in *The Addisonian Tradition in France: Passion and Objectivity in Social Observation* (Rutherford: Fairleigh Dickinson UP, 1990), Ralph A. Nablow found a group of pseudo-journalists in 18th-century France excited by the prospects of objectivity for opening the door to truth. For the most part, however, accounts of journalism in Britain, France, and other European countries have found little use for objectivity as an organizing concept. In continental Europe in particular, the emphasis has been on bias, distortion, and ideology and the longstanding preference for editorializing over reporting.

The Invention of Journalism

During the late 1990s, a small but significant literature began to address the question of when and where modern journalism or journalism as we know it today might be said to have been "invented." One need not take the term *invented* too literally to see how it helps to bring journalism even closer to the center of the stage. In the literature in question, journalism is theorized as a set of discursive practices governed by both internal and external power relations. That is, there are power relations between news reports, leaders, and commentaries, for example, as well as between journalism and other genres. Though influenced, somewhat sycophantically, by the writings of the French philosophers Michel Foucault and Pierre Bourdieu, there is nothing particularly novel about this assumption. It was the basis of Lennard J. Davis's brilliant study *Factual Fictions: The Origins of the English Novel* (New York: Columbia University Press, 1983), which saw journalism materializing from the fragmentation of what, in early modern Europe, Davis believed was an undifferentiated "news/novels discourse." But (not without loss) the present literature shifts our attention forward in time and argues that this process of differentiation did not occur simultaneously or independently in different countries or throughout the world. Journalism is seen, not as a universal discourse, but as one arising within a particular Western setting and then undergoing a process of cultural diffusion from there. This perspective obviously has major implications for understanding the relationship between Western and non-Western journalism, especially insofar as the diffusion is also regarded as hegemonic in nature.

The pioneer of this approach has been Jean Chalaby, first in an article entitled "Journalism as an Anglo-American Invention" in the *European Journal of Communication* 11 (1996), 303–26, and then in *The Invention of Journalism* (New York: St. Martin's Press, 1998). Michael Schudson has pointed out in a review in the *American Historical Review* that it is important to consider both publications, because Chalaby's approach changed significantly between them. In the earlier article, Chalaby equated the "invention" of journalism with the relatively sudden rupture (*à la* Foucault) of a highly polemical and politicized news discourse in early 19th-century Europe into two distinct discourses: a new, fact-centered, news-oriented, and depoliticized discourse in the Anglo-American world and a continuation of journalism as political ideology in France. (It was not simply in France that 19th-century newspapers continued to emphasize opinion over news; until 1873, Greek papers were called "views-papers" rather than newspapers, reflecting the extent to which opinions were freely intermingled with facts.) Again, there is nothing particularly original about this thesis or its explanation in terms of the varying operation of market and political forces. In his initial treatment of the supposedly revolutionary Anglo-American journalism, Chalaby retailed much the same story as Schudson and Schiller and the historiography of objectivity. What makes his thesis controversial, indeed provocative, and thus recommended reading is the degree of emphasis placed on discontinuity: between past and present and between information and opinion. As if this were not enough, however, Chalaby went even further in *The Invention of Journalism* by concentrating on the transformation of political discourse in mid-19th-century Britain and framing the "invention" of journalism much more explicitly as a deterioration of public discourse.

For readers interested in pursuing Chalaby's general line of enquiry, Martin Conboy's *Journalism: A Critical History* (London: Sage, 2004) looked promising. Like Chalaby, Conboy analyzes journalism primarily as discourse and seemed to offer a history transcending the focus on particular countries and periods, which continues to govern journalism history. In the end, however, he restricts himself to Britain, at times even to London, and falls into a similarly Whiggish or rather Habermasian motif (the Whigs wrote in terms of steady progress, Habermas in terms of a rise and fall) regarding the public sphere. His work is still well worth reading, but conceives the "invention" question too narrowly.

Published the same year as Conboy's book was Paul Starr's smoothly written *The Creation of the Media: Political Origins of Modern Communication* (New York: Basic Books, 2004). Though primarily concerned with the United States, it includes a broader geographic perspective and develops a more sophisticated explanatory framework. Starr describes many of the same differences between Anglo-American and French journalism as the early Chalaby, but draws a greater contrast between British and American journalism. While journalism is not his main focus, it is frequently woven into his account. His main argument is that during the 18th, 19th, and early 20th centuries, Americans made a significantly different set of "constitutive choices" about their media system than Europeans. This different groundwork helps to explain differences in American journalism, which then influenced journalism elsewhere. Although many of the different choices made by Americans concerned technology, they also involved issues such as freedom of expression and factors such as the design and operation of commercial media. Despite long discussions of technology, Starr ends up emphasizing two of the more prominent themes in the historiography of American media: the hope that communication would enable Americans to build a nation on a continental scale; and the commitment, albeit far from total, to its development as a liberal republic. By linking these themes to journalism, Starr's work provides a rich context for reconsidering its "invention" as a modern discursive form.

The Professionalization of Journalism

The "invention" paradigm has several obvious shortcomings. It usually leaves off long before the present day and has little to say about working journalists and their struggle for some level of professionalization. This quest has taken quite different forms in different countries. In France, it involved a campaign for accreditation to counter the loss of credibility suffered by French journalists in World War I. In Britain, it was spearheaded during the 1890s by the Institute of Journalists, but had to compete against the movement for trade unionism. In the United States, it dates from the 1880s and was closely tied to the rise of modern news reporting.

Apart from chapters in books like those of Schudson and Schiller mentioned above, most of the literature on the professionalization of journalism is to be found in periodicals. In the case of the United States, however, there are several excellent book-length treatments of the subject. In *Taking Their Place: Journalists and the Making of an Occupation* (Westport, Conn.: Greenwood Press, 1997), Patricia L. Dooley used prospectuses issued by new newspapers, transcripts from libel trials, and biographies of publishers and editors to show that claims about professionalism were initially tied to a new insistence in the late 19th century on journalism's role in exposing corruption and wrongdoing in politics and business. Dooley's account dovetails nicely with Christopher Wilson's *The Labor of Words: Literary Professionalism in the Progressive* (Athens: University of Georgia Press, 1985), which focused more narrowly on four writers-cum-journalists in the Progressive era: Jack London, Upton Sinclair, David Graham Phillips, and Lincoln Steffens. Wilson argued that these authors repudiated the prevailing view of literature as aloof from the struggles of life in favor of taking an active role in the affairs of the nation. According to Wilson, this transition was only possible because of the rise of mass journalism and the implication is that the acceptance of a new "responsibility to the American public" transformed journalism as well. In Wilson's account, this new ideal began to suffer from exhaustion by World War I and works such as Ronald T. Farrar's *A Creed for My Profession: Walter Williams, Journalist to the World* (Columbia: University of Missouri Press, 1998) confirm this analysis. In Williams, a journalist-turned-academic, one can see the beginnings of a shift away from professionalism as a more idealistic self-fashioning toward the more mundane tasks of providing journalists with better education and codes of ethics.

That the late 19th-century pursuit of professionalism in journalism was not simply an American or even Western phenomenon is clear from studies such as Joan Judge's *Print and Politics: "Shibao" and the Culture of Reform in Late Qing China* (Stanford, Calif.: Stanford University Press, 1996), which looks at how journalists such as Liang Qichao turned to professionalization as a form of protection against state controls. For more current examples of the role of professionalism in highly authoritarian regimes, works such as Jane Leftwich Curry's *Poland's Journalists: Professionalism and Politics* (Cambridge: Cambridge University Press, 1990) are still relatively useful. Based on interviews with 249 Polish journalists, Curry found that in the absence of autonomy, journalists use professionalism as a form of resistance, but still function primarily as political actors, manipulating information in accordance with state ideology. In such regimes, professionalism is more concerned with establishing control over entrance and membership and isolating non-professional influences.

Journalism and the Internet

During the past decade, the production of books concerned with the impact of the Internet on journalism has become a veritable cottage industry which threatens to overwhelm the field of journalism history. Choosing from among them is difficult, because most have a relatively short shelf life, quickly becoming dated by new developments in the Internet itself. Apart from their narrow research base, they have tended to be uncritical, under-theorized, and biased toward discontinuity and progress.

Initially, the main concern of works on journalism and the Internet was with the differences between, and respective advantages and disadvantages of, traditional print-based newspapers and digitalized news on the Worldwide Web. In *Digitizing the News: Innovation in Online Newspapers* (Cambridge, Mass.: MIT Press, 2004), for example, Pablo J. Boczkowski emphasizes how web-based journalism makes possible a more user-centered news experience and introduces elements of broadcast journalism into traditional print formats. He does not, however, compare their respective merits in terms of creating a visual map of current reality, giving citizens a common basis for understanding that reality, or having an impact on its political architects. A similar weakness underlies works such as Stephen D. Cooper's *Watching the Watchdogs: Bloggers as the Fifth Estate* (Spokane, Wash.: Marquette, 2006), which address the impact of blogging on journalism. Cooper argues typically that bloggers have become a legitimate factor in media criticism and explores their potential as independent news gatherers. Not surprisingly, he has no difficulty finding anecdotal evidence of bloggers who have successfully contested the accuracy of particular claims made by mainstream journalists. But his sample does not include cases where bloggers got it wrong and he provides little reason for thinking that bloggers could provide error-free news on a regular basis themselves.

While these works remain useful starting points for exploring the impact of the Internet on journalism, they need to be supplemented by several related types of study. The first need is for a realistic perspective on cyberspace generally, which, like the traditional media environment, is also governed by forces of political economy. Of continuing use in this regard is Jack Goldsmith and Tim Wu's *Who Controls the Internet?: Illusions of a Borderless World* (New York: Oxford University Press, 2006), which effectively dispels earlier romantic views of the Internet. It is also necessary to avoid taking discontinuity as a tacit assumption, especially in areas such as journalism ethics where online journalism is thought by some to have its unique issues. One of the strengths of Robert I. Berkman and Christopher A. Shumwat's *Digital Dilemmas: Ethical Issues for Online Media Professionals* (Ames: Iowa State University Press, 2003) is that they trace the evolution of codes of journalism ethics before considering current ethical issues associated with online journalism.

Finally, there is a need for works which stand back and try to understand the significance of cyberspace from a more philosophical perspective. This literature is more speculative and abstract, but of more lasting value and relevance. One of the more provocative examples of the genre is Jodi Dean's *Publicity's Secret: How Technoculture Capitalizes on Democracy* (Ithaca, N.Y.: Cornell University Press, 2002). Dean's thesis is that rapid, information-oriented communication, which online news and blogging would typify, has become a new ideology and that what she calls "communicative capitalism" has, among other things, co-opted the idea of a democratic public. For Dean, indeed, there no longer is a public and cyberspace has been one of the main forces in its destruction. While this pessimistic assessment is certainly not the final word on the fate of the public or its common interest, studies on journalism and the Internet need to ascend at times to such planes of enquiry if they are to contribute to the larger field of journalism history.

REFERENCE TOOLS

Bibliographies

Asante, Clement E. *Press Freedom and Development: A Research Guide and Selected Bibliography*. Westport, Conn.: Greenwood Press, 1997.

Caswell, Lucy Shelton, ed. *Guide to Sources in American Journalism History*. New York: Greenwood Press, 1989.

Cates, Jo A. *Journalism: A Guide to the Reference Literature*, 3rd ed. Westport, Conn.: Libraries Unlimited, 2004.

Lent, John A. *Women and Mass Communications in the 1990s: An International Annotated Bibliography*. Westport, Conn.: Greenwood Press, 1999.

Linton, David. *The Twentieth-Century Newspaper Press in Britain: An Annotated Bibliography*. London: Mansell, 1994.

Parker, Elliott S. *Asian Journalism: A Selected Bibliography on Journalism in China and Southeast Asia.* Metuchen, N.J.: Scarecrow Press, 1979.

Sloan, Wm. David. *American Journalism History: An Annotated Bibliography.* New York: Greenwood Press, 1989.

Wolseley, Roland Edgar, and Isabel Wolseley. *The Journalist's Bookshelf: An Annotated and Selected Bibliography of United States Print Journalism.* Indianapolis, Ind.: R. J. Berg, 1986.

Dictionaries and Encyclopedias

Applegate, Edd. *Literary Journalism: A Biographical Dictionary of Writers and Editors.* Westport, Conn.: Greenwood Press, 1996.

Ashley, Perry J. *American Newspaper Journalists,* 4 vols. Chicago: Gale Research, 1983ff.

Blanchard, M. A., ed. *History of the Mass Media in the United States: An Encyclopedia.* Chicago: Fitzroy-Dearborn, 1998.

Bryant, Mark, and Simon Henage. *Dictionary of British Cartoonists and Caricaturists, 1730–1980.* Aldershots, Hants., U.K.: Scolar Press, 1994.

Chadwick, Ruth. *The Concise Encyclopedia of Ethics in Politics and the Media.* San Diego, Calif.: Academic Press, 2001.

Downs, R. B., and J. B. Downs. *Journalists of the United States: Biographical Sketches of Print and Broadcast News Shapers from the 17th Century to the Present.* London: McFarland, 1991.

Griffiths, Dennis, ed. *The Encyclopedia of the British Press 1422–1992.* New York: St. Martin's Press, 1992.

Harnett, Richard M. *Wirespeak: Codes and Jargon of the News Business.* San Mateo, Calif.: Shorebird Press, 1997.

Hudson, Robert V. *Mass Media: A Chronological Encyclopedia of Television, Radio, Motion Pictures, Magazines, Newspapers, and Books in the United States.* New York: Garland, 1987.

Kaul, Arthur J. *American Literary Journalists, 1945–1995.* Detroit, Mich.: Gale Research, 1997.

McKerns, Joseph P., ed. *The Biographical Dictionary of American Journalism.* Westport, Conn.: Greenwood Press, 1989.

Murray, Michael D., ed. *Encyclopedia of Television News.* Phoenix, Ariz.: Oryx Press, 1998.

Paneth, Donald, ed. *The Encyclopedia of American Journalism.* New York: Facts on File, 1983.

Riley, Sam G. *American Magazine Journalists,* 4 vols. Chicago, Ill.: Gale Research, 1983ff.

Roth, Mitchel P. *Historical Dictionary of War Journalism.* Westport, Conn.: Greenwood Press, 1997.

Taft, William H., ed. *Encyclopedia of Twentieth-Century Journalists*. New York: Garland, 1986.

Wilson, John. *Understanding Journalism: A Guide to Issues*. London: Routledge, 1996.

Source Books and Anthologies

Ashdown, Paul, ed. *James Agee, Selected Journalism*. Knoxville: University of Tennessee Press, 1985.

Barrineau, Nancy Warner, ed. *Theodore Dreiser's Ev'ry Month*. Athens: University of Georgia Press, 1996.

Belford, Barbara. *Brilliant Bylines: A Biographical Anthology of Notable Newspaperwomen in America*. New York: Columbia University Press, 1986.

Blackett, R. J. M., ed. *Thomas Morris Chester, Black Civil War Correspondent: His Dispatches from the Virginia Front*. Baton Rouge: Louisiana State University Press, 1989.

Blaney, Retta, ed. *Journalism: Stories from the Real World*. Golden, Colo.: North American Press, 1995.

Burlingame, Michel, ed. *Lincoln's Journalist: John Hay's Anonymous Writings for the Press, 1860–1864*. Carbondale: Southern Illinois Press, 1998.

Connery, Thomas B. *A Sourcebook of American Literary Journalism: Representative Writers in an Emerging Genre*. New York: Greenwood Press, 1992.

Halberstam, David, ed. *The Best American Sports Writing of the Century*. Boston, Mass.: Houghton Mifflin, 1999.

Hammond, William M., ed. *Reporting Vietnam: American Journalism 1959–1975*. 2 vols., New York: Library of America, 1998.

Keever, Beverly Ann Deepe, Carolyn Martindale, and Mary Ann Weston, eds. *U.S. News Coverage of Racial Minorities: A Sourcebook, 1934–1996*. Westport, Conn.: Greenwood Press, 1997.

Kerrane, Kevin, and Ben Yagoda, eds. *The Art of Fact: A Historical Anthology of Literary Journalism*. New York: Scribner, 1997.

Knight, Bill, and Deckle McLean, eds. *Literature's Heritage in the Press*. Macomb: Western Illinois University Press, 1996.

Library of America. *Reporting Civil Rights: Part One: American Journalism, 1941–1963* and *Reporting Civil Rights: Part Two: American Journalism, 1963–1973*. New York: 2003.

Ricchiardi, Sherry, and Virginia Young. *Women on Deadline: A Collection of America's Best*. Ames: Iowa State University Press, 1991.

Signorielli, Nancy, ed. *Women in Communication: A Biographical Sourcebook*. Westport, Conn.: Greenwood Press, 1996.

Silvester, Christopher. *The Penguin Book of Columnists*. London: Viking, 1997.

Sims, Norman, ed. *Literary Journalism in the Twentieth Century*. New York: Oxford University Press, 1990.

Sloan, W. David, Cheryl Sloan Wray, and C. Joanne Sloan. *Great Editorials: Masterpieces of Opinion Writing*. Northport, Ala.: Vision, 1997.

Interviews of Journalists

Braden, Maria. *She Said What? Interviews with Women Newspaper Columnists*. Lexington: University Press of Kentucky, 1993.

Knudson, Jerry W. *In the News: American Journalists View Their Craft*. Wilmington, Del.: SR Books, 2000.

Ricchiardi, Sherry, and Virginia Young. *Women on Deadline: A Collection of America's Best*. Ames: Iowa State University Press, 1991.

Autobiographies

Bradlee, Ben. *A Good Life: Newspapering and Other Adventures*. New York: Simon and Schuster, 1995.

Brinkley, David. *David Brinkley: Memoir*. New York: Alfred A. Knopf, 1995.

Des Champs, Jean. *The Life and "Mémoires secrets" of Jean Des Champs (1707–1767): Journalist, Minister, and Man of Feeling*. Amsterdam: APA-Holland University, 1990.

Duster, Alfreda M., ed. *Crusade for Justice: The Autobiography of Ida B. Wells*. Chicago, Ill.: University of Chicago Press, 1970.

Harsch, Joseph C. *At the Hinge of History: A Reporter's Story*. Athens: University of Georgia Press, 1993.

Steffens, Lincoln. *The Autobiography of Lincoln Steffens*. Berkeley, Calif.: Heyday Books, 2005.

Stillman, William James. *The Autobiography of a Journalist, William James Stillman*. Boston, Mass.: Houghton, 1901.

White, William Allen. *The Autobiography of William Allen White*. New York: Macmillan, 1946.

Woods, Donald. *Asking for Trouble: Autobiography of a Banned Journalist*. London: v. Gollancz, 1980.

Websites

Gale press reference database: www.pressreference.com.

Media History Monographs: An Online Journal of Media History: http://facstaff.elon.edu/dcopeland/mhm/mhm.htm.

Newspaper Association of America: www.naa.org.

HISTORICAL STUDIES

General and Comparative

Barker, Hannah, and Simon Burrows, eds. *Press, Politics and the Public Sphere in Europe and North America: 1760–1820*. Cambridge: Cambridge University Press, 2002.

Botein, Stephen, Jack R. Censer, and Harriet Ritvo. "The Periodical Press in Eighteenth-Century English and French Society: A Cross-Cultural Approach." *Comparative Studies in Society and History* 23, no. 3 (1981): 464–90.

Boyd-Barrett, Oliver, and Terhi Rantanen. *The Globalization of News*. London: Sage, 1998.

Byrne, Jeb. "The Comparative Development of Newspapers in New Zealand and the United States in the Nineteenth Century." *American Studies International* 37, no. 1 (1999): 55–70.

Canel, María José. *Morality Tales: Political Scandals and Journalism in Britain and Spain in the 1990s*. Creskill, N.J.: Hampton Press, 2006.

Chalaby, Jean K. "Journalism as an Anglo-American Invention: A Comparison of the Development of French and Anglo-American Journalism, 1830s–1920s." *European Journal of Communication* 11, no. 3 (1996): 303–26.

———. *The Invention of Journalism*. Houndmills, Basingstoke, Hampshire: Macmillan Press, 1998.

Conboy, Martin. *Journalism: A Critical History*. London: Sage, 2004.

Desmond, Robert William. *Crisis and Conflict: World News Reporting Between Two Wars, 1920–1940*. Iowa City: University of Iowa Press, 1982.

Deuze, Mark. "National News Cultures: A Comparison of Dutch, German, British, Australian, and U.S. Journalists." *Journalism and Mass Communication Quarterly* 79, no. 1 (2002): 134–49.

Eisenstein, Elizabeth L. *Grub Street Abroad: Aspects of the French Cosmopolitan Press from the Age of Louis XIV to the French Revolution*. Oxford: Clarendon Press, 1992.

Kevin, Deirdre. *Europe in the Media: A Comparison of Reporting, Representation, and Rhetoric in National Media Systems in Europe*. Mahwah, N.J.: Lawrence Erlbaum Associates, 2003.

Leth, Goran. "A Protestant Public Sphere: The Early European Newspaper Press." *Studies in Newspaper and Periodical History* (1993): 67–90.

Ogbondah, Chris W. "The Sword Versus the Pen: A Study of Military-Press Relations in Chile, Greece, and Nigeria." *Gazette* 44, no. 1 (1989): 1–26.

Smith, Anthony. *The Newspaper: An International History*. London: Thames & Hudson, 1979.

Starr, Paul. *The Creation of the Media: Political Origins of Modern Communications*. New York: Basic Books, 2004.

Stephens, Mitchell. *A History of News: From the Drum to the Satellite*. New York: Viking, 1988.

Winston, Brian. *Messages: Free Expression, Media and the West from Gutenberg to Google*. London: Routledge, 2005.

By Country or Region

Africa

Burrowes, Carl Patrick. *Power and Press Freedom in Liberia, 1830–1970: The Impact of Globalization and Civil Society on Media-Government Relations*. Trenton, N.J.: Africa World Press, 2004.

Dare, Olatunji, and Adidi Uyo, eds. *Journalism in Nigeria: Issues and Perspectives*. Victoria Island, Lagos: Nigerian Union of Journalists, Lagos State Council, 1996.

Edeani, D. O. "Role of Development Journalism in Nigeria's Development." *Gazette* 52, no. 1 (1993): 123–44.

Eribo, Festus, and Enoh Tanjong, eds. *Journalism and Mass Communication in Africa: Cameroon*. Lanham, Md.: Lexington Books, 2002.

Faringer, G. L. *Press Freedom in Africa*. New York: Praeger, 1991.

Israel, Adrienne M. "The Afrocentric Perspective in African Journalism: A Case Study of the *Ashanti Pioneer*, 1939–1957." *Journal of Black Studies* 22, no. 3 (1992): 411–28.

Kasoma, Francis P. "The Independent Press and Politics in Africa." *Gazette* 54, nos. 4–5 (1997): 295–310.

Martin, Robert. "Building Independent Mass Media in Africa." *Journal of Modern African Studies* 30, no. 2 (1992): 331–40.

Matovu, Jacob. "Mass Media as Agencies of Socialization in Uganda." *Journal of Black Studies* 20, no. 3 (1990): 342–61.

M'Bayo, R., C. Onwumechili, and R. Nwanko, eds. *Press and Politics in Africa*. New York: Mellen Press, 2000.

Ormond, Roger. *Watchdog or Poodle? The Press in South Africa*. Oxford: Nuffield College, 1991.

Pratt, Cornelius B. "Ethics in Newspaper Editorials: Perceptions of Sub-Sahara African Journalists." *Gazette* 46 (1990): 17–40.

Ramaprasad, Jyotika. "A Profile of Journalists in Post-Independence Tanzania." *Gazette* 63, no. 6 (2001): 539–55.

Switzer, Les. "Bantu World and the Origins of a Captive African Commercial Press in South Africa." *Journal of Southern African Studies* 14, no. 3 (1988): 351–70.

Switzer, Les, ed. *South Africa's Alternative Press: Voices of Protest and Resistance, 1880s–1960s*. Cambridge: Cambridge University Press, 1997.

Switzer, Les, and Mohamed Adhikari, eds. *South Africa's Resistance Press: Alternative Voices in the Last Generation under Apartheid*. Athens: Ohio University Center for International Studies, 2000.

Uwechue, Ralph, ed. *Makers of Modern Africa: Profiles in History*. 2nd ed., London: Africa Books Limited, 1991.

Asia

Gunaratne, Shelton A. ed., *Handbook of the Media in Asia*. New Delhi: Sage, 2000.

———. "Asian Philosophies and Authoritarian Press Practice: A Remarkable Contradiction." *The Public* 12 (2005): 2–16.

Latif, A., ed. *Walking the Tightrope: Press Freedom and Professional Standards in Asia*. Singapore: AMIC, 1998.

Lee, Kwang-rin. "Newspaper Publication in the Late Yi Dynasty." *Korean Studies* 12 (1988): 62–72.

Lent, John A. "The Perpetual See-Saw: Press Freedom in the ASEAN Countries." *Human Rights Quarterly* 3, no. 1 (1981): 62–77.

Richstad, Jim. "Asian Journalism in the Twentieth Century." *Journalism Studies* 1, no. 2 (2000): 273–84.

Romano, Angela, and Michael Bromley, eds. *Journalism and Democracy in Asia*. London: Routledge Curzon, 2005.

Salam, S. A. *Mass Media in Bangladesh: Newspapers, Radio and Television*. Dhaka: South Asian News Agency, 1997.

Szende, Andrew. *From Torrent to Trickle: Managing the Flow of News in Southeast Asia*. Singapore: Institute of Southeast Asian Studies, 1986.

Wong, Kokkeong. "Asian-based Development Journalism and Political Elections: Press Coverage of the 1999 Elections in Malaysia." *Gazette* 66, no. 1 (2004): 25–40.

Australia

Goff, Victoria. "Convicts and Clerics: Their Roles in the Infancy of the Press in Sydney, 1803–1840." *Media History* 4, no. 2 (1998): 101–20.

Griffen-Foley, Bridget. "'The Crumbs are Better Than a Feast Elsewhere': Australian Journalists on Fleet Street." *Journalism History* 28, no. 1 (2002): 26–37.

Little, Janine. "'The Innocence in Her Beautiful Green Eyes': Speculations on Seduction and the 'Feminine' in the Australian News Media." *Pacific Journalism Review* 12, no. 1 (2006): 131–45.

Putnis, Peter. "Reuters in Australia: The Supply and Exchange of News, 1859–1877." *Media History* 10, no. 2 (2004): 67–88.

Canada

Beaven, Brian P. N. "Partisanship, Patronage, and the Press in Ontario, 1880–1914: Myths and Realities." *Canadian Historical Review* 64, no. 3 (1983): 317–51.
Buxton, William, and Catherine McKercher. "Newspapers, Magazines and Journalism in Canada: Towards a Critical Historiography." *Acadiensis* 28, no. 1 (1998): 103–26.
Cumming, Carman. *Secret Craft: The Journalism of Edward Farrer*. Toronto, Ont.: University of Toronto Press, 1992.
Houston, Susan E. "'Little Steam, a Little Sizzle and a Little Sleaze': English-language Tabloids in the Interwar Period." *Papers of the Bibliographical Society of Canada* 40, no. 1 (2002): 37–60.
Keel, Vernon. "Community Values in the Law and Practice of Journalism in Canada." *American Review of Canadian Studies* 28, nos. 1–2 (1998): 29–52.
Rutherford, Paul. *A Victorian Authority: The Daily Press in Late Nineteenth-Century Canada*. Toronto, Ont.: University of Toronto Press, 1982.
Sotiron, Minko. *From Politics to Profits: The Commercialization of Canadian Daily Newspapers, 1890–1920*. Montreal, Que.: McGill-Queen's University Press, 1997.
Stabile, Julie. "The Economics of an Early Nineteenth-Century Toronto Newspaper Shop." *Papers of the Bibliographical Society of Canada* 41, no. 1 (2003): 43–76.

China

Fitzgerald, J. "The Origins of the Illiberal Party Newspaper: Print Journalism in China's Nationalist Revolution." *Republican China* 22, no. 2 (1996): 1–22.
Goodman, Bryna. "Networks of News: Power, Language and Transnational Dimensions of the Chinese Press, 1850–1949." *China Review* 4, no. 1 (2004): 2–9.
Hung, Chang-Tai. "Paper Bullets: Fan Changjiang and New Journalism in Wartime China." *Modern China* 17, no. 4 (1991): 427–68.
Judge, Joan. "Public Opinion and the New Politics of Contestation in the Qing, 1904–1911." *Modern China* 20, no. 1 (1994): 64–91.
———. "The Factional Function of Print: Liang Qichao, *Shibao*, and the Fissures in the Late Qing Reform Movement." *Late Imperial China* 16, no. 1 (1995): 120–40.

———. *Print and Politics: "Shibao" and the Culture of Reform in Late Qing China*. Stanford, Calif.: Stanford University Press, 1996.

Knight, Alan, and Yoshiko Nakano, eds. *Reporting Hong Kong: Foreign Media and the Handover*. New York: St. Martin's Press, 1999.

MacKinnon, Stephen R. "Press Freedom and the Chinese Revolution in the 1930s." 174–88 in Jeremy Popkin, ed., *Media and Revolution: Comparative Perspectives*. Lexington: University of Kentucky Press, 1995.

———. "Toward a History of the Chinese Press in the Republican Period." *Modern China* 23, no. 1 (1997): 3–32.

Mittler, Barbara. *A Newspaper for China? Power, Identity and Change in Shanghai's News Media (1872–1912)*. Cambridge, Mass.: Harvard University Press, 2004.

Narramore, Terry. "The Nationalists and the Daily Press: The Case of the *Shen Bao*, 1927–1934." 106–32 in John Fitzgerald, ed., *The Nationalists and Chinese Society, 1923–1937*. Melbourne: University of Melbourne Press, 1989.

———. *Making the News in Shanghai: Shen Bao and the Politics of Newspaper Journalism 1912–1937*. Canberra: Australian National University, 1993.

Polumbaum, Judy. "Tribulations of China's Journalists After a Decade of Reform." 33–68 in Chin-chuan Lee, ed., *Voices of China: The Interplay of Politics and Journalism*. New York: Guilford Press, 1990.

———. "Outpaced by Events: Learning, Unlearning, and Relearning to be a Journalist in Post-Cultural Revolution China." *Gazette: The International Journal for Mass Communication Studies* 48, no. 2 (1991): 129–46.

Stranahan, Patricia. "The Last Battle: Mao and the Internationists' Fight for the *Liberation Daily*." *China Quarterly* no. 123 (1990): 521–37.

———. *Molding the Medium: The Chinese Communist Party and the Liberation Daily*. Armonk, N.Y.: M. E. Sharpe, 1990.

Tan, Frank. "The People's Daily: Politics and Popular Will—Journalistic Defiance in China During the Spring of 1989." *Pacific Affairs* 63, no. 2 (1990): 151–69.

Vittinghoff, Natascha. "Unity vs. Uniformity: Liang Qichao and the Invention of a New Journalism for China." *Late Imperial China* 23, no. 1 (2002): 91–143.

Wagner, Rudolf G. "The Role of the Foreign Community in the Chinese Public Sphere." *China Quarterly* 142 (1995): 423–43.

———. "The *Shenbao* in Crisis: The International Environment and the Conflict Between *Guo Songtag* and the *Shenbao*." *Late Imperial China* 20, no. 1 (1999): 107–43.

———. "The Early Chinese Newspapers and the Chinese Public Sphere." *European Journal of East Asian Studies* 1, no. 1 (2001): 1–33.

Wagner, Rudolf G., ed. *Joining the Global Public: Word, Image, and City in the Early Chinese Newspapers 1870–1910*. New York: Suny Press, 2003.

Wang, L. Sophia. "The Independent Press and Authoritarian Regimes: The Case of the *Dagong bao* in Republican China." *Pacific Affairs* 67, no. 2 (1994): 216–41.

Yoon, Seungjoo. "Literati-journalists of the Chinese Progress (Shiwu Bao) in Discord, 1896–1898." 48–76 in Rebecca Karl and Peter Zarrow, eds., *Rethinking the 1898 Reform Period: Political and Cultural Change in Late Qing China*. Cambridge, Mass.: Harvard University Press, 2002.

Zhang Volz, Yong. "Journalism as a Vocation: Liang Qichao and the Contested Ideas of Journalism, 1890s–1900s." Paper presented to the annual meeting of the International Communication Association in 2005.

Eastern Europe

Aumente, Jerome. *Eastern European Journalism: Before, During and After Communism*. Cresskill, N.J.: Hampton Press, 1999.

Curry, Jane L. *Poland's Journalists: Professionalism and Politics*. New York: Cambridge University Press, 1990.

Hester, Al, and Kristina White, eds. *Creating a Free Press in Eastern Europe*. Athens: University of Georgia Press, 1993.

France

Censer, Jack R. *The French Press in the Age of Enlightenment*. London: Routledge, 1995.

Darnton, Robert, and Daniel Roche, eds. *Revolution in Print: The Press in France, 1775–1800*. Berkeley: University of California Press, 1989.

de la Motte, Dean, and Jeannene M. Przyblyski, eds. *Making the News: Modernity and the Mass Press in Nineteenth-Century France*. Amherst: University of Massachusetts Press, 1999.

Gelbert, Nina. *Feminine and Opposition Journalism in Old Regime France: "Le Journal des Dames."* Berkeley: University of California Press, 1987.

Gough, Hugh. *The Newspaper Press in the French Revolution*. London: Routledge, 1988.

Gruder, Vivian R. "Political News as Coded Messages: The Parisian and Provincial Press in the Pre-Revolution, 1787–1788." *French History* 12, no. 1 (1998): 1–24.

Hanley, Wayne. "News from the Front: Bonaparte's Dispatches and the Press." *Consortium on Revolutionary Europe 1750–1850: Selected Papers* (1999): 72–82.

LeHir, Marie-Pierre. "The Société des Gens de Lettres and French Socialism: Association as Resistance to the Industrialization and Censorship of the Press." *Nineteenth-Century French Studies* 24, nos. 3–4 (1996): 306–18.

Murray, William James. *The Right-Wing Press in the French Revolution, 1789–92*. London: Boydell Press for the Royal Historical Society, 1986.

Nablow, Ralph A. *The Addisonian Tradition in France: Passion and Objectivity in Social Observation*. Rutherford: Fairleigh Dickinson University Press, 1990.

Popkin, Jeremy D. "The Newspaper Press in French Political Thought, 1789–99." *Studies in Eighteenth-Century Culture* 10 (1981): 113–33.

———. *News and Politics in the Age of Revolution: Jean Luzac's Gazette de Leyde*. Ithaca, N.Y.: Cornell University Press, 1989.

Thogmartin, Clyde. *The National Daily Press of France*. Birmingham: Summa, 1998.

Thompson, Victoria. "Splendeurs et misères des journalistes: Female Imagery and the Commercialization of Journalism in July Monarchy France." *Proceedings of the Annual Meeting of the Western Society for French History* 23 (1996): 361–8.

Todd, Christopher. *Political Bias, Censorship and the Dissolution of the "Official" Press in Eighteenth-Century France*. Lewiston, N.Y.: Edward Mellen Press, 1991.

Trinkle, Dennis A. *The Napoleonic Press: The Public Sphere and Oppositionary Journalism*. Lewiston, N.Y.: Edwin Mellen Press, 2002.

Germany

Bond, M. A. "A. L. von Schlözer: A German Political Journalist. Theory and Practice in the Light of the French Revolution." *European Studies Review* 6, no. 1 (1976): 61–72.

Boyer, Dominic. *Spirit and System: Media, Intellectuals, and the Dialectic in Modern German Culture*. Chicago: University of Chicago Press, 2005.

———. "Gender and the Solvency of Professionalism: Eastern German Journalism Before and After 1989." *East European Politics and Societies* 20, no. 1 (2006): 152–79.

Foster, Frances C. "Images of the Press in German Literature In and After 1848." *German Life and Letters* 49, no. 4 (1996): 422–37.

Hardt, Hanno. "Sites of Reality: Constructing Press Photography in Weimar Germany, 1928–1933." *Communication Review* 1, no. 3 (1996): 373–402.

Moran, Daniel. *Toward the Century of Words: Johann Cotta and the Politics of the Public Realm in Germany, 1795–1832*. Berkeley: University of California Press, 1990.

Oppen, Karoline von. *The Role of the Writer and the Press in the Unification of Gemany, 1889–1990*. New York: P. Lang, 2000.

Popkin, Jeremy. "Political Communication in the German Enlightenment: Gottlob Benedikt von Schirach's *Politische Journal*." *Eighteenth-Century Life* 20, no. 1 (1996): 24–41.

Retalleck, James. "From Pariah to Professional? The Journalist in German Society and Politics, from the Late Enlightenment to the Rise of Hitler." *German Studies Review* 16, no. 2 (1993): 175–223.

Sieberg, Heinz-Otto. "The French Revolution as Mirrored in the German Press and in Political Journalism (1789–1801)." *History of European Ideas* 13, no. 5 (1991): 509–24.

Smaldone, William T. "Friedrich Stampfer and the Fall of the Weimar Republic." *Historian* 64, nos. 3–4 (2002): 687–703.

Willnat, Lars. "The East German Press during the Political Transformation of East Germany." *Gazette* 48, no. 3 (1991): 193–208.

Great Britain

Barker, Hannah. *Newspapers, Politics and Public Opinion in Late Eighteenth-Century England*. Oxford: Clarendon Press, 1998.

———. *Newspapers, Politics and English Society 1695–1855*. Oxford: Clarendon Press, 1998.

Black, Jeremy. *The English Press in the Eighteenth-Century*. Philadelphia: University of Pennsylvania Press, 1987.

———. *The English Press 1621–1861*. Sutton: Stroud, Gloucestershire, 2001.

Bourne, Richard. *Lords of Fleet Street: The Harmsworth Dynasty*. London: Unwin Hyman, 1990.

Boyce, George, James Curran, and Pauline Wingate, eds. *Newspaper History from the Seventeenth Century to the Present Day*. London: Constable, 1978.

Brake, Laurel, Aled Jones, and Lionel Madden, eds. *Investigating Victorian Journalism*. London: Macmillan, 1990.

Brown, David. "Compelling but not Controlling? Palmerston and the Press, 1846–1855." *History* 86, no. 281 (2001): 41–61.

Brownless, Nicholas. "Spoken Discourse in Early English Newspapers." *Media History* 11, nos. 1–2 (2005): 69–85.

Connell, Liam. "The Scottishness of the Scottish Press: 1918–1939." *Media, Culture & Society* 25, no. 2 (2003): 187–207.

Cross, Nigel. *The Common Writer: Life in Nineteenth-Century Grub Street*. New York: Cambridge University Press, 1985.

Curran, James, and Jean Seaton. *Power without Responsibility*. London: Routledge, 2003.

Dwyer, John. "The *Caledonian Mercury* and Scottish National Culture, 1763–1801." *Journal of History and Politics* 7 (1989): 147–69.

Ferdinand, C. Y. *Benjamin Collins and the Provincial Newspaper Trade in the Eighteenth Century*. New York: Clarendon Press, 1997.

Hampton, Mark. *Visions of the Press in Britain, 1850–1950*. Urbana: University of Illinois Press, 2004.

Harding, Jason. *The Criterion: Cultural Politics and Periodical Networks in Inter-war Britain*. Oxford: Oxford University Press, 2002.

Harris, Michael. "Timely Notices: The Use of Advertising and Its Relationship to News During the Late Seventeenth Century." *Prose Studies* 21, no. 2 (1998): 141–56.

Harris, Michael, and Alan Lee, eds. *The Press in English Society from the Seventeenth to the Nineteenth Centuries*. Rutherford, N.J.: Fairleigh Dickinson University Press, 1986.

Harris, Robert. *A Patriot Press: National Politics and the London Press in the 1740s*. New York: Oxford University Press, 1993.

Higgins, Michael. "Substantiating a Political Public Sphere in the Scottish Press." *Journalism* 7, no. 1 (2006): 25–44.

Hollingsworth, Mark. *The Press and Political Dissent*. London: Pluto Press, 1986.

Jones, Aled. *Powers of the Press: Newspapers, Power and the Public in Nineteenth-Century England*. Brookfield, Vt.: Scolar, 1996.

Mathison, Hamish. "Tropes of Promotion and Wellbeing: Advertisement and the Eighteenth-Century Scottish Periodical." *Prose Studies* 21, no. 2 (1998): 206–25.

———. "Robert Hepburn and the Edinburgh *Tatler*: A Study in an Early British Periodical." *Media History* 11, nos. 1/2 (2005): 147–61.

Mayne, Alan. *The Imagined Slum: Newspaper Representation in Three Cities, 1870–1914*. New York: Leicester University Press, 1993.

Potter, Simon J. "Communication and Integration: The British and Dominions Press and the British World, c. 1876–1914." *Journal of Imperial and Commonwealth History* 31, no. 2 (2003): 190–206.

Raymond, Joad, ed. *News, Newspapers, and Society in Early Modern Britain*. London: F. Cass, 1999.

Snoddy, Raymond. *The Good, the Bad and the Unacceptable: The Hard News About the British Press*. London: Faber, 1992.

Spector, Robert Donald. *Political Controversy: A Study in Eighteenth-Century Propaganda*. New York: Greenwood Press, 1992.

Startt, James D. *Journalists for Empire: The Imperial Debate in the Edwardian Stately Press, 1903–1913*. New York: Greenwood Press, 1991.

Sutherland, James. *The Restoration Newspaper and Its Development*. New York: Cambridge University Press, 1986.

Taylor, S. J. *The Great Outsiders: Northcliffe, Rothermere, and the Daily Mail*. London: Weidenfeld and Nicholson, 1996.

Wiener, Joel H., ed. *Innovators and Preachers: The Role of the Editor in Victorian England*. Westport, Conn.: Greenwood Press, 1985.

Winkler, K. T. "The Forces of the Market and the London Newspaper in the First Half of the Nineteenth Century." *Journal of Newspaper and Periodical History* 4, no. 2 (1988): 22–35.

Wilson, Keith M. *A Study in the History and Politics of the Morning Post 1905–1926*. Lewiston, N.Y.: Edwin Mellen Press, 1990.

Greece

Daremas, Georgios, and Georgios Terzias. "Televisualization of Politics in Greece." *Gazette* 62, no. 2 (2000): 117–31.

Papathanassopoulos, Stylianos. "Media Commercialization and Journalism in Greece." *European Journal of Communication* 16, no. 4 (2001): 505–21.

Zaharopoulos, T., and E. M. Paraschos. *Mass Media in Greece: Power Politics and Privatization*. Westport, Conn.: Praeger, 1993.

India

Bayly, C. A. *Empire and Information: Intelligence Gathering and Social Communication in India, 1780–1870*. New York: Cambridge University Press, 1996.

Hirschmann, Edwin. "An Editor Speaks for the Natives: Robert Knight in 19th Century India." *Journalism Quarterly* 63, no. 2 (1986): 260–67.

———. "The Hidden Roots of a Great Newspaper: Calcutta's *Statesman*." *Victorian Periodicals Review* 37, no. 2 (2004): 141–60.

Jeffrey, Robin. *India's Newspaper Revolution: Capitalism, Politics and the Indian Language Press*. New York: St. Martin's Press, 2000.

Parthasarthy, Rangaswami. *Journalism in India: From the Earliest Times to the Present Day*. New Delhi: Sterling, 1997.

Peers, Douglas M. "Liberty vs. Authority in a Colonial Society: Freedom of the Press in India During the Revolutionary Period." *Consortium on Revolutionary Europe 1750–1850: Proceedings* 20 (1990): 780–88.

———. "'Those Noble Exemplars of the True Military Tradition': Constructions of the Indian Army in the Mid-Victorian Press." *Modern Asian Studies* 31, no. 1 (1997): 109–42.

Ireland

Delacroix, Jacques, and Glenn R. Carroll. "Organizational Foundings: An Ecological Study of the Newspaper Industries of Argentina and Ireland." *Administrative Science Quarterly* 28, no. 2 (1983): 274–91.

Foley, Michael. "Colonialism and Journalism in Ireland." *Journalism Studies* 5, no. 4 (2004): 373–85.

Horgan, John. *Irish Media: A Critical History Since 1922*. London: Routledge, 2001.

Oram, Hugh. *The Newspaper Book: A History of Newspapers in Ireland, 1649–1983*. Dublin: MO Books, 1983.

Italy

Caprotti, Federico. "Information Management and Fascist Identity: Newsreels in Fascist Italy." *Media History* 11, no. 3 (2005): 177–91.

Mancini, P. "Political Complexity and Alternative Models of Journalism: The Italian Case." 64–78 in James Curran and M. J. Park, eds. *De-Westernizing Media Studies*. London: Routledge, 2000.

Michaelis, Meir. "Mussolini's Unofficial Mouthpiece: Telesio Interlandi, *Il Tevere* and the Evolution of Mussolini's Anti-Semitism." *Journal of Modern Italian Studies* 3, no. 3 (1998): 217–40.

Morris, Penelope. "Giovanna Zangrandi: Negotiating Fascism." *Italian Studies* 53 (1998): 94–121.

Porter, William E. *The Italian Journalist*. Ann Arbor: University of Michigan Press, 1983.

Japan

Altman, Albert A. "The Press and Social Cohesion during a Period of Change: The Case of Early Meiji Japan." *Modern Asian Studies* 15, no. 4 (1981): 865–76.

Cooper-Chen, Anne. *Mass Communication in Japan*. Ames: Iowa State University Press, 1997.

De Lange, William. *A History of Japanese Journalism: Japan's Press Clubs as the Last Obstacle to a Mature Press*. Richmond, Surrey: Japan Library, 1998.

Feldman, Ofer. *Politics and the News Media in Japan*. Ann Arbor: University of Michigan Press, 1993.

Groemer, Gerald. "Singing the News: Yomiuri in Japan During the Edo and Meiji Periods." *Harvard Journal of Asiatic Studies* 54, no. 1 (1994): 233–61.

Haruhara, Akihiko. "English-language Newspapers in Japan." *Japan Quarterly* 41, no. 4 (1994): 474–84.

Hirose, Hidehiko. "The Development of Discussions on Journalism in Postwar Japan." *Media Culture & Society* 12 (1990): 465–76.

Hoare, J. E. "The 'Bankoku Shimbun' Affair: Foreigners, the Japanese Press and Extraterritoriality in Early Meiji Japan." *Modern Asian Studies* 9, no. 3 (1975): 289–302.

Huffman, James L. *Creating a Public: People and Press in Meiji Japan.* Honolulu: University of Hawai'i Press, 1997.

Kakegawa, Tomiko, and A. M. Cohen. "The *Japan Chronicle* and Its Editors: Reflecting Japan to the Press and the People, 1891–1940." *Japan Forum* 13, no. 1 (2001): 27–40.

Kasza, Gregory J. *The State and the Mass Media in Japan, 1918–1945.* Berkeley: University of California Press, 1988.

Kim, Young C. *Japanese Journalists and Their World.* Charlottesville: University Press of Virginia, 1981.

Krauss, Ellis S. "Changing Television News in Japan." *Journal of Asian Studies* 57, no. 3 (1998): 663–92.

Lee, Jung Bock. *The Political Character of the Japanese Press.* Seoul: Seoul National University Press, 1985.

Miller, J. Scott. "Japanese Shorthand and Sokkibon." *Monumenta Nipponica* 49, no. 4 (Winter 1994): 476.

Oblas, P. B. "On Japan and the Sovereign Ghost-State: Hugh Byas, Journalist-Expert, and the Manchurian Incident." *Journalism History* 29, no. 1 (2003): 32–42.

O'Connor, Peter. "Endgame: The English-language Press Networks of East Asia in the Run-up to War, 1936–1941." *Japan Forum* 13, no. 1 (2001): 63–76.

Yamamoto, Taketoshi. "The Press Clubs of Japan." *Journal of Japanese Studies* 15, no. 2 (1989): 371–88.

Latin America

Britton, John A. *Carleton Beals: A Radical Journalist in Latin America.* Albuquerque: University of New Mexico Press, 1987.

Buckman, Robert. "Cultural Agenda of Latin American Newspapers and Magazines: Is U.S. Domination a Myth?" *Latin American Research Review* 25, no. 2 (1990): 134–55.

Cole, Richard R. *Communication in Latin America: Journalism, Mass Media, and Society.* Wilmington, Del.: Scholarly Resources, 1996.

González, Aníbal. *Journalism and the Development of Spanish American Narrative.* Cambridge: Cambridge University Press, 1993.

Knudson, Jerry W. "Veil of Silence: The Argentine Press and the Dirty War, 1976–1983." *Latin American Perspectives* 24, no. 6 (1997): 93–112.

Kodrich, Kris. *Tradition and Change in the Nicaraguan Press: Newspapers and Journalists in a New Democratic Era.* Lanham, Md.: University Press of America, 2002.

Lawson, Chappell H. *Building the Fourth Estate: Democratization and the Rise of a Free Press in Mexico.* Berkeley: University of California Press, 2002.

Leiken, Robert S. *Why Nicaragua Vanished: A Story of Reporters and Revolutionaries*. Lanham, Md.: Rowman & Littlefield, 2003.

Salwen, Michael B. *Radio and Television in Cuba: The Pre-Castro Era*. Ames: Iowa State University Press, 1994.

Salwen, Michael B. and Bruce Garrison. *Latin American Journalism*. Hillsdale, N.J.: Lawrence Erlbaum Associates, 1991.

Uribe-Uran, Victor M. "The Birth of a Public Sphere in Latin America During the Age of Revolutions." *Comparative Studies in Society and History* 42, no. 2 (2000): 425–57.

Waisbord, Silvio R. *Watchdog Journalism in South America: News, Accountability, and Democracy*. New York: Columbia University Press, 2000.

Zamora, Lois Parkinson. "Novels and Newspapers in the Americas." *NOVEL: A Forum on Fiction* 23, no. 1 (1989): 44–62.

Middle East

Frenkel, Erwin. *The Press and Politics in Israel: The Jerusalem Post from 1932 to the Present*. Westport, Conn.: Greenwod Press, 1994.

Mellor, Noha. *The Making of Arab News*. Lanham, Md.: Rowman & Littlefield, 2005.

Meyers, Oren. "Israeli Journalism During the State's Formative Era: Between Ideological Affiliation and Professional Consciousness." *Journalism History* 31, no. 2 (2005): 88–97.

Shahidi, Hossein. "From Mission to Profession: Journalism in Iran, 1979–2004." *Iranian Studies* 39, no. 1 (2006): 1–28.

Sowerwine, James. "The Turkish Press and Its Impact on Foreign Policy, 1961–1980." *Journal of South Asian and Middle Eastern Studies* 23, no. 4 (2000): 37–61.

Netherlands

Deuze, Mark. *Journalists in the Netherlands: An Analysis of the People, the Issues and the (Inter-)national Environment*. Amsterdam: Aksant, 2002.

New Zealand

Byrne, Jeh. "The Comparative Development of Newspapers in New Zealand and the United States in the Nineteenth Century." *American Studies International* 37, no. 1 (1999): 55–70.

Day, Patrick. *The Making of the New Zealand Press: A Study of the Organizational and Political Concerns of New Zealand Newspaper Controllers*. Wellington: Victoria University Press, 1990.

Harvey, Ross. "Bringing the News to New Zealand: The Supply and Control of Overseas News in the Nineteenth Century." *Media History* 8, no. 1 (2002): 21–34.

Philippines

Roces, Mina. "Filipino Identity in Fiction, 1945–1972." *Modern Asian Studies* 28, no. 2 (1994): 279–315.
Rosario-Braid, Florangel, and Ramon R. Tuazon. "Communication Media in the Philippines: 1521–1986." *Philippine Studies* 47, no. 3 (1999): 291–318.
Sussman, Gerald. "Politics and the Press: The Philippines Since Marcos." *Philippine Studies* 36, no. 4 (1988): 494–505.
Youngblood, Robert L. "Government-Media Relations in the Philippines." *Asian Survey* 21, no. 7 (1981): 710–28.

Portugal

Agee, Warren Kendall. *A Frustrated Fourth Estate: Portugal's Post-Revolutionary Mass Media.* Columbia: University of South Carolina, 1984.

Russia/Soviet Union

Balmuth, Daniel. *The Russian Bulletin, 1863–1917: A Liberal Voice in Tsarist Russia.* New York: Peter Lang, 2000.
Blium, Arlen Viktorovich. "Forbidden Topics: Early Soviet Censorship Directives." *Book History* 1, no. 1 (1998): 268–82.
Brooks, Jeffrey. *Thank You, Comrade Stalin! Soviet Public Culture from Revolution to Cold War.* Princeton, N.J.: Princeton University Press, 1999.
Ekecrantz, Jan, and Kerstin Olofsson, eds. *Russian Reports: Studies in Post-Communist Transformation of Media Journalism.* Stockholm: Almqvist and Wiksell International, 2002.
Jones, Adam. "The Russian Press in the Post-Soviet Era: A Case Study of *Izvestia.*" *Journalism Studies* 3, no. 3 (2002): 359–75.
Kenez, Peter. *The Birth of the Propaganda State: Soviet Methods of Mass Mobilization, 1917–29.* Cambridge: Cambridge University Press, 1985.
Leone, Matthew. *Closer to the Masses: Stalinist Culture, Social Revolution, and Soviet Newspapers.* Cambridge, Mass.: Harvard University Press, 2004.
McNair, Brian. *Glasnost, Perestroika, and the Soviet Media.* London: Routledge, 1991.
McReynolds, Louise. "Autocratic Journalism: The Case of the St. Petersburg Telegraph Agency." *Slavic Review* 49, no. 1 (1990): 48–57.

——. *The News Under Russia's Old Regime: The Development of a Mass-Circulation Press*. Princeton, N.J.: Princeton University Press, 1991.

——. "The Russian Intelligentsia in the Public Sphere: The Mass-Circulation Press and Political Culture, 1860–1917." *Communication Review* 1, no. 1 (1995): 83–100.

Mueller, Julie Kay. "Soviet Journalists: Cadres or Professionals?" *Russian History* 23, nos. 1–4 (1996): 277–93.

——. "Staffing Newspapers and Training Journalists in Early Soviet Russia." *Journal of Social History* 31, no. 4 (Summer 1998): 851–73.

Neuberger, Joan. "Stories of the Street: Hooliganism in the St. Petersburg Popular Press." *Slavic Review* 48, no. 2 (1989): 177–94.

Norton, Barbara T., and Jehanne M. Gheith, eds. *An Improper Profession: Women, Gender, and Journalism in Late Imperial Russia*. Durham, N.C.: Duke Univerity Press, 2001.

Rosenkrans, Ginger. "Evolution of Russian Newspapers from Perestroika to 1998." *Journal of Government Information* 28, no. 5 (2001): 549–60.

Ruud, Charles A. "The Printing Press as an Agent of Political Change in Early Twentieth-Century Russia." *Russian Review* 40, no. 4 (1981): 378–95.

Wedgwood Benn, David. "The Russian Media in Post-Soviet Conditions." *Europe-Asia Studies* 48, no. 3 (1996): 471–9.

Scandinavia

Esaisson, Peter. "120 Years of Swedish Election Campaigns: A Story of the Rise and Decline of Political Parties and the Emergence of the Mass Media as Power Brokers." *Scandinavian Political Studies* 14, no. 3 (1991): 261–78.

Laursen, John Christian. "Censorship in the Nordic Countries, ca. 1750–1890: Transformation in Law, Theory, and Practice." *Journal of Modern European History* 3, no. 1 (2005): 100–17.

Ney, Birgitta. "The Woman Reporter Goes Street Haunting: On the Work of Women Reporters in the Swedish Daily Press 1900–1910." *Media History* 7, no. 1 (2001): 41–6.

United States

Alexander, John K. *The Selling of the Constitutional Convention: A History of News Coverage*. Madison, Wis.: Madison House, 1990.

Altschull, J. Herbert. *From Milton to McLuhan: The Ideas Behind American Journalism*. New York: Longman, 1990.

Benjaminson, Peter. *Death in the Afternoon: America's Newspaper Giants Struggle for Survival*. Kansas City, Mo.: Andrews, McMeel, and Parker, 1984.

Baldasty, Gerald J. *The Commercialization of the News in the Nineteenth Century*. Madison: University of Wisconsin Press, 1992.

Brown, Joshua. *Beyond the Lines: Pictorial Reporting, Everyday Life, and the Crisis of Gilded Age America*. Berkeley: University of California Press, 2002.

Brown, Walt. *John Adams and the American Press: Politics & Journalism at the Birth of the Republic*. Jefferson, N.C.: McFarland, 1995.

Clark, Charles E. *The Public Prints: The Newspaper in Anglo-American Culture, 1665–1740*. New York: Oxford University Press, 1994.

Copeland, David. *Colonial American Newspapers: Character and Content*. Newark: University of Delaware Press, 1997.

———. *Debating the Issues in Colonial Newspapers*. Westport, Conn.: Greenwood Press, 2000.

Dicken-Garcia, Hazel. *Journalistic Standards in Nineteenth-Century America*. Madison: University of Wisconsin Press, 1989.

Dillon, Michael. "'Satanic Journalism and Its Fate': The Scripps Chain Strikes Out in Buffalo." *American Journalism* 20, no. 2 (2003): 57–82.

Evenson, Bruce J. *When Dempsey Fought Tunney: Heroes, Hokum, and Storytelling in the Jazz Age*. Knoxville: University of Tennessee Press, 1996.

———. "'Saucepan Journalism' in an Age of Indifference: Moody, Beecher, and Brooklyn's Gilded Press." *Journalism History* 27, no. 4 (2001/2002): 165–77.

Foerstel, Herbert N. *From Watergate to Monicagate: Ten Controversies in Modern Journalism and Media*. Westport, Conn.: Greenwood Press, 2001.

Ghiglione, Loren. *The American Journalist: Paradox of the Press*. Washington, D.C.: Library of Congress, 1990.

Heald, Morrell. *Transatlantic Vistas: American Journalists in Europe, 1900–1940*. Kent, Ohio: Kent State University Press, 1988.

Humphrey, Carol Sue. *The Press of the Young Republic, 1783–1833*. Westport, Conn.: Greenwood Press, 1996.

Jackaway, Gwenyth L. *Media at War: Radio's Challenge to Newspapers, 1924–1939*. Westport, Conn.: Praeger, 1995.

Kaplan, Richard. "The Economics of Popular Journalism in the Gilded Age: The Detroit *Evening News* in 1873–1888." *Journalism History* 21 (1995): 65–78.

Kielbowicz, Richard B. *News in the Mail: The Press, the Post Office & Public Information, 1700–1860s*. New York: Greenwood Press, 1989.

Lawson, Linda. *Truth in Publishing: Federal Regulation of the Press's Business Practices, 1880–1912*. Carbondale: Southern Illinois University Press, 1993.

Nerone, John. *Violence Against the Press: Policing the Public Sphere in U.S. History*. New York: Oxford University Press, 1994.

Nerone, John, and Kevin G. Barnhurst. "U.S. Newspaper Types, the Newsroom, and the Division of Labor, 1750–2000." *Journalism Studies* 4, no. 4 (2003): 435–49.

Nord, David Paul. "The Evangelical Origins of Mass Media in America, 1815–1835." *Journalism Monographs* no. 88 (1984): 30.

———. *Communities of Journalism: A History of American Newspapers and Their Readers.* Urbana: University of Illinois Press, 2001.

Olasky, Marvin N. *Central Ideas in the Development of American Journalism: A Narrative History.* Hillsdale, N.J.: Lawrence Erlbaum Associates, 1991.

Osthaus, Carl R. 1994. *Partisans of the Southern Press: Editorial Spokesmen of the Nineteenth Century.* Lexington: University Press of Kentucky, 1994.

Pasley, Jeffrey L. *"The Tyranny of Printers": Newspaper Politics in the Early American Republic.* Charlottesville: University Press of Virginia, 2001.

Ritchie, Donald A. *American Journalists: Getting the Story.* New York: Oxford University Press, 1997.

Rutenbeck, Jeff. "The Triumph of News over Ideas in American Journalism: The Trade Journal Debate, 1872–1915." *Journal of Communication Inquiry* 18 (1994): 63–79.

Schiller, Dan. *Objectivity and the News: The Public and the Rise of Commercial Journalism.* Philadelphia: University of Pennsylvania Press, 1981.

Schudson, Michael. *Discovering the News: A Social History of American Newspapers.* New York: Basic Books, 1978.

Sloan, Wm. David, and Julie Hedgepeth Williams. *The Early American Press, 1690–1783.* Westport, Conn.: Greenwood Press, 1994.

Smythe, Ted Curtis. *The Gilded Age Press, 1865–1900.* Westport, Conn.: Praeger, 2003.

Stevens, John D. *Sensationalism and the New York Press.* New York: Columbia University Press, 1991.

Tucher, Andie. *Froth & Scum: Truth, Beauty, Goodness, and the Ax Murder in America's First Mass Medium.* Chapel Hill: University of North Carolina Press, 1994.

Tunstall, Jeremy. *The Media Were American: U.S. Media in Decline.* New York: Oxford University Press, 2007.

Turner, Hy B. *When Giants Ruled: The Story of Park Row, New York's Great Newspaper Street.* New York: Fordham University Press, 1999.

Walach, Glenn. "'A Depraved Taste for Publicity': The Press and Private Life in the Gilded Age." *American Studies* 39 (1998): 31–57.

Ward, Hiley H. *Mainstreams of American Media History: A Narrative and Intellectual History.* Boston, Mass.: Allyn and Bacon, 1997.

Weaver, David H., and G. Cleveland Wilhoit. *The American Journalist: A Portrait of U.S. News People and Their Work.* Bloomington: Indiana University Press, 1991.

———. *The American Journalist in the 1990s: U.S. News People at the End of an Era*. Mahwah, N.J.: Lawrence Erlbaum Associates, 1996.

Williams, Julie Hedgepeth. *The Significance of the Printed Word in Early America: Colonists' Thoughts on the Role of the Press*. Westport, Conn.: Greenwood Press, 1999.

SPECIFIC TOPICS

Advertising

DeLorme, Denise E., and Fred Fedler. "An Historical Analysis of Journalists' Attitudes toward Advertisers and Advertising's Influence." *American Journalism* 22, no. 2 (2005): 7–40.

Shaw, Steven J. "Colonial Newspaper Advertising: A Step toward Freedom of the Press." *Business History Review* 33, no. 3 (Autumn 1959): 409–20.

Advice Columns

Barnard, Rita. "The Storyteller, the Novelist, and the Advice Columnist: Narrative and Mass Culture in *Miss Lonelyhearts*." *NOVEL: A Forum on Fiction* 27, no. 1 (Autumn 1993): 40–61.

Hendley, W. Clark. "Dear Abbey, Miss Lonelyhearts, and the Eighteenth Century: The Origins of the Newspaper Advice Column." *Journal of Popular Culture* 11, no. 2 (1977): 345–52.

McKinstry, John A., and Asako Nakajima McKinstry. *Jinsei Annai: "Life's Guide" Glimpses of Japan Through a Popular Advice Column*. New York: M. E. Sharpe, 1991.

Shissler, Ada Holland. "'If You Ask Me': Sabiha Sertel's Advice Column, Gender Equity, and Social Engineering in the Early Turkish Republic." *Journal of Middle East Women's Studies* 3, no. 2 (Spring 2007): 1–30.

African American Journalism

Broussard, Jinx Coleman, and John Maxwell Hamilton. "Covering a Two-Front War: Three African American Correspondents During World War II." *American Journalism* 22, no. 3 (2005): 33–54.

Hutton, Frankie. *The Early Black Press in America, 1827 to 1860*. Westport, Conn.: Greenwood, 1993.

Rhodes, Jane. *Mary Ann Shadd Cary: The Black Press and Protest in the Nineteenth Century*. Bloomington: Indiana University Press, 1998.

Streitmatter, Rodger. *Raising Her Voice: African-American Women Journalists Who Changed History*. Lexington: University Press of Kentucky, 1994.

Washburn, Patrick S. *A Question of Sedition: The Federal Government's Investigation of the Black Press During World War II*. New York: Oxford University Press, 1986.

Wilson, Clint C., II. *Black Journalists in Paradox: Historical Perspectives and Current Dilemmas*. New York: Greenwood, 1991.

Wolseley, Roland. *The Black Press, U.S.A.* 2nd ed., Ames: Iowa State University Press, 1990.

Agenda-Setting

Davie, William R., and T. Michael Maher. "Maxwell McCombs: Agenda-setting Explorer." *Journal of Broadcasting and Electronic Media* 50, no. 2 (June 2006): 358–64.

McCombs, Maxwell. "A Look at Agenda-setting: Past, Present and Future." *Journalism Studies* 6, no. 4 (November 2005): 543–57.

Agricultural Journalism

Fry, John J. *The Farm Press, Reform, and Rural Change, 1895–1920*. New York: Routledge, 2005.

Pawlick, Thomas. *The Invisible Farm: The Worldwide Decline of Farm News and Agricultural Journalism Training*. Chicago, Ill.: Burnham, 2001.

Alternative Journalism

Kessler, Lauren. *The Dissident Press: Alternative Journalism in American History*. Beverly Hills, Calif.: Sage, 1984.

Streitmatter, Rodger. *Unspeakable: The Rise of the Gay and Lesbian Press*. Boston, Mass.: Faber and Faber, 1995.

American Revolution

Bailyn, Bernard, and John B. Hench, eds. *The Press and the American Revolution*. Worcester, Mass.: American Antiquarian Society, 1980.

Humphrey, Carol Sue. *"This Popular Engine": New England Newspapers During the American Revolution, 1775–1789*. Newark: University of Delaware Press, 1992.

Larkin, Edward. "Inventing an American Public: Thomas Paine, the *Pennsylvania Magazine*, and American Revolutionary Discourse." *Early American Literature* 33, no. 3 (1998): 250–76.
Leonard, Thomas C. "News for a Revolution: The Exposé in America, 1768–1773." *Journal of American History* 67, no. 1 (1980): 26–40.

Anonymity

Artese, B. "'Speech Was of No Use': Conrad, a New Journalism, and the Critical Abjection of Testimony." *Novel* 36, no. 2 (Spring 2003): 176–97.
Liddle, Dallas. "Salesmen, Sportsmen, Mentors: Anonymity and Mid-Victorian Theories of Journalism." *Victorian Studies* 41, no. 1 (1997): 31–68.

Associations, Institutes, Societies, Unions

Cryle, Denis. "The Empire Press Union and Antipodean Communications: Australian-New Zealand Involvement 1909–1950." *Media History* 8, no. 1 (2002): 49–62.
———. "A British Legacy? The Empire Press Union and Freedom of the Press, 1940–1950." *History of Intellectual Culture* 4, no. 1 (2004).
Hampton, Mark. "Journalists and the 'Professional Ideal' in Britain: The Institute of Journalists, 1884–1907." *Historical Research* 72, no. 178 (1999): 183–201.
Loenz, Alfred Lawrence. "The Whitechapel Club: Defining Chicago's Newspapermen in the 1890s." *American Journalism* 15, no. 1 (1998): 83–102.
Mytton-Davies, Cynric. *Journalist Alone: The Story of the Freelance and the Freelance Section of the Institute of Journalists.* London: Institute of Journalists, 1968.
Pratte, Paul Alfred. *Gods Within the Machine: A History of the American Society of Newspaper Editors, 1923–1993.* Westport, Conn.: Praeger, 1995.

Atomic Bomb

Asada, Sadao. "The Mushroom Cloud and National Psyches: Japanese and American Perceptions of the A-Bomb Decision, 1945–1995." *Journal of American-East Asian Relations* 4, no. 2 (1995): 95–116.
Mohan, Uday, and Sanho Tree. "Hiroshima, the American Media, and the Construction of Conventional Wisdom." *Journal of American-East Asian Relations* 4, no. 2 (1995): 141–60.

Torney-Parlicki, Prue. "'Whatever the Thing May Be Called': The Australian News Media and the Atomic Bombing of Hiroshima and Nagasaki." *Australian Historical Studies* 31, no. 114 (2000): 49–66.
Washburn, Patrick. "The Office of Censorship's Attempt to Control Press Coverage of the Atomic Bomb During World War II." *Journalism Monographs* no. 120 (1990): 1–43.

Bias and Distortion

Alterman, Eric. *What Liberal Media? The Truth About Bias and the News.* New York: Basic Books, 2003.
Cohen, Jeff, and Norman Solomon. *Through the Media Looking Glass: Decoding Bias and Blather in the News.* Monroe, Me.: Common Courage Press, 1995.
Goldberg, Bernard. *Bias: A CBS Insider Exposes How the Media Distort the News.* Washington, D.C.: Regnery, 2001.
Kuypers, Jim A. *Press Bias and Politics: How the Media Frame Controversial Issues.* Westport, Conn.: Praeger, 2002.
Miljan, Lydia A., and Barry Cooper. *Hidden Agendas: How Journalists Influence the News.* Vancouver: University of British Columbia Press, 2003.
Olasky, Marvin N. *Prodigal Press: The Anti-Christian Bias of the American News Media.* Westchester, Ill.: Crossway Books, 1988.
Shoemaker, Pamela J. *Gatekeeping.* Newbury Park, Calif.: Sage, 1991.
Weaver, Paul H. *News and the Culture of Lying.* New York: Free Press, 1994.

Blogs

Barlow, Aaron. *Blogging America: The New Public Sphere.* Westport, Conn.: Praeger, 2008.
Cooper, Stephen D. *Watching the Watchdog: Bloggers as the Fifth Estate.* Spokane, Wash.: Marquette Books, 2006.
Hewitt, Hugh. *Blog: Understanding the Information Revolution That's Changing Your World.* Nashville, Tenn.: Nelson Books, 2005.
Kline, David, and Dan Burstein. *Blog! How the Newest Media Revolution is Changing Politics, Business, and Culture.* New York: CDS Books, 2005.
Perlmutter, David D. *Blogwars.* Oxford: Oxford University Press, 2008.
Rodzvilla, John, ed. *We've Got Blog: How Weblogs Are Changing Our Culture.* New York: Basic Books, 2002.
Tremayne, Mark. *Blogging, Citizenship, and the Future of Media.* London: Routledge, 2007.

Broadcast Journalism

Bliss, Edward. *Now the News: The Story of Broadcast Journalism*. New York: Columbia University Press, 1991.

Blum, David. *Tick . . . Tick . . . Tick: The Long Life and Turbulent Times of 60 Minutes*. New York: HarperCollins, 2004.

Boyer, Peter J. *Who Killed CBS? The Undoing of America's Number One News Network*. New York: St. Martin's Press, 1989.

Crook, Tim. *International Radio Journalism: History, Theory, and Practice*. London: Routledge, 1998.

Curtin, Michael. *Redeeming the Wasteland: Television Documentary and Cold War Politics*. New Brunswick, N.J.: Rutgers University Press, 1995.

Edwards, Bob. *Edward R. Murrow and the Birth of Broadcast Journalism*. Hoboken, N.J.: Wiley, 2004.

Franklin, Bob. *Newszak and News Media*. London: Arnold, 1997.

Hilmes, Michelle. *Radio Voices: American Broadcasting, 1922–1952*. Twin Cities: University of Minnesota Press, 1997.

Jackaway, Gwenyth L. *Media at War: Radio's Challenge to the Newspapers, 1924–1939*. Westport, Conn.: Praeger, 1995.

Murray, Michael D. *The Political Performers: CBS Broadcasts in the Public Interest*. Westport, Conn.: Praeger, 1994.

Nash, Knowlton. *Prime Time at Ten: Behind-the-camera Battles of Canadian TV Journalism*. Toronto, Ont.: McClelland and Stewart, 1987.

Reuven, Frank. *Out of Thin Air: The Brief Wonderful Life of Network News*. New York: Simon & Schuster, 1991.

Rosteck, Thomas. *See It Now Confronts McCarthyism*. Tuscaloosa: University of Alabama Press, 1994.

Turner, Graeme. *Ending the Affair: The Decline of Television Current Affairs in Australia*. Sydney: University of New South Wales Press, 2005.

Wallis, Roger. *The Known World of Broadcast News: International News and Electronic Media*. London: Routledge, 1990.

Business Journalism

McCusker, John J. *The Beginnings of Commercial and Financial Journalism: The Commodity Price Currents, Exchange Rate Currents, and Money Currents of Early Modern Europe*. Amsterdam: NEHA, 1991.

———. "The Demise of Distance: The Business Press and the Origins of the Information Revolution in the Early Modern Atlantic World." *American Historical Review* 110, no. 2 (2005): 295–321.

Parsons, D. W. *The Power of the Financial Press: Journalism and Economic Opinion in Britain and America*. Aldershot, England: E. Elgar, 1989.

Pines, Burton Yale, and Timothy Lamar. *Out of Focus: Network Television and the American Economy*. Washington, D.C.: Regnery, 1994.

Poovey, Mary. "Writing about Finance in Victorian England: Disclosure and Secrecy in the Culture of Investment." *Victorian Studies* 45, no. 1 (2002): 17–41.

Porter, Dilwyn. "City Editors and the Modern Investing Public: Establishing the Integrity of the New Financial Journalism in Late Nineteenth-Century London." *Media History* 4, no. 1 (1998): 49–60.

Reilly, Kevin S. "Dilettantes at the Gate: *Fortune* Magazine and the Cultural Politics of Business Journalism in the 1930s." *Business and Economic History* 28, no. 2 (1999): 213–22.

Steeples, Douglas W. *Advocate for American Enterprise: William Buck Dana and the Commercial and Financial Chronicle, 1865–1910*. Westport, Conn.: Greenwood Press, 2002.

Vissink, H. G. A. *Economic and Financial Reporting in England and the Netherlands: A Comparative Study over the Period 1850 to 1914*. Assen/Maastricht, Netherlands: Van Gorcum, 1985.

Yarrow, Andrew L. "The Big Postwar Story: Abundance and the Rise of Economic Journalism." *Journalism History* 32, no. 2 (2006): 58–76.

Caricature, Cartoons

Alba, Victor. "The Mexican Revolution and the Cartoon," *Comparative Studies in Society and History* 9, no. 1 (1967): 121–36.

Barrett, Ross. "On Forgetting: Thomas Nast, the Middle Class, and the Visual Culture of the Draft Riots." *Prospects* 29 (2004): 25–55.

Coupe, W. A. "The German Cartoon and the Revolution of 1848." *Comparative Studies in Society and History* 9, no. 2 (1967): 137–67.

Donald, Diana. *The Age of Caricature: Satirical Prints in the Reign of George III*. New Haven, Conn.: Yale University Press, 1996.

Douglas, Roy. *The World War, 1939–1945: The Cartoonists' Vision*. New York: Routledge, 1990.

Goldstein, Robert Justin. *Censorship of Political Caricature in Nineteenth-Century France*. Kent, Ohio: Ohio State University Press, 1989.

Kunzle, David. "Between Broadsheet Caricature and *Punch*: Cheap Newspaper Cuts for the Lower Classes in the 1830s." *Art Journal* 43, no. 4 (1983): 339–46.

McCauley, Anne. "Caricature and Photography in the Second Paris Empire." *Art Journal* 43, no. 4 (1983): 355–60.

Smith, Kirsten M., ed. *The Lines Are Drawn: Political Cartoons of the Civil War*. Athens, Ga.: Hill Street Press, 1999.

Censorship

Clegg, Cyndia. *Press Censorship in Elizabethan England*. Cambridge: Cambridge University Press, 1997.

———. *Press Censorship in Jacobean England*. Cambridge: Cambridge Univesity Press, 2001.

Curry, Jane Leftwich, ed. and trans. *The Black Book of Polish Censorship*. New York: Random House, 1984.

Goldstein, Robert Justin. *Political Censorship of the Arts and the Press in Nineteenth-Century France*. New York: St. Martin's Press, 1989.

———. *Censorship of Political Caricature in Nineteenth-Century France*. Kent, Ohio: Kent State University Press, 1989.

Lambert, Sheila. "State Control of the Press in Theory and Practice: The Role of the Stationers' Company before 1640." In R. Myers and M. Harris, eds., *Censorship and Control of Print in England and France, 1600–1900*. Winchester, U.K.: St. Paul's Bibliographies, 1992.

McElligott, Jason. "'A Couple of Hundred Small Squabbling Tradesmen'? Censorship, the Stationers' Company, and the State in Early Modern England." *Media History* 11, nos. 1/2 (2005): 87–104.

Morris, Wayne. "Stalin's Famine and the American Journalists." *Continuity* 18 (1994): 69–78.

Mostyn, Trevor. *Censorship in Islamic Societies*. London: Saqi Books, 2002.

Myers, Robin, and Michael Harris, eds. *Censorship and the Control of Print in England and France (1600–1910)*. Winchester, U.K.: St. Paul's Bibliographies, 1992.

Popkin, Jeremy. "International Gazettes and Politics of Europe in the Revolutionary Period." *Journalism Quarterly* 62, no. 3 (1985): 482–8.

Siebert, Fred S. *Freedom of the Press in England, 1476–1776*. Urbana: University of Illinois Press, 1952.

Sweeney, Michael S. *Secrets of Victory: The Office of Censorship and the American Press and Radio in World War II*. Chapel Hill: University of North Carolina Press, 2001.

Tolbert, Jane T. "Censorship and Retraction: Théophraste Renaudot's *Gazette* and the Galileo Affair, 1631–33." *Journalism History* 31, no. 2 (Summer 2005): 98–105.

Central Intelligence Agency (CIA)

Chamorro, Edgar. "Packaging the Contras: A Case of CIA Disinformation." *Radical America* 21, nos. 2–3 (1987): 72–9.

Dee, Juliet. "Legal Confrontations between Press, Ex-CIA Agents and the Government." *Journalism Quarterly* 66, no. 2 (1989): 418–26.

Johnson, Loch. "The CIA and the Media." *Intelligence and National Security* 1, no. 2 (1986): 143–69.

Columnists

Barbas, Samantha. *The First Lady of Hollywood: A Biography of Louella Parsons*. Berkeley: University of California Press, 2005.

Gordon, Lynn D. "Why Dorothy Thompson Lost Her Job: Political Columnists and the Press Wars of the 1930s and 1940s." *History of Education Quarterly* 34, no. 3 (1994): 281–303.

Riley, Sam G. *The American Newspaper Columnist*. Westport, Conn.: Praeger, 1998.

Stacks, John F. *Scotty: James B. Reston and the Rise and Fall of American Journalism*. Boston, Mass.: Little, Brown, 2003.

Weiner, Richard. "The Doctors: An Historical Overview of Syndicated Columnists, from Dr. William Brady to Dr. George Crane." *American Journalism* 14, nos. 3–4 (1997): 530–38.

Committee on Public Information (CPI)

Vaughn, Stephen. *Holding Fast the Inner Lines: Democracy, Nationalism, and the Committee on Public Information*. Chapel Hill: University of North Carolina Press, 1979.

Coverage, General Topics

Adelman, Richard C., and Lois M. Verbrugge. "Death Makes News: The Social Impact of Disease on Newspaper Coverage." *Journal of Health and Social Behavior* 41, no. 3 (2000): 347–67.

Alali, A. Odasuo, and Kelvin Eke Kenoye, eds. *Media Coverage of Terrorism: Methods of Diffusion*. Newbury Park, Calif.: Sage, 1991.

Cohen, Akiba A., Hanna Adoni, and Charles R. Bantz. *Social Conflict and Television News*. Newbury Park, Calif.: Sage, 1990.

Davies, Owen. "Newspapers and the Popular Belief in Witchcraft and Magic in the Modern Period." *Journal of British Studies* 37, no. 2 (1998): 139–65.

Gilboa, Eytan. *Media and Conflict: Framing Issues, Making Policy, Shaping Opinions*. Ardsley, N.Y.: Transnational Publishers, 2002.

Leckie, Barbara. *Culture and Adultery: The Novel, the Newspaper, and the Law, 1857–1914*. Philadelphia: University of Pennsylvania Press, 1999.

MacDonald, Michael. "Suicide and the Rise of the Popular Press in England." *Representations* no. 22 (1988): 36–55.

Neuzil, Mark, and William Kovarik. *Mass Media and Environmental Conflict: America's Green Crusades.* Beverly Hills, Calif.: Sage, 1996.

Savage, Gail. "Erotic Stories and Public Decency: Newspaper Reporting of Divorce Proceedings in England." *Historical Journal* 41, no. 2 (1998): 511–28.

Simon, Rita J., and Susan H. Alexander. *The Ambivalent Welcome: Print Media, Public Opinion and Immigration.* Westport, Conn.: Praeger, 1993.

Small, Melvin. *Covering Dissent.* New Brunswick, N.J.: Rutgers University Press, 1994.

Wallace, James. *Liberal Journalism and American Education, 1914–1941.* New Brunswick, N.J.: Rutgers University Press, 1991.

Weston, Mary Ann. *Native Americans in the News: Images of Indians in the Twentieth Century.* Westport, Conn.: Greenwood Press, 1996.

Coverage, Specific Events

Bredin, Jean-Denis. *The Affair: The Case of Alfred Dreyfus.* New York: George Braziller, 1986.

Goren, Dina. "Communication Intelligence and the Freedom of the Press: The *Chicago Tribune*'s Battle of Midway Dispatch and the Breaking of the Japanese Naval Code." *Journal of Contemporary History* 16, no. 4 (1981): 663–90.

Hardt, Hanno. "Reading the Russian Revolution: International Communication Research and the Journalism of Lippmann and Merz." *Mass Communication & Society* 5, no. 1 (2002): 25–39.

Kane, Daniel. "Each of Us in His Own Way: Factors Behind Conflicting Accounts of the Massacre at Port Arthur." *Journalism History* 3, no. 1 (2005): 23–33.

Leff, Laurel L. "A Tragic 'Fight in the Family': *The New York Times*, Reform Judaism, and the Holocaust." *American Jewish History* 88, no. 1 (2000): 3–51.

———. "On the Inside Pages: The Holocaust in the *New York Times*, 1939–1945." *Harvard International Journal of Press/Politics* 5, no. 2 (2000): 52–72.

Zelizer, Barbie. *Covering the Body: The Kennedy Assassination, the Media, and the Shaping of Collective Memory.* Chicago: University of Chicago Press, 1992.

———. *Remembering to Forget: Holocaust Memory Through the Camera's Eye.* Chicago: University of Chicago Press, 1998.

Crimes and Trials, Coverage of

Anthony, David. "The Helen Jewett Panic: Tabloids, Men, and the Sensational Public Sphere in Antebellum New York." *American Literature* 69, no. 3 (1997): 487–514.

Chiasson, Lloyd, Jr., ed. *The Press on Trial: Crimes and Trials as Media Events.* Westport, Conn.: Greenwood Press, 1997.

Ericson, Richard V., Patricia M. Naranek, and Janet B. L. Chan. *Representing Order: Crime, Law, and Justice in the News Media.* Toronto, Ont.: University of Toronto Press, 1991.

Grabosky, Peter N. *Journalism and Justice: How Crime is Reported.* Sydney: Pluto Press, 1989.

Knelman, Judith. "Transatlantic Influences on the Reporting of Crime: England vs. America vs. Canada." *American Periodicals* 3 (1993): 1–10.

Krajicek, David J. *Scooped! Media Miss Real Story on Crime While Chasing Sex, Sleaze, and Celebrities.* New York: Columbia University Press, 1998.

Lotz, Roy. *Crime and the American Press.* New York: Praeger, 1991.

McCormick, Christopher Ray. *Constructing Danger: The Mis/representation of Crime in the News.* Halifax, N.J.: Fernwood, 1995.

Rodrick, Anne Baltz. "'Only a Newspaper Metaphor': Crime Reports, Class Conflict, and Social Criticism in Two Victorian Newspapers." *Victorian Periodicals Review* 29, no. 1 (1996): 1–18.

Criticism of the Press

Entman, Robert M. *Democracy Without Citizens: Media and the Decay of American Politics.* New York: Oxford University Press, 1989.

Fallows, James M. *Breaking the News: How the Media Undermine American Democracy.* New York: Pantheon, 1996.

Hachten, William A. *The Troubles of Journalism: A Critical Look at What's Right and Wrong with the Press.* Mahwah, N.J.: Lawrence Erlbaum Associates, 2005.

Hampton, Mark. "Censors and Stereotypes: Kingsley Martin Theorizes the Press." *Media History* 10, no. 1 (2004): 17–28.

Kennedy, William V. *The Military and the Media: Why the Press Cannot Be Trusted to Cover a War.* Westport, Conn.: Praeger, 1993.

Marzolf, Marion. *Civilizing Voices: American Press Criticism, 1880–1950.* New York: Longman, 1991.

Paulos, John. *A Mathematician Reads the Newspaper*. London: Penguin, 1996.
Whitfield, Stephen J. "From Publick to Pseudo-events: Journalists and their Critics." *American Jewish History* 72, no. 1 (1982): 52–81.

Danish Cartoon Controversy

Goldstone, Brian. "Violence and the Profane: Islamism, Liberal Democracy, and the Limits of Secular Discipline." *Anthropological Quarterly* 80, no. 1 (2007): 207–35.
Naim, C. M. "A Clash of Fanaticisms." *Comparative Studies of South Asia, Africa and the Middle East* 26, no. 3 (2006):41–6.

Design

Harter, Eugene C. *Boilerplating America: The Hidden Newspaper*. Lanham, Md.: University Press of America, 1991.
Nerone, John. "Visual Mapping and Cultural Authority: Design Changes in U.S. Newspapers, 1920–1940." *Journal of Communication* 45, no. 2 (1995): 9–43.
Tobias, Jenny. "Truth to Materials: Modernism and U.S. Television News Design Since 1940." *Journal of Design History* 18, no. 2 (2005): 179–90.

Education and Training

Beasley, Maurine. "Women in Journalism Education: The Formative Period, 1908–1930." *Journalism History* 13, no. 1 (1986): 10–18.
Bronstein, Carolyn, and Stephen Vaughn. "Willard G. Bleyer and the Relevance of Journalism Education." *Journalism & Mass Communication Monographs* no. 166 (1998): 36.
Boylan, James. *Pulitzer's School: Columbia University's School of Journalism, 1903–2003*. New York: Columbia University Press, 2003.
Gaunt, Philip. "The Training of Journalists in France, Britain and the U.S." *Journalism Quarterly* 65, no. 3 (1988): 582–8.
Mueller, Julie Kay. "Staffing Newspapers and Training Journalists in Early Soviet Russia." *Journal of Social History* 31, no. 4 (1998): 851–73.
Reese, Stephen D. "The Progressive Potential of Journalism Education: Recasting the Academic versus Professional Debate." *Harvard International Journal of Press Politics* 4, no. 4 (1999): 70–94.
Sloan, W. David, ed. *Makers of the Media Mind: Journalism Educators and Their Ideas*. Hillsdale, N.J.: Lawrence Erlbaum Associates, 1990.

Ethics

Banning, Stephen A. "'Truth is Our Ultimate Goal': A Mid-19th Century Concern for Journalism Ethics." *American Journalism* 16, no. 1 (1999): 17–39.

Belsey, Andrew, and Ruth Chadwick, eds. *Ethical Issues in Journalism and the Media*. New York: Routledge, 1992.

Christians, Clifford G., John P. Ferré, and P. Mark Fackler. *Good News: Social Ethics and the Press*. New York: Oxford University Press, 1993.

Cronin, Mary M. and James B. McPherson. "Pronouncements and Denunciations: An Analysis of State Press Association Ethics Codes from the 1920s." *Journalism and Mass Communication Quarterly* 72, no. 4 (1995): 890–901.

Fuller, Jack. *News Values: Ideas for an Information Age*. Chicago, Ill.: University of Chicago Press, 1996.

Hausman, Carl. *Crisis of Conscience: Perspectives on Journalism Ethics*. New York: HarperCollins, 1992.

Plaisance, Patrick Lee. "A Gang of Pecksniffs Grows Up: The Evolution of Journalism Ethics Discourse in *The Journalist* and *Editor and Publisher*." *Journalism Studies* 6, no. 4 (2005): 479–91.

Russell, Nicholas. *Morals and the Media: Ethics in Canadan Journalism*. Vancouver: University of British Columbia Press, 2006.

Seib, Philip M. *Journalism Ethics*. Fort Worth, Tex.: Harcourt Brace College Publishers, 1997.

Solomon, Norman, and Jeff Cohen. *Wizards of Media Oz: Behind the Curtain of Mainstream News*. Monroe, Me.: Common Courage Press, 1997.

Wheeler, Tom. *Phototruth or Photofiction?: Ethics and Media Imagery in the Digital Age*. Mahwah, N.J.: Lawrence Erlbaum Associates, 2002.

Etymology

Mattauch, H. "A Contribution to the Early History of the Terms 'Journaliste' and 'Journalisme,'" *Romance Notes* 8, no. 2 (1967), 310–14.

Federal Bureau of Investigation (FBI)

Cecil, Matthew. "'Press Every Angle': FBI Public Relations and the 'Smear Campaign' of 1958." *American Journalism* 19, no. 1 (2002): 39–58.

Farnsworth, Stephen J. "Seeing Red: The FBI and Edgar Snow." *Journalism History* 28, no. 3 (2002): 137–45.

Theoharis, Athan. "The FBI, the Roosevelt Administration, and the 'Subversive' Press." *Journalism History* 19, no. 1 (1993): 3–10.

Feuilletons

Dianina, Katia. "The Feuilleton: An Everyday Guide to Public Culture in the Age of the Great Reforms." *Slavic and East European Journal* 47, no. 2 (2003), 187–210.

Ryan-Hayes, Karen. "Marina Lebedeva's 'MEZHDU NAMI, ZHENSHCHI-NAMI' Feuilletons." *Slavic and East European Journal* 36, no. 2 (1992), 172–88.

Fictional Reporters

Daniel, Douglass K. *Lou Grant: The Making of TV's Top Newspaper Drama.* Syracuse, N.Y.: Syracuse University Press, 1996.

Film Treatments

Ehrlich, Matthew C. *Journalism in the Movies.* Urbana: University of Illinois Press, 2004.

Good, Howard. *The Drunken Journalist: The Biography of a Film Stereotype.* Lanham, Md.: Scarecrow Press, 2000.

Ness, Richard R. *From Headline Hunter to Superman: A Journalism Filmography.* Lanham, Md.: Scarecrow Press, 1997.

Saltzman, Joe. *Frank Capra and the Image of the Journalist in American Film.* Los Angeles, Calif.: Annenberg School for Communication, 2002.

Foreign Correspondents

Bjork, Ulf Jonas. "The Commercial Roots of Foreign Correspondence: The New York *Herald* and Foreign News, 1835–1839." *American Journalism* 11, no. 2 (1994): 102–15.

Edwards, Julia. *Women of the World: The Great Foreign Correspondents.* Boston, Mass.: Houghton Mifflin, 1988.

Emery, Michael C. *On the Front Lines: Following America's Foreign Correspondents Across the Twentieth Century.* Washington, D.C.: American University Press, 1995.

Hannerz, Ulf. *Foreign News: Exploring the World of Foreign Correspondents.* Chicago, Ill.: University of Chicago Press, 2004.

Hosley, David H. *As Good as Any: Foreign Correspondence on American Radio, 1930–1940.* Westport, Conn.: Greenwood Press, 1984.

Freedom of the Press

Cortner, Richard C. *The Kingfish and the Constitution: Huey Long, the First Amendment, and the Emergence of Modern Press Freedom in America.* Westport, Conn.: Greenwood Press, 1996.

Dunham, Corydon B. *Fighting the First Amendment: Stanton of CBS vs. Congress and the Nixon White House.* Westport, Conn.: Praeger, 1997.

Lewis, Anthony. *Make No Law: The Sullivan Case and the First Amendment.* New York: Random House, 1991.

Merrill, John C. *The Dialectic in Journalism: Toward Responsible Use of Press Freedom.* Baton Rouge: Louisiana State University Press, 1989.

Nerone, John C., ed. *Last Rights: Revisiting Four Theories of the Press.* Urbana: University of Illinois Press, 1995.

Sanford, Bruce W. *Don't Shoot the Messenger: How Our Growing Hatred of the Media Threatens Free Speech for All of Us.* New York: Free Press, 1999.

Schwartz, Bernard. *Freedom of the Press: Constitutional Issues.* New York: Facts on File, 1992.

Weaver, Russell L. *The Right to Speak Ill: Defamation, Reputation, and Free Speech.* Durham: Carolina Academic Press, 2006.

Great Awakening

Lambert, Frank. *Pedlar in Divinity: George Whitefield and the Transatlantic Revivals, 1737–1770.* Princeton, N.J.: Princeton University Press, 1994.

———. *Inventing the "Great Awakening."* Princeton, N.J.: Princeton University Press, 1999.

O'Brien, Susan. "A Transatlantic Community of Saints: The Great Awakening and the First Evangelical Network, 1735–1755." *American Historical Review* 91, no. 4 (October 1986): 811–32.

Historiography

Brennan, Bonnie. "Toward a History of Labor and News Work: The Use of Oral Sources in Journalism History." *Journal of American History* 83, no. 2 (1996): 571–9.

Curran, James. "Media and the Making of British History, c. 1700–2000." *Media History* 8, no. 2 (2002): 135–54.

Dooley, Brendan. "From Literary Criticism to Systems Theory in Early Modern Journalism History." *Journal of the History of Ideas* 51, no. 3 (1990): 461–86.

Emery, Michael. "The Writing of American Journalism History." *Journalism History* 10, nos. 3–4 (1983): 38–93.

Rogers, Everett M., and Steven H. Chaffee. "Communication and Journalism from 'Daddy' Bleyer to Wilbur Schramm: A Palimpsest." *Journalism Monographs* 148 (1994): 1–52.

Sloan, Wm. David. "Historians and the American Press, 1900–1945." *American Journalism* 3, no. 3 (1986): 154–66.

Zelizer, Barbie. *Taking Journalism Seriously: News and the Academy*. Thousand Oaks, Calif.: Sage, 2004.

Hoaxes

Thornton, Brian. "The Moon Hoax: Debates About Ethics in 1835 New York Newspapers." *Journal of Mass Media Ethics* 15, no. 2 (2000): 89–110.

Whalen, Stephen, and Robert E. Bartholomew. "The Great New England Airship Hoax of 1909." *New England Quarterly* 75, no. 3 (2002): 466–76.

Horserace Journalism

Freedman, Eric, and Frederick Fico. "Whither the Experts? Newspaper Use of Horse Race and Issue Experts in Coverage of Open Governors' Races in 2002." *Journalism and Mass Communication Quarterly* 81, no. 3 (2004): 498–510.

Iyengar, Shanto, Helmut Norpoth, and Kyu S. Hahn. "Consumer Demand for Election News: The Horserace Sells," *Journal of Politics* 66, no. 1 (2004): 157–75.

Littlewood, Thomas B. *Calling Elections: The History of Horse-Race Journalism*. Notre Dame, Ind.: University of Notre Dame Press, 1999.

Human Interest Stories

Fine, Gary Alan, and Ryan D. White. "Creating Collective Attention in the Public Domain: Human Interest Narratives and the Rescue of Floyd Collins." *Social Forces* 81, no. 1 (2002): 57–85.

Russell, Frank. "Folklore in a Hurry: The Community Experience Narrative in Newspaper Coverage of the Loma Prieta Earthquake," *Journal of American Folklore* 116, no. 460 (2003): 159–75.

Hutchins Commission

Blanchard, Margaret A. "The Hutchins Commission, the Press and the Responsibility Concept." *Journalism Monographs*, no. 49 (1977).
McIntyre, Jerilyn S. "Repositioning a Landmark: The Hutchins Commission and Freedom of the Press." *Critical Studies in Mass Communication* 4, no. 2 (1987): 136–60.

Illustrated Journalism

Dowling, Peter. "Truth Versus Art in Nineteenth-Century Graphic Journalism: The Colonial Australian Case." *Media History* 5, no. 2 (1999): 109–25.
Hogarth, Paul. *Artists on Horseback: The Old West in Illustrated Journalism, 1857–1900*. New York: Watson-Guptill, 1972.

Inoculation Controversy

Furtwangler, Albert. "Franklin's Apprenticeship and the Spectator." *New England Quarterly* 52, no. 3 (1979): 377–96.
Jeske, Jeffrey. "Cotton Mather: Physico-Theologian." *Journal of the History of Ideas* 47, no. 4 (1986): 583–94.
Van De Wetering, Maxine. "A Reconsideration of the Inoculation Controversy." *New England Quarterly* 58, no. 1 (1985): 46–67.

Internet

Berkman, Robert I., and Christopher A. Shumwat. *Digital Dilemmas: Ethical Issues for Online Media Professionals*. Ames: Iowa State University Press, 2003.
Boczkowski, Pablo J. *Digitizing the News: Innovation in Online Newspapers*. Cambridge, Mass.: MIT Press, 2004.
Dean, Jodi. *Publicity's Secret: How Technoculture Capitalizes on Democracy*. Ithaca, N.Y.: Cornell University Press, 2002.
Gant, Scott. *We're All Journalists Now: The Transformation of the Press and the Reshaping of the Law in the Internet Age*. New York: Free Press, 2007.
Goldsmith, Jack, and Tim Wu. *Who Controls the Internet?: Illusions of a Borderless World*. New York: Oxford University Press, 2006.
Salwen, Michael B., Bruce Garrison, and Paul D. Driscoll, eds. *Online News and the Public*. Mahwah, N. J.: Lawrence Erlbaum Associates, 2005.

Interviewing

Nilsson, Nils Gunnar. "The Origin of the Interview." *Journalism Quarterly* 48, no. 4 (1971): 707–13.

Rubery, Matthew. "Wishing to be Interviewed in Henry James's *The Reverberator.*" *The Henry James Review* 28, no. 1 (2007): 57–72.

Schudson, Michael. "Question Authority: A History of the News Interview in American Journalism, 1860s–1930s." *Media, Culture & Society* 16, no. 4 (1994): 565–87.

Tucher, Andie. "In Search of Jenkins: Taste, Style, and Credibility in Gilded-Age Journalism." *Journalism History* 27, no. 2 (2001): 50–55.

Inverted Pyramid

Errico, Marcus. "The Evolution of the Summary News Lead." *Media History Monographs* 1, no. 1 (1997–98).

Mindich, David T. Z. "Edwin M. Stanton, the Inverted Pyramid, and Information Control." *Journalism Monographs* no. 140 (1993): 1–31.

Pöttker, Horst. "News and Its Communicative Quality: The Inverted Pyramid—When and Why Did It Appear?" *Journalism Studies* 4, no. 4 (2003): 485–96.

Investigative Journalism

Aucoin, J. L. "The Re-emergence of American Investigative Journalism 1960–75." *Journalism History* 21 (1995): 3–15.

———. "The Early Years of IRE: The Evolution of Modern Investigative Journalism." *American Journalism* 12, no. 4 (1995): 425–43.

de Burgh, Hugo, ed. *Investigative Journalism: Context and Practice.* New York: Routledge, 2000.

Ettema, James S., and Theodore L. Glasser. *Custodians of Conscience: Investigative Journalism and Public Virtue.* New York: Columbia University Press, 1998.

Lawler, Philip F. *The Alternative Influence: The Impact of Investigative Reporting Groups on America's Media.* Lanham, Md.: University Press of America, 1984.

Olmsted, Kathryn S. *Challenging the Secret Government: The Post-Watergate Investigations of the CIA and the FBI.* Chapel Hill: University of North Carolina Press, 1996.

Tichi, Cecelia. *Exposes and Excesses: Muckraking in America, 1900–2000.* Philadelphia: University of Pennsylvania Press, 2004.

Jefferson, Thomas

Golden, A. L., et al. "Thomas Jefferson's Perspectives on the Press as an Instrument of Political Communication." *American Behavioral Scientist* 37 (1993): 194–99.

Knudson, Jerry W. *Jefferson and the Press: Crucible of Liberty*. Columbia: University of South Carolina Press, 2006.

Jonson, Ben

Nevitt, Marcus. "Ben Jonson and the Serial Publication of News." *Media History* 11, nos. 1/2 (2005): 53–68.

Sellin, Paul R. "The Politics of Ben Jonson's *Newes from the New World Discover'd in the Moone*." *Viator* 17 (1986): 321–37.

Journalists, Selected Individual

Alsop, Joseph W., Jr.

Almquist, Leann Grabavoy. *Joseph Alsop and American Foreign Policy: The Journalist as Advocate*. Lanham, Md.: University Press of America, 1993.

Yoder, Edwin M., Jr. *Joe Alsop's Cold War: A Study of Journalistic Influence and Intrigue*. Chapel Hill: University of North Carolina Press, 1995.

Anderson, Paul Y.

Lambeth, Edmund B. "The Lost Career of Paul Y. Anderson." *Journalism Quarterly* 60, no. 3 (Autumn 1983): 401–6.

Banks, Elizabeth

Onslow, Barbara. "New World, New Woman, New Journalism: Elizabeth Banks, Transatlantic Stuntwoman in London." *Media History* 7, no. 1 (2001): 7–15.

Besant, Annie

Mortimer, Joanne Stafford. "Annie Besant and India 1913–1917." *Journal of Contemporary History* 18, no. 1 (1983): 61–78.

Bly, Nellie

Kroeger, Brooke. *Nellie Bly: Daredevil, Reporter, Feminist.* New York: Times Books, 1994.

Lutes, Jean Marie. "Into the Madhouse with Nellie Bly: Girl Stunt Reporting in Late Nineteenth-Century America." *American Quarterly* 54, no. 2 (2002): 217–53.

Roggenkamp, Karen. "To Turn a Fiction into Fact: Nellie Bly, Jules Verne, and Trips Around the World." *Journal of the American Studies Association of Texas* 31 (2000): 19–46.

Cobbett, William

Gunzenhauser, Bonnie J. "Reading the Rhetoric of Resistance in William Cobbett's *Two Penny Trash.*" *Prose Studies* 25, no. 1 (2002): 84–101.

Lemrow, Lynne. "William Cobbett's Journalism for the Lower Orders." *Victorian Periodicals Review* 15, no. 1 (1982): 11–20.

Coleman, Kit

Freeman, Barbara M. *Kit's Kingdom: The Journalism of Kathleen Blake Coleman.* Ottawa, Ont.: Carleton University Press, 1989.

Davis, Richard Harding

Lubow, Arthur. *The Reporter Who Would be King: A Biography of Richard Harding Davis.* New York: Scribner, 1992.

Stephens, Rodney. "Shattered Windows, German Spies, and Zigzag Trenches: World War I Through the Eyes of Richard Harding Davis." *Historian* 65, no. 1 (2002): 43–73.

Defoe, Daniel

Backscheider, Paula R. *Daniel Defoe: His Life.* Baltimore, Md.: Johns Hopkins University Press, 1989.

Novak, Maximilian E. *Daniel Defoe, Master of Fictions: His Life and Ideas.* Oxford: Oxford University Press, 2001.

West, Richard. *Daniel Defoe: The Life and Strange, Surprising Adventures.* New York: Carroll and Graf, 1998.

Dunne, Finley Peter

Morath, Max. "Translating Mister Dooley: A New Examination of the Journalism of Finley Peter Dunne." *Journal of American Culture* 27, no. 2 (2004): 147–56.

Duranty, Walter

Luciuk, Lubomyr, ed. *Not Worthy: Walter Duranty's Pulitzer Prize and the New York Times*. Kingston, Ont.: Kashtan Press, 2004.
Taylor, S. J. *Stalin's Apologist: Walter Duranty, the New York Times's Man in Moscow*. New York: Oxford University Press, 1990.

Ebbut, Norman

McDonough, Frank. "*The Times*, Norman Ebbut and the Nazis, 1927–37." *Journal of Contemporary History* 27, no. 3 (1992): 407–24.

Field, Kate

Scharnhorst, Gary. "Kate Field and the New York *Tribune*." *American Periodicals* 14, no. 2 (2004): 159–78.

Franklin, Benjamin

Frasca, Ralph. "Benjamin Franklin's Printing Network and the Dissemination of Moral Virtue in Early America." *Michigan Academician* 27, no. 2 (1995): 125–34.
Furtwangler, Albert. "Franklin's Apprenticeship and the *Spectator.*" *New England Quarterly* 52, no. 3 (1979): 377–96.
Leonard, Thomas C. "Recovering 'Wretched Stuff' and the Franklins' Synergy." *New England Quarterly* 73, no. 2 (1999): 444–55.
Smith, Jeffrey Alan. *Franklin and Bache: Envisioning the Enlightened Republic*. New York: Oxford University Press, 1990.

Gilman, Charlotte Perkins

Knight, Denise D. "Charlotte Perkins Gilman, William Randolph Hearst and the Practice of Ethical Journalism." *American Journalism* 11 (1994): 336–47.

Lane, Ann J. *To Herland and Beyond: The Life and Work of Charlotte Perkins Gilman*. New York: Pantheon Books, 1990.

Greeley, Horace

Williams, Robert Chadwell. *Horace Greeley: Champion of American Freedom*. New York: New York University Press, 2006.

Hale, Sarah J.

Okker, Patricia. *Our Sister Editors: Sarah J. Hale and the Tradition of Nineteenth-Century American Women Editors*. Athens: University of Georgia Press, 1995.

Hemingway, Ernest

Cote, William E. "Correspondent or Warrior? Hemingway's Murky World War II 'Combat' Experience." *Hemingway Review* 22, no. 1 (2002): 88–104.

Harrison, S. L. "Hemingway as Negligent Reporter: New Masses and the 1935 Florida Hurricane." *American Journalism* 11, no. 1 (1994): 11–19.

Kobler, J. F. *Ernest Hemingway: Journalist and Artist*. Ann Arbor, Mich.: UMI Research Press, 1985.

Stonebeck, H. R. "Hemingway's Happiest Summer—'The Wildest, Most Beautiful, Wonderful Time Ever'; or, the Liberation of France and Hemingway." *North Dakota Quarterly* 64, no. 3 (1997): 184–220.

Watson, William Braasch. "Joris Ivens and the Communists: Bringing Hemingway into the Spanish Civil War." *Hemingway Review* 10, no. 1 (1990): 2–18.

Lippincott, Sara Jane

Garrett, Paula K. "An 'Unprotected' Pilgrim; or, a New Woman in the Old World: Grace Greenwood's Self-Sexualization in the Popular Press 1875–76, 1878–79." *Women's Writing* 11, no. 2 (2004): 303–23.

Lippmann, Walter

Diggins, John Patrick. "From Pragmatism to Natural Law: Walter Lippmann's Quest for the Foundations of Legitimacy." *Political Theory* 19, no. 4 (1991): 519–38.

Riccio, Barry D. *Walter Lippmann: Odyssey of a Liberal*. New Brunswick, N.J.: Transaction, 1994.

Steel, Ronald. *Walter Lippmann and the American Century*. Boston, Mass.: Little, Brown, 1980.

McWilliams, Carey

Richardson, Peter. *American Prophet: The Life and Work of Carey McWilliams*. Ann Arbor: University of Michigan Press, 2005.

Mencken, H. L.

Harrison, S. L. "Mencken: Magnificent Anachronism." *American Journalism* 13, no. 1 (1996): 60–78.

Rodgers, Marion Elizabeth. *Mencken, the American Iconoclast: The Life and Times of the Bad Boy of Baltimore*. New York: Oxford University Press, 2006.

Parton, Sara Willis

Pettengill, Claire C. "Against Novels: Fanny Fern's Newspaper Fictions and the Reform of Print Culture." *American Periodicals* 6 (1996): 61–91.

Warren, Joyce W. "Fanny Fern, Performative Incivilities and Rap." *Studies in American Humor* 3, no. 6 (1999): 17–36.

Pearson, Drew

Feldstein, Mark. "Fighting Quakers: The 1950s Battle Between Richard Nixon and Drew Pearson." *Journalism History* 30, no. 2 (2004): 76–90.

Weinberg, Steve. "Avenging Angel or Deceitful Devil? The Evolution of Drew Pearson, a New Kind of Investigative Journalist." *American Journalist* 14, nos. 3–4 (1997): 283–302.

Ralph, Julian

Lancaster, Paul. *Gentleman of the Press: The Life and Times of an Early Reporter, Julian Ralph of the Sun*. Syracuse, N.Y.: Syracuse University Press, 1992.

Snow, Edgar

Farnsworth, Robert M. *From Vagabond to Journalist: Edgar Snow in Asia, 1928–1941*. Columbia: University of Missouri Press, 1996.

Thomas, S. Bernard. *Season of High Adventure: Edgar Snow in China*. Berkeley: University of California Press, 1996.

Steinbeck, John

Sullivan, Christopher C. "John Steinbeck, War Reporter: Fiction, Journalism and Types of Truth." *Journalism History* 23 (1997): 16–23.

Stone, I. F.

Blissert, Julie Harrison. "Guerrila Journalist: I. F. Stone and Tonkin." *Journalism History* 23, no. 3 (1997): 102–13.

Cottrell, Robert C. *Izzy: A Biography of I. F. Stone*. New Brunswick, N.J.: Rutgers University Press, 1992.

Swisshelm, Jane Grey

Hoffert, Sylvia D. *Jane Grey Swisshelm: An Unconventional Life, 1815–1884*. Chapel Hill: University of North Carolina Press, 2004.

Wells, Ida B.

Davidson, Sue. *Getting the Real Story: Nellie Bly and Ida B. Wells*. Seattle, Wash.: Seal Press, 1992.

White, Theodore H.

Hoffmann, Joyce. *Theodore H. White and Journalism as Illusion*. Columbia: University of Missouri Press, 1995.

White, William Allen

Griffith, Sally Foreman. *Home Town News: William Allen White and the Emporia Gazette*. New York: Oxford University Press, 1989.

Wilkes, John

Sainsbury, John. *John Wilkes: The Lives of a Libertine*. Burlington, Vt.: Ashgate, 2006.

Labor Journalism

Faue, Elizabeth. *Writing the Wrongs: Eva Valesh and the Rise of Labor Journalism*. Ithaca, N.Y.: Cornell University Press, 2002.
Spencer, David R. "Divine Intervention: God, Working People, Labour Journalism." *Journalism History* 25, no. 3 (1999), 90–98.

Labor Practices

Bohere, G. *Profession, Journalist: A Study on the Working Conditions of Journalists*. Geneva: International Labour Office, 1984.
Hardt, Hanno, and Bonnie Brennen, eds. *Newsworkers: Toward a History of the Rank and File*. Minneapolis: University of Minnesota Press, 1995.

Labor Relations

Brasch, Walter, ed. *With Just Cause: Unionization of the American Journalist*. Lanham, Md.: University Press of America, 1991.
McKercher, Catherine. *Newsworkers United: Labor, Convergence, and North American Newspapers*. Lanham, Md.: Rowman & Littlefield, 2002.

Language

Brownlees, Nevitt. "Spoken Discourse in Early English Newspapers." *Media History* 11, nos. 1–2 (2005): 69–86.
Fowler, Roger. *Language in the News: Discourse and Ideology in the Press*. London: Routledge, 1991.
Lasky, Melvin J. *The Language of Journalism*. New Brunswick, N.J.: Transaction, 2000.

Literature and Journalism

Brake, Laurel. *Subjugated Knowledges: Journalism, Gender, and Literature in the Nineteenth Century*. Washington Square, N.Y.: New York University Press, 1994.

Campbell, Kate, ed. *Journalism, Literature, and Modernity: From Hazlitt to Modernism.* Edinburgh: Edinburgh University Press, 2000.
Davis, Lennard J. *Factual Fictions: The Origins of the English Novel.* New York: Columbia University Press, 1983.
Drew, John M. L. *Dickens the Journalist.* New York: Palgrave Macmillan, 2003.
Fishkin, Shelley Fisher. *From Fact to Fiction: Journalism and Imaginative Writing in America.* Baltimore: Johns Hopkins University Press, 1985.
González, Aníbal. *Journalism and the Development of Spanish American Narrative.* Cambridge: Cambridge University Press, 1993.
Good, Howard. *Acquainted with the Night: The Image of Journalists in American Fiction, 1890–1930.* Metuchen, N.J.: Scarecrow Press, 1986.
Knight, Bill, and Deckle McLean, eds. *The Eye of the Reporter: Literature's Heritage in the Press.* Macomb: Western Illinois University Press, 1996.
Leckie, Barbara. *Culture and Adultery: The Novel, the Newspaper, and the Law 1857–1914.* Philadelphia: University of Pennsylvania Press, 1999.
Shapiro, Stephanie. *Reinventing the Feature Story: Mythic Cycles in American Literary Journalism.* Baltimore, Md.: Apprentice House, 2005.
Treglown, Jeremy, and Bridget Bennett, eds. *Grub Street and the Ivory Tower: Literary Journalism and Literary Scholarship from Fielding to the Internet.* Oxford: Clarendon Press, 1998.
Weber, Ronald. *Journalism, Writing, and American Literature.* New York: Gannett Center for Media Studies, 1987.

Lynching

Perloff, Richard M. "The Press and Lynchings of African Americans." *Journal of Black Studies* 30, no. 3 (2000): 315–30.
Smith, Reed W. "Southern Journalists and Lynching: The Statesboro Case Study." *Journalism and Communication Monographs* 7, no. 2 (2005): 51–92.

Magazines, General

Endres, Kathleen L. "Women and the 'Larger Household': The 'Big Six' and Muckraking." *American Journalism* 14, nos. 3–4 (1997): 262–82.
Schneirov, Matthew. *The Dream of a New Social Order: Popular Magazines in America, 1893–1914.* New York: Columbia University Press, 1994.
Tebbel, John, and Mary Ellen Zuckerman. *The Magazine in America, 1741–1990.* New York: Oxford University Press, 1991.
Thom, Mary. *Inside MS.: 25 Years of the Magazine and the Feminist Movement.* New York: Henry Holt and Company, 1997.

Magazines, Selected Individual

Catholic Worker

Piehl, Mel. *Breaking Bread: "The Catholic Worker" and the Origin of Catholic Radicalism in America*. Philadelphia: Temple University Press, 1982.

Gentleman's Magazine

Ram, Titia. *Magnitude in Marginality: Edward Cave and 'The* Gentleman's Magazine,' *1731–1754*. Amersfoort: Gottmann & Fainsilber Katz, 1999.

Ladies' Home Journal

Damon-Moore, Helen. *Magazines for the Millions: Gender and Commerce in the* Ladies' Home Journal *and the* Saturday Evening Post. Albany: State University of New York Press, 1994.
Scanlon, Jennifer. *Inarticulate Longings: The* Ladies' Home Journal, *Gender, and the Promises of Consumer Culture*. New York: Routledge, 1995.

The Masses

Fishbein, Leslie. *Rebels in Bohemia: The Radicals of* The Masses, *1911–1917*. Chapel Hill: University of North Carolina Press, 1982.
Jones, Margaret C. *Heretics & Hellraisers: Women Contributors to* The Masses, *1911–1917*. Austin: University of Texas Press, 1993.

New Republic

Levy, David. *Herbert Croly and "The* New Republic." Princeton, N.J.: Princeton University Press, 1985.
Seideman, David. *"The New Republic": A Voice of Modern Liberalism*. New York: Praeger, 1986.

New Yorker

Cory, Mary F. *The World Through a Monocle: The* "New Yorker" *at Midcentury*. Cambridge, Mass.: Harvard University Press, 1999.

The March of Time

Fielding, Raymond. *The March of Time, 1935–1951*. New York: Oxford University Press, 1978.

Medical Journalism

Copeland, David A. "'A Receipt Against the PLAGUE': Medical Reporting in Colonial America." *American Journalism* 11, no. 3 (1994): 219–41.

Corbett, Julia B., and Motomi Mori. "Medicine, Media, and Celebrities: News Coverage of Breast Cancer, 1960–1995." *Journalism and Mass Communication Quarterly* 76 (1999): 229–49.

Payne, J. G., and K. A. Mercuri. "Crisis in Communication: Coverage of Magic Johnson's AIDS Disclosure." In S. Ratzan, ed., *AIDS: Effective Health Communication for the 90s*. London: Taylor and Francis, 1993.

Payne, J. G., D. Dornbusch, and V. Demco. "Media Coverage of the Mad Cow Issue." In S. Ratzan, ed., *Mad Cow Crisis: Health and the Public Good*. London: University College of London Press, 1997.

Tomes, Nancy. "Epidemic Entertainments: Disease and Popular Culture in Early Twentieth-Century America," *American Literary History* 14, no. 4 (2002), 625–52.

Muckrakers, American

Applegate, Edd. *Journalistic Advocates and Muckrakers: Three Centuries of Crusading Writers*. Jefferson, N.C.: McFarland, 1997.

Brady, Kathleen. *Ida Tarbell: Portrait of a Muckraker*. New York: Seaview/Putnam, 1984.

Digby-Junger, Richard. *The Journalist as Reformer: Henry Demarest Lloyd and Wealth Against Commonwealth*. Westport, Conn.: Greenwood Press, 1996.

Kennedy, Samuel V. III. *Samuel Hopkins Adams and the Business of Writing*. Syracuse: Syracuse University Press, 1999.

Kochersberger, Robert C., ed. *More than a Muckraker: Ida Tarbell's Lifetime in Journalism*. Knoxville: University of Tennessee Press, 1994.

Miraldi, Robert. *Objectivity and the New Muckraking: John L. Hess and the Nursing Home Scandal*. Columbia, S.C.: AEJMC, 1989.

———. *Muckraking and Objectivity; Journalism's Colliding Traditions*. New York: Greenwood Press, 1990.

———. "Charles Edward Russell: 'Chief of the Muckrakers.'" *Journalism Monographs* no. 150 (1995): 27.

———. *The Pen Is Mightier: The Muckraking Life of Charles Edward Russell.* New York: Palgrave Macmillan, 2003.

Neuzil, Mark. "Hearst, Roosevelt, and the Muckrake Speech of 1906: A New Perspective." *Journalism and Mass Communication Quarterly* 73, no. 1 (1996): 29–39.

Thornton, Brian. "Muckraking Journalists and Their Readers: Perceptions of Professionalism." *Journalism History* 21, no. 1 (1995): 29–41.

Tichi, Cecelia. *Exposes and Excess: Muckraking in America, 1900–2000.* Philadelphia: University of Pennsylvania Press, 2004.

Wilson, Harold S. "Circulation and Survival: *McClure's Magazine* and the Strange Death of Muckraking Journalism." *Western Illinois Regional Studies* 11, no. 1 (1988): 71–81.

Muckrakers, Japanese

Stone, Alan. "The Japanese Muckrakers." *Journal of Japanese Studies* 1, no. 2 (1975): 385–407.

Myth

Koch, Tom. *The News as Myth: Fact and Context in Journalism.* New York: Greenwood Press, 1990.

Lule, Jack. *Daily News, Eternal Stories: The Mythological Role of Journalism.* New York: Guilford Press, 2000.

Rivers, Caryl. *Slick Spins and Fractured Facts: How Cultural Myths Distort the News.* New York: Columbia University Press, 1996.

New Journalism

Marzolf, Marion T. "American 'New Journalism' Takes Root in Europe at End of the Nineteenth Century." *Journalism Quarterly* 61 (1984): 529–36, 691.

Wiener, Joel. *Papers for the Millions: The New Journalism in Britain, 1850s to 1914.* New York: Greenwood Press, 1988.

Newsbooks

Cogswell, Thomas. "'Published by Authoritie': Newsbooks and the Duke of Buckingham's Expedition to the Ile de Ré." *Huntingdon Library Quarterly* 67, no. 1 (2004): 1–25.

O'Hara, D. A. "English Newsbooks and the Outbreak of the Irish Rebellion of 1641." *Media History* 9, no. 3 (2003): 179–93.

Peacey, Jason. "'The Counterfeit Silly Curr': Money, Politics, and the Forging of Royalist Newspapers During the English Civil War." *Huntingdon Library Quarterly* 67, no. 1 (2004): 27–57.

Raymond, Joad. *The Invention of the Newspaper: English Newsbooks, 1641–1649.* Oxford: Oxford University Press, 1996.

Tubb, Amos. "Mixed Messages: Royalist Newsbook Reports of Charles I's Execution and of the Leveler Uprising." *Huntingdon Library Quarterly* 67, no. 1 (2004): 59–74.

News, Concepts of

Alexander, Jeffrey C. "The Mass Media in Systemic, Historical, and Comparative Perspective." In Elihu Katz and Tamás Szecskö, eds. *Mass Media and Social Change.* Beverly Hills, Calif.: Sage, 1981.

Cohen, S., and J. Young, eds. *The Manufacture of News: Social Problems, Deviance and the Mass Media.* London: Constable, 1973.

Newsletters

Arblaster, Paul. "Posts, Newsletters, Newspapers: England in a European System of Communications." *Media History* 11, nos. 1/2 (2005): 21–36.

Cust, Richard. "News and Politics in Early Seventeenth-Century England." *Past and Present,* no. 112 (1986): 60–90.

De Vivo, Filipo. "Paolo Sarpi and the Uses of Information in Seventeenth-Century Venice." *Media History* 11, nos. 1/2 (2005): 37–51.

Levy, F. J. "How Information Spread Among the Gentry, 1550–1640." *Journal of British Studies* 21 (1982): 11–34.

News Management

Weiss, W. Michael. "Government News Management, Bias, and Distortion in American Press Coverage of the Brazilian Coup of 1964." *Social Science Journal* 34, no. 1 (1997): 35–55.

Newspapers, Selected Individual

New-England Courant

Fireoved, Joseph. "Nathaniel Gardner and the *New-England Courant.*" *Early American Literature* 20, no. 3 (1985–1986): 214–35.

Sloan, W. David. "The *New-England Courant*: Voice of Anglicanism." *American Journalism* 7 (1991): 108–41.

———. "Chaos, Polemics, and America's First Newspaper." *Journalism Quarterly* 70 (1993): 666–81.

New York Herald Tribune

Kluger, Richard. *The Paper: The Life and Death of the 'New York Herald Tribune'*. New York: Knopf, 1986.

New York Times

Barton, Michael. "Journalistic Gore: Disaster Reporting and Emotional Discourse in the *New York Times*, 1852–1956." In Peter N. Stearns and Jan Lewis, eds., *An Emotional History of the United States*. New York: New York University Press, 1998.

Hays, Robert G. *A Race at Bay: New York Times Editorials on "The Indian Problem," 1860–1900*. Carbondale: Southern Illinois University Press, 1997.

Hindman, Elizabeth Banks. "Jayson Blair, *The New York Times*, and Paradigm Repair." *Journal of Communication* 55, no. 2 (2005): 225–41.

Howden, William D. "Seeing Social Class in the Sermons of *The New York Times*." *ATQ* 14, no. 4 (December 2000): 313–33.

Leff, Laurel. *Buried by the Times: The Holocaust and America's Most Important Newspaper*. New York: Cambridge University Press, 2005.

Mnookin, Seth. *Hard News: Twenty-one Brutal Months at the New York Times and How They Hanged the American Media*. New York: Random House, 2004.

The Times of London

Crawford, Martin. *The Anglo-American Crisis of the Mid-nineteenth Century: The Times and America, 1850–1862*. Athens: University of Georgia Press, 1987.

Evans, Harold. *Good Times, Bad Times*. London: Weidenfeld and Nicholson, 1983.

Martel, Gordon, ed. The Times *and Appeasement: The Journals of A. L. Kennedy, 1932–1939*. Cambridge, U.K.: Cambridge University Press for the Royal Historical Society, 2000.

Winkworth, Stephen. *Room Two More Guns: The Intriguing History of the Personal Column of* The Times. London: Allen and Unwin, 1986.

Newsreels

Bowles, Brett. "Newsreels, Ideology, and Public Opinion Under Vichy: The Case of *La France en March.*" *French Historical Studies* 27, no. 2 (2004): 419–63.

Fielding, Raymond. *The American Newsreel, 1911–1967.* Norman: University of Oklahoma Press, 1972.

Mould, David. *American Newsfilm, 1914–1919: The Underexposed War.* New York: Garland, 1983.

Novels, Newspaper

Law, Graham. "Before Tillotsons: Novels in British Provincial Newspapers, 1855–1873." *Victorian Periodicals Review* 32, no. 1 (1999): 43–79.

Law, Graham, and Norimasa Morita. "The Newspaper Novel: Towards an International History." *Media History* 6, no. 1 (2000): 5–17.

Objectivity

Hackett, Robert A., and Yuezhi Zhao. *Sustaining Democracy? Journalism and the Politics of Objectivity.* Toronto, Ont.: Garamond Press, 1998.

Kaplan, Richard L. *Politics and the American Press: The Rise of Objectivity, 1865–1920.* New York: Cambridge University Press, 2002.

Knowlton, Steven R., and Karen L. Freeman, eds. *Fair and Balanced: A History of Journalistic Objectivity.* Northport, Ala.: Vision, 2005.

McKinzie, Bruce Wayne. *Objectivity, Communication, and the Foundation of Understanding.* Lanham, Md.: University Press of America, 1994.

Mindich, David T. Z. *Just the Facts: How "Objectivity" Came to Define American Journalism.* New York: New York University Press, 1998.

Ognianova, Ekaterina. "Objectivity Revisited: A Spatial Model of Political Ideology and Mass Communication." *Journalism and Mass Communication Monographs* no. 159 (1996): 36.

Reeb, Richard H., Jr. *Taking Journalism Seriously: 'Objectivity' as a Partisan Cause.* Lanham, Md.: University Press of America, 1999.

Schiller, Dan. *Objectivity and the News: The Public and the Rise of Commercial Journalism.* Philadelphia: University of Pennsylvania Press, 1981.

Schudson, Michael. *Origins of the Ideal of Objectivity in the Professions: Studies in the History of American Journalism and American Law, 1830–1940.* New York: Garland, 1990.

Pacifica

Land, Jeff. *Active Radio: Pacifica's Brash Experiment.* Minneapolis: University of Minnesota Press, 1999.

Lasar, Matthew. *Pacifica Radio: The Rise of an Alternative Network.* Philadelphia: Temple University Press, 1999.

Pamphlets

Halasz, Alexandra. *The Marketplace of Print: Pamphlets and the Public Sphere in Early Modern England.* Cambridge: Cambridge University Press, 1997.

Nussdorfer, Laurie. "Print and Pageantry in Baroque Rome." *Sixteenth Century Journal* 29, no. 2 (1998): 439–64.

Parmalee, Lisa Ferraro. "Printers, Patrons, Readers, and Spies: Importation of French Propaganda in Late Elizabethan England." *Sixteenth Century Journal* 25, no. 4 (1994): 853–72.

Raymond, Joad. *Pamphlets and Pamphleteering in Early Modern Britain.* Cambridge: Cambridge University Press, 2003.

Streckfuss, Richard. "News Before Newspapers." *Journalism and Mass Communication Quarterly* 75, no. 1 (1998): 84–97.

Voss, Paul J. *Elizabethan News Pamphlets: Shakespeare, Marlowe and the Birth of Journalism.* Pittsburgh, Pa.: Duquesne University Press, 2001.

Parliamentary Reporting, Origins of

Lowe, William C. "Peers and Printers: the Beginning of Sustained Press Coverage of the House of Lords in the 1770s." *Parliamentary History* 7, no. 2 (1988): 241–56.

Sparrow, Andrew. *Obscure Scribblers: A History of Parliamentary Journalism.* London: Politico, 2003.

Thomas, Peter D. G. "The Beginning of Parliamentary Reporting in Newspapers, 1768–1774." *English Historical Review* 74, no. 293 (1959): 632–36.

Penny Press

Crouthamel, James L. *Bennett's New York Herald and the Rise of the Popular Press.* Syracuse, N.Y.: Syracuse University Press, 1989.

Fermer, Douglas. *James Gordon Bennett and the New York Herald: A Study of Editorial Opinion in the Civil War Era, 1854–1867.* New York: St. Martin's Press, 1986.

Huntzicker, William E. *The Popular Press, 1833–1836*. Westport, Conn.: Greenwood Press, 1999.

Nerone, John. "The Mythology of the Penny Press." *Critical Studies in Mass Communication* 4 (1987): 376–404.

Risley, Ford. "The Savannah *Morning News* as a Penny Paper: Independent, but Hardly Neutral." *American Journalism* 16, no. 4 (1999): 19–36.

Saxton, Alexander. "Problems of Class and Race in the Origins of the Mass Circulation Press." *American Quarterly* 36, no. 2 (1984): 211–34.

Steele, Janet E. *The Sun Shines for All: Journalism and Ideology in the Life of Charles A. Dana*. Syracuse, N.Y.: Syracuse University Press, 1993.

Pentagon Papers

Ungar, Sanford J. *The Papers & the Papers: An Account of the Legal and Political Battle over the Pentagon Papers*. New York: Columbia University Press, 1989.

Photojournalism

Brennen, Bonnie, and Hanno Hardt, eds. *Picturing the Past: Media, History, and Photography*. Urbana: University of Illinois Press, 1999.

Hannigan, William. *Picture Machine: The Rise of American Newspictures*. New York: Henry N. Abrams, 2004.

Harrison, Martin. *Young Meteors: British Photojournalism, 1957–1965*. London: Jonathan Cape, 1998.

Kozol, Wendy. *Life's America: Family and Nation in Postwar Photojournalism*. Philadelphia, Pa.: Temple University Press, 1994.

Mraz, John. *Photographing Political Power in Mexico*. Storrs: University of Connecticut, 1997.

Petro, Patrice. *Joyless Streets: Women and Melodramatic Representation in Weimar Germany*. Princeton, N.J.: Princeton University Press, 1989.

Taylor, John. *Body Horror: Photojournalism, Catastrophe, and War*. New York: New York University Press, 1998.

Political Economy

Cohen, Elliott D., ed. *News Incorporated: Corporate Media Ownership and Its Threat to Democracy*. Buffalo, N.Y.: Prometheus, 2005.

Compton, James Robert. *The Integrated News Spectacle: A Political Economy of Cultural Performance*. New York: P. Lang, 2004.

Curran, James, Angus Douglas, and Gary Whannel. "The Political Economy of the Human Interest Story." In Anthony Smith, ed., *Newspapers and Democracy: International Essays on a Changing Medium*. Cambridge, Mass.: MIT Press, 1980.

Gaunt, Philip. *Choosing the News: The Profit Factor in News Selection*. New York: Greenwood Press, 1990.

Political Journalism

Jamieson, Kathleen Hall, and Paul Waldman. *The Press Effect: Politicians, Journalists, and the Stories That Shape the Political World*. New York: Oxford University Press, 2003.

Niven, David. "An Economic Theory of Political Journalism." *Journalism and Mass Communication Quarterly* 82, no. 2 (2005): 247–63.

Popular Culture

Dahlgren, Peter, and Colin Sparks, eds. *Journalism and Popular Culture*. London: Sage, 1992.

Hartley, John. *Popular Reality: Journalism, Modernity, Popular Culture*. London: Arnold, 1996.

Practices

Clayman, Steven E. "Displaying Neutrality in Television News Interviews." *Social Problems* 35, no. 4 (1988): 474–92.

Good, Howard. *The Journalist as Autobiographer*. Metuchen, N.J.: Scarecrow Press, 1993.

Monmonier, Mark. *Maps with the News: The Development of American Journalistic Cartography*. Chicago, Ill.: University of Chicago Press, 1989.

Peterson, Mark Allen. "Getting to the Story: Unwriteable Discourse and Interpretive Practice in American Journalism." *Anthropological Quarterly* 74, no. 4 (2001): 201–11.

Reisner, A. E. "The News Conference: How Daily Newspaper Editors Construct the Front Page." *Journalism Quarterly* 69 (1992): 971–86.

Presidential Press Coverage, U.S.

Allen, Craig. *Eisenhower and the Mass Media: Peace, Prosperity, and Prime-Time TV*. Chapel Hill: University of North Carolina Press, 1993.

Hertsgaard, Mark. *On Bended Knee: The Press and the Reagan Presidency.* New York: Farrar, Straus, and Giroux, 1988.

Kiousis, Spiro. "Killing the Messenger: An Exploration of Presidential Newspaper Coverage and Public Confidence in the Press." *Journalism Studies* 3, no. 4 (2002): 557–72.

Liebovich, Louis W. *Bylines in Despair: Herbert Hoover, The Great Depression, and the U.S. News Media.* Westport, Conn.: Praeger, 1994.

Ponder, Stephen. "The Presidency Makes News: William McKinley and the First Presidential Press Corps, 1897–1901." *Presidential Studies Quarterly* 24 (1994): 823–36.

———. *Managing the Press: Origins of the Media Presidency, 1897–1933.* New York: St. Martin's Press, 1999.

Ritchie, Donald A. "'The Loyalty of the Senate': Washington Correspondents in the Progressive Era." *Historian* 51, no. 4 (1989): 574–91.

Smith, Carolyn. *Presidential Press Conferences: A Critical Approach.* Westport, Conn.: Praeger, 1990.

Spear, Joseph. *Presidents and the Press: The Nixon Legacy.* Cambridge, Mass.: MIT Press, 1984.

Steele, Richard W. *Propaganda in an Open Society: The Roosevelt Administration and the Media, 1933–1941.* Westport, Conn.: Greenwood Press, 1985.

———. *Press Gallery: Congress and the Washington Correspondents.* Boston, Mass.: Harvard University Press, 1991.

———. *Reporting from Washington: The History of the Washington Press Corps.* Oxford: Oxford University Press, 2005.

Summers, Mark Wahlgren. *The Press Gang: Newspapers and Politics, 1865–1878.* Chapel Hill: University of North Carolina Press, 1994.

Turner, Kathleen J. *Lyndon Johnson's Dual War: Vietnam and the Press.* Chicago, Ill.: University of Chicago Press, 1985.

White, Graham J. *FDR and the Press.* Chicago: University of Chicago Press, 1979.

Winfield, Betty Houchin. *FDR and the News Media.* New York: Columbia University Press, 1994.

Printing Press

Davis, Natalie Zemon. "Printing and the People." In Chandra Mukerji and Michael Schudson, eds., *Rethinking Popular Culture: Contemporary Perspectives in Cultural Studies.* Berkeley: University of California Press, 1991.

Eisenstein, Elizabeth L. *The Printing Press as an Agent of Change: Communications and Cultural Transformation in Early-Modern Europe,* 2 vols. Cambridge: Cambridge University Press, 1979.

Griffiths, Jeremy, and D. Pearsall, eds. *Book Production and Publishing in Britain, 1375–1475*. Cambridge: Cambridge University Press, 1989.

Martin, Henri-Jean. *The History and Power of Writing*, trans. Lydia G. Cochrane. Chicago, Ill.: University of Chicago Press, 1994.

Professionalization

Banning, Stephen A. "The Professionalization of Journalism: A Nineteenth-Century Beginning." *Journalism History* 24, no. 4 (1998–99): 157–63.

Dooley, Patricia L. *Taking their Political Place: Journalists and the Making of an Occupation*. Westport, Conn.: Greenwood Press, 1997.

Dzur, Albert W. *Democratic Professionalism: Citizen Participation and the Reconstruction of Professional Ethics, Identity, and Practice*. Mahwah, N.J.: Lawrence Erlbaum Associates, 2008.

Farrar, Ronald T. *A Creed for My Profession: Walter Williams, Journalist to the World*. Columbia: University of Missouri Press, 1998.

Wilson, Christopher. *The Labor of Words: Literary Professionalism in the Progressive Era*. Athens: University of Georgia Press, 1985.

Public Journalism

Black, Jay. *Mixed News: The Public/Civic/Communitarian Journalism Debate*. Hillsdale, N.J.: Lawrence Erlbaum Associates, 1997.

Charity, Arthur. *Doing Public Journalism*. New York: Guilford Press, 1995.

Coleman, Renita, and Ben Wasike. "Visual Elements in Public Journalism Newspapers in an Election Campaign: A Content Analysis of the Photographs and Graphics in Campaign 2000." *Journal of Communication* 54, no. 3 (2004): 456–73.

Corrigan, Don H. *The Public Journalism Movement in America: Evangelists in the Newsroom*. Westport, Conn.: Praeger, 1999.

Fee, Frank E., Jr. "Reconnecting with the Body Politic: Toward Disconnecting Muckrakers and Public Journalists." *American Journalism* 22, no. 3 (2005): 77–102.

Glasser, Theodore L. *The Idea of Public Journalism*. New York: Guilford Press, 1999.

Lambeth, Edmund B., Philip E. Meyer, and Esther Thorson, eds. *Assessing Public Journalism*. Columbia: University of Missouri Press, 1998.

Merritt, Davis. *Public Journalism and Public Life: Why Telling the News is Not Enough* 2nd ed., Mahwah, N.J.: Lawrence Erlbaum Associates, 1998.

Rosen, Jay. *Getting the Connections Right: Public Journalism and the Troubles in the Press*. New York: Twentieth Century Fund, 1996.

———. *What Are Journalists For?* New Haven, Conn.: Yale University Press, 1999.

Public Relations

Ewen, Stuart. *PR! A Social History of Spin.* New York: Basic Books, 1996.
Kitch, Carolyn. "'A Genuine, Vivid Personality': Newspaper Coverage and Construction of a 'Real' Advertising Celebrity in a Pioneering Publicity Campaign." *Journalism History* 31, no. 3 (2005): 122–37.
Ponder, Stephen. "Presidential Publicity and Executive Power: Woodrow Wilson and the Centralizing of Government Information." *American Journalism* 11, no. 3 (1994): 257–69.

Public Sphere

Goran, Leth. "A Protestant Public Sphere: The Early European Newspaper Press." *Studies in Newspaper and Periodical History* (1993): 67–90.
Habermas, Jürgen. *The Structural Transformation of the Public Sphere: An Inquiry into a Concept of Bourgeois Society,* trans. Thomas Burger. Cambridge, Mass.: MIT Press, 1989.
Örnebring, Henrik, and Anna Maria Jönsson. "Tabloid Journalism and the Public Sphere: A Historical Perspective on Tabloid Journalism." *Journalism Studies* 5, no. 3 (2004): 283–95.
Raymond, Joad. "The Newspaper, Public Opinion, and the Public Sphere in the Seventeenth Century." *Prose Studies* 21, no. 2 (1998): 109–40.
Zaret, David. *Origins of Democratic Culture: Printing, Petitions, and the Public Sphere in Early Modern England.* Princeton, N.J.: Princeton University Press, 2000.

Publishers, Selected Individual

Hearst, William Randolph

Nasaw, David. *The Chief: The Life of William Randolph Hearst.* Boston, Mass.: Houghton Mifflin, 2000.
Proctor, Ben K. *William Randolph Hearst: The Early Years, 1863–1910.* New York: Oxford University Press, 1998.

Luce, Henry R.

Baughman, James L. *Henry R. Luce and the Rise of the American News Media.* Boston, Mass.: Twayne, 1987.

Griffith, Thomas. *Harry and Teddy: The Turbulent Friendship of Press Lord Henry R. Luce and His Favorite Reporter, Theodore H. White*. New York: Random House, 1995.
Herzstein, Robert Edwin. *Henry R. Luce, Time, and the American Crusade in Asia*. Cambridge: Cambridge University Press, 2005.

Newnes, George

Jackson, Kate. *George Newnes and the New Journalism in Britain, 1880–1910: Culture and Profit*. Burlington, Vt.: Ashgate, 2001.

Pulitzer, Joseph

Brian, Denis. *Pulitzer: A Life*. New York: J. Wiley, 2001.
Juergens, George. *Joseph Pulitzer and the* New York World. Princeton, N.J.: Princeton University Press, 1966.

Science Journalism

Goldsmith, Maurice. *The Science Critic: A Critical Analysis of the Popular Presentation of Science*. New York: Routledge & Kegan Paul, 1986.
Irwin, Alan, and Brian Wynne, eds. *Misunderstanding Science? The Public Reconstruction of Science and Technology*. Cambridge: Cambridge University Press, 1996.
Murray, David, Joel Schwartz, and S. Robert Lichter. *It Ain't Necessarily So: How Media Make and Unmake the Scientific Picture of Reality*. Lanham, Md.: Rowman & Littlefield, 2001.
Nelkin, Dorothy. *Selling Science: How the Press Covers Science and Technology*. Rev. ed., New York: Freeman, 1995.

Scopes Trial

Caudill, Edward. "The Roots of Bias: An Empiricist Press and Coverage of the Scopes Trial." *Journalism Monographs* 114 (1989): 1–37.
Clarke, Constance Areson. "Evolution for John Doe: Pictures, the Public, and the Scopes Trial Debate." *Journal of American History* 87, no. 4 (2000): 1275–1303.
Wood, L. Maren. "The Monkey Trial Myth: Popular Culture Representations of the Scopes Trial." *Canadian Review of American Studies* 32, no. 2 (2002): 147–64.

Social Constructionism

Johnson-Cartee, Karen S. *News Narratives and News Framing: Constructing Political Reality*. Lanham, Md.: Rowman & Littlefield, 2005.

Reese, Stephen D., Oscar H. Gandy, Jr., and August E. Grant. *Framing Public Life: Perspectives on Media and Our Understanding of the Social World*. Mahwah, N.J.: Lawrence Erlbaum Associates, 2001.

Tuchman, Gaye. *Making News: A Study in the Construction of Reality*. New York: Free Press, 1978.

Sociology

McNair, Brian. *The Sociology of Journalism*. London: Arnold, 1998.

Sources

Soley, Lawrence C. *The News Shapers: The Sources Who Explain the News*. New York: Praeger, 1992.

Strentz, Herbert. *News Reporters and News Sources: Accomplices in Shaping and Misshaping the News*. Ames: Iowa State University Press, 1989.

Spies, Journalists as

Crary, Catherine Snell. "The Tory and the Spy: The Double Life of James Rivington." *William and Mary Quarterly* Third Series 16, no. 1 (1959): 61–72.

French, David. "Spy Fever in Britain, 1900–1915." *Historical Journal* 21, no. 2 (1978): 355–70.

Greenspan, Nicole. "News, Intelligence, and Espionage at the Exiled Court of Cologne: The Case of Henry Manning." *Media History* 11, nos. 1–2 (2005): 105–26.

Johnson, Chalmers. *An Instance of Treason: Ozaki Hotsumi and the Sorge Spy Ring*. Stanford, Calif.: Stanford University Press, 1964.

Sports Journalism

Anderson, William B. "Does Cheerleading Ever Stop? Major League Baseball and Sports Journalism." *Journalism and Mass Comunication Quarterly* 78, no. 2 (2001): 355–82.

Baker, William J. "Press Games: Sportswriters and the Making of American Football." *Review in American History* 22, no. 3 (1994): 530–7.

Berryman, Jack W. "The Tenuous Attempts of Americans to 'Catch-up With John Bull': Specialty Magazines and Sporting Journalism, 1800–1835."

Canadian Journal of History of Sport and Physical Education 10, no. 1 (1979): 33–61.

Fontain, Charles. *Sportswriter: The Life and Times of Grantland Rice.* New York: Oxford University Press, 1994.

Hardin, Marie. "Stopped at the Gate: Women's Sports, 'Reader Interest,' and Decision Making by Editors." *Journalism and Mass Communication Quarterly* 82, no. 2 (2005): 62–77.

Hardin, Robin. "Crowning the King: Grantland Rice and Bobby Jones." *Georgia Historical Quarterly* 88, no. 4 (2004): 511–29.

Harris, Michael. "Sport in the Newspapers Before 1750: Representations of Cricket, Class and Commerce in the London Press." *Media History* 4 (1998): 19–28.

Inabinett, Mark. *Grantland Rice and His Heroes: The Sportswriter as Mythmaker in the 1920s.* Knoxville: University of Tennessee Press, 1994.

Lamb, Chris. "Affaire Jake Powell: The Minority Press Goes to Bat Against Segregated Baseball." *Journalism and Mass Communication Quarterly* 76 (1999): 21–34.

Messenger, Christian K. "Football as Narrative." *American Literary History* 7, no. 4 (1995): 726–39.

Oriard, Michael. *Reading Football: How the Popular Press Created an American Spectacle.* Chapel Hill: University of North Carolina Press, 1993.

Rader, Benjamin. *In Its Own Image: How Television Has Transformed Sports.* New York: Free Press, 1984.

Reel, Guy. "Richard Fox, John L. Sullivan, and the Rise of Modern American Prize Fighting." *Journalism History* 27, no. 2 (2001): 73–85.

Sowell, Michael. "The Myth Becomes the Mythmaker: Bat Masterson as a New York Sports 'Writer'." *Journalism History* 26, no. 1 (2000): 2–14.

Tabloids

Baum, Matthew A. "Sex, Lies, and War: How Soft News Brings Foreign Policy to the Inattentive Public," *American Political Science Review* 96, no. 1 (2002), 91–109.

Prichard, Peter. *The Making of McPaper: The Inside Story of 'USA Today.'* Kansas City, Mo.: Andrews, McMeel & Parker, 1987.

Telegraph

Blondheim, Menahem. *News Over the Wires: The Telegraph and the Flow of Public Information in America, 1844–1897.* Cambridge, Mass.: Harvard University Press, 1994.

———. "The Click: Telegraphic Technology, Journalism, and the Transformations of the New York Associated Press." *American Journalism* 17, no. 4 (2000): 27–52.

Kielbowicz, Richard B. "News Gathering by Mail in the Age of the Telegraph: Adapting to a New Technology." *Technology and Culture* 28, no. 1 (1987): 26–41.

Standage, Tom. *The Victorian Internet: The Remarkable Story of the Telegraph and the Nineteenth Century's Online Pioneers*. New York: Walker and Company, 1998.

Vietnam War

Hallin, Daniel C. "The Media, the War in Vietnam, and Political Support: A Critique of the Thesis of an Oppositional Media." *Journal of Politics* 46, no. 1 (1984): 2–24.

Hammond, William M. *Reporting Vietnam: Media and Military at War*. Lawrence: University Press of Kansas, 1998.

Huebner, Andrew J. "Rethinking American Press Coverage of the Vietnam War, 1965–68." *Journalism History* 31, no. 3 (2005): 150–61.

Landers, James. "Specter of Stalemate: Vietnam War Perspectives in *Newsweek*, *Time*, and *U.S. News & World Report*, 1965–1968." *American Journalism* 19, no. 3 (2002): 13–38.

Mascaro, Thomas A. "The Peril of the Unheeded Warning: Robert F. Rogers' 'Vietnam: It's a Mad War.'" *Journalism History* 28, no. 4 (2003): 182–90.

Patterson, Oscar III. "Television's Living Room War in Print: Vietnam in the News Magazines." *Journalism Quarterly* 61, no. 1 (1984): 35–9, 136.

———. "If the Vietnam War Had Been Reported Under Gulf War Rules." *Journal of Broadcasting and Electronic Media* 39 (1995): 20–29.

Steinman, Ron. *Inside Television's First War: A Saigon Journal*. Columbia: University of Missouri Press, 2002.

Turner, Kathleen J. *Lyndon Johnson's Dual War: Vietnam and the Press*. Chicago: University of Chicago Press, 1985.

Tuttle, Jon. "How You Get That Story: Heisenberg's Uncertainty Principle and the Literature of the Vietnam War." *Journal of Popular Culture* 38, no. 6 (2005): 1088–98.

Wyatt, Clarence R. "'At the Cannon's Mouth': The American Press and the Vietnam War." *Journalism History* 13, nos. 3–4 (1986): 104–13.

Violence

Sussman, Leonard R. "Dying (and Being Killed) on the Job: A Case Study of World Journalists, 1982–1989." *Journalism Quarterly* 68, nos. 1–2 (1991): 195–9.

Woodbury, Marda Liggett. *Stopping the Presses: The Murder of Walter W. Liggett.* Minneapolis: University of Minnesota Press, 1998.

War Correspondents

Beckett, I. F. W. *The American Civil War: The War Correspondents.* Phoenix Mill, N.H.: Sutton, 1993.

Bjork, Ulf Jonas. "Latest from the Canadian Revolution: Early War Correspondence in the *New York Herald*, 1837–1838." *Journalism Quarterly* 71, no. 4 (1994): 851–58.

Cockett, R. B. "'In Wartime Every Objective Reporter Should Be Shot': The Experience of British Press Correspondents in Moscow, 1941–45." *Journal of Contemporary History* 23, no. 4 (1988): 515–30.

Elwood-Akers, Virginia. *Women War Correspondents in the Vietnam War, 1961–1975.* Metuchen, N.J.: Scarecrow Press, 1988.

Hankinson, Alan. *Man of Wars, William Howard Russell of The Times.* London: Heinemann, 1982.

Knightley, Phillip. *The First Casualty: From the Crimea to Vietnam: The War Correspondent as Hero, Propagandist, and Myth Maker.* New York: Harcourt Brace Jovanovich, 1975.

Lambert, Andrew D., and Stephen Badsey. *The Crimean War.* Dover: A. Sutton, 1994.

Lande, Nathaniel. *Dispatches from the Front: A History of the American War Correspondent.* New York: Oxford University Press, 1995.

McLaughlin, Greg. *The War Correspondent.* Sterling, Va.: Pluto, 2002.

Morrison, David E. *Journalists at War: The Dynamics of News Reporting During the Falklands Conflict.* London: Sage, 1988.

Pedelty, Mark. *War Stories: The Culture of Foreign Correspondents.* New York: Routledge, 1995.

Walker, Dale L. *Januarius MacGahan: The Life and Campaigns of an American War Correspondent.* Athens: Ohio University Press, 1988.

Wartime, Journalism in

Allan, Stuart, and Barbie Zelizer, eds. *Reporting War: Journalism in Wartime.* London: Routledge, 2004.

Connelly, Mark, and David Welch, eds. *War and the Media: Reportage and Propaganda, 1900–2003.* London: I. B. Tauris, 2005.

Gjelten, Tom. *Sarajevo Daily: A City and Its Newspaper Under Siege.* New York: HarperCollins, 1995.

Mercer, Derrik, Geoff Mungham, and Kevin Williams. *The Fog of War: The Media on the Battlefield.* London: Heineman, 1987.

Smith, Jeffery A. *War and Press: The Problem of Prerogative Power*. New York: Oxford University Press, 1999.
Sonnenberg, Rhonda. *Still We Danced Forward: World War II and the Writer's Life*. Washington, D.C.: Brassey's, 1998.
Torney-Parlicki, Prue. *Somewhere in Asia: War, Journalism and Australia's Neighbours, 1941–75*. Sydney: University of New South Wales Press, 2000.

Watergate

Woodward, Bob, and Carl Bernstein. *The Final Days*. New York: Simon and Schuster, 1994.
Woodward, Bob. *Shadow: Five Presidents and the Legacy of Watergate*. New York: Simon and Schuster, 2000.

Women and Journalism

Abramson, Phyllis Leslie. *Sob Sister Journalism*. Westport, Conn.: Greenwood Press, 1990.
Beasley, Maurine Hoffman. *Eleanor Roosevelt and the Media: A Public Quest for Self-Fulfillment*. Urbana: University of Illinois Press, 1987.
———. "The Women's National Press Club: Case Study in Professional Aspirations." *Journalism History* 15, no. 4 (1988): 112–20.
———. "Women and Journalism in World War II: Discrimination and Progress." *American Journalism* 12, no. 3 (1995): 321–33.
Beasley, Maurine Hoffman, and Shelia J. Gibbons. *Taking Their Place: A Documentary History of Women and Journalism*. Washington, D.C.: American University Press, 1993.
Burt, Elizabeth V. "A Bid for Legitimacy: The Woman's Press Club Movement, 1881–1900." *Journalism History* 23, no. 2 (1997): 72–84.
Cairns, Kathleen A. *Front-Page Women Journalists, 1920–1950*. Lincoln: University of Nebraska Press, 2003.
Carter, Cynthia. *News, Gender and Power*. London: Routledge, 1998.
Collins, Jean E. *She Was There: Stories of Pioneering Women Journalists*. New York: J. Messner, 1980.
Demeter, Richard L. *Primer, Presses and Composing Sticks: Women Printers of the Colonial Period*. Hicksville, N.Y.: Exposition Press, 1979.
Gottlieb, Agnes Hooper. "Networking in the Nineteenth Century: Founding of the Woman's Press Club of New York." *Journalism History* 21, no. 4 (1995): 156–63.
———. *Women Journalists and the Municipal Housekeeping Movement: 1868–1914*. Lewiston, N.Y.: Edwin Mellen Press, 2001.

——. "Grit Your Teeth, Then Learn to Swear: Women in Journalistic Careers, 1850–1926." *American Journalism* 18, no. 1 (2001): 53–72.

Hosley, David H. *Hard News: Women in Broadcast Journalism*. New York: Greenwood Press, 1987.

Lutes, Jean Marie. "Sob Sisterhood Revisited." *American Literary History* 15, no. 3 (2003): 504–32.

Marzolf, Marion. *Up from the Footnote: A History of Women Journalists*. New York: Hastings House, 1977.

Mills, Kay. *A Place in the News: From the Women's Pages to the Front Page*. New York: Columbia University Press, 1990.

Onslow, Barbara. *Women of the Press in Nineteenth-century Britain*. London: Macmillan, 2000.

Randall, Margaret. "Reclaiming Voices: Notes on a New Female Practice in Journalism." *Latin American Perspectives* 18, no. 3 (1991): 103–13.

Ross, Ishbel. *Ladies of the Press: The Story of Women in Journalism by an Insider*. New York: Harper, 1936. Republished by Arno Press, 1974.

Sanders, Marlene, and Marcia Rock. *Waiting for Prime Time: The Women of Television News*. Urbana: University of Illinois Press, 1988.

Schilpp, Madelon Gordon, and Sharon L. Murphy. *Great Women of the Press*. Carbondale: Southern Illinois University Press, 1983.

Sebba, Anne. *Battling for News: The Rise of the Woman Reporter*. London: Hodder & Stoughton, 1993.

Steiner, Linda. "Do You Belong in Journalism? Definitions of the Ideal Journalist in Career Guidance Books." *American Journalism* 11, no. 4 (1994): 321–35.

Streitmatter, Rodger. *Raising Her Voice: African-American Women Journalists Who Changed History*. Lexington: University Press of Kentucky, 1994.

Tusan, Michelle Elizabeth. *Women Making News: Gender and Journalism in Modern Britain*. Urbana: University of Illinois Press, 2005.

World War I

Audoin-Rouzeau, Stéphane. *Men at War, 1914–1918: National Sentiment and Trench Journalism in France during the First World War*, trans. Helen McPhail. Providence, R.I.: Berg, 1993.

Collins, Ross F. "'Cossacks Marching to Berlin!': A New Look at French Journalism During the First World War." *American Journalism* 18, no. 4 (2001): 29–44.

Cornebise, Alfred. *"The Stars and Stripes": Doughboy Journalism in World War I*. Westport, Conn.: Greenwood Press, 1984.

——. *Ranks and Columns: Armed Forces Newspapers in American Wars*. Westport, Conn.: Greenwood Press, 1993.

Kornweibel, Theodore, Jr. "'The Most Dangerous of All Negro Journals': Federal Efforts to Suppress the *Chicago Defender* during World War I." *American Journalism* 11, no. 2 (1994): 154–68.

Lorenz, Alfred Lawrence. "Ralph W. Tyler: The Unknown Correspondent of World War I." *Journalism History* 31, no. 1 (2005): 2–12.

O'Brien, Paul. *Mussolini in the First World War: The Journalist, the Soldier, the Fascist.* Oxford: Berg, 2005.

Whalen, Robert K. "'The Commonwealth of Peoples to Which We Racially Belong': The National Press and the Manufacturing of an Arms Race." *Historian* 63, no. 2 (2001): 335–56.

World War II

Bishop, Ronald. "To Protect and Serve: The 'Guard Dog' Function of Journalism in Coverage of the Japanese-American Internment." *Journalism and Communication Monographs* 2, no. 2 (2000): 65–103.

Blanchard, Margaret A. "Freedom of the Press in World War II." *American Journalism* 12, no. 3 (1995): 342–58.

Friedman, Barbara. "'The Soldier Speaks': Yank Coverage of Women and Wartime Work." *American Journalism* 22, no. 2 (2005): 63–82.

Garrett, Greg. "It's Everybody's War: Racism and the World War Two Documentary." *Journal of Popular Film and Television* 22 (Summer 1994): 70–78.

Goldman, Aaron L. "Press Freedom in Britain During World War II." *Journalism History* 22, no. 4 (1997): 146–55.

Marcellus, Jane. "Bo's'n's Whistle: Representing 'Rosie the Riveter' on the Job." *American Journalism* 22, no. 2 (2005): 83–108.

Mizuno, Takeya. "Self-censorship by Coercion: The Federal Government and the California Japanese-Language Newspapers from Pearl Harbor to Internment." *American Journalism* 17, no. 3 (2000): 31–57.

Perry, Ernest L., Jr. "It's Time to Force a Change: The African-American Press' Campaign for a True Democracy During World War II." *Journalism History* 28, no. 2 (2002): 85–95.

Roeder, George, Jr. *The Censored War: American Visual Experience During World War Two.* New Haven, Conn.: Yale University Press, 1993.

Sharp, Patrick B. "From Yellow Peril to Japanese Wasteland: John Hersey's 'Hiroshima.'" *Twentieth Century Literature* 46, no. 4 (2000): 434–52.

Somers, Paul P., Jr. "'Right in the Fuhrer's Face': American Editorial Cartoons of the World War II Period." *American Journalism* 13, no. 3 (1996): 333–53.

Sweeney, Michael S. "Censorship Missionaries of World War II." *Journalism History* 27, no. 1 (2001): 4–13.

Tobin, James. *Ernie Pyle's War: America's Eyewitness to World War II.* New York: The Free Press, 1997.

Tombs, Isabelle. "Scrutinizing France: Collecting and Using Newspaper Intelligence During World War II." *Intelligence and National Security* 17, no. 2 (2002): 105–26.

Voss, Frederick. *Reporting the War: The Journalistic Coverage of World War II.* Washington, D.C.: Smithsonian Institution Press, 1994.

Yang, Mei-ling. "Creating the Kitchen Patriot: Media Promotion of Food Rationing and Nutrition Campaigns on the American Home Front During World War II." *American Journalism* 22, no. 3 (2005): 55–75.

Yellow Journalism

Campbell, W. Joseph. *Yellow Journalism: Puncturing the Myths, Defining the Legacies.* Westport, Conn.: Praeger, 2001.

Milton, Joyce. *The Yellow Kids: Foreign Correspondents in the Heyday of Yellow Journalism.* New York: Harper and Row, 1989.

About the Author

Ross A. Eaman (born in Ottawa, Canada, in 1945) studied American history at the University of Toronto and specialized in intellectual history and the philosophy of history at Queen's University in Kingston, Ontario, obtaining his Ph.D. in 1978. In 1980, he joined the full-time faculty in the School of Journalism (now Journalism and Communication) at Carleton University in Ottawa to teach the history of communication in the school's new mass communication program. During the 1980s, he coordinated a CBC Oral History Project in association with the National Archives of Canada, the Institute of Canadian Studies at Carleton, and the Canadian Broadcasting Corporation. He has published books and articles on the history of the media and the CBC, with special emphasis on the history and role of audience research. He has also submitted evidence to parliamentary committees on broadcasting and served as an advisor to the auditor general in relation to public broadcasting. In addition to the history of journalism, his current research interests include communication and the built environment and communication and international crises.